COLONIAL CONSEQUENCES

Essays in Irish Literature and Culture

D0760651

TO MY SISTER, ALLISON

COLONIAL CONSEQUENCES

Essays in Irish Literature and Culture

John Wilson Foster

THE LILLIPUT PRESS
1991

First published in 1991 by
THE LILLIPUT PRESS LTD
4 Rosemount Terrace, Arbour Hill,
Dublin 7, Ireland

A CIP record for this title
is available from
The British Library.

ISBN 0 946640 46 7
ISBN 0 946640 47 5 (pbk)

The Lilliput Press receives financial assistance from
The Arts Council/An Chomhairle Ealaíon, Ireland.

Jacket design by The Graphiconies (Bortoli)
Set in 10.5 on 12 Bembo by
Seton Music Graphics Ltd of Bantry
and printed in Ireland by Betaprint Ltd of Dublin

CONTENTS

INTRODUCTION

These pieces, written over a period of sixteen years, begin collectively as articles in literary criticism and end as essays in cultural criticism. Although I was unaware of it until I reread them, the shift in interest, scope and method reflects a reorientation in Anglo-American critical pursuit during the same period, when the interdisciplinary, cultural and even ideological have been increasingly prized over the more modest quarry of prior criticism. My graduate instruction during the second half of the 1960s at the University of Oregon, which I attended at the invitation of the Milton scholar Kester Svendsen, was conducted during the fag-end of New Criticism – the form prior criticism largely took – and I watched it being locally stubbed out and made seem irrelevant (when everything had to be 'relevant' or perish) amid the headier activities of anti-Vietnam War protesters, Black Panthers, draft-dodgers, and Ken Kesey and his Merry Pranksters, all of whom made Eugene a counter-culture staging post on Highway 99 running from California to the half-legendary asylum of British Columbia.

But in fact I had already crossed the bounds of New Criticism by having studied aesthetics during the first half of the 1960s under Philip Hobsbaum, the English critic and poet then galvanizing the inert body of Ulster poetry into life from his post at Queen's University, Belfast. Being reserved in such matters, I met the poet Michael Longley only once and merely passed in the street the distinctive figure of Stewart Parker, the playwright (at that time a poet and, like me, Hobsbaum's research student), and I failed to meet at all Seamus Heaney or Derek Mahon: all of these writers were starting to go their own ways, fledged in a confidence that may not have come to them natively. As a postgraduate student, I studied jointly under Hobsbaum and the philosopher W. B. Gallie, and plied between two neighbouring departmental doors along University Square. American New Criticism, therefore, seemed to me, still under the influence of these two teachers when I went to Oregon, rather unadventurous, however much I admired the Chicago Aristotelians and the Southern ex-Fugitives, especially John Crowe Ransom, who gave a memorable reading at the university (as did Auden and Vozneshenski).

I

But just in case I should succumb to the formulas of American critical practice (useful in graduate examinations), Someone or Something decreed that I should meet the fiction writer and raconteur Benedict Kiely, who began a year-long stint as writer-in-residence as I arrived in Eugene. The greatest Revival figures aside, I had read no Irish writers, with the exceptions of Brendan Behan and Brian Moore, whose novel *The Lonely Passion of Judith Hearne* is set in Belfast and coupled life and literature for me in the most obvious and liberating way. (For a year or two, I was too busy reading Jack Kerouac, Lawrence Lipton and Christmas Humphreys and trying to offend the good burghers of Belfast with a struggling beard and an American war surplus combat jacket.) It was Benedict Kiely who in his infectious style and with his customary generosity of knowledge led me to the work of Irish writers as living men and women; I recall his gloom when he got word that his friend Myles na gCopaleen (Flann O'Brien) had died in Dublin. This one-man ambience set at naught the anti-intentionalist and anti-biographical approach I was being taught beyond the dim and swarming interior of Maxie's Tavern where Kiely held court. He also showed for the culture (Protestant and Catholic alike) of the province we both came from an affection and respect surprising to me, for in my heart I had always despised it a little.

However, I had term-papers to write after Kiely went back east. In American graduate school one serves a professional apprenticeship, and I am grateful for mine. One of my papers, a redefinition of topographical poetry, I was encouraged to 'send out', and it appeared in the severe pages of *The Journal of English and Germanic Philology* the year I left Oregon and returned to Belfast. As a run-through for a history of the genre (which I never wrote), I constructed a scale-model, published as 'The Topographical Tradition in Anglo-Irish Poetry' and printed below. It is not an entirely cold-blooded piece and the print of my background can be seen in my choice of Northern topographicalists to exemplify the localizing of a once-stately genre.

Before leaving Oregon, I had departed the then polished lawns of critical theory – the feminists, Lacanians, New Marxists and deconstructionists were as yet indecipherable on the horizon – for the rougher fields of folklore and Irish literature. A quarrel with J. Barre Toelken, the folklorist and balladeer, gave way to a friendship and collaboration. He had disputed the folk credentials of Woody Guthrie and Bob Dylan, but I was a fierce defender of these men and was the first in Ireland, I believe, to sing on stage the songs of Dylan (1963) and in his style (simultaneous guitar and mouth-harp, deadpan face, voice laden with premature world-weariness). I was writing my own songs, inspired by Dylan's, some of which caught the ears of Judy Collins and the Elektra record company, but song-writing faltered as my criticism grew more confident. Toelken introduced me to academic folklore (as well as to his Navajo ex-relatives in southern Utah and the desolate, extraterrestrial formations of Monument Valley) and we published papers on its theory. This collaboration, together with the social anthropology I had learned from Rosemary Harris when I was an undergraduate at Queen's University, stood me in good stead when I came later to engage with the Irish Cultural Revival.

In the meantime there was the Ulster literature Ben Kiely had urged me to read. My doctoral dissertation was a minimalist effort, but back in Northern Ireland I began afresh and quickly wrote *Forces and Themes in Ulster Fiction* (1974), the first word of that title acquiring special meaning in Belfast, in which, even in the university district, one would lie abed and hear nightly gunfire and explosions. If that was stimulation of a rather desperate kind, a quieter kind was the awareness that almost all serious criticism of Ulster literature was pioneering; for a couple of years, it seemed as if Seamus Deane, Terence Brown and I were writing all of it. Indeed, it is easy to forget that less than twenty years ago most criticism of Irish writers was written by Americans, and that 'Irish writers' meant almost exclusively the Big Names of the Revival. While Irish critics owe these scholars a great debt, they tended to perpetuate whatever view of Ireland their chosen writer himself versified or dramatized. (Fiction writers tended to get short shrift.) There is now a number of Irish-born critics scanning all of Irish literature and doing so with eyes properly capable of narrowing.

While I was engaged on *Ulster Fiction*, my Canadian wife and I moved to Dublin in 1972, unaware of the events in Derry that would cause that day to be known as Bloody Sunday. Despite the tolerant and unfocused zest of Dublin (once the anger over Bloody Sunday subsided), it was hard in those days to escape one's tribal membership or the Troubles a hundred miles north. One evening in May 1974, my wife and I had an arrangement to meet Benedict Kiely for a drink before we went on to a reading by Seamus Heaney in St Stephen's Green. That afternoon I had stood on D'Olier Street and heard the heart-stilling stereophony of two loyalist car-bombs, one on Nassau Street, the other in Parnell Square, that killed twenty-two passers-by. We met in the Shelbourne Hotel, Heaney included, and after some hesitation he decided to go ahead with the reading. It took place amid a chorus of keening ambulances, and was what the occasion required – a ministration, an assuagement, to use a Heaney word.

By going on with the reading, Heaney redressed what he later diagnosed as a serious dereliction when he *didn't* read one evening in 1972 after an IRA blitz in Belfast. In 'The Interesting Case of Nero, Chekhov's Cognac and a Knocker', the first essay in *The Government of the Tongue* (and whose opening I have mimicked above), Heaney modestly omits mention of the evening the reading *did* go on.

After four years away from North America, two of them a *post facto* obligation to the Fulbright Commission, I left Dublin for the University of British Columbia. This became a domicile and workplace. In Vancouver, against a backdrop of startling mountains and kettles of soaring eagles, I wrote the literary essays below, with the exceptions of the two on the subject of Heaney. I completed 'The Poetry of Seamus Heaney' before setting out for the Pacific Northwest and had the pleasure of giving it in person to the poet, only to have him read it in my presence, with its occasional strictures, during my visit to Glanmore, a novel and chastening experience. 'Heaney's Redress' I have written specially for this volume and it takes up the 'story' from *North* (1975). In the new essay I take for granted the excellence of many individual poems in order to concentrate on the aesthetic order they compose in cumulation. Whereas in 'Post-War Ulster Poetry' (1985) I emphasize Heaney's Britishness, in the new essay I return to the Irishness to which I directed English readers in 1974.

In Vancouver I also worked on the apparently neutral subject of novels of the Revival. But by the time my study was coming to a close, interpretations of this movement were being revised by Southern Irish nationalist critics, whereas *Fictions of the Irish Literary Revival* (1987) is an obliquely Northern view of that astonishing release of literary energy. I finished the book just as my perspective on literature was becoming more broadly cultural. This was due in part to my reading the new French-inspired critical theory, in part to my acquaintance with the French art historian Serge Guilbaut, a colleague at the University of British Columbia. But it was also due to my reading the provocative, pioneering pamphlets of the Field Day Theatre Company of Derry, whose directorate includes Seamus

Deane, Brian Friel, Tom Paulin and Seamus Heaney. In my talk 'The Critical Condition of Ulster', delivered to the International Association for the Study of Anglo-Irish Literature, at Queen's University in 1985, I grappled with the Field Day pamphleteers, themselves inspired by international theory. This conference was a turning-point, in terms not just of my work but of the frequency of my return visits to Ireland and the degree of my involvement in a place I had once shown a clean pair of heels. In 1986 I began a year as Research Fellow at the Institute of Irish Studies, Queen's University, during which I immersed myself in the sundry research interests of my colleagues there, one result being the essay 'New Realism', printed below. It was then, too, that I began to benefit from vigorous conversations in Belfast and Dublin with Edna Longley, Liam Kennedy, Liam O'Dowd, Terence Brown, Gerald Dawe and others.

From 1985, my cultural readings have been excited less by critical theory than by the changing political weather in Ireland. For several years now, a lively cultural debate has been conducted in Ireland, often within earshot of bomb-blast and variously responsive to political fall-out. The debate has seemed for a while to have been won by pluralists and revisionists, particularly among historians, who question nationalist and anglophobic readings of past and present events in Ireland. However, pluralism and revisionism are themselves being energetically contested. Meanwhile, several influential commentators have managed to carry a traditional and hostile attitude to Northern Protestant culture safely away from the swaying edifice of Irish nationalism. It has been in this context and others that I have felt the need to offer some sympathetic explanation of the peculiar pressures operating historically on that culture.

It's as well to volunteer the tribal allegiances that may lie behind such yieldings and sympathies, to anticipate from some quarter Nietzsche's question, 'Who speaks?' These allegiances press upon all Irish critics and in turn must be subjected to the circumspection of argument and print. I was reared on the prejudices and perspectives, virtues and vices, of lower middle-class loyalism and Nonconformism in east Belfast. My eldest brother, one of the first Northern Irish children to benefit from the Butler Education Act (1944, but extended to Northern Ireland only in 1947), was the first member of my connection to have daytime secondary education and to attend university. My own avoidance of Irish literature at university – made easy by a curriculum that looked east across the water – and my absorption in the 'abstruser musings' of aestheticians may well have been attempts to distance myself from my background. If to some degree I have recently assumed qualified, defensive pride in my ancestry, I hope of course that with all my circling I have nevertheless, to adapt John Montague, failed to return.

The peculiar challenge to cultural criticism in Ireland is to establish and hold a meeting-ground for civil conversation while both acknowledging the legitimate imperatives of difference and advancing the legitimate claims of one's community, whose deep fears and honourable desires one is better equipped to understand and articulate than any outsider. Organized terror reinforces the challenge when it causes one to host feelings and sentiments more extreme than one would ordinarily wish, and of a different kind also: thus, for example, a belief in individuality (which in my own case, ironically, is part of a Dissenter inheritance) can be overmastered by the exigencies of group peril and held in troubling abeyance. One can even feel an immodest desire to be spokesman and apologist instead of the singular commentator one's education has fitted one to be.

The critic in Ireland, particularly in Northern Ireland, is engaged therefore in a parley with himself as well as with his counterparts. (Out of the first parley the gifted among us have made poetry.) However burdensome, it is nevertheless the best defence against the terrorizing of argument and the misgovernment of the tongue to which we in Ireland are given. A certain strain, a weakness for 'solutionism', for blueprints and multiple projections, are perhaps inevitable, under the circumstances, in any mapping of contemporary Irish culture, and I see them in my own. But if conducting one's education in public is commonly a risky thing to do, I'm not sure it is entirely a vice in a traditionally prejudgmental society.

The shared etymology of 'crisis' and 'critic' seems especially apt in Ireland, but the literary critic is concerned as much with continuity as with turning-point or climax. Much of the literature discussed below is relatively innocent of our current predicament, and I find I haven't pursued the coincidence (or is it causality?) of twenty years of civil commotions and political rupture and twenty identical years of literary accomplishment. Place and poetry loom large in the following essays, in Ulster but elsewhere in the island too, and before as well as after the events of the late 1960s. Regionalism is a fitfully theoretical underpinning that makes counterparts of the literary and cultural pieces: the last essay, for example, returns us to the first. (My title for the volume pluralizes one given to a poem by John Hewitt, exponent of regionalism.) Regionality expresses continuity in time; but I see it as no mere contraction in figurative space: rather should it be a progressive critique of modernism as it accepts the benefits of modernity. Meanwhile, for pressing local reasons, the realistic acknowledgment of Ulster's regionality is a necessary posture in our present difficulties.

Vancouver – Belfast 1991

1

THE TOPOGRAPHICAL TRADITION IN ANGLO-IRISH POETRY

Quintessentially an eighteenth-century form, topographical poetry nevertheless had its origin in Sir John Denham's 'Cooper's Hill' (1642/55) and panted on, long after its heyday, well into the nineteenth century. Dr Johnson's definition of the form – under one of its several aliases – is succinct. 'Local poetry', says Johnson, is 'a species of composition . . . of which the fundamental subject is some particular landscape, to be poetically described, with the addition of such embellishment as may be supplied by historical retrospection or incidental meditation.'[1]

An adequate definition, however, must account for the *manner* in which the description of the locality on the one hand, and the meanings attached to it through retrospection and meditation on the other, are blended. I have tried to do this elsewhere, listing five structural characteristics of the genre: the creation of three-dimensional space, the use of space as a patterning device, the use of time-projections, the use of extended metaphor, and the development of a controlling moral vision.[2] These features are present throughout the long history of topographical poetry, but their substance and meaning alter, as we shall see, in response to the changing nature of society and changing conceptions of poetry from Denham's time to the nineteenth century. Change and adaptation were slow, however, and the genre retained its basic identity, along with most of the georgic motifs and formulas uniquely combined in the founding poems: 'Cooper's Hill', Waller's 'On St James's Park' (1661), Pope's 'Windsor Forest' (1713) and Dyer's 'Grongar Hill' (1726).[3] Generic inertia thereafter ensured the steady shunting of topographical poetry, with its increasingly outmoded neoclassicism, from the main line of English poetry into local yet quaint and fascinating sidings.

Topographical poetry is a minor but intriguing strain of Anglo-Irish poetry. In the beginning it was expressly political after the manner of Denham, Waller and Pope, and in being so mirrored the political relationship of Ireland to England. Thus, to the extent that the seventeenth- and eighteenth-century ruling classes in England and Ireland were socially continuous, early topographical poetry in Ireland is indistinguishable from the genre in England. In another sense, the Irish poems are blatant imitations of the English poems, as the political and class structure in Ireland was an imitation of its English model. In yet a third sense, the parallel with English topographical poetry was quite legitimate, not only because the genre is self-imitative anyway, but also because in the parallel was the beginning of that process of 'localization' that characterizes the history of the topographical genre: that is, the choice of localities increasingly distant from London, and the increase in local matter at the partial expense of the capacity of the localities to symbolize larger entities such as the nation or world. Even if we choose to regard the early poems by James Ward and Henry Jones as merely Irish facsimiles of English originals, we are less likely so to regard the later poems by William Hamilton Drummond and William Drennan, even though the latter retain the formulaic structure of the genre. This is partly because later topographical poems, full of local matter, became absorbed into appropriate regional poetic traditions, of which the Ulster tradition was one.

In discussing the topographical tradition in Ireland, I have taken no account of the influence, if any, of the Gaelic topographical tradition on Anglo-Irish poetry. Research in this direction is possibly required, but Anglo-Irish topographical poems seem adequately accounted for within the English tradition. Anglo-Irish topographical poets tend to be Protestant, unionist and conservative, but this description becomes less relevant as topographical poetry replaces its political bias with aesthetic, scientific and theological biases. Keeping in mind Johnson's definition, I want in fact to trace the changing meanings of landscape in Anglo-Irish topographical poetry. I do so roughly chronologically, but the meanings of landscape tend not to exclude one another; instead they accumulate, with emphases rather than exclusive concerns distinguishing period from period. All the forms and themes of subsequent topographical poetry can even be said to exist, embryonically or fully-fledged, in 'Cooper's Hill' and 'Windsor Forest'.

Development of these embryonic themes and forms takes place under the influence of altering poetic norms and of wider social

interests and disciplines, in particular surveying and topography, landscape painting and gardening, travel and the picturesque cult, and
geology. In each case, these interests and disciplines will be found to
have peculiarly Irish versions: topographical poetry, despite its fluc-
tuating imaginative value, is cultural documentation of startling
inclusiveness.

I

As it happens, Ireland can lay slender claim to the first topographical
poet. Denham was born in Dublin in 1615 where his father was the
Chief Baron of the Exchequer and his mother the daughter of Sir
Garret Moore, Baron Mellefont and Viscount Drogheda. In 1617,
however, 'before the Foggy Air of that Climate, could influence, or
any way adulterate his Mind, he was brought from thence' to
England.[4] Denham's life is included in Webb's *Compendium of Irish
Biography* (1878) and O'Donoghue's *The Poets of Ireland* (1912), and
his poetry in Charles Read's *The Cabinet of Irish Literature* (rev. ed.
1904). It would be unhealthy, though, to claim 'Cooper's Hill', a
poem majestically concerned with the history of the realm, as an Irish
poem. What is certain is that amidst the poem's georgic motifs, we
can discern a clear structural pattern (woven by the five characteristics
I have mentioned) that became a model for subsequent topographical
poems.

Denham stands on Cooper's Hill on the Berkshire-Surrey border
and contemplates the northern prospect. He focuses on three prominent points of interest: St Paul's to the distant right, Windsor Castle
(on Windsor Hill) to the closer left, and the ruins of Chertsey Abbey
(on St Anne's Hill) to his immediate right. Against the Thames Valley
these compose a topographical dialectic, but more importantly they
compose – when contemplated historically – a political dialectic. The
Chertsey ruins and the feverish activity around St Paul's, visible from
Cooper's Hill, summon up the imbalance of power between Crown
and subjects before the signing of Magna Charta at Runnymede.
Standing on the hill in 1642, at a time of renewed political unrest,
Denham insists that Charles I's reign (symbolized by Windsor Castle)
represents a refinement of the spirit of Runnymede. Magna Charta
and Charles's reign were both triumphs for harmony, peace and
moderation, qualities enshrined in the contemporary cosmic (and

therefore political as well as topographical) ideal of *concordia discors* and embodied in the view from Cooper's Hill considered *in toto*.[5]

In Denham's fashion, early topographical poets create a *landscape of polity*: that is to say, they abstract from the landscape or townscape features that have political significance, or they invest natural features with political meaning. Topographically and politically, the poets are on the edge of this landscape: they give us merely a 'prospect of power'. Like Denham, Waller in 'On St James's Park' stands at a distance from, and looks towards, topographical symbols of central power that guarantee harmony and moderation. The view, like that from Cooper's Hill, is a microcosm of the realm through history. Both poems are reservedly royalist and Tory. Pope's 'Windsor Forest' also constructs a microcosm of the realm from close to its centre (in the wake of the Treaty of Utrecht, his 'Runnymede'), but this poem in addition represents the beginning of a movement away from spare London locations of power towards more luxuriant locations of retreat and respite from affairs of Court and parliament, a movement continued in Samuel Garth's 'Claremont' (1715). The same ambivalence is evidenced by the first genuinely Irish topographical poem, 'Phoenix Park' (1718) by James Ward.

Ward opens his poem with what looks like provincial self-consciousness:

> Shall *Cooper's Hill* majestic rise in Rhyme,
> Strong as its basis, as its Brow sublime?
> Shall *Windsor-Forest* win immortal Praise,
> It self outlasting in its Poet's Lays;
> And thou, O *Phoenix-Park*, remain so long
> Unknown to Fame, and unadorn'd in song?[6]

Evidently not; but Ward is not being provincial: Pope alludes to Denham, and Garth to both Denham and Pope, a device that became standard procedure in topographical poetry. Equally standard were the invocation of the *genius loci* and the poet's assertion of the claims to Parnassus of his own neck of the woods (the 'local pride' motif). 'Phoenix Park' sports many other topographical formulas, including a division of the poet's walk through the park into parts of the day, the exotic episode, the retirement motif, the hymn to peace and stability, and the 'picturesque' motif (using the Liffey as Denham and Pope used the Thames):

Deep in the Vale old *Liffey* rolls his Tides,
Romantic Prospects crown his rev'rend Sides;
Now thro' wild Grotts, and pendant Woods he strays,
And ravish'd at the Sight his Course delays,
Silent, and calm – now with impetuous Shock,
Pours his swift Torrent down the steepy Rock;
The tumbling Waves thro' airy Channels flow,
And loudly roaring, smoak, and foam below.

In the park, Ward encounters 'A Fabrick rais'd in peaceful *Charles's* Reign', and so joins Denham and Waller in making early topographical poetry, in terms of inspiration, a Caroline form. Ward describes that part of the park 'Where Vet'ran Bands discharg'd from War retire' to relive past campaigns, such as the recent wars with France (1702–13) and to discuss 'how bravely *Marlbro*' fought'. For Ward, peace and stability are Tory and royalist qualities, but there is an Irish dimension to his political and Denhamesque version of *concordia discors*. Like Windsor Forest, Phoenix Park was a spacious, variegated rural area within sight of the governing city of the island (Dublin to Windsor's London).[7] Although Ward fashions the park into a microcosm, not only of Ireland but, like Pope's Windsor Forest, of the entire realm, that he does so is due to the negative factor expressed by Edmund Curtis: 'In the period 1714 to 1760 Ireland had little or no political history.'[8] If Ward's gaze was thus naturally directed outside Ireland for the political *meaning* of his park, the fact that he nevertheless chose the Dublin park to *describe*, that he was content to let it 'stand in' for Windsor Forest, was due to the extent to which the Protestant Ascendancy was, in Curtis's words, 'a replica on a small scale of that of England'. Therefore, though Ward explicitly celebrates the post-Civil War and post-Utrecht realm, he is implicitly celebrating Hanoverian Ireland. 'At least in 1714,' writes Curtis, 'our country, after the unrest of a hundred and fifty years, reached an equilibrium which lasted for some fifty years. Unjust as was the established order, it gave peace and security for such gains as men could make or such education as their minds could take advantage of.' The Ascendancy of the Protestants made possible the composition of topographical poetry in Ireland, even though the Irish poet (like the Ascendancy itself) sought social and political inspirations in England.

While falling far short of 'Cooper's Hill' and 'Windsor Forest', 'Phoenix Park' is a better poem than Garth's 'Claremont'. Ward's sense of topography is superior to Garth's, not merely in terms of varieties of terrain but also in terms of perspective:

> Here on the Mount a ruin'd Tow'r I spy,
> A sweet Amusement to the distant Eye,
> Forward it starts, approaching to be seen,
> And cheats me of the sinking Lands between.

Written about the time poets were discovering landscape painting and gardening, 'Phoenix Park' is a small but distinct contribution to the development of visual composition in landscape poetry. In addition, Ward established Irish versions of the topographical motifs (e.g. praise for St Patrick, the island's absence of 'noxious Creatures', and 'Hybernia's' greenness) that became obligatory for Irish loco-descriptive poets.

II

Visually, 'Phoenix Park' is also a better poem than 'Rath-Farnham' (1749) by the hapless Henry Jones. Like Denham, and unlike Ward, who moves in allegorical fashion through his park, Jones is stationary on a prominence, near Rathfarnham Castle outside Dublin, letting his 'roving Eye' and the flight of his Muse (cf. Denham's Muse and 'wandring eye') do his walking for him as he contemplates four topographical features in orderly succession. The description from a hilltop of one prospect after another (which in combination form a landscape) is the basic visual principle of topographical poetry. Even did we not know that Denham in later life became Surveyor General of the Works, nor the word 'survey' so frequently appear in topographical poetry, we ought still to appreciate the similarity between the methods of early surveyors and those of topographical poets. To survey is to overlook, to see the whole from the vantage-point of an elevated position: surveyor and poet alike established a 'station' on a hill from which they could survey the land bounded by other chosen prominences. The poet swivels his 'Eye' (almost always in the impersonal singular, as though it were an instrument) as the surveyor swivels *his* eye and the alidade on his theodolite or circumferentor. The surveyor measures angles and distances, as the poet, through a kind of 'measurement in thought', contemplates historical and political meanings and associations. We can even diagram early topographical poems, and the result looks remarkably like the 'triangulations' of early surveyors.

The rise of topographical poetry coincides with the acceleration of scientific surveying, which suggests the science's influence on the poetry.[9] There were in turn socio-economic spurs to the development of surveying: in England during the sixteenth and seventeenth centuries it was enclosure; in Ireland during the seventeenth century it was the Cromwellian Settlement, during which Sir William Petty produced, in the so-called Down Survey, the first scientific mapping out of Ireland. Practical and theoretical map-making and surveying developed apace throughout the eighteenth century, indirectly resulting in such poems as Richard Jago's 'Edge Hill' (1767). Ireland contributed several texts on surveying during that century, among them Robert Gibson's *A Treatise of Practical Surveying* (1752; 2nd ed. Dublin 1763), Peter Callan's *A Dissertation on the Practice of Land-Surveying in Ireland* (Drogheda 1758) and Benjamin Noble's *Geodaesia Hibernica* (Dublin 1763). Callan is unintentionally whimsical, setting out to rid Ireland of fraudulences and anomalies in surveying: his picture of the island swarming with dissembling surveyors is positively Carletonesque. It is clear from his book, however, that surveying in Ireland was closely connected with the outrageous land situation and with the incidence of confiscation, forfeiture and reapportionment. The book by Gibson (d. 1760), on the other hand, was a genuine contribution to the science and was the first English surveying text to be published in North America, where it passed through twenty-one editions.[10]

Using prominences like a surveyor, Jones makes four 'eye-shifts', which plot the poem's narrative and structure its philosophy. Less literally, however, prominences enable him to escape the hazardous lowlands of Callanesque Ireland. The landscape is a metaphor for the harmony-in-inequality of human society:

> As in the moral World we, wond'ring, see
> Such diff'rent Stations, yet such just Degree;
> Which all contribute wisely to sustain
> The mutual Intercourse, and social Chain,
> Whose Links in regular Gradation fall,
> Whilst all in one, and each depends on all:
> Wise Nature, thus, proportions her Degrees,
> From shrubs to Cedars, and from Brooks to Seas.[11]

This is standard eighteenth-century fare, illustrating how Denham's use of landscape as a metaphor for *concordia discors* and fundamental principles of government degenerated into a partisan metaphor for social class. The established highborn and the grasping lowborn both justified inequality, but the lowborn had to admit in their justification their own lowly position if they were to have a chance of improving it. When he remarks that 'lesser Hills upon those Mountains wait', Jones is expediently imagining himself a lesser hill and the Earl of Chesterfield (to whom his book of poems is dedicated) as a mountain. Jones was a bricklayer born near Drogheda in 1721 who came to the attention of Philip Stanhope, fourth Earl of Chesterfield, when he addressed a poem of welcome to the new Lord Lieutenant in 1745. Chesterfield (who was largely responsible for the planting of Phoenix Park) took Jones to London where his tragedy *The Earl of Essex* enjoyed great success. Later, in the words of O'Donoghue, Jones 'gave way to dissipation and drink' and was cast off by Chesterfield after borrowing money from a servant. After a two-day binge, Jones was run over and fatally injured in St Martin's Lane in 1770.

Jones's social career made him exaggerate the panegyric formulas of topographical poetry. Of the four prospects in 'Rath-Farnham' – a view of fair Eblana (Dublin) in the distance, the Lord Chancellor's residence to the east, the home of Mr Baron Mountney ('My Patron, Guide, and let me add, my Friend'), and Rathfarnham Castle itself[12] – two evince Jones's self-insinuation into high society. But the deferential allusions to Mountney and the Lord Chancellor also reflect that change of emphasis in topographical poetry signalled as early as Garth's 'Claremont', Ward's 'Phoenix Park' and the description of Trumbull's retirement at the close of 'Windsor Forest': that is, the diversion from central seats of power to gentlemen's seats of retirement and leisure. Harmony and order remain as values but exchange their currency. Jones does declare of Dublin: 'And Health and Peace are her's [*sic*] – for *Stanhope* reigns' (cf. Pope: 'And peace and plenty tell, a STUART reigns'), but like Pope he half turns his back upon state affairs, attracted by the private estates of the powerful. The topographical locale is no longer wholly a microcosm of the often bloody realm, but a microcosm also of polite human society. The *landscape of taste* (embracing notions of art, wit and manners) succeeds the landscape of polity. Jones speaks of Rathfarnham Castle's 'rich Embellishments' displaying 'true Taste', while 'teeming Nature' thrives in the valley below. He praises the warm sheltered climate and the exotic blooms in the grounds of William Palmer (to whom the poem is dedicated) and concludes: 'Lo! Nature, here, and Art for ever vie;/And Art the Mind, and Nature charms the Eye.' The artistic garden, set amidst a larger and more natural landscape, is the topographical poet's new locale, and is very different from Denham's expansive, natural prospect.

Like his contemporaries, Denham had a literary interest in wild nature (the picturesque motif), but he had little sense – literary or otherwise – of man-shaped landscape. The concern with artistic *vis-à-vis* natural landscape coincides with the rise half a century later of Whiggism in politics, Shaftesbury's philosophy in aesthetics and ethics, the cult of Italian landscape painting, and an English style in landscape gardening. Sir John Vanbrugh (1664–1726), who landscaped Claremont estate in Surrey, did much to break the domination of French and Dutch formalities in the English garden and worked, as Edward Malins tells us, in a climate of opinion characterized by the Whig benevolence of the Earl of Shaftesbury (1671–1713).[13] Vanbrugh demonstrated how nature, instead of having artistic will imposed upon her, could be shaped to resemble artistic conceptions. The ideal in all things became a balance between art and nature, passion and mind, reason and imagination, and gentlemen sought to reproduce this balance in their estates. Other philosophers and landscapes followed in the wake of Shaftesbury and Vanbrugh. William Kent (1684–1748) and Capability Brown (1715–83) took Vanbrugh's development of an English or 'Natural' style still farther, while Shaftesbury's *Characteristics* (1711) was followed in 1725 by an *Inquiry into the Original of our Ideas of Beauty and Virtue* from the pen of County Down-born Francis Hutcheson (1694–1746).[14]

Through the researches of Edward Malins, we know that in the theory and practice of landscaping, 'the work of Irishmen, principally Jonathan Swift and Patrick Delany, was simultaneous with that of their English counterparts, with whom they were in close touch'.[15] Rev. Patrick Delany, fellow and tutor at Trinity College, heard the views of his friend Swift, who, like Pope, desired greater freedom in landscaping, and in 1724 started to improve a small estate called Delville, at Glasnevin outside Dublin, which is now part of the Botanic Gardens. Delany is thus credited by Malins with introducing the modern style of gardening into Ireland. In accordance with the fashionable significance attached to landscape, Delville became the centre of an artistic and intellectual coterie (including, among others, Swift, Tickell and Addison), comparable with the Worcestershire estate owned by William Shenstone and lengthily versified in James Woodhouse's 'The Leasowes' (1764).[16] The coterie, withdrawn for self-protection from the wider public, is imaged in the garden surrounded by less cultivated landscape.

Malins claims that the natural topography of Ireland was easily adaptable to the new style of gardening: 'In Ireland, where so much rolling, lake-begirt natural landscape was available, it was popular and cheaper to lay out a garden by making use of these natural advantages, rather than create Baroque *parterres* and elaborate *allées . . .*'.[17] Other Irish estates and gardens were landscaped after Delville in deference to the new style: they included Dangan, near Trim; Market Hill, Co. Armagh; Sir Arthur Gore's at Killala, Co. Mayo; Lord Orrery's at Caledon, Co. Tyrone, and, presumably, those of Henry Jones's rich friends. Yet 'Rath-Farnham' itself is an old-fashioned poem, and reads more like an augury than a celebration of that pre-picturesque tradition of aesthetics that created the landscape of taste.

III

Denham, though visualizing through the filter of poetic convention rather than actually seeing, wrote in 'Cooper's Hill' of the 'steep horrid roughness of the Wood' that 'Strives with the gentle calmness of the flood'. Pope and Ward have similar and obligatory picturesque passages. But it was John Dyer who in 'Grongar Hill' and 'The Country Walk' (both 1726) raised the motif to the status of a pervasive tone and theme. There is something of 'L'Allegro' and 'Il Penseroso' in Dyer's poems, with their snappy, four-beat couplets and vivid chiaroscuro, but it has been established that Dyer, who was a painter, was influenced by the seventeenth-century Italian landscape painters Claude Lorraine (1600–82) and Salvator Rosa (1615–73), whose work was then becoming popular in England. Under the influence of painting, poets and non-poets alike began to appreciate, judge, even see landscapes pictorially as well as politically and literarily. Simultaneously, an aesthetic of emotion was developed alongside an aesthetic of pictorial composition. By a species of pathetic fallacy, feelings were thought not only to be kindled by the landscape but also to reside in the landscape: hence the exaggeration in picturesqueness, as though landscape features were solidified feelings of awe, delight, melancholy and wonder.

What had been mere literary motif became a philosophy: the landscape of taste became the *landscape of feeling*. The socio-aesthetic theories of Pope, Shaftesbury and Hutcheson – with their emphases on taste, good sense and human capability – gave way to Burke's *Enquiry into the Origin of Our Ideas of the Sublime and Beautiful* (1757) that took account of the asocial feelings of individual men and nature's immensity independent of mankind. Burke stimulated a new generation of landscapers, including Sir Humphrey Repton (1752–1818), who sought the picturesque qualities of roughness, irregularity and surprise. The Popian balance between art and nature tilted towards nature. The picturesque-lover – busily doctoring his garden to resemble wild nature – really, however, desired the *illusion* of remote landscape recently touched only by the hand of time. Moreover, the feelings aroused were stylized and programmed: it came as no surprise when Sir Uvedale Price in his *Essays on the Picturesque* (1794) simply added another watertight category – the picturesque – to Burke's beauty and sublimity.

The cult of the picturesque began in what Malins calls the 'romantic-poetic' garden, but soon topographical poets, like other lovers of landscape, left the estates and gardens and sought their locales in fashionably 'remote' areas, so continuing the move away from centre that began with the landscape of taste. The demand for poems about outer locations presented opportunities for regional poets hitherto wholly at a disadvantage if they could not travel to London, as Henry Jones did. Irish poets were especially equipped to capitalize, because Ireland had the kind of landscape that not only appealed to landscapers but also evoked picturesque feelings. The picturesque hand of time, in the guise of castles and abbeys, ruined or otherwise, was evident everywhere on the island, and often these were located (originally for purposes of defence or contemplation) in picturesquely remote areas. Killarney in particular inspired poems, among them John Leslie's 'Killarney' (1772), Joseph Atkinson's 'Killarney' (1798) and later Charles Hoyle's 'Three Days at Killarney' (1828).[18]

These poems retain conservative political associations, but in order, one feels, to sell copies as well as to further a certain view of society: Leslie dedicates his poem to Lord Viscount Townshend, the Lord Lieutenant, Atkinson to the Earl of Moira, while Hoyle acknowledges the Earl of Kenmare. Balance and conservatism in government are matched by these qualities in feeling, with delight carefully balanced by melancholy, awe by cosy contentment. In style, too, the heroic couplet and iambic pentameter are retained long after their heyday, in order to accommodate, in an increasingly middle-brow fashion, the familiar topographical motifs, including in Leslie and Atkinson the staghunt (a rural sport inherited from 'Cooper's Hill') and the call to patriotism (British patriotism, of course). There are local versions of the 'Commerce' motif: Leslie bemoans the inability of Kenmare's harbours to attract foreign shipping; less graciously, Atkinson encouraged English workers to come to Killarney so that 'our rude peasants, by example wise,/Shall see new manufactures round them rise'.

Atkinson and Leslie are conscious of landscape poetry, painting and gardening, and see Killarney through these media. Unlike the landscapers of taste, however, they see art and nature in alternation, even in conflict:

> The craggy heights and tufted hills oppose
> This cultured sight, and wilder scenes disclose;
> Tho' unembellish'd by laborious art,
> Their native wonders greater charms impart,

writes Atkinson when looking at a cultivated part of Killarney. And Leslie, for whom 'Majestick Nature's artless symmetry' unites the 'Wonderful, Sublime, and Fair,' notes that 'Nature and Art their diff'rent claims maintain,/Divide their empire, and alternate reign.' Neither poet, of course, wants his nature *too* wild. Leslie asks us to behold 'the rude masonry of rocky piles' that forms Killarney's islands:

> Grotesque and various, from the deep they rise,
> And catch by turns, new forms to mock our eyes.

But he assures us that Killarney sports no alpine horrors, 'No massy fragments, pendant from on high/With hideous ruin strike the aching eye.' (Cf. Denham: 'no stupendious precipice denies/Access, no horror turns away our eyes'.)

The grotesque and various might be fully appreciated only by acquaintance with landscape poetry and painting, but first they had to be seen, and this entailed travel to relatively remote regions. 'The awakening in England to an appreciation of landscape,' claims

Christopher Hussey, 'was a direct result of the Grand Tour fashionable with the aristocracy after the isolation of the country from the rest of Europe during the greater part of the seventeenth century.'[19] Englishmen abroad became familiar with the landscapes and paintings that were to form models for picturesque theorists and landscapers. During the middle and late eighteenth century, the connoisseur and collector of paintings, engravings and etchings became prominent, injecting the note of snobbery that sounds throughout the picturesque movement. In this burgeoning of connoisseurship and travel, the Irish Ascendancy participated, while the hapless native Irish travelled in Ireland only for the lowlier purposes of finding food and employment.

Travel abroad encouraged travel at home. It can be said that the cult of the picturesque created modern tourism, which still depends heavily on 'selling' picturesque scenery. It was in the eighteenth century that places such as Killarney generated their modern reputations, and they did so partly through picturesque engravings, prints and etchings. Atkinson counsels us to consult by way of compensation, should we not be able to get to Killarney, Jonathan Fisher's prints in *The Beauties of Ireland*. He may be referring here to Fisher's *Scenery of Ireland* (1795), more probably to *A Picturesque Tour of Killarney* (Dublin 1789). In twenty aquatints and six engravings, Fisher seeks in the latter 'to lead the curious (who visit the Lake) to points of view, where the sublime and beautiful are most picturesquely combined; and which often might be hastily passed by, if the Painter's observation did not induce a more critical examination'. Fisher's aquatints, however, are appealingly underplayed, without that overcharging common to the picturesque: like Leslie and Atkinson, he plainly eschews the wilder shores of the cult. Other favourite haunts of the painter and etcher were the Giant's Causeway and Cashel, as we can see from Rosalind M. Elmes's *Catalogue of Irish Topographical Prints and Original Drawings* (Dublin 1943).

More informative than prints were the descriptions of tours in Ireland by doughty and industrious individuals. These mushroomed during the picturesque period, and included William Rufus Chetwood's *A Tour through Ireland* (1746), Richard Pococke's *Tour in Ireland* (1752), John Bush's *Hibernia Curiosa* (1767) and Arthur Young's famous tours in Ireland in 1776, 1777 and 1778. Young bristles with practicality, but does permit himself this of Killarney (proving how standard such observations must then have been):

'Soon entered the wildest and most romantic country I had any where seen; a region of steep rocks and mountains . . . There is something magnificently wild in this stupendous scenery, formed to impress the mind with a certain species of terror.' Topographical poets, too, frequently fell into this rhetoric that had once been fresh and which afterwards became the traveloguese of tourist operators.

Travel depended on such practical affairs as the state of the roads and the existence of road-maps. Road-books and road-maps began to appear in Ireland at the time interest in the picturesque was running high. According to Sir Herbert Fordham, there were no road-books in Ireland before 1647 (coincidentally within five years of 'Cooper's Hill'), when a surveyor produced one.[20] Few followed until 1763. In 1778, George Taylor and Andrew Skinner published their pioneering and ambitious *Maps of the Roads of Ireland*, much used by subsequent topographers. It was not, however, until late in the century that road-books actually printed in Dublin began appearing, beginning with the *Post-Chaise Companion: or Traveller's Directory through Ireland* (1784). William W. Seward's directory, *Topographia Hibernica* (Dublin 1795), appearing a year after Price's *Essays on the Picturesque*, has a picturesque bias when treating Killarney, which he describes as 'astonishingly sublime' and striking 'the timid with awe'. But Seward's book is useful as well as rhapsodic, and topographical poets, like everyone else, plainly availed of it.

Interest in the picturesque was maintained well into the nineteenth century, and in a sense its vocabulary and mode of vision have never been totally abandoned. William Carr in 'Rosstrevor' (Newry 1810) writes of ivy-mantl'd piles and Gothic grandeur and of the picturesque prospect from the top of the Mournes, this last an attempt no doubt to honour both the basic and climactic situation in topographical poetry (the view from a hilltop) and the local pride motif (one senses a regionalist desire to rival Leslie's and Atkinson's Mangerton). Carr's poem has many of the standard formulas, as well as a passing celebration of the recent Act of Union (*his* Runnymede?), without which Ireland 'must drooping then to gradual ruin tend'. The poet's only concession to Romanticism is in leaving his pentameters unrhymed and in including a recollection of his own childhood.

IV

All along, an aspect of 'Cooper's Hill' quite different from the picturesque motif was influencing topographical poetry: the methodical and informative manner in which Denham described and contemplated features of the landscape. We have already noted the resemblance to early surveying; some poets fastened on this approach of Denham's, importing into their poetry an increasingly scientific vision until their poems resembled versified ordnance survey maps. Moreover, topography became more widely interpreted to mean not only the physical layout, but also the history, biology and geology of a locality. In the hands of amateur scientists and poetasters, the fine symbolic balance between feature and meaning in 'Cooper's Hill' was upset, and, in compensation, readers were given more topographical information and lengthier discussion of its significance; in short, the landscape became increasingly literal.

Whereas 'Cooper's Hill', 'Windsor Forest' and 'Phoenix Park' had – as befits their classical origins – a strongly pagan cast, subsequent topographical poetry was largely Christian. A Christian outlook coexisted with a scientific outlook; indeed, to achieve a harmony of the two was frequently the point of the poem. It is clear that the topographical genre fell under the spell of the physico-theological movement that began with Thomas Burnet, John Ray and William Derham.[21] This movement was in part an attempt to square the account of the earth's origin in Genesis with that presented by contemporary geology. An astonishing number of topographical poets were clergymen, including, among many others, Ward, Dyer, Jago, Hoyle, William Lisle Bowles, Thomas Maurice and William Hamilton Drummond. Many later poets were also enthusiastic amateur scientists. From these twin interests was created in the poetry a *landscape of divine phenomena*, that is, a landscape that was scientifically intriguing and yet the handiwork of God.

The physico-theological debates were conducted during what Karl Alfred Von Zittel calls the second Age of Geology, i.e. from the Middle Ages until around 1790.[22] However, the establishment of modern geology during the 'Heroic Age of Geology' (1790–1820) made the position of Christian scientists more difficult, particularly concerning the formation of the earth's crust and the dating of fossils. One might be forgiven for imagining that contemporary Ulster, with its contentious Protestant divines, might be a hotbed for physico-theological debate.* What is certain is that during a period that

---

* Peter Brooke has, since this essay appeared, retrieved for us the physico-theological debate in early-nineteenth-century Ulster that rather lazily I merely speculated about: 'Religion and Secular Thought 1800–75' in *Belfast: The Making of the City*, eds J.C. Beckett et al. (Belfast: Appletree Press 1983).

coincides with both the heroic age of geology and the late flowering of the picturesque, Ulster produced a large number of topographical poems written by, among others, William Drennan, William Hamilton Drummond, James Stuart, Thomas Beggs, Samuel Thomson, William Carr and John McKinley.[23] That Ulster was one of the beneficiaries of the localization of the topographical genre is not unconnected with the fact that in possessing the Antrim coast and the Giant's Causeway, she was close to the centre of the picturesque cult and the geological debates (the picturesque and geologically interesting place occasionally being one and the same). And despite their distance in time and space from the original topographical poets, the Ulster poets remained conscious of the national genre in which they worked. Thomson (1766–1816), a Templepatrick, Co. Antrim schoolmaster, laments:

> O had I Denham's classic skill
> Or Dyer's soft descriptive quill,
> The beauties of the verdant Lyle
> Should echo round my native isle,
> Great Pope had lofty Windsor's groves . . .

And in his preface to 'Clontarf' (1822), Drummond repeats Johnson's definition with which this paper opened, and credits Denham with having originated what Drummond calls 'loco-descriptive poetry'.

Of the Ulster poets, Rev. William Hamilton Drummond (1778–1865) is with Drennan (1754–1820) the most interesting. Durling calls Drummond 'an outstanding local poet' in his survey of the genre. It must be said, though, that the readability of 'The Giant's Causeway' (1811) is less that of an epic poem than that of a scientific thriller.[24] Despite, perhaps indeed because of, the poem's epic apparatus (it occupies an entire volume, is divided into three Books, has a long preface and a hundred pages of geological and historical notes), 'The Giant's Causeway' is the versification of hard matter by a first-rate intellect and a second-rate imagination. To compare Drummond's poem with Jago's 'Edge Hill' (1767) is nevertheless to uncover successive and exciting layers of the history of geology. Jago follows slavishly Burnet's theory of the role of the biblical Flood in the formation of the earth's crust, a theory presented in the *Sacred Theory of the Earth* (1681–9). Jago also uses the fossil theories of John Woodward (1665–1722), and 'the most famous English representative of the religious school of geologists', as Von Zittel calls him) and the theories of John Ray (1627–1705) regarding the action of water, both Diluvialists like Burnet.

Writing forty years after Jago, Drummond has access to post-Diluvialist thought during the heroic age of geology. The action of water was still held paramount by the Neptunists, headed by A.G. Werner (1750–1817), but the latter were now opposed by the Vulcanists, whose chief theorist was James Hutton (1726–97). According to Hutton, the strata of the earth's present crust are the debris of an antecedent earth, worn down by the elements, carried into the oceanic abysses and there laid horizontally down, fused and consolidated by subaqueous heat, and afterwards elevated to their present altitude, and broken and dislocated into their present form.

For both factions of geology, the Giant's Causeway was a convenient case-study, an open secret of the earth's subterranean workings. Drummond tells us that 'philosophers' began to attend to the Causeway, after a fifty-year respite, when in 1740 two beautiful engravings of the phenomenon came to public attention (another instance of the geological and picturesque combining). To Drummond, as topographical poet as well as amateur geologist and clergyman, the Causeway is a microcosm of the earth's crust and of God's handiwork, just as for Denham the Thames valley was a microcosm of the realm. Like Denham, Drummond discusses the history and mythology of his locality in Book One, and in Book Two describes the folkways of the area (a georgic motif Durling calls 'the genre sketch'). In Book Three, Drummond versifies three main theories of the Causeway's origin – Neptunism, Vulcanism and the vertical-force theory of Rev. William Richardson (1740–1820), an Irish geologist and rector of Moy – 'without having professed a decided attachment to any'. Richardson apart, Irish geologists played an eminent role in the formulation and application of Neptunism and Vulcanism. Three workers mentioned by Drummond are Richard Kirwan (1733–1812), the Galway chemist and geologist, author of *Elements of Mineralogy*, whose criticism of the Huttonian theory involved him in a heated controversy and whom Drummond calls 'Neptunian KIRWAN, green Ierne's pride'; John Templeton (1766–1825), the Belfast botanist and meteorologist; and the unfortunate William Hamilton (b. 1755), the Londonderry antiquarian and geologist whose *Letters Concerning the Northern Coast of the County of Antrim* professed a volcanic theory of the basalts, and who was assassinated (as a clergyman of the Established Church and magistrate) in 1797.

Drummond's poem was followed in 1819 by a poem of the same name from the pen of John McKinley, who assures us that despite the similarities of content and treatment, part of his poem was written before Drummond published his and that in any case he, McKinley, would not presume to emulate Drummond since he was only six months at school![25] Like Drummond's, McKinley's poem is got up in the garb of a classical epic, further evidence of how the topographical poem, always partial to expansiveness, paradoxically belittled itself through bloated ambition and a purely mechanical notion of epic scale. McKinley follows Drummond in combining geology with a picturesque appreciation of the embattled capes, impending cliffs, and 'surge-scoop'd antres, thunder-splinter'd spires' of the Antrim coast.

The Huttonian theory towards which Drummond and McKinley incline taught that geological formations succeed one another in an endless sequence of decay, upheaval and consolidation. The need for constant renewal accorded with the Christian belief that the present earth is sinful and imperfect, while the geological concept of 'renovation' was evidence that God's benevolent hand was still upon the planet. Where Drummond would differ from Hutton would be over the latter's majestically soulful claim that in the fate of the earth's crust 'we find no vestige of a beginning – no prospect of an end'. The Christian poets preferred the notion of Doomsday, and many of them used it as a convenient climax for their poems.

Of renovation, McKinley (though it could have been Drummond) writes:

> Hail, Renovation! thou whose plastic care
> Can worlds on worlds from age to age repair.

As a moral and spiritual notion, renovation was a bridge between science and Christianity. It also bridged these with political vision. Joseph Atkinson, exhorting hard-working Englishmen to come to Killarney, desires to see among the Irish, as a result, 'in their neat cots a renovated race'. From beginning to end, topographical poetry was an ameliorist genre that promulgated the idea that things are always in the process of getting better. It was also a conservative genre that desired equilibrium and steady progress, harmony and moderation, states achievable only through vigilance (such as that of the topographical poet from the vantage-point of his elevated position) and the will to check as well as to reform. At the centre of the genre was

26

the realization that these states paradoxically proceed from discord, excess and imbalance. The notions of amelioration, upheaval and dynamic equilibrium are all contained in the concept of renovation which one can easily imagine Denham embracing: 'Cooper's Hill', like Drummond's 'The Giant's Causeway', depicts a universe in which certain climactic events propel the earth and human society forward. Throughout the genre, the abstract metaphors for the ideal of harmony and equilibrium (polity, taste, feeling, divinity and geological curiosity) alter as society changes, and along with them the kind of landscape in which these states are vested. But the states themselves, along with the genre's structure and motifs, endure; in this way, the history of topographical poetry enacts its own philosophy.

[1974]

NOTES

1. *The Works of Samuel Johnson* (Dublin 1793), p. 55.
2. 'A Redefinition of Topographical Poetry', *Journal of English and Germanic Philology*, LXIX (1970), 394–406.
3. Dwight L. Durling, in the final chapter of his *Georgic Tradition in English Poetry* (New York: Columbia University Press 1935), briefly annotates a list of georgic motifs that were absorbed into topographical poetry: the didactic episode, seasons of the year, parts of the day, the genre sketch, scientific facts or theories in episode, the use of natural history, the exotic episode, the patriotic panegyric, the moral episode, the narrative episode, themes of benevolence and humanitarianism, and divine immanence in nature. Other topographical formulas, including the use of rural sports and the modesty, retirement and local pride motifs, are discussed in R.A. Aubin's standard history of the genre, *Topographical Poetry in Eighteenth-Century England* (New York: MLA 1936).
4. Gerard Langbaine, *English Dramatic Poets* (1691), quoted by Theodore Howard Banks Jr in the introduction to his authoritative edition of *The Poetical Works of Sir John Denham* (New Haven: Yale University Press 1928), p. 3. 'Cooper's Hill' first appeared in 1642, and in revised editions in 1655 and 1668. In 1969, Brendan O Hehir published a critical edition of the poem, *Expans'd Hieroglyphicks* (Berkeley: University of California Press).
5. All students of 'Cooper's Hill' are indebted to Earl R. Wasserman for his masterly explication of the political contexts and meanings of the poem and of the principle of *concordia discors* in *The Subtler Language: Critical Readings of Neoclassic and Romantic Poems* (Baltimore: Johns Hopkins Press 1959).
6. 'Phoenix Park' appeared in *A Miscellany of Poems* (Dublin 1718). Rev. James Ward, according to O'Donoghue, was a Trinity College graduate.
7. Ward is writing long before Phoenix Park was developed and planted around 1745.
8. *A History of Ireland* (London: Methuen, sixth edn 1950), p. 292.
9. For the history of modern surveying, consult Sir Herbert Fordham, *Some Notable Surveyors and Map-Makers of the Sixteenth, Seventeenth, and Eighteenth Centuries and*

their Work (Cambridge: University Press 1929) and A.W Richeson, *English Land Measuring to 1800: Instruments and Practices* (Cambridge, Mass.: MIT Press 1966). (In 'The Measure of Paradise: Topography in Eighteenth-Century Poetry,' *Eighteenth-Century Studies* IX, 2 [1975–6], I have explored the relationship between surveying and topographical poetry – JWF.)

10. Richeson, p. 201. (Ireland, incidentally, also had its instrument makers; consult Thomas H. Mason, 'Dublin Opticians and Instrument Makers,' *Dublin Historical Record* VI [1944], 133–49. Mason speculates that the city's instrument makers were 'kept busy in supplying the wants of surveyors of lands during the redistribution which took place subsequent to the Williamite War in Ireland' – JWF.)

11. 'Rath-Farnham' appeared in Jones's *Poems on Several Occasions* (Dublin 1749).

12. Richard Mountney (1707–68) was an Irish judge and classical scholar who was one of the Barons of the Exchequer. Rathfarnham Castle was built by Archbishop Loftus in 1587, but its military importance during the English Civil War interrupted its religious associations.

13. Edward Malins, *English Landscaping and Literature 1660–1840* (London: Oxford University Press 1966), p. 20.

14. Hutcheson's grandfather had emigrated to Co. Down from Ayrshire, presumably during the Plantation of Ulster. Francis was born near Saintfield, was educated in Scotland, returned to Ulster for a time, lived in Dublin, and later became Professor of Moral Philosophy at Glasgow University.

15. 'Landscape Gardening by Jonathan Swift and his Friends in Ireland,' *Garden History* II (1973), 69.

16. Poems by several poets of the Delville circle, including Swift, Parnell and Delany, can be found in *Miscellaneous Poems, Original and Translated, by Several Hands*, an anthology published by Matthew Concanen in London in 1724. This book, which has been claimed as the first Irish poetry anthology, also includes Ward's 'Phoenix Park'.

17. 'Landscape Gardening by Jonathan Swift and his Friends in Ireland', 82.

18. John Leslie, *Killarney: A Poem* (London 1772): Leslie (d. 1778) was tutor to Lord Clanwilliam and also wrote 'Phoenix Park' (1772), a copy of which I have yet to see; Joseph Atkinson, *Killarney, A Poem* (Dublin 1798): Atkinson was born in Dublin in 1743, was a soldier and intimate friend of Thomas Moore, and died in England in 1818, although a slab was erected to his memory in Monkstown church, Co. Dublin; Charles Hoyle, *Three Days at Killarney; with Other Poems* (London 1828): Rev. Charles Hoyle was vicar of Overton, near Marlborough.

19. *The Picturesque* (London: Putnam's 1927), p. 12.

20. 'The Road-Books and Itineraries of Ireland, 1647 to 1850, A Catalogue', *The Bibliographical Society of Ireland* II (1923), 66.

21. See Basil Willey, *The Eighteenth-Century Background* (London: Chatto and Windus 1957), chapter II.

22. *History of Geology and Palaeontology*, trans. M.M. Ogilvie-Gordon (London: Scott 1901).

23. An account of the Ulster poets is given by John Hewitt in *Ulster Poets 1800–50* (a paper read to the Belfast Literary Society in 1950) which includes the quotation from Thomson I have used. To this period also belongs the Co. Meath poet Anna Liddiard, author of *Mount Leinster or The Prospect* (Dublin 1819).

24. *The Giant's Causeway: A Poem* (Belfast 1811). Drummond, a controversial essayist and sermonizer, was born in Larne, Co. Antrim and educated in Belfast and Glasgow, after which he became Pastor of the Second Congregation in Belfast.

25. John McKinley, *The Giant's Causeway, A Poem* (Belfast 1819; Dublin 1821). McKinley, from Co. Antrim, was said to have been an ancestor of President McKinley of the United States.

2

THE GEOGRAPHY OF IRISH FICTION

The Irish are possessed by place. In part, such possession is a practical necessity, a way of separating common and identical names by attaching them genitivally to a uniqueness of place: Johnston of Bally-kilbeg, O'Sullivan of Beare. But from the beginning, even before the practical necessity, the self and the places it came from and inhabits are bound. 'A notable characteristic of Irish tales', wrote Jeremiah Curtin, 'is the definiteness of names and places in a majority of them. In the Irish myths we are told who the characters are, what their condition of life is, and where they lived and acted; the heroes and their fields of action are brought before us with as much definiteness as if they were persons of today or yesterday.'[1] Later, names and placenames make equal demands upon the poet. In 'Easter 1916', it is the obligatory bardic recital of euphonic names that cuts short the poet's moral self-interrogation. And in 'Under Ben Bulben', the poet brings his name and native place together in appropriate fusion after a lifetime's exploration of both: 'Under bare Ben Bulben's head/In Drumcliff churchyard Yeats is laid.'

In its preoccupation with place as an unseverable aspect of self, Irish fiction is a descendant of the Irish mythic tale. Certainly 'setting' is an inadequate word to describe the attention Irish writers lavish upon geographic location and topography. As in the case of poets ('An ancestor was rector there') and mythmakers, the fiction writer's preoccupation with place is a preoccupation with the past without which Irish selfhood is apparently inconceivable. The past is constantly made contemporary through an obsession with remembered place. The spirit of Edna O'Brien's epigraph to *A Pagan Place* (1970), a quotation from Brecht, is highly appropriate to the novel and our case: 'I carry a brick on my shoulder in order that the world may know what my house was like.'[2] This has an un-Irish economy to it, however: the Irishman usually tries to carry his entire house around with him. It is not entirely voluntary. A recurring theme in the Irish novel is the attempt to escape what Sean O'Faolain in *Bird Alone* (1936) calls the 'cave of self'. Even when the self appears to have emerged from its cave, it still inhabits what O'Faolain in the same novel calls the 'shell of self', which for my purposes I will take to mean place transformed into the memory of place and therefore transportable. When this theme is conscious, we have that recurring Irish topophobia, hatred of the place that ensnares the self.

Yet precisely in the memory of place lies the degree of freedom of self the Irish writer enjoys. If the physical reality of Ireland has stamped itself heavily upon Irish novels and stories, the fiction in turn has put its signatures upon the physical reality. Again, the precedent is in myth: 'A mythology in the time of its greatest vigor puts its imprint on the whole region to which it belongs; the hills, rivers, mountains, plains, villages, trees, rocks, springs, and plants are all made sacred.'[3] What was sacred for the community in myth is sacred to the individual writer in literature; Irish writers tend to have almost totemic relations with one or two places. Writers have appropriated the real Ireland and turned its places over into imaginative and fictional landscapes of often great and magical beauty. I do not mean merely imaginary and fictitious landscapes, for they are fashioned from the world of the geographers and topographers. Occasionally they can be found on the map. Irish writers have created an Ireland astonishingly richer than the Ireland of real existence, but this love of place, what Gaston Bachelard calls 'topophilia', is really a love of self which only in the short run contravenes the theme of self-escape. Ultimately, the Irish writer's concern with place is evidence of a subjectivity he is unwilling or unable to transcend. The richer the imagination the more expansive and decorative the captivity.[4]

'The geography of Irish fiction', then, is an essentially ambiguous phrase, implying both real and fictional place. We feel more comfortable with the first, imagining that fiction writers simply *utilize* real places and that the fictional Ireland can be fitted over the real Ireland like a film. If we can use a textbook geography of Ireland as a guide to the fiction, then equally might we use the fiction as a guide to Ireland, since most of the island from Rathlin to Cahirciveen is re-created somewhere in novel or story. This has already been attempted, for literature as a whole, by Susan and Thomas Cahill in their interesting book, *A Literary Guide to Ireland* (1973). This is a literary survey of Irish geography, complete with a map showing the places to be found in the works of particular authors. The map and text omit Ulster, however, for the Cahills consider their literary Ireland to bounded by Patrick Kavanagh country in the north-east, Yeats country in the north-west, O'Flaherty country in the west, and Somerville and Ross country in the south. In order to survey in like fashion the places that have occurred in fiction, we should want references to novelists and storywriters that the Cahills leave out, including John Broderick, Francis MacManus, Brinsley MacNamara, Walter Macken and James Plunkett. We should also want to reinstate Ulster, to map and describe, for example, the Co. Fermanagh of Anne Crone, the Rathlin Island of Michael McLaverty and the Co. Down of St John Ervine.

Perhaps we should also want to establish the *frequency* with which particular places occur in the fiction; if you like, a demography as well as geography of Irish fiction. Why certain places – Dublin, Belfast, Cork, Derry – attract writers is easily explained by the statistics of population and commerce. But the frequency of occurrence of other places – Galway, Aran – cannot be so explained. In these cases we are faced with the imaginative potency of place that often seems inversely related to actual social importance. Certainly their potency has to do with the force of fictional repetition, perhaps more so with the force of fictional achievement (by virtue of which Joyce's Galway, say, in 'The Dead' carries an immense impact). What is important for us to realize, however, is that place in Irish fiction (*pace* the Cahills) is *essentially* fictional and imaginative and packs the power of individual and communal dream. Galway, Aran, Connemara: these have functioned as a kind of otherworld, representations of lonely and barren spaces to which the Irish literary imagination has had frequent recourse. They are places of solitude and retreat (flight and succour), of passion and of timelessness, and they exist in the west, in a permanent recess of the Irish psyche. Less dreamlike, Dublin, Cork and Belfast, the crowded eastern places, are equally places of the imagination. For this reason, one can easily envisage a fictional geography of Ireland written by someone who was totally an armchair traveller.

What holds for geography holds equally for topography. Certainly Ireland's amazingly varied and swift-changing topography from farthest Rosses to thronging city streets is reflected in the fiction. Even when it is difficult to ascertain exactly where in Ireland a particular novel or scene is meant to be set, the force of place frequently remains through the novel's dependence upon creating and distinguishing *kinds* of landscape. For example, rural Irish novels set among small farmers often derive their plots from the deeply rooted ancestral bonds families have with particular fields and townlands, and from the uprooting force of land-hunger and its effects, land-grabbing or forced migration. In such fiction, as in real life, the distinction between green and fertile lowland and poor, often barren upland is paramount. So important, indeed, are such distinctions that kinds of terrain – town and country, lowlands and uplands, island and mainland, lake and river – carry imaginative values in the fiction. The critic's task is to understand these values, to 'uncode', in Seamus Heaney's phrase, 'all landscape'.

When the novelist creates place, he is using a form of language. In order to understand his places, we need a study of the rhetoric of place in Irish fiction, the rhetoric of landscape and townscape, of geography and topography. Part of such a study would be what Bachelard calls 'topoanalysis': 'the systematic psychological study of the sites of our intimate lives'.[5] Certain sites that recur in Irish fiction offer themselves for analysis – confessional, church, haggard, garden, river, pub, cottage. And beyond these, the communal sites I have already mentioned, including the west. In this chapter, I have only room to discuss sketchily the meanings of love and aversion, past and present, self-captivity and attempted self-emancipation as they are generated by specific and generic places in Irish fiction.

The strategy of escape from place and past is well known to the Irish. It involves departure from the land, urbanization and in many cases emigration. The salient statistics, masking crucial implications for Irish psychology behind the obvious social import, are readily available. In 1841 one-fifth of the Irish population lived in towns and villages, but in 1961 three-fifths of the population did so; the country population has been at least halved in most areas during the past century; only Dublin and Belfast have to any significant degree absorbed rural migrants, emigration having been approximately equal to the natural increase of other towns (though the growth of towns has been greater in Northern Ireland than in the Republic); emigration was well established before the Famine, but the 50 per cent fall in Irish population since the Famine makes Ireland a demographic freak: six million people have been lost by Ireland since 1845, chiefly to Britain and

North America.[6] This population movement is fictionally reflected in what in *Forces and Themes in Ulster Fiction* (1974) I called a scenario of locations: the land – the ghetto – suburbia – overseas cosmopolis – return to the land. I called this scenario topographical rather than geographical since although I was thinking initially of the movement of real people and fictional characters from the land into Belfast and thence to England or America, I was also thinking of the applicability of the scenario to Irish fiction as a whole. The scenario is not, therefore, meant to be a closed system, nor primarily a way of defining Ulster or Ulster fiction, but a model by which I believe we can organize, on one level at least, a great deal of Irish fiction. For the fact is that the actual or projected shift in settings within novels and within authors' canons echoes the direction and sequence of the scenario. Also, there is a relationship between the stages of the scenario on the one hand and theme, plot, character and style on the other. Thirdly, and most important for my purposes here, the scenario is a strategy of escape from past, place and self.

A novel that ruthlessly dramatizes forces of bondage upon the land and the attempted flight of the hero is Patrick Kavanagh's *Tarry Flynn* (1948). It is also a novel that provides an ideal link between my Ulster scenario and the rest of Irish fiction. *Tarry Flynn* has clear affinities with the rural naturalism of more northerly novels by Shan Bullock, Michael McLaverty and John O'Connor. And its lyrical fantasy, while unique in the nature and power of its poetry, is the same response of author and hero to rural deprivation that we find in other Ulster and Irish fiction.

Tarry languishes in thrall to the social forces of pre-war rural Ireland (in this case Cavan in 1935): poverty and land-greed, sibling rivalry, rivalry between generations, enforced or habituated celibacy and bachelorhood, cultural deprivation. The documentary underpinning of the novel is substantial, and passages such as these, suggesting the land's opposing tendencies to captivate and expel, could almost have come out of Conrad Arensberg's *The Irish Countryman* (1937):

A great row was going on in McArdle's kitchen. The four sons were arguing with their father and mother for money. These four sons were all over forty but they were treated as babies by their parents. That may have been why when they appeared at Drumnay cross-roads or in the discussions in Magan's pub they were so aggressive and spoke with airs of such domineering authority.

[His sisters] should go and try to make a living elsewhere, but when he thought of them sympathetically, where could they go unless to England to be nurses? They were too proud to do that. So there wasn't much chance of Tarry having a clear house into which to bring a wife.

Tarry Flynn is a surgical portrayal of a society by an insider who has since gained the objectivity of an outsider. Tarry himself is a product of this society, of the clay that binds and mesmerizes him. Unlike the other characters, however, he seeks to escape the clay by taking flight, and his promiscuous daydreaming is the first tentative trial of the wings of poetry and fantasy. 'Ah, clay! It was out of clay that wings were made. He stared down at the dry little canyons in the parched earth and he loved that dry earth which could produce a miracle of wings.' Kavanagh's scalding hatred and submissive love of the earth provide the novel's uneasy balance between rural naturalism and poetic fantasy, an uneasy balance that characterizes a great deal of rural Irish fiction. Kavanagh's achievement, like Synge's in *The Playboy of the Western World*, is his ability to retain the buoyancy of fancy while unstintingly diagnosing an ailing society.

If, then, Tarry is in part product of his society, he is also in part parish freak, for his drying wings are God-given and mysterious, like Kavanagh's own poetic talent. Tarry's story is, like the visit of the sin-hunting Redemptorists to Dargan, and − against the more sober background of most Irish novels of rural life − like *Tarry Flynn* itself, 'a story of life in a townland of death'. Amidst the wrangling and scheming, mere illusion of activity and purpose disguising the paralysis, a pulse of genuine life will beat, for the novel is one of sunshine and fitful epiphany:

Standing in the doorway of the stable he felt good and terribly strong. A man is happy and poetic in health and strength. The stable in summer with the dust of last year's straw on the floor was to Tarry the most romantic place he knew. Sitting in the manger smoking and reading was paradise. But he had work to do now . . .

Walking through the meadow in summer was a great excitement. The simple fantastic beauty of ordinary things growing − marsh-marigolds, dandelions, thistles and grass. He did not ask things to have a meaning or to tell a story. To be was the only story . . .

The sun had come out through the haze and the morning was very warm. The cackle of morning had ceased. The songs of the birds were blotted out by the sun.

But at least we can explain the deadening clay out of which the apparent miracle of wings bursts. For Tarry is a not untypical case of arrested puberty, a 27-year-old whose only alternatives to perennial boyhood and wishful thinking in a familistic community are instant old age upon accession to marriage and the land, and migration in search of maturity. At the novel's end, Tarry opts for the latter and follows a well-trodden path out of the rural parish. But he cannot escape past or place. With true Irish perversity, he transforms the Cavan fields of his childhood and enslaved youth even as he passes through them into the dream landscape of memory that will forever haunt him. The memory of this imaginative landscape might liberate him into song (as it did Kavanagh) or it might bind him permanently to that impotent and pathetic fantasy that brightens the dull lives of many rural Irish characters. Either way, the self will not have been emancipated. *Tarry Flynn*, the fruit of Tarry's flight, is the song of a caged and colourful bird.

To where will Tarry's wings fly him? To Parnassus, if we believe Tarry is Kavanagh, and also more prosaically to Dublin. Dublin in rural Irish fiction is frequently a place of worldly and minatory energies. When at the close of John McGahern's *The Dark* (1965) Mahoney warns his son on the eve of his departure for Dublin about the strangeness of the city, he is hinting at the temptations to which Baba in Edna O'Brien's *The Country Girls* (1960) and Emma in *A Pagan Place* succumb. (We recall, too, that Tarry Flynn leaves Dargan behind a pied piper of a worldly uncle, visiting tempter in the rural demi-paradise.) Yet at the same time Dublin is a promise of freedom that concludes many novels about the repressions of country and provincial life. One thinks, for example, of Benedict Kiely's three novels held together by the severe illness common to their respective and similar heroes: *Honey Seems Bitter* (1954), *There Was An Ancient House* (1955) and *Dogs Enjoy the Morning* (1968). In all three, the young hero 'suffers' from sexual inexperience, social isolation and worthless spiritual innocence, all of which are presented as forms of sickness of the mind and soul metaphorized in his actual bodily sickness. The constraints of seminary are in each case exchanged for those of hospital and, at the novel's end, after solitude, virginity and clerical dedication have been discarded, for the prospect of Dublin and freedom. In the context, seminary and hospital are, like Edna O'Brien's convent and John McGahern's barracks (in *The Barracks*, 1963), peculiarly rural symbols of bondage.

In such novels as these in which the heroes flee rural constraint, as well as in novels where urbanized heroes – often 'returned Americans' – come back to their native fields, the division between town and country is more important than it has been in real life. Speaking of the Ireland up to 1918, one historian has said: 'The tension between town and country, which many historians detect on the continent, barely existed in Ireland. Irish towns were overwhelmingly rural . . . Ireland cannot be imprisoned in the urban historians' synthetic straitjacket of "town versus country".'[7] If Irish towns became less rural after 1918, they remained fairly intimate with the surrounding countryside that can still even today be seen from the streets of the two largest, Dublin and Belfast. They continued to exhibit the features of overgrown villages, being personal, neighbourly and communal, features that characterize the towns and cities of predominantly urban novels, even the Dublin of *Ulysses* (1922) and Flann O'Brien's *At Swim-Two-Birds* (1939). (Consider how frequent and essential conversational street scenes are in Irish novels, for instance.) Only with reservation, then, could we claim that in reality or in fiction Ireland has developed a peculiarly urban consciousness. We would be thinking of the Anglo-Irish upper class who have always commuted physically and spiritually between Dublin and London and perhaps of the middle and working classes of Dublin and Belfast. But we would not be thinking, even in these cases, of urban depression or impersonalization: indeed, Dublin in urban novels tends to exhibit not so much these features as airless provincialism.

How, then, could the Irish city fulfil the promise of freedom and self-escape that tantalizes the heroes who turn their faces towards Dublin in *The Dark*, *The Country Girls*, *There Was An Ancient House* and *Honey Seems Bitter*, and towards Belfast in Ervine's *The Foolish Lovers* (1920) and McLaverty's *Call My Brother Back* (1939)? For of course it does not. Disenchantment sets in on the heels of the promise in *The Country Girls*. The illusion left intact in O'Brien's novel is generated by the possibility of a life outside Ireland, dashed temporarily by the break with Mr Gentleman but reinstated by the strange young foreigner who makes Cait at least momentarily forget herself and her troubles at the novel's close. And this hints at the magnitude of the problem facing the fictional hero in Irish novels. The parochialism of the countryside (for example, Tarry Flynn's Dargan) might be left behind, but urban provincialism is hardly the answer. The place to be escaped is not only Dargan or even Cork,

Belfast or Dublin, but Ireland itself, which, regarded as a whole, exhibits paradoxically a nationwide provincialism. What is more provincial than Irish nationalism or Ulster loyalism? Writers and their heroes may not always take the next logical step incisively spelled out at the end of *A Portrait of the Artist as a Young Man* (1916), but many of them have explicitly or implicitly accepted that exile of one kind or another is necessary. What happens when the step is not taken is poignantly demonstrated in Frank O'Connor's underestimated *Dutch Interior* (1940). This novel is uncompromisingly urban in imagery (a comparative rarity in Irish fiction because of that), yet the implication is that nowhere in Ireland, inside or outside the town, is there possibility of escape from the cave and shell of self. While about it, O'Connor has created a Cork city of striking imagination.

Dutch Interior is a novel about furniture and people who have the passive repose of furniture; it is about rooms and stairways, about windows and doorways, about streets, lanes and roads, and about light and shade. Objects and spaces are arranged and lighted in the series of painterly, sculptural and architectural tableaux that compose the novel. Characters and surroundings are caught in the paralysed gestures of portraiture: they are equal components in a curious poetics of space.

The novel opens with young Peter Devane climbing the stairs of the large house in which his mother chars. The house is far grander than his family's and affords him daydreams of the raised and distant. The house with its rooms and stairwell is the privacy of the self's possibility in circumstances other than his own. Yet after reaching the attic, Peter is overcome by 'the sense of isolation, of height and forgottenness, windowless walls'. The isolate self is imaged in the dead-end of the attic, that mere, and blind, illusion of superiority and advantage. Some time after, from the drawing-room – high and windowed enough for him to see the vistas of departing opportunity – he watches a ship leaving the harbour. Later on in the novel, when Devane's personality has withered, we realize that he has 'missed the boat', watched life itself depart.

The novel's other hero, Stevie Dalton, also inhabits the inter-spaces of light and architecture. He is doomed to watch, through doorways and windows, love and life beaten down (Peter Devane and the Beautiful Miss Maddens grown old and mad). He is imprisoned in his home by a paranoid and bitter father who shackles his doors with locks and bolts and rails at his son's use of a candle by which to read. In any case, beyond the darkness and walls of home is the crossroads, an arena of further darkness, high walls and illusory spaciousness through which tantalizing lights of trams appear and disappear.

Dutch Interior creates interlocking spaces of captivity: there is the domestic interior relieved by the doors, windows and skylights that alluringly give on to the larger spaces beyond; but beyond are the restrictive spaces of street and road that converge on the crossroads, a familiar and intimate Irish space made hostile and confining in O'Connor's novel; and even if these spaces should be escaped, there is the confining darkness alleviated only by the unendorsed promise of candlelight, firelight, gaslight and moonlight. Peter Devane's definition of character provides the theme of *Dutch Interior*: 'Character is personality gone to seed . . . When 'tis all shaped and limited by circumstances, and there isn't a kick left in it . . . '. All the 'characters' in the novel and in the Ireland of real life are suddenly transformed by Devane's remark. O'Connor uses hostile space to image the dead and circumstantial forces of family, religion and nationalism bearing in upon the sensitive self.[8] On almost every page of *Dutch Interior*, shape and lighting define the hopelessness of life in O'Connor's Ireland. Only gestures towards real life are possible: the older Peter Devane's passionate singing of the opera he had left unfinished years before; the older Stevie's love-child he will never be able to acknowledge.

The first part of *Dutch Interior* seems to be set in the years before the Troubles (1910–20?) and the second part sometime in the 'thirties. Rebellion, the break with Britain and the Civil War all take place during the novel's time-span, but only in the silent corridor of time between the novel's two parts, for they are never mentioned. They do not need to be, for paralysis and unfulfilment have survived the Troubles intact. There are possibilities only for those who, like the returned American, Gus Devane, are at home with the inward-looking patriotism and political opportunism of post-revolutionary Ireland. The others are caught in slow and barren decay. Only death appears to offer escape. And so Ned Dalton, the martyr, 'lived on, released from the grip of circumstance, fixed in the eternal gesture of the rebel'. But how ironic that Stevie Dalton should imagine freedom as a frozen archetype and think of his brother precisely in the painterly terms in which O'Connor has captured his view of twentieth-century Ireland! Ned, after all, has simply become one with the past that is indistinguishable from circumstance, 'the past', as Stevie has already mused, 'that will not be quiet; the dead who will not rest;

images of desire and loss that rise for ever on our paths; lost fatherlands'.

To portray the self locked in an eternally present past, O'Connor creates in *Dutch Interior* a sense of timelessness. To portray the self simultaneously trapped in an inescapable place, he creates a sense of placelessness. Cork is never specified as the novel's setting since O'Connor wants to capture a nationwide provincialism that is both pre-revolutionary nationalism that has failed and post-revolutionary nationalism that has been perverted. This provincialism inhabits the countryside no less than the city, the novel seems to say. *Dutch Interior* is not, then, an exploration of the constrictions of urban life, but an exploration of the Irish self and the hostile spaces it both creates and is forced to inhabit. These spaces are the intimate ones of house, road and town, located, almost accidentally, in a fictional Cork and Ireland of O'Connor's imagination.

In writing a novel whose hero flees the land and seeks the town, or flees the town and seeks a new life overseas, the author is apt to be drawing upon the facts or aspirations of his own life. One might mention, almost as random examples, some fiction writers who left the land for Dublin, whether to gain greater cultural and social freedom, to be closer to the commercial hub of their craft, or to have the stimulation of other writers' company: Edna O'Brien, John McGahern, Patrick Kavanagh, Liam O'Flaherty, Patrick Boyle, Benedict Kiely, Flann O'Brien, Brinsley MacNamara and Walter Macken. Journeying as he did from Tyrone to Dublin down a colourful length of early-nineteenth-century Ireland, William Carleton is surely the archetypal figure of the Irish fiction writer trekking from the land into the city where he will dream the countryside he has left into a fictional landscape of character and anecdote.

Some writers, of course, including McGahern and Edna O'Brien, have found it necessary to leave Dublin for England. And some have gone even farther, seeking freedom of imagination outside the British Isles: James Joyce, Samuel Beckett, Francis Stuart, Brian Moore, Aidan Higgins. Of these, Joyce presents an anomalous case. *A Portrait of the Artist* closes with Dedalus's decision to go into exile. Contemporary readers might have been led to expect a follow-up novel set on the Continent, but of course that never materialized: Joyce resolutely refused to enact (except indirectly in the third episode of *Ulysses*) the stages of his own exile through his settings or chief characters. Perhaps the figure of a wandering Dublin Jew as well as Joyce's growing universality of style and expanding concept of fiction did the job more satisfactorily. Other novelists have not opted for such subtle geographical 'sublimation'. For example, the novels of Brian Moore and Edna O'Brien, viewed as sequences, have thus far mirrored, with some expected distortions, the authors' own movements. Edna O'Brien was born in Co. Clare and moved to Dublin and then London, a direction reflected in her canon, from *The Country Girls* through *The Girl with Green Eyes* (1962), *August is a Wicked Month* (1965) to *Casualties of Peace* (1966). Moore, born in Belfast, has lived in Montreal, New York City and southern California, and all of these have become settings for, respectively, *Judith Hearne* (1955), *The Luck of Ginger Coffey* (1960), *An Answer from Limbo* (1962) and *Fergus* (1971).

These novels by O'Brien and Moore often depict their heroes' flight from home and from Ireland. But the flight is a hopeless irony, for Ireland and home survive in memory. The remembrance of Ireland and the home town or parish begins by being passive but soon becomes active, an obsession indistinguishable from an attempt to exorcize place and past. This attempt is likewise doomed to fail. Perhaps we could regard the authors' own struggle to exorcize Ireland as more successful, since it at least issues in creativity, but the compulsive repetition of the rite and the fact that more blatant exorcisms appeared well along the respective canons (Moore's *The Emperor of Ice-Cream*, 1965, and O'Brien's *A Pagan Place*) suggest that the novelists do not consider that they have achieved a greater degree of self-emancipation than their heroes.

The contest between place and self is crucial in Irish fiction. So powerful is it that it is not unusual for it to be a death-struggle, for the fictional self to be so bound to place that the self is destroyed when it is sundered from place. What makes the theme so pervasive is the fact that the Irish have such a localized sense of place that the archetypal trauma of the separation from place can quite easily occur inside Ireland itself. This is evidenced by Richard Power's *The Hungry Grass* (1969). Power has created in this novel a priest who endures kinds of exile: from the 'deep, green soft-layered places' of Rosnagree, his family home and native parish; from post-revolutionary Ireland which has degenerated into political jobbery and bureaucratic squabbling; and from his political relations who batten upon the recently independent country. Father Conroy has been banished to Kilbride, the poorest parish in the diocese – 'bare hills peopled with sheep and boulders' – in part because he was thought to have been a red priest during a labour dispute at the time of the Civil War. Conroy spends the novel trying to make his way back to Rosnagree by locating those he considers its rightful heirs, his dead brother's anglicized children. This takes the ailing priest to England where he almost dies: easy enough in these English scenes to believe with Octavio Paz that permanent exile is the same as a death sentence, as it has proved for Father Conroy's brother Owen. But the priest's sense of orphanhood and exile is most deeply felt in Kilbride itself and drives him to fantasy, panic and illness. When he returns to Rosnagree for the annual reunion of the diocesan priests who had been ordained together, 'like an emigrant returning to seek nourishment at his root', and there dies, it is as though to confirm the repeated lesson of the Irish novel and short story – that place is life. But all along, Rosnagree and the memory of its natural beauty have held Conroy's weak self in thrall. We should be equally justified in regarding complete exile as life and place as a fatality. The geography of Irish fiction, as *The Hungry Grass* demonstrates once more, is a scenario of spiritual and intellectual entrapment, imagined escape, and fantasy or death. It is the beguiling beauty of real and fictional Ireland that tends to obscure this profound reality.

[1975]

NOTES

1. Jeremiah Curtin, *Myths and Folk-Lore of Ireland* (Boston: Little, Brown 1890), p. 11.
2. Actually, Brecht has borrowed from Hierocles, whose pedant carries a brick in his pocket as a specimen when he offers his house for sale.
3. Curtin, p. 12.
4. Joyce and Beckett come to mind as writers who did achieve self-transcendence by artistic self-effacement. In any case Joyce's places – Dublin and Ireland – are expanded into mythic universes with the richness of an entire world. By a process of intension rather than expansion, Beckett has synthesized out of France and Ireland a wholly imaginative landscape. And could either writer have achieved artistic self-effacement and created his resonant universe by remaining in Ireland? In this essay I am concerned with writers who have tackled the problems of place without the genius of Joyce or Beckett.
5. Gaston Bachelard, *The Poetics of Space* (Boston: Beacon Press 1972), p. 8.
6. I am indebted for these statistics to T.W. Freeman's *Ireland: A General and Regional Geography* (London: Methuen 1972).
7. Joseph Lee, *The Modernisation of Irish Society, 1848–1918* (Dublin: Gill and Macmillan 1973), pp. 97–9.

8. Readers might compare the way Joyce in several stories in *Dubliners*, and most notably in 'The Dead', employs the interaction of indoors and outdoors (connected by windows) and of darkness and light to image the sensitive self beset by these same dead and hostile forces. Like the chief characters in *Dutch Interior*, Gabriel Conroy has failed to escape Ireland, except in the most superficial sense of adopting certain continental habits of dress and literary taste.

3

IRISH MODERNISM

I

The difficulties in detecting the first stirrings of what became the Modernist movement in literature are increased, not diminished, by those scandalous suggestions (scandalous because so brazen and various) that the movement sprang adult from the womb. I need hardly remind students of literature of those precise dates on which the world was supposed to have changed. Yeats elected 1900; Woolf 1910, in or about December; Lawrence 1915; Willa Cather 1922. Writers surely offer such dates in mock-historical accuracy, to confound the cultural historians, and the intention may itself be a Modernist ploy. Modernism was meant by many writers, after all, to travesty cultural movements, to be a movement to end movements, in whose floruit was waged, suitably, the war to end wars.

Contemporary critics, shed of irony, suggest Modernist beginnings as splendidly precise as the writers'. One strong candidate is 1880. In that same year, on an island largely shielded from Europe, Standish James O'Grady published Volume Two of his *History of Ireland*. Although this high nonsensical work was a good deal laughed at by the Anglophile historians of Trinity College, Dublin, it more inarguably set in motion the Irish Literary Revival than, say, Brandes's essays of 1883 or the Post-Impressionist Exhibition did Modernism. That Revival gave to European literature writers whose names were they erased from its history would seriously impoverish it.

The Irish Literary Revival was, as it happens, co-terminous with Modernism's innings – shall we say 1880 until, as Kermode suggests for Modernism, 1925, with the years of high accomplishment in each case the latter fifteen?[1]

This seems an odd coincidence in the light of the Revival's dedication to the restoration to Ireland of its so-called Heroic Period

44

(variously dated from the Iron Age to the Middle Ages) and to the championing of the primitive present, alleged vestige of that Heroic Period. In being so dedicated, the Revival was a belated Irish expression of Romanticism. This makes the coincidence odder, though it is diminished somewhat (but in such a way as to complicate the picture) by the fact that several Revival writers express a note of modernity in their work: that note of irony and scepticism, for instance, we hear in Synge, O'Casey and the middle Yeats, though it may have been sounded first by George Moore, who brings it to one triumphant conclusion with the eloquent malice of *Hail and Farewell* (1911–14). In Joyce, though not in Moore, who in any case was born too early, irony and scepticism became cultural artifice and lucid indifference, a terminus that by a far different route Yeats also reached. Joyce, it seems, is incontrovertibly a Modernist, even in his earlier, more naturalistic and realistic years. After him came Flann O'Brien and Samuel Beckett, second- or third-generation Modernists who nevertheless wrote in the distant wash and wake of the Revival.

As usual, Yeats writing at the tension-point of literature is the crux. One Yeats placed the unionist landowner O'Grady among the Olympians and acknowledged him as cultural ethnarch, father of the Revival whom he, Yeats, succeeded. Another Yeats wrote admiringly of the deracinated 'last romantics', of whom he accounted himself one, inheritors of a mood which, in his own words,

Edgar Poe found in a wine-cup, and [which] passed into France and took possession of Baudelaire, and from Baudelaire passed to England and the Pre-Raphaelites, and then again returned to France, and still wanders the world, enlarging its power as it goes, awaiting the time when it shall be, perhaps, alone, or, with other moods, master over a great new religion, and an awakener of the fanatical wars that hovered in the grey surges, and forget the winecup where it was born.[2]

Perhaps I can show the identity of these two Yeatses while attempting to explain the coincidence of Irish Revivalism and international Modernism and making larger claims of a fitful native Modernism than have been so far advanced for Ireland. Ireland is not charted in Bradbury and McFarlane's geography of Modernism, nor Dublin enrolled among its cities, yet Joyce and Yeats are weightily indexed. But I do not want my claims to run in one direction only. Using the Irish case, I would like to weaken, or at least adjust, the claims of international Modernism upon us, in Ireland at any rate, and in the light of Irish cultural reality, having – perversely – claimed the Irish Revival as itself more generously Modernist than previously thought. The conjunction of Revivalism and Modernism may throw light on the latter and sceptical shadow on its orthodoxy.

II

No paradox or incongruity need exist, of course, if we make capacious enough our definition of Modernism, if, for example, we offer this: 'In short' – in short! –

Modernism was in most countries an extraordinary compound of the futuristic and the nihilistic, the revolutionary and the conservative, the naturalistic and the symbolistic, the romantic and the classical. It was a celebration of a technological age and a condemnation of it; an excited acceptance of the belief that the old régimes of culture were over, and a deep despairing in the face of that fear; a mixture of convictions that the new forms were escapes from historicism and the pressures of the time with convictions that they were precisely the living expressions of these things.[3]

The 'formal desperation' which has been seen as a Modernist characteristic seems to have infected its diagnosis whose epidemic of binary oppositions is its own symptom of despair. One wonders if the bewildering diversity of so-called Modernist works does not make Modernism, like Romanticism, a vagrant and essentially contested concept.

Be that as it may, it would be difficult to regard as Modernist, in its slackest definition, certain important features of the Irish Revival: the preoccupation with heroism ('Whatever is not heroic is not Irish,' AE declared), the call for patriotic sacrifice, the obstinate nativism; though its primitivism, its sense of a beginning and of an ending (that is, its apocalyptic view of history) would give less trouble. The backward look of Modernism has been pointed out by some critics, though they prefer to speak of synchronicity, of synthesized contemporaneity and antiquity. This was certainly the aim of the Irish Revivalists, though perhaps only Joyce – no ostensible Revivalist – and Yeats turned manifesto into achieved art. In reviving, the Irish did not think of themselves as bringing out, dusting off, and winding up – one definition of Revival – but as living again, as fully as ineradicable time would permit. For O'Grady and the cultural nationalists he fathered, what had happened between the bardic rendition of the Heroic Period and the imminent recovery of the Heroic Period at the close of the nineteenth century was a bad dream or a case of suspended animation; it had not in a sense happened at all. The well of Irish legendry had been capped by Christianity and successive philistine invasions and was now being reopened by a generation that claimed to be the bards' legitimate and even, where the imagination was concerned, immediate successors.

One thinks of that significant tendency of Modernism to vault over nineteenth-century Realism, Naturalism and Romanticism, to vault over even Renaissance humanism in search of the countering artifice of eternity, that lucid indifference. It is at its most conscious a kind of internal contest and it is waged with greatest understanding in the pages of an Irishman, in *Dubliners* (1914), *A Portrait of the Artist as a Young Man* (1916) and *Ulysses* (1922). We make much of the medieval bent of Joyce's mind, a mind happiest, it seems, working in terms of analogue, structure, law, rhetoric, authority. Stephen Dedalus believes his monkish learning may be a handicap, 'held no higher by the age he lived in than the subtle and curious jargons of heraldry and falconry'.[4] Like Joyce's, his monkish learning is, of course, a strength, but only, I believe, when it addressed, painfully, what Joyce in 'The Universal Literary Influence of the Renaissance' identified as the chief legacies of that cultural watershed – compassion and realism.[5] Solve Joyce's treatment of pity, charity and compassion, a chief conceptual arena in his work, and you have solved much of him – his point of view, his dialectic, the relation of his constructs to the world in which we live and die.

I do not mean to underestimate the medievalism – or Modernism – of Joyce's mind. His medievalism was a Christian one which he displaced into secularism, and in doing so moved back as well as forward, back to the pagan structures of Irish art. Ostensibly he dismissed, actually he absorbed the medieval Irish sagas and heroic romances upon whose translation and adaptation the Irish Literary Revival rested. Despite their fitful, startling realism, the splendid stories of the Cuchulain, Fenian, Mythological and Historical cycles must ultimately be understood in terms of narrative structure and code. The stories proceed by formula and convention, by rhetorical commonplaces, set-pieces, genealogies, etymologies, inventories, word-games, runs, teichoscopies, rhapsodies, lays, kennings (the latter being an esoteric form of speech concocted by bards and thought by some to be a – rather Joycean – form of erudite slang). The Irish sagas are cultural encyclopedias. Speech in them is not so much self-expression as incantation, song, spell, prophecy. Prophecy provides a prior arrangement of the narrative and a mnemonic cue for composer and reciter, and the result is a form of narrative foreclosure very different from the modern, realistic – but not Modernist – conception of fiction. It is not surprising that in such narratives the will and individuality of the characters are thematically at the mercy of outside forces. The relationship between these forces can perhaps best be described by the physicist's phrase 'sympathetic resonance', of which the arch-waves of Erin that invariably roar in response to battle-strokes delivered against Conchubar's shield (in the Cuchulain Cycle) are merely the most vivid example that comes to mind. The sympathetic resonance takes place at a high frequency of motif, seme and formula. The result is that the world of the hero tales is a unified field that not even the brutal factionalism or the heroic solitude and enterprise, that theme and character often illustrate, can fragment. Or, to put it in homelier fashion, as James Stephens did when discussing the violence of the tales: it's a give-and-take world, and there is no great harm in it.

Readers of Lévi-Strauss, Barthes and Joyce would be at ease in this old narrative dispensation. Many Revivalists were not so at ease and they shamelessly altered the old stories, not for Modernist but for romantic nationalist reasons. Ironically it was Joyce – the counter-Revivalist – who was most faithful to the old stories. Where the romantic Revivalists edited out the comic grotesqueries, for example, Joyce swooped on them as matter for parody (think of the portrait of the Citizen in *Ulysses*); where the romantic Revivalists humanized and historicized the old stories, Joyce retained their spirit and structure, their tenebrous indifference. James Stephens – in whom Joyce sensed a kindred spirit and whom in 1927 he invited to complete *Finnegans Wake* (1939) in the event of his own death – was possibly the closest in temperament of all Revivalists to the old writers. *Irish Fairy Tales* (1920) is a misnomered masterpiece that rewrites the ancient Fenian and Mythological tales, but its swift intersecting planes of narrative slicing across expected continuities suggest the influence of Cubism, in which we know Stephens was interested. When Stephens attempted to combine the old stories with psychological realism, as in his novels *Deirdre* (1923), and *In the Land of Youth* (1924), the result was calamitous. At his best, Stephens exhibits those medieval and perennial qualities of Irish mentality and art in which authority, eschatology and correspondence cuckoo philosophy and science out of the nest, in which chronophobia flourishes, and supererogation – of which Joyce is a laureate – makes expressive plurality inescapable, part of the territory, no mere Modernist prescription.

Irish mentality and art happily – or unhappily – accord with twentieth-century European artistic mentality, in part because Joyce, Yeats and the Revivalists helped to shape the European twentieth century. (Though they did not accord with the nineteenth-century artistic mentality, as Matthew Arnold's essay on Celtic literature will tell you at a glance.[6] It was then, understandably, a sportive and dangerous thing, to be reduced to, and kept as, a 'note' and carefully administered in small but essential doses to English writers, a tonic in medical and musical senses, you might say.) But in part it is pure coincidence. The archaic inventiveness of Joyce and other Catholic (or in the case of Stephens, poor) Irish writers is given impetus by a sense of linguistic orphanhood, one more among the orphanhoods on which Joyce eloquently brooded. Confronted by Joyce's stylistic and linguistic plurality – a Modernist characteristic – Hugh Kenner attributes it to Joyce's Pyrrhonism, a fundamental scepticism that leads him to adopt a variety of disguises in place of any central or stable certainty.[7] But the whole truth involves the Irish comic tradition and, beyond that, the deep, often subliminal sense of linguistic deprivation many Irish writers feel. The native mode of expression has been lost, a foreign tongue has been grafted on to the remnant of the old. The Irish writer's linguistic *brio* may be a disguised double act of revenge – an attempt to enliven the foreign tongue with the energy of the native (a revenge of impurity) and to colonize in turn, if not the English, then tracts of English literature, as in fact the Irish have done this century. The Irish writer has an enviable linguistic freedom. One, he is, at the very least in the Hugh MacDiarmid sense, bilingual. Two, if the English language is not his, he owes no obligation to rules and regulations that, moreover, have been allied in England to that class structure to which the Irishman is foreigner or victim. But the freedom can be hazardous because it can lead to irresponsibility, monomania, diseased subjectivity.

III

The Ascendancy had imposed that class structure on Ireland, but inefficiently, among other reasons because there was no vigorous bourgeoisie to complete a hierarchy. The absence of a vigorous bourgeoisie probably explains in part the absence of a vigorous realist tradition (indeed a reputable novel tradition) in Irish literature, and this may have facilitated the Revival triumph of Romanticism, its return to medieval literature, and its fitful Modernism. The Irish Literary Revival was largely a flight from reality, especially on the part of Protestant intellectuals whose life and heritage had rarely been depicted with seriousness and realism. The Protestant Revival – and most important Revivalists were Protestant – was an unearned class apostasy. The Revivalists called into question the two class cultures to which they belonged: that of landlordism and the gentry, and that of the mercantile middle class. Only the latter did they reject outright. They rejected the landlord class only for what they considered it had become, while nursing hopes for a return to what they thought it had been, a cultivated nobility. Their prescription was an imaginary feudalism made up of a gallant aristocracy, a fey peasantry, and a troubadourish or patronized artistry. This flight from reality helps to make of Yeats the qualified Modernist (and the great poet) he is, but one might with some perplexity regret the flight while honouring the achievement it enabled.

The Revivalists' desire to be ancestrally Irish obliged them to evade the reality of anglicized Ireland, a reality their own class had entrenched. This amounted to a denial of self at the level of class. In a sense the denial proved an impossibility. The Irish Literary Revival, dominated by the Anglo-Irish, was what Foucault has called a 'fellowship of discourse' whose function it is 'to preserve or to reproduce discourse, but in order that it should circulate within a closed community, according to strict regulations, without those in possession being dispossessed by this very distribution'.[8] From the raw materials of a peasant folklore and a bardic literature in another language, the Anglo-Irish *littérateurs* amassed what Foucault terms 'the property of discourse'. Even when the theme of Revival literature, like that of political nationalism, was selflessness, the assumed and collectively egotistic function of the Revivalists was that of culture-givers. When Standish James O'Grady forfeited leadership of the

Revival by failing to follow his cultural premises to their political conclusion (he remained a unionist) and their literary conclusion (he maintained that the heroic romances ought not to be dramatized), Yeats became his successor, inviting writers to change direction, indefatigably prefacing and introducing the works of the chosen, bestowing his approval here, withholding it there (as in the case of James Cousins and the middle O'Casey). Successively O'Grady and Yeats led a clerisy whose ultimate social base was manorial, in which dissident voices as articulate as their own were remarkably few.

This clerisy is at once uniquely Irish (or Anglo-Irish) and the figure in a recurring European cultural pattern; either way it is relevant to any claim that Yeats and other Protestant Revivalists were Modernists. Consider the case of John Millington Synge. Synge was much influenced by the Breton writer Anatole le Braz, whom he read the year before he travelled to the Aran Islands. Le Braz celebrates in his works a rather medieval peasantry very like the Aran Islanders, a legend-loving, credulous yet humorous people, steeped in Catholicism and an elder paganism. A refrain in *Au Pays des Pardons* (1894) – a book whose influence is visible in *Riders to the Sea* (1904) and *The Aran Islands* (1907) – is Le Braz's fear of the extinction of age-old customs, beliefs and communities at the hands of merchants, tourists, trains, machines and other symptoms of bourgeois civilization. Yet in the interstices of civilized interference endures a way of life so old and unchanging that it creates in the writer 'that feeling of being in a new-made land, a world scarce wakened out of chaos'. In Breton society are both changelessness and change, beginning and end. Le Braz disapproves of modernization as strongly as Synge. One student of Breton nationalism has claimed that it was in order to shield Brittany from the modernizing influences of French culture that members of the Breton clerico-aristocratic right were converted to the regionalist ideas that strengthened ethnic minority nationalism in Brittany around the time Le Braz was most involved in the affairs of his native region.[9] Unlike Le Braz, such Bretons were exclusively French-speaking, yet it was remarked as early as 1919 that 'their lack of the language paradoxically heightens their sense of being threatened in their Bretonness'.[10] A claim could be made that many exclusively Anglophone Irish Revivalists similarly were political or cultural nationalists chiefly because, and to the extent that they were, enemies of capitalism and bourgeois industrialism, and not because of undiluted nationalist impulses. Several of the Revivalists, including

Yeats and O'Grady, were, when they were political at all, right-wing and aristocratic in sympathy. (One might wish to note the rightward bias in the political thinking of several major Modernist writers whose Modernism ironically inverts their anti-modernization.)

We would, of course, have to exclude Synge from generalizations about aristocratic-right-wing tendencies in Irish Revivalism (and he did learn Gaelic), but the connection in his life and work between cultural nationalism and anti-modernization remains intact. It is a connection that was reinforced through the influence of Le Braz, though of course Synge met Irish cultural nationalists before he read the Breton. (Le Braz, as it happened, played a role in the Breton Revival not unlike that of Douglas Hyde in its Irish counterpart. The recovery of the old language and of the region's submerged history and racial pride, and, for some, the maintenance of Catholicism, were all important in the Breton Revival as they were in the Irish, but some Revivalists went further and encouraged separatism. Le Braz was the first director of the Union Régionaliste Bretonne, an avowedly non-partisan and non-sectarian alliance between intellec-tuals and members of Brittany's upper classes begun in 1898 'to develop by the revival of Breton sentiment all forms of Breton activity'.[11] The following year – the year Synge himself visited Brittany – Le Braz resigned as director when some members at the second annual URB congress attacked the Third Republic, just as Douglas Hyde resigned the presidency and his membership of the Gaelic League because of its espousal of Irish nationalism.)

Besides the overt resemblances between Breton and Irish nation-alism, there was a comparable millenarianism directed by intellectual prophets. (These and other millenarianisms would surely have to be taken into account when we examine the 'apocalyptic, crisis-centred views of history' said to be a feature of the Modernist age.[12]) What Jack Reece, drawing upon other social philosophers, has deduced from Breton millenarianism could, I think, be said to some degree of the Anglo-Irish millenarianism of the Irish Revival. Reece sets the Breton phenomenon within a recurring European pattern that has led Anthony D. Smith to theorize that a leading historical function of nationalism has been to resolve 'the crisis of the intelligentsia'. Such a crisis, says Reece,

arises out of the threat to the social dependencies of a traditional order that is being undermined by modernizing currents. Among these dependencies the intellectuals, by virtue of their superior educational attainments and their broad cultural experience, are particularly cognizant of the peril in which they are placed by the conjunction of the old and the new. Indeed, their vulnerability is perhaps greater than that of any other dependent group. Long the most articulate exponents of the ideological world view that gave the traditional order its theoretical legitimacy, they had received substantial moral and material rewards from those whose interests they served. Such intellectuals thus find themselves doubly threatened: from above by the collapsing debris of the old order and from below by the builders of the new one, who are determined to sweep away all those whose fortunes are tied to the traditional holders of power. According to Karl Mannheim, the social thinker to whom Smith is most heavily in debt, these intellectuals may extricate themselves from their dangerous situation by following either of two courses of action. They may seek affiliation with one of the various groups that are struggling to dominate the emergent social order or, through scrutiny of their social moorings, they may seek to rise above their particular class interests and forge a new mission for themselves as the detached guardians of the moral and material objectives of the people as a whole.[13]

In the case of the Irish intellectuals, mostly Protestant, the collapse of the old order – be it the Ascendancy, whose heyday was the century before the Act of Union, or the landlord class, dangerously corrupt by the late nineteenth century – exceeded in import the danger from builders of a new order, many of whom had indeed been in recent history Protestants. As for the two methods of extrication from the predicament, both were attempted by the versatile leaders of the Revival. Yeats's and AE's and Synge's admiration for aristocrat, peasant and artist, for example, embodied several social options, and only from the petty bourgeois class that emerged later did they withhold all admiration and support. Unifying the various social adaptations and ploys was, of course, the desire of the chief Revivalists to be the detached guardians of the moral objectives of the Irish people as a whole. Joyce, it might be said, did not feel the same need to extricate himself since he owed no more than dubious emotional allegiance to the old order and was in any case a middle-class Catholic; besides, he aligned himself with no social group and therefore felt far less the resonances of group and class peril (though his racial allegiance he felt strongly on occasion).

IV

One way in which the Protestant Revivalists sought to rise above their class interests was by exploring the mystical and the occult. Mystical rites were required preparation for envisioning Heroic Ireland, but it is probable that they simultaneously satisfied the cruder need of some Protestants for ritual discipline, a need normally satisfied for the less demanding by Free Masonry and for the more orthodox by Anglicanism. (Not irrelevantly, Yeats noted that Irish country people 'often attribute magical powers to Orangemen and to Freemasons'.[14]) Anglo-Irish Protestants shared with Catholics a detestation of puritanism, for which unscriptural ceremony is corrupt, a disdain Yeats expresses in 'The Curse of the Fires and of the Shadows', one of the stories in *The Secret Rose* (1897). At any rate, the fact is that the most famous leaders of Irish literary transcendentalism were Protestant – Yeats, AE, John Eglinton, James Stephens, James and Margaret Cousins, Charles Johnston. According to Gretta Cousins, Charlotte Despard, an Englishwoman, 'was one of the rare Catholics who were Theosophists'. That the most responsive and intellectual members of a declining ruling social class would turn to a mysticism ritually organized by rank (one co-opting the hierarchical society of Heroic Ireland) does not seem surprising: it was in part a withdrawal through unconscious pique into esotericism, in part – and this could be ventured, *mutatis mutandis*, of the whole Anglo-Irish Revival – an attempt to regain leadership (intellectual and cultural where moral and social leadership had faltered) by concealing new symbols of power in cabbalistic language and gesture. Perhaps too the mystical advocates of self-transcendence found peculiarly receptive listeners among Anglo-Irish Protestants. Stephens, AE, Yeats, Synge – all were preoccupied with the transience of the self and the natural order and with the need to escape both. It is possible that the themes of self-escape and self-denial reflected the uncertainty of the Anglo-Irish in any new Ireland, perhaps their sense of guilt, even self-hatred.

Yeats's interest in the occult was bound up with his early symbolism, which takes fictional form in the so-called apocalyptic stories of the 1890s, 'Rosa Alchemica', 'The Adoration of the Magi' and 'The Tables of the Law', in the stories of *The Secret Rose* and in the *Stories of Red Hanrahan* (1905). In these fictions we are in the mood whose beginning Yeats ascribed to Poe. Yeats's symbolist heroes court unreality, a Paterian and exclusive world of beauty and spirituality, and risk being 'thrown fatally out of key with reality', incurring 'penalties which are not to be taken lightly'.[15] If there is anything to Edmund Wilson's distinction – the romantic hero is at war with society while the symbolist hero is in flight from it (a distinction difficult to maintain in Ireland where unreal and quixotic insurrections have been commonplace; the Easter Rising is one such and has symbolist overtones) – and if there is anything to the claim that symbolism is a component of Modernism, then symbolism might well be the key to the apparent paradox of Modernism's uneasy relationship with modernization. It is possible that we have two kinds of symbolism in mind, however, when *Ulysses*, written by a man indifferent to modernization, is described as 'the most characteristic Symbolist novel'.[16]

I adduce the mysticism, symbolism, millenarianism and anti-modernization of the Irish Revivalists as evidence of a cultural unreality and self-transformation. Shape-changing is of course an archaic phenomenon in the Celtic literature the Revivalists championed. It is a Druid craft and necessity; which is to say it is the poetic craft and necessity. In the old literature, the Druids, poetry and Ireland herself all survive the centuries by adaptive transformation. Yeats, like Stephens and Joyce, assumes it as theme and form, little guessing perhaps that the entire Revival was a remarkable exercise in shape-changing. In its multitude of guises, flights and masks, it is what defines the Revival. Little wonder that the versatile writers of the Revival can invade Modernism, which has been seen by some in terms of displacement, accommodations and plurality.

We find shape-changing supremely in folklore. In returning to the Irish folktale and saga, the Revivalist fiction writers were, in the absence of a native novel tradition, returning by necessity to the foundations of narrative, ignoring an advanced narrative realism that barely existed for them in helpful or hindering form. Once again, here was a happy coincidence, since twentieth-century pioneers such as Picasso, Stravinsky and Eliot were, as we have been told, inquiring into the nature and foundations of their mediums. Yeats's interest in folklore was largely romantic, though he half-heartedly imitated the structure of folktale in his early fictions; folklore was the art of a diminishing peasantry: a spade is poetry, he said, the machine is prose and a *parvenu*. Folklore was also the diminishing record of the Irish belief in the supernatural. He scorned scholars who approached folklore scientifically and compiled motifs like grocery lists. We now know (from Hyde and his successors) that many Irish folktales are international narrative forms largely independent of local and expressive concerns and have been generated according to a mainly internal 'genetic' programme of type and motif. Propp has distinguished 'text' from 'tale'.[17] What the teller gives us is a text but this may include more than one tale or render a tale imperfectly.

In the transmission of traditional narratives (many of which were collected and published as part of the Revival), the storyteller's freedom of expression is limited and regulated. Motifs, runs and other migratory formulas are not his invention and their deployment should comply with the laws of folk narrative (which might through Anderson's Law of Self-correction put right any egregious error).[18] The ability of Gaelic storytellers to memorize after one hearing novella-length tales and keep them in the memory for years until asked to recite them suggests not only that the tellers had phenomenal memories but also that the tales were self-memorizing in the sense that one link suggested the next, not only by association or contiguity but by a delimitation of sequential possibilities that grew increasingly severe as the tale progressed. To tell a story is to re-count it, to pay out the chain of motifs.

One is reminded, of course, of talk of the autonomy of the Modernist fictive structure, of the autotelic species of literature, of which the international folktale is surely one. I find Fletcher and Bradbury's distinction between pre-Modernist and Modernist self-consciousness of form (the earlier works draw attention to the autonomy of the narrator, Modernist works to the autonomy of the text) inadequate as a definition of Modernist narrative reflexiveness, since the folktale frequently draws attention to itself. 'One of the great themes of the Modernist novel has been ... the theme of the art of the novel itself,' they say;[19] but one thinks of those Irish tales in which the pursuit of a story *is* the story; the story must be found and completed before the enveloping story can itself be completed. One thinks, too, of that folktale character, the man who has no story and who had better find one before the tale is through.

So while staking Modernist claims to the narrative introversion of the Irish folktale as it is mimicked by Irish writers, notably Stephens, who was powerfully interested in the dynamics of story-telling, I am wondering if the Modernist autonomy of text is new except perhaps in its high incidence – which may, of course, be sufficiently definitive – within the tradition of the novel.

V

There is method in my heterodoxy. The Irish critic must bridle his enthusiasm for Irish Modernism with the reflection that no reputable body of realist fiction appeared in Ireland until the Revival had spent itself. The European chronology was therefore reversed. When it did appear, realism (in the hands of Frank O'Connor, Sean O'Faolain and others) was dwarfed by the Revival and could not fulfil itself because it was in truth romantic feedback and frustration, a diseased retractive subjectivity in disguise. This has been a serious matter in a country where realism, literary, political, psychological, is in desperately short supply, where fantasy impinges cruelly, maimingly, on reality. So much in Ireland militates against realism: the rurality, the unsophistication, the lack of a vigorous middle class, the political instability. 'We [Irish] cannot become philosophic like the English,' Yeats quoted, 'our lives are too exciting.'[20] We Irish can barely afford such excitement nowadays.

Yeats saw no excitement in the only Ireland O'Faolain regarded as real: the Catholic, English-speaking, democratic, petit-bourgeois world created by Daniel O'Connell in the nineteenth century; this Ireland was a wave of Yeats's 'filthy modern tide'. He did not take under his notice the Ulster Protestant equivalent. Yet these are the only two Irelands that exist today, and their horns are locked. They are the basic, inescapable data, the forces of life, the disordered surfaces of living upon which literary naturalism and realism in the hands of a great writer need to go to work.

It is for tactical reasons, then, that I stress Joyce's realism and naturalism, his laureateship of O'Connellite Ireland. I do so knowing that the Irish genius has not thus far been for a final realism. In *Dubliners*, *A Portrait* and *Ulysses*, the contest between symbolism and realism recurs, and even if the upshot is synthesis, I choose to emphasize the symbolism's rejection. Joyce thought 'The Adoration of the Magi' and 'The Tables of the Law' were 'work worthy of the great Russian masters', and indeed they are powerful stories of a kind. Joyce has Stephen Hero repeat them by heart as he passes through the throng of Yeats's impure multitude. Young Joyce read Joachim of Flora in Marsh's Library, seeking to re-enact the transport of the narrator of 'The Tables of the Law', who is shown a subversive book of Joachim's by Owen Aherne. *Stephen Hero*, *Dubliners*, *A Portrait*, *Ulysses* all reveal the temptations that esotericism, monasticism, prophecy and secret sinfulness represent for many of Joyce's major characters. In all, the temptations are resisted or surmounted. In *Ulysses*, Stephen decides not to visit his Uncle Richie Goulding's house, and thinks: 'Houses of decay, mine, his and all. You told the Clongowes gentry you had an uncle a judge and an uncle a general in the Army. Come out of them, Stephen. Beauty is not there. Nor in the stagnant bay of Marsh's Library where you read the fading prophecies of Joachim Abbas.' As an alternative to the symbolist tempters, we are given the impure Bloom, 'the prophet of sanity, realism, and a secular decency unsupported by dogma', as one critic puts it, 'and he passes his ministry on to Stephen'.[21]

Joyce is a great Modernist, encompassing. The period symbolism I have been talking about is part of his work; even when it is thematically and stylistically rejected, it remains inerasable in each text in which it occurs. Nevertheless, I prefer to regard his work as narrative dialectic, as endlessly amenable and extrusive, as ultimate realism rather than ultimate symbolism, though both are necessary stages in the dialectic to whose synthesis they may each claim superior contribution. Having said that, I remind myself of the biographical irony. Yeats did not flee Ireland; he remained to fight. Joyce sequestered himself in Europe, blinding himself with monkish tenacity.

[1981]

NOTES

1. Frank Kermode, cited by Malcolm Bradbury and James McFarlane, 'The Name and Nature of Modernism' in *Modernism 1890–1930*, eds Bradbury and McFarlane (Harmondsworth: Penguin Books 1976), p. 32.
2. *The Savoy*, April 1896, quoted by Robert O'Driscoll, '*The Tables of the Law*: A Critical Text', *Yeats Studies* 1 (1971), 90.
3. Bradbury and McFarlane, 'The Name and Nature of Modernism' in *Modernism 1890–1930*, p. 46.
4. *A Portrait of the Artist as a Young Man* (Harmondsworth: Penguin Books 1960), p. 179.
5. 'The Universal Literary Influence of the Renaissance' in Louis Berrone, ed., *James Joyce in Padua* (New York: Random House 1977), pp. 19–23.
6. *On the Study of Celtic Literature* (1867).
7. *Joyce's Voices* (Berkeley: University of California Press 1978).
8. Michel Foucault, *The Archaeology of Knowledge* (New York: Harper and Row 1976), p. 225.
9. Jack E. Reece, *The Bretons Against France: Ethnic Minority Nationalism in Twentieth-Century Brittany* (Chapel Hill: University of North Carolina Press 1977), p. 52.
10. Maurice Marchal, quoted by Reece, p. 29.
11. Quoted from the URB charter by Reece, p. 54.
12. Bradbury and McFarlane in *Modernism 1890–1930*, p. 20.
13. Reece, pp. 39–40.
14. 'Witches and Wizards and Irish Folk-Lore' in Lady Gregory, *Visions and Beliefs in the West of Ireland* (Gerrards Cross: Colin Smythe 1970), p. 302.

15. Edmund Wilson, *Axel's Castle: A Study in the Imaginative Literature of 1870 to 1930* (New York: Charles Scribner's Sons 1931), p. 34.
16. Melvin J. Friedman, 'The Symbolist Novel: Huysman to Malraux' in *Modernism 1890–1930*, p. 456. By other contributors to this collection of essays (John Fletcher and Malcolm Bradbury, 'The Introverted Novel'), *Ulysses* is called 'the Modernist novel *par excellence*', p. 405.
17. Vladimir Propp, *Morphology of the Folktale* (Bloomington: Indiana University Research Center in Anthropology, Folklore and Linguistics 1958).
18. Stith Thompson, *The Folktale* (Berkeley: University of California Press 1977), p. 437.
19. Fletcher and Bradbury, 'The Introverted Novel' in *Modernism 1890–1930*, p. 396.
20. Introduction to *The Oxford Book of Modern Verse*, rpt in *W. B. Yeats: Selected Criticism*, ed. A. Norman Jeffares (London: Pan Books 1976), p. 219.
21. Joseph C. Voelker, '"Proteus" and the *Vaticinia* of Marsh's Library: Joyce's Subjunctive Selves', *Eire-Ireland* XIV, 4 (1979), p. 139.

4

POST-WAR ULSTER POETRY:
THE ENGLISH CONNECTION

I

'Since Congreve and Sterne there has always been at least one major Irish star on the British literary scene.' It would be imprecise to say that A. Alvarez *claims* this in his review of Seamus Heaney's *Field Work*.[1] I think he laments it. One senses that Alvarez praises another Irish poet the more ('the gifted, underrated Thomas Kinsella') because he has, according to Alvarez, 'departed for America, disappeared into the interior, and has scarcely been heard from since'. In the light of the fact that Kinsella lives in a large American city (Philadelphia) and has published steadily, and that Alvarez presumably owns a library ticket, one wonders at first what he can mean. But what he means is that the *English* have not heard from Kinsella, and to say this while including himself is to betray the very provincialism Alvarez proceeds to attack.

For it is Alvarez's contention that the British 'are comfortable with Heaney' – the current major Irish star – 'because he himself is comfortably in a recognizable tradition'. That tradition is English, still capable of Victorian ornamentation, uneasy with Modernism, cosy and unambitious, and its prevailing vice is 'a monotony of the mundane'. Heaney's work, we are told, 'challenges no presuppositions, does not upset or scare, is mellifluous, craftsmanly, and often perfect within its chosen limits. In other words, it is beautiful minor poetry, like Philip Larkin's . . .'. Alvarez is not wrong in implying that Heaney is as British as he's Irish (I will argue something of the sort myself), but the terms in which he couches the poet's Britishness and Irishness seem contradictory. He sees in abundance in Heaney 'a gift which the English distrust in one another but expect of the Irish: a fine way with the language. What in Brendan Behan, for instance, was a brilliant, boozy gift of the gab is transformed by Heaney into rich and sensuous rhetoric. He is a man besotted with words and, like all lovers, he wants to display the beauties and range and subtleties of his beloved.' To liken Heaney to Behan, via an alcoholic metaphor, is absurd, especially when Alvarez also sees Heaney as allusive, intensely literary, even at times downright pedantic. But having done so, he then turns round and accuses Heaney of being too discreet, steady and reliable, in a word, *English*. Moreover, it seems unfair that the gifted Heaney, as it transpires, is the distrustable Heaney, the trustable being the cosier and less ambitious. A difficult man, Alvarez; almost as difficult as Geoffrey Grigson, who has denied the very possibility of an Irish poetry written in English.[2]

In Alvarez's reaction to Heaney we glimpse the tangled relations between English and Irish writers, which may be as tangled as those between the English and Irish peoples. To the English, and rightly, the Irish writer is both an exotic and a familiar, as the Irish people are both British and not British, provincial citizens of the archipelago and at the same time strange, troublesome, and backward colonists. The ambivalence of the English writers towards their Irish counterparts, that odd mixture of envy and admiration, respect and condescension, can be found at least as early as Sidney's *Apologie for Poetrie* (1595), in which occurs the remark: 'In our neighbour country Ireland, where truly learning goeth very bare, yet are their poets held in a devout reverence.' Praise for the exalted position of the poet in Ireland is accompanied by the charge of cultural poverty. A compromise status for the Irish writer is that of overseas citizen: the Irish writer has a special passport entitling him to behave in ways unacceptable from holders of ordinary passports, but that special passport has of course been issued from the Colonial Office and may be revoked at any time. Alvarez rings the changes on this arrangement by revoking Heaney's special passport *and* carpeting him for travelling with an ordinary passport.

The inconsistency is not all on the one side. Irish writers want to avail themselves of the hospitality of English readers and at the same time maintain the refuge of difference against the day when the critical going gets rough. 'I have never been much considered by the English critics', Patrick Kavanagh began his 'Author's Note' to his *Collected Poems*, in a tone poised between truculence and self-pity, between anglophobia and unrequited love. Such ambivalence, on both sides of the Irish Sea, is concentrated in Northern Ireland, a province geographically Irish but constitutionally British. The career of Ulster poetry since the war, written as it has been by those who think of themselves as primarily Irish as well as by those who think of themselves as primarily Northern Irish (i.e. British), is a vivid case-study in the history of Anglo-Irish literary relations, with their mutual incursions, and their two-way traffic in poetic reputation and critical reception. I content myself in what follows with drawing attention to what I believe are the high-points of that case-study; if I stress the 'English dimension' of this chapter in Anglo-Irish literary history, it is because the 'Irish dimension' has been amply accounted for elsewhere.[3]

II

In the 1940s, in the absence of Auden and despite the tetchy vigilance of Grigson and *New Verse*, there was a bout of enthusiasm in Britain for Celticism as a pseudo-geographic strain of the dominant Romanticism of the period. It was claimed that there was a 'Welsh Renaissance' (one imagines the youthful Kingsley Amis waiting in gleeful ambuscade) and also a 'Scottish Renaissance', but that 'the Irish, especially in *The Bell*, have been busy, but more traditionally'.[4] *Poetry Scotland* (a regional counterforce, though not a poetic counter-force, to *Poetry London*), encouraging the Irish, published John Hewitt, Maurice James Craig and Donagh MacDonagh in their second number (1944). It was, however, an indecisive showing, especially since Hewitt, despite his presence here and later in *A New Romantic Anthology* (1949), edited by Stefan Schimanski and Henry Treece, was if anything closer to the Grigson camp in which he found himself when Grigson anthologized him in his *Poetry of the Present* (1949).

In the words of Robert Herring, written at the end of the war, the Celt is a Romantic, endowed with a sense 'of the mystery of Man': 'the difference between English and Celtic love-poetry, for instance, is that between sentiment and passion and the Celtic passion is not only personal but directed to the divinity enshrined in the person'.[5] When Celts mobilize, Irish poets are an obvious group to conscribe, but it appears that there was token resistance to conscription. In 1942 the Ulster poet Robert Greacen co-edited with Alex Comfort *Lyra: An Anthology of New Lyric*. Of the Irish poets represented in the volume (all of whom were from Ulster), the editors wrote: 'The Irish-Ulster group, who are more like a school than any of the others, includes Greacen, McFadden, Gallen and Brook (who is English). They are evolving something which again is new, a form of poetic realism.'[6] But the company the Ulster poets were keeping rendered suspect such an enterprise. The anthology was published by Wrey Gardiner, editor of *Poetry Quarterly*, home to many of the 1940s neo-Romantics, and included such prominent members of that band as G. S. Fraser, Alex Comfort, Nicholas Moore, Tambimuttu, Henry Treece and Vernon Watkins, as well as Robert Herring and Gardiner himself. There was a Preface by Herbert Read, and in 'A Word from the Editors' Comfort and Greacen described their anthology as 'a contribution to a new romanticism'. In fact, the Ulster poets, like their co-anthologized, flourish a hackneyed Romantic enervation that the war seems to have encouraged in contemporary poets:

> Not world as world is, but world as wish is
> but the long suffering of 'I' at last lost, lip-puffed-by:
> dreams no doubt – there is no need of courage
>
> nor of anything but dreaming, in a dream.
>> (Gallen, 'A Little Lyricism on a New Occasion')

> Whin and thistle and the weeds of a wan winter
> You are fit symbols for this time of tearing war
>> (Greacen, 'Lines for Friends expecting a Baby at Christmas 1941')

> What can we say who have said it all already?
> Who have seen the years fall
> Like leaves or tears on to a million coffins
> Returning dully to the blissful womb;
> What can we say, here, by the hardening fire,
> As the clock ticks history, and the flowers drip blood?
>> (McFadden, 'Poem for To-Day')

McFadden's is meant, of course, to be brass-tack sentiment, and one of his three poems, 'Gaudeamus Igitur', is mock-Romantic, but realism and end-of-the-tether rhetoric are not one and the same, and Greacen is surely in error when he suggests in a recent and otherwise valuable reminiscence that McFadden gave up Romanticism abruptly in 1939 on Greacen's recommendation.[7] There is no distinction in theme, matter or style to be made between the Ulster contributions to *Lyra* and the English, Scottish and Welsh contributions of the kind that the phrase 'poetic realism' would seem to invite.

On the evidence of *Lyra*, Ulster poetry in the 1940s written by the newcomers was hardly distinguishable from British neo-Romanticism at large, even though they wrote out of a discouraging wartime in Belfast. (This apparently is how the Ulster poets wanted it. According to Terence Brown, they display 'an iconoclastic irritation with the Irish mode' available to them, McFadden in particular believing that 'an emulation of contemporary English experiments is the only possible way forward for Irish poets'.)[8] In the light of this, it seems odd that *Lyra* did not include W. R. Rodgers, especially since Greacen in his reminiscence admits that he and the others were very aware of Rodgers 'and the stir made by his first collection, *Awake! and Other Poems*' (1941).[9]

Rodgers, indeed, became one of only two Irish poets of his generation to enjoy a substantial British and American reputation, the other being Louis MacNeice, another Ulsterman. *Awake! and Other Poems* appeared in England and America to great acclaim, and the poet was heralded by some as the new Auden. The joyous use of words ('a fine way with the language'!) is the immediate quality of Rodgers's verse, and the reader, like the poet, is an astonished host to lines both buoyed and weighted by alliteration, assonance, puns and breakneck rhythms and charged with exclamatory and imperative urgency. Such poetry unfortunately contributes to the English stereotype of the word-besotted Irish bard for whom reason is low on the totem-pole of priorities.

Although he was an Ulster Protestant (indeed, a Presbyterian minister who forsook the collar of the cleric for the collar on a pint of Guinness), Rodgers thought of himself as thoroughly Irish:

> O these lakes and all gills that live in them,
> These acres and all legs that walk on them,
> These tall winds and all wings that cling to them,
> Are part and parcel of me, bit and bundle,
> Thumb and thimble.

Perhaps Rodgers's self-advertising Irishness dismayed Greacen and the Ulster poets, even though they too were wartime neo-Romantics. Yet Rodgers shares linguistic verve and dash with his contemporaries George Barker and Dylan Thomas, two poets Kenneth Rexroth thought it natural to bracket with the Ulsterman in his resourceful Introduction to The New British Poets (1949). Given Barker's part-Irish ancestry and Thomas's Welshness, perhaps we could say that what the three poets share is Celticness, though this is debatable. Despite the fact that the 'thirties poets were his initial, acknowledged inspiration,[10] Rodgers's reliance on the unconscious (by way of association and suggestion) and his lack of political commitment mark him as a post-Auden British Romantic. And the obtrusively apocalyptic theme and tone of many of the poems in Awake! and Other Poems associate him with Henry Treece, J. F. Hendry and the poets of the Apocalyptic anthologies, The New Apocalypse (1939), The White Horseman (1941) and The Crown and the Sickle (1944), which briefly, but only briefly (thankfully), lit up the sky over the English poetry scene.[11]

III

In short, Rodgers was a sitting duck for the new generation of poets (Kingsley Amis, Robert Conquest, Philip Larkin, John Wain and others) that was beginning to make its presence felt in British poetry. The year after Rodgers's second (and last) volume, *Europa and the Bull and Other Poems*, appeared in 1952, Amis tried to make ribbons of Rodgers's verse in *Essays in Criticism*. The punning title of Amis's piece struck the attitude: 'Ulster Bull: The Case of W. R. Rodgers'.[12]

Taking the opening four lines of 'Europa and the Bull' as text, Amis concluded after some elementary Empsonian analysis that whereas attention to the meaning of Rodgers's verse is disastrous, attention to the sound is in the end equally disastrous. For Amis, Rodgers's poems – and by association the poems of New Romanticism for which he let them conveniently stand – were so many 'word-salads'. In a poem entitled 'Here is Where', Amis seemed to mock Rodgers and his ilk:

> *Here, where the ragged water*
> *Is twilled and spun over*
> *Pebbles backed like beetles,*
> *Bright as beer-bottles*
> *Bits of it like snow beaten*
> *Or milk boiling in saucepan* . . .
>
> Going well so far, eh? . . .

In 'Wrong Words', possibly with Rodgers in mind, Amis rounded on poets who are 'Too fluent, drenching with confectionery/One image, one event's hard outline'.

But though in 'Ulster Bull', Amis dissociated Rodgers's verse from the first Romanticism, Amis himself acidly rewrote a chief Romantic text in 'Ode to the East-North-East-by-East Wind' in which he makes a tough-minded attack on Shelley's poetic egotism. The assault on Shelley seems sincere enough, originating possibly in Leavis's downgrading of that poet, but it would be a mistake to take such a poem too seriously. Still, Amis and the other-Movement poets were generally (Larkin having apparently come out of his Yeats phase) against Romanticism. In a poem of just that title, Amis expressed a desire for temperateness and realism in verse as in life. Romanticism is equated in this poem with anarchy, reminding us of the Movement's penchant for an order (masquerading as consensus) that was challenged by Rodgers's (as by Thomas's) love of duality, trinity and in the end fecund dishevelment and 'throughotherness'. (Far from believing in order, Rodgers seemed to hold a millenarian view of history not as continuity but as a series of ruptures. His world is full of prophecies, revelations, catastrophes, redemptions, resurrections, myths, dreams and mysteries.)[13] In later years, Amis and Larkin developed a sympathy for right-wing politics,[14] but we can see a disdain for the left as early as 'Against Romanticism', which concludes:

> Let the sky be clean of officious birds
> Punctiliously flying on the left;
> Let there be a path leading out of sight,
> And at its other end a temperate zone:
> Woods devoid of beasts, roads that please the foot.

Mention of Dylan Thomas is a reminder that Movement reaction against Romanticism entailed reaction against the immensely popular Welsh poet, who died in 1953. In *Poets of the 1950s* (1955), the first anthology of Movement verse, D. J. Enright wrote of Thomas:

The rich and brilliant imagery in which his work abounds almost blinds the critic to its deficiency in intellectual conviction. Perhaps the kind of admiration which Thomas received encouraged him to leave 'thinking' to the *New Verse* poets; but poetry is like the human body in needing bones as well as flesh and blood. Poetry must possess (and honour) its own kind of logic, however elusive it may be; and Welsh rhetoric seems a deadly enemy to all varieties of logic, even the poetic.[15]

'Our new poets', claimed Enright, are 'moderate' (Amis would have said 'temperate'), both in technique and in attitude, 'and of course moderation lacks the immediate popular appeal of the extremes', i.e. of the bards, Romantics, Apocalyptics and Celts. Thomas, of course, had been reproved before the Movement came into being by Grigson and also by Robert Graves. More to my point, he had also been attacked by Orwell, who was something of a hero to members of the Movement. In the Movement's assault on extremism, especially of anarchist and leftist varieties, we might detect stirrings of Orwell's anti-Stalinism and Cold War anti-communism.[16] The facts of life in post-war Britain seemed to indicate a circumspect realism. A Shelleyan Romanticism was bound to be a casualty under conditions in which social order, after the recent catastrophe, was trying to reassert itself. Indeed, any Romanticism was bound to be a casualty and so Rodgers's heady verse came under attack (not just for its lack of merit but also for its colouration and ideology) in the changed and sober circumstances of post-war Britain.

Much has been made, rightly, of the provincial stance of the Movement poets, their suspicion of the metropolis. The provincial stance came perhaps from a natural wish on the part of young writers to settle alternative sites for themselves away from the established centre of literary power, which was London. It came too, perhaps, from the fact that the young writers were the New University Wits, as Van O'Connor early nicknamed them, who needed university posts after graduation, most of these being in the provinces. Their provincialism was, then, both necessary and strategic, and consisted as much in the 'metropolitanization' of the provinces (through links with London via publishers, readers and critics, as well as via the BBC and journals) as in the creation of regional alternatives to London (for settings and subject-matter). Provincialism, in any case, implies, even entails, a metropolis from which it derives its values and standards.

This is a largely English perspective on the Movement. From a Scottish, Welsh and Irish perspective, the Movement was English in three vivid ways – its writers were mostly English nationals, they attended Oxford or Cambridge, and they were, at least temporarily, associated after graduation with the English academy. The Movement may have been provincial in one sense or another, but it was also anti-regionalist, the regions (Scotland, Wales and Ireland) being associated with Romanticism and Celticism; in short, with Enright's 'extremes', poetic and geographic. The equation of regionalism with Romantic Celticism had been established in the 1940s by the neo-Romantics themselves. Neo-Romanticism was even on occasions seen hopefully as a force in 'the revival and revitalisation of nationalist and regional cultures'.[17] In this light, the Movement can be viewed as much as a reaction as a revolution, an English, centralist reaction against a brief, regional interregnum, a Commonwealth between king-ships (in which Dylan Thomas played a benign Cromwell). Critics have already drawn attention to the Little Englandism of the Move-ment, and Morrison has correctly linked it in its international context to the Movement's provincialism in an English context.[18] Anti-regionalism may have been as much an aspect of post-imperial (as well as post-war) tristesse as provincialism and xenophobia.[19] We see an aggressive insularity at work in an interview with Larkin, who may himself have been unaware of it at that precise moment. 'So you don't ever feel the need to be at the centre of things?' he was asked. 'You don't want to see the latest play, for instance?' 'Oh no,' he replied,

I very much feel the need to be on the periphery of things. I suppose when one was young one liked to be up to date. But I very soon got tired of the theatre. I count it as one of the great moments of my life when I first realized one could actually walk out of a theatre. I don't mean offensively – but go to the bar at the interval and not come back. I did it first at Oxford: I was watching *Playboy of the Western World* and when the bell rang at the interval I asked myself: 'Am I enjoying myself? No, I've never watched such stupid balls.' So I just had another drink and walked out into the evening sunshine.[20]

Is it a coincidence that the play he was watching when his great moment occurred was an internationally acclaimed, extravagantly *Irish* play?

This might help to explain Kavanagh's neglect by the English at the time of the Movement. Alvarez to the contrary, there was no English desire for an Irish star in their firmament between Behan and Heaney, between, say, 1955 and 1975. For his part, Kavanagh knew the poetry of the Movement was hostile to his own work. His impatience with Movement verse anticipated Alvarez's strictures in his Preface to his 1962 anthology, *The New Poetry*:

> I say to hell
> With all reasonable
> Poems in particular
> We want no secular
> Wisdom plodded together
> By concerned fools.[21]

It might also help to explain – since the Movement held sway for some time – the later neglect of Kinsella and John Montague. True,

Kinsella and Montague write a verse responsive to Modernism and therefore more welcome in America, where they have sought their largest audience outside Ireland, than in England. But the naturalness of their choice of America may be as culturally (even racially) explicable as it is poetically explicable. If Kinsella and Montague were (as far as an English readership is concerned) victims of the Movement, they have been victims too of partition, being, as they are, too unambiguously Irish. Since the Movement, with its implicit redefinition of Britishness as a cultural nationality radiating from its English core, there has been little English interest in southern Irish writers.[22] (Exceptions such as Edna O'Brien and William Trevor are fiction writers who do not threaten English political sensibilities in the manner of a Montague or English aesthetic sensibilities in the manner of a Kinsella.) Certainly the Irish poets most highly regarded in England today are from Northern Ireland.

IV

If what I have said is true, it is all the more hilarious to stumble upon, in Iain Fletcher and G. S. Fraser's Introduction to their 1953 anthology, *Springtime: An Anthology of Young Poets*, this inspired inaccuracy: 'Irish poets, like Mr Larkin, though writing in Standard English, reflect another regional value, that of rootedness.'[23] This about the future and firmly English author of 'The Importance of Elsewhere', a poem which begins, 'Lonely in Ireland since it was not home'! For rooted and regionalist are precisely what Larkin is not, even if we decide to label England as a region. In his work there is no Wordsworthian attachment to place: 'Nothing, like something, happens anywhere', as he ends the ironically titled 'I Remember, I Remember', a line that also disavows revelation. In Larkin there is no romantic memory of beginnings or fond recalls of boyhood. Coventry is 'only where my childhood was unspent', he says in the same poem.[24]

It is not easy to picture Larkin in Belfast (the city whose postmark his poems to Fraser and Fletcher would have borne), but he spent five years there as a librarian at Queen's University (failing to overlap with the student Heaney by only two years). The city's lack of those romantic and literary associations clinging to Dublin would have gratified him, as would its awkward poise of relationship with England

and Ireland, but most of all, it seems its foreignness appealed. Belfast lay on the far side of that mere provincialism Amis exploited in Swansea. Larkin being Larkin, he found the city's strangeness familiar, its difference congenial. Belfast, whose 'fifties sights, sounds and smells I can corroborate,

> Their draughty streets, end-on to hills, the faint
> Archaic smell of dockland, like a stable,
> The herring-hawker's cry, dwindling . . .

became one of the several 'elsewheres' that have underwritten Larkin's poetic, and, he would no doubt claim, his real existence.

'After finishing my first books,' Larkin has said, 'say by 1945, I thought I had come to an end. I couldn't write another novel, I published nothing. My personal life was rather harassing. Then in 1950 I went to Belfast, and things reawoke somehow. I wrote some poems, and thought, These aren't bad, and had that little pamphlet *XX Poems* printed privately. I felt for the first time I was speaking for myself. Thoughts, feelings, language cohered and jumped.'[25] Thirteen of *XX Poems*, printed in Belfast, reappeared in *The Less Deceived* (1955). The seminal collection of post-war English poetry, the volume that changed the direction of British poetry, was, then, largely written in Belfast. It was this city's undeceived, unromantic, unEnglish (and yet unIrish) provincialism, its negative identity (unavailable as it is to any English perspective on Ireland or England), that was the poetry's inspiration.

Another English poet arrived at Queen's University to teach English in the early 1960s. Along with Edward Lucie-Smith, Peter Redgrove and others, Philip Hobsbaum was a leading light in the Group, Cambridge's delayed answer to Oxford's Movement. Movement and Group poetry seem to me indistinguishable except by merit. The title poem of Hobsbaum's first volume of verse, *The Place's Fault and Other Poems* (1964), in which he recalls, unlike Larkin, his childhood (and with distaste), reverses Larkin's judgment in 'I Remember, I Remember' that his unspent childhood was not 'the place's fault'. The reversal is nevertheless a salute to Larkin. Hobsbaum was aware of following in Larkin's footsteps to Belfast, and he offered as epigraph to his second volume (*In Retreat and Other Poems*, 1966) the opening line of 'The Importance of Elsewhere': 'Lonely in Ireland, since it was not home'.

Hobsbaum played a large part in the inspiriting of Ulster poetry; unlike Larkin, Hobsbaum was pedagogical, proselytic and convivial, and his role as catalyst has been by now fully acknowledged.[26] Through Hobsbaum, rather than Larkin, the values of the Movement were carried to Belfast (if I may risk a vector theory of literary influence), putting paid to any Romantic residue in Ulster poetry of the time.[27] Perhaps it was more like a devolution of poetical power. Like Alvarez after him, Hobsbaum has tried to appropriate the work of Heaney (one of Hobsbaum's Belfast Group) in the name of an essentially English tradition. Hobsbaum claimed the wedding sequence of *Wintering Out* (1972) as the best of Heaney thus far, and placed it firmly within 'the central line of English poetry', a line allegedly extended by the Group poet, Redgrove.[28] We can, of course, bridle at the confident sweep of the claim, the blindness to Heaney's Irishness, but that is not to deny that Ulster poetry since and including Heaney's carries the imprint of Movement and Group verse.

V

We discover it, for example, in Derek Mahon's unease with the academy and its familiars, the critic-as-sutler and the writer-in-residence. Larkin's 'Posterity' finds its equivalent in Mahon's 'I Am Raftery'. Mahon and Larkin share an almost pedantic nurturing of ignorance, a versed bravado leading in each case to pervasive, even reflex paradox of tone and attitude. Larkin's purely assumed philistinism in 'A Study of Reading Habits' – 'Get stewed:/Books are a load of crap' – has its fellow in Mahon's excellent 'Rock Music' (*The Hunt by Night*):

> The ocean glittered quietly in the moonlight
> While heavy metal rocked the discotheques;
> Space-age Hondas farted half the night,
> Fired by the prospect of fortuitous sex.
> I sat late at the window, bland with rage,
> And listened to the tumult down below,
> Trying to concentrate on the printed page
> As if such obsolete bumf could save us now.

Like Larkin, the Ulster poets, Mahon, Ormsby and Muldoon, specialize in versifying sentiments to which every bosom returns an echo.

The Movement influence I would define broadly as the studied concern for the techniques of poetry behind the pretence (possibly at times a genuine fear or conviction) that poetry in these times and in the real world doesn't matter. Mahon's lines

> And all the time I have my doubts
> About this verse-making . . .
> All farts in a biscuit tin, in truth –
> Faint cries, sententious or uncouth.[29]

and his fear that the Ulster poets, ostensibly concerned about the Troubles, are really 'middle-class cunts', strike the attitude vividly. The refusal of bardism, then, with a concomitant dedication to the craft of verse. Indeed, the refusal of bardism may be a rearguard action of regret, pique and self-pity against society's disregard for poets, which is how we might read 'I Am Raftery' and 'Rock Music'.[30] If that disregard is a post-war phenomenon, we might care to allow no essential difference between the Movement reaction and that of a writer who preceded the Movement, Samuel Beckett. Mahon, who admires Beckett, especially the Beckett of the trilogy, may be the mediating figure here rather than solely being a provincial post-Movementeer. Mahon's picture of himself as 'Scribbling on the off-chance,/Darkening the page' is an unacknowledged image from *Molloy*.[31] Beckett as much as Larkin has encouraged in Mahon what the Ulster poet calls 'the love-play of the ironic conscience'. To complicate things still further, what Geoffrey Thurley observes in Larkin – 'a residual self-distrust leavened by wit' – and about Larkin – 'eliminating the bogus is in fact Larkin's chosen profession' – are equally true for Mahon.[32] But Thurley would explain this in terms of what he claims is the poetic harvest of the English intellectualist tradition begun by Eliot, Richards and Empson – irony, scepticism, doubt, failure of nerve, loss of faith in literature itself.

Moreover, even if Mahon, Ormsby and Muldoon have learned from the Movement, there is a specifically Ulster context for their irony and scepticism, for the eloquent displacements their nervousness has caused. The Ulster poets are mostly from the urban working class or lower middle class or from their rural equivalents, and are not to the literary manner born, and this bears some resemblance to the class situation of the Movement writers.[33] But some are Catholics in a Protestant archipelago and all are triply provincial – self-conscious (like all British provincials) before London, but self-conscious too (as colonials) before the mainland, as well as self-conscious (as literary men) before Dublin. They are, then, going to be uneasy about their role as poets and about their readership. However, that unease has probably been reinforced by their inheritance of Movement values. Likewise, their refusal of a too evident Irishness, indicated by their Ulsterness, was stiffened no doubt by the Movement refusal of bardism. This refusal suggests some discomfiture with place, even a kind of rootlessness, though in the Ulster poets it doesn't have Larkin's succinctness of expression.

As luck would have it, the kind of unease I am talking about has mingled in the Ulster poets with their political unease over the progress of the Troubles in Northern Ireland. For many observers, this has been a happy conjunction, for it has put a welcome brake on any reflex, extreme or ancestral response to a difficult situation. The Movement quality of moderation, rooted in a rejection of 1940s Romanticism and romantic nationalism as well as in Orwell's 'advocacy of quietism',[34] even the Movement failure of nerve, if that was what it was, have permitted or encouraged a poetry in Ulster angularly at odds with the brutal facts of life and history there.[35] (On the other hand, there is no trace of Movement anti-leftism in Ulster poetry, but then 'right' and 'left' hold little meaning in Northern Ireland.) One senses conscience at work in an almost Nonconformist way; John Holloway once referred to the Nonconformist background of many of the Movement writers,[36] and while this might account in small part, and in Arnoldian terms, for the philistinism of the Movement (largely affected), it might also suggest an anglicizing or protestantizing of Catholic writers in Northern Ireland (to match the hibernicization in other regards of Ulster Protestant writers).[37]

This is not the whole story, of course. Some of the Ulster writers, from James Simmons on, have taken a blunt, no-nonsense approach to life and literature in Ulster. It puts to work, half-ironically, the stereotype of the 'honest Ulsterman' (the Northern equivalent of Myles na gCopaleen's plain people of Ireland). It crosses this stereotype with the stereotype of the American tough guy. Simmons, Michael Foley, Ormsby and Muldoon are all enamoured of Americanism that reaches them second-hand or is turned by them into the second-hand by parody or imitation. One recalls, of course, the well-publicized liking of Amis and Larkin for American jazz, which goes hand in hand with their refusal to be deceived by mandarin flummery. Yet *The Honest Ulsterman*, a highly successful and long-lived magazine, begun by Simmons and for which Foley has written, may owe more of its no-nonsense literary posture to the English magazine *The Review*, edited by Ian Hamilton, both magazines carrying blunt reviews and on occasions pseudonymous satires and parodies.[38] Hamilton and Alvarez were enemies of the Movement, but the chief influence on the first volume of poetry by the present editor of *The Honest Ulsterman*, Frank Ormsby, would seem to have been Larkin.* Larkin's droll self-deprecation lightens *A Store of Candles* (1977), as well as his humorous and precise observation of the mundane, his awareness of the strength of absence and elsewhere. Like Larkin, Ormsby has several poems that offer a jocularly detailed description or narrative capped by an irony that is apparently accepted but conceals a blank misgiving, a sense of loss. Larkin's 'Sunny Prestatyn' suggests the formula and it is put to good use in Ormsby's 'Spot the Ball' and 'Ornaments'.

VI

The Movement was famously repudiated by Alvarez in his anthology, *The New Poetry*, which brought its poets before their readers for a public caning and to benefit from the example of two American visitors to the school, Berryman and Lowell. Although he had been associated with it in earlier years, Alvarez considered the Movement tame, monotonous and fearful of the heart of darkness.[39] We might have thought that Heaney would have satisfied Alvarez. After all, Alvarez is an admirer of Ted Hughes, and Heaney's notion of poetry as a raid into the dark is actually Hughes's, as is Heaney's location of meaning deep underfoot accessible in some sense through wells, ponds, divining-rods, burial-chambers, bog-holes.[40] However, Alvarez has chosen to stress the Movement rather than Hughesian side of Heaney, and I cannot quarrel with him for doing so, since I preceded him in his choice.[41] Let me just supplement my earlier observation by suggesting that Heaney's early affinities with Larkin, though more surprising than Larkin's affinities with the more filtered personalities of Mahon and Ormsby, are there, despite the presence in his verse of the violence from which Larkin would run a mile. Like Larkin, Heaney has cultivated his 'elsewhere', and Heaney's being lost, unhappy and at home in Denmark (see 'The Tollund Man') puts me in mind of Larkin's being lost, unhappy and at home in Belfast. Read Larkin's 'MCMXIV', a poem that captures with the dim precision of an old photograph a turning-point in his country's

* Ormsby gave up editorship of the magazine in 1989.

history (the line of volunteers outside the recruiting offices in August 1914), and you might well think of Heaney's Irish equivalent, 'Linen Town', which captures an afternoon in Belfast before the 1798 rebellion in the same way and to the same end. Perhaps this is to say no more than this: that Larkin injected post-war British poetry with the now pervasive feelings of regret, nostalgia, loss, unease and reticence, that he established as expected practice in poetry a public but guarded self-inquisition.

If Alvarez has spurned Heaney, the new men in England, Blake Morrison, Andrew Motion and Craig Raine, are much taken with him. In 1982 Motion and Morrison promoted Heaney to father-figure in their anthology, *The Penguin Book of Contemporary British Poetry*. This compilation is meant to register 'a reformation of poetic taste' and a decisive break with the Movement and its ageing members. The Ulster poets constitute a vanguard fleet: six out of the twenty poets represented in the anthology are from a province of a million and a half people. However, the connections I have tried to establish between Ulster and Movement poetry throw the enterprise in some doubt, apart from the fact that the anthology is actually duller than the one it is meant to replace, Alvarez's *The New Poetry*, itself a perverse demonstration of dullness enlivened by its editor's polemical Preface. In their rather laboured and term-paperish Introduction, Motion and Morrison, needing a break with the Movement, invent a geologic fault. The new poets, it seems, are not inhabitants of their own lives so much as intrigued observers, 'inner émigrés' (Heaney's phrase). But if this does not fit Larkin, it fits no one. It seems odd that Morrison does not see to what extent he has re-imported into English Poetry – Ulsterized certainly – many of the values, standards and postures of a poetry he earlier chronicled.

Nevertheless, for the post-Movement poets and critics, Ulster poetry has rehabilitated the regionalism that the Movement scorned (but not the romantic regionalism of the 1940s), and does so in a way that is both model and inspiration for mainland verse: Tony Harrison, for example, has extended Heaney's probings of dialect and language-place connections. Through a cursory, even reflex reading of the Northern Irish political situation, Ulster poetry also permits for the post-Movement writers reinstatement of the leftist, working-class and anti-authoritarian perspectives to which the Movement was in reality hostile. Above all, then, Ulster poetry is *useful* to the English writers, helping them to turn English provincialism (in the honorific sense of indicating a lower-class background in the North or Midlands) into an authentic regionalism in the way that the Liverpool poets of the 'sixties might have done but in the event could not do. No doubt for a very brief time, Belfast is in some sense for these writers the British capital (as Liverpool was twenty years ago). Motion has made his obligatory pilgrimage there and commemorates it in verse; his 'Leaving Belfast' (in *The Pleasure Steamers*, 1978, and dedicated to Raine) can be set beside Raine's 'Flying to Belfast, 1977' (included in the Penguin collection). The 'Belfast poem' is now a small tradition among English poets, for different reasons to those which prompted Larkin's 'The Importance of Elsewhere'. For all, Belfast is strange and unfamiliar, but whereas the Motion and Raine poems are to-ings and fro-ings and wine-tastings of fear between flights, Larkin thrived on his separateness in Belfast, for it productively cleft his life into *here* and *there*.

It is a nice irony that in the service of homage as well as the principles of regionalism and anti-authoritarianism, the English poets have culturally bound Ulster more firmly to a Britain that will always be the dominant country in the enforced partnership of English-Irish contiguity. Perhaps this realization (if it wasn't that Alvarez touched a nerve) prompted Heaney – Motion and Morrison's captain – to stage a one-man mutiny. Suddenly he has seen *The Penguin Book of Contemporary British Poetry* as a colonialist venture. (The effect of their captain's mutiny on the morale of the other Irish crew-members, Muldoon, Paulin, McGuckian, Mahon and Longley, I don't know.) In *An Open Letter* (1983, Field Day pamphlet No. 2), Heaney politely but firmly refuses the adjective 'British':

> As empire rings its curtain down
> > This 'British' word
> Sticks deep in native and *colon*
> > Like Arthur's sword.

He admits that he has spoken out only after what he regards in himself as typical dithering, and he is characteristically aware of the irony in his stance:

> Yet doubts, admittedly, arise
> When somebody who publishes
> In LRB and TLS,
> > *The Listener* –
> In other words, whose audience is,
> > Via Faber,

A British one, is characterized
As British.

But he is nonetheless defiant:

> be advised
> My passport's green.
> No glass of ours was ever raised
> To toast *The Queen*.

Permission to reprint Heaney's poems having been sought and granted, permission fees presumably having been paid, Heaney's demurral cannot be seen as a case of his usual reticence and circumspection. One senses instead political pressure unrelated to the original literary decision to appear in the anthology. *An Open Letter* must be seen in the context of increased polarization of postures in Northern Ireland, and of the reversion to origins and heritages of which this polarization is cause or effect. Behind the understandable ambivalence towards Britain felt by all the Irish, one suspects the specific pressures on Heaney from his own tribe. He is talking in this pamphlet not so much to Motion and Morrison as to his own, and he is making appropriate anti-colonialist noises, but noises which are not only comfortless but also unHeaney-like, poetically as well as politically.[42] More than some influential others in Ireland, Heaney knows how tangled are the literary as well as political relations between Ireland and Britain, how unavailable they are to the simplicities of doggerel, as the past forty years, especially in Ulster, have once more shown.

[1985]

NOTES

1. A. Alvarez, 'A Fine Way with the Language', *The New York Review of Books* (8 March 1980).
2. As reported by Graham Martin in *The Review* I, No. 8 (August 1963), 18.
3. By Terence Brown, for instance, in his *Northern Voices: Poets from Ulster* (Dublin: Gill and Macmillan 1975).
4. Robert Herring, 'Reflections on Poetry prompted by the Poets of 1939–1944', *Transformation Three*, eds Stefan Schimanski and Henry Treece (London: Lindsay Drummond Ltd 1945), 183.
5. Herring, p. 183.
6. *Lyra: An Anthology of New Lyric* (Billericay, Essex: Grey Walls Press 1942), p. 13.
7. Robert Greacen, 'The Belfast Poetry Scene 1939–1945', *The Honest Ulsterman* (Winter 1984), p. 19.

8. Brown, pp. 128, 132. At the same time, Greacen wanted Ulster poetry to 'act as the bridgehead between Ireland and Great Britain, and to suck the best out of the English, the Gaelic and the Anglo-Irish culture', quoted by Brown, p. 129.

9. Greacen, p. 21.

10. Quoted to this effect in *The Poet Speaks: Interviews with Contemporary Poets*, ed. Peter Orr (London: Routledge & Kegan Paul 1966), p. 207.

11. There are two valuable memoirs of the 'forties poetry scene in London: Wrey Gardiner's *The Dark Thorn* (1946) and Derek Stanford's *Inside the Forties* (1977).

12. 'Ulster Bull: The Case of W. R. Rodgers', *Essays in Criticism* III, No. 4 (October 1953), 470–5.

13. I discuss Rodgers's world-view in more detail in 'The Dissidence of Dissent: John Hewitt and W. R. Rodgers', printed below.

14. However, Larkin told an *Observer* interviewer, 'I've always been right-wing'; the interview is reprinted in Philip Larkin, *Required Writing: Miscellaneous Pieces 1955–1982* (London: Faber and Faber 1983), p. 52.

15. *Poets of the 1950s: An Anthology of New English Verse*, ed. D. J. Enright (Tokyo: Kenkyusha Ltd), pp. 8–9.

16. Blake Morrison has already made this very point, in *The Movement: English Poetry and Fiction of the 1950s* (Oxford: Oxford University Press 1980), p. 93.

17. See Herring's article in *Transformation Three*; the quotation, however, is from Denys Val Baker's article, 'A Review of War-Time Reviews', also in *Transformation Three*, 199.

18. Morrison, pp. 60–2.

19. Larkin's 'Homage to a Government' accrues a deeper post-imperial sadness when we set it beside 'Going, Going' (both from *High Windows*, 1974). Larkin alludes to the first poem in his *Observer* interview just before proclaiming the right-wing nature of his politics, *Required Writing*, p. 52.

20. *Required Writing*, p. 55.

21. This is from Kavanagh's poem 'To Hell with Commonsense', reprinted in his *Collected Poems* (New York: Norton 1973), p. 155. Kavanagh includes an unflattering reference to Enright in his poem 'Sensational Disclosures'. Kavanagh was often co-author of his own neglect; for example, he declined the opportunity to appear in the Faber anthology *Contemporary Irish Poets* (1949), eds Robert Greacen and Valentin Iremonger: Greacen, 'I Followed a Dream' (autobiography), unpublished MS.

22. When reviewing *The Oxford Book of Contemporary Verse*, edited by Enright, in *The Irish Times*, Montague took the opportunity to denounce the provincialism of the Movement and of recent English poets generally. Montague, born in the USA, grew up in Ulster, but he is not a Northern Irish writer in the way Heaney, Muldoon or Longley are Northern Irish. This is partly to do with the fact that he is closer generationally to pre-partition Ireland, that his politics are (or seem) more republican than theirs, and that his education pre-dates the Butler Education Act, from which Heaney, Muldoon and Longley, as British subjects, benefited.

23. *Springtime: An Anthology of Young Poets*, eds G. S. Fraser and Iain Fletcher (London: Peter Owen 1953), p. 12. In the 'Editors' Introduction', Larkin is grouped with the 'Regionalists'!

24. 'Tell me a bit about your childhood,' the *Observer* interviewer asked Larkin.

'Oh, I've completely forgotten it,' he replied. *Required Writing*, p. 47.

25. From an interview with *Paris Review*, reprinted in *Required Writing*, p. 68.

26. See Derek Mahon, 'Poetry in Northern Ireland', *20th Century Studies* (November 1970), 90–1; also my article on Heaney, 'The Poetry of Seamus Heaney', printed below.

27. The Ulster neo-Romantics of the 1940s fell silent around 1947 or 1948 and kept their heads down for a quarter of a century until the Movement was no longer recognizable as such. After *The Undying Day* (1948), Greacen did not publish a full-length volume of poetry until *A Garland for Captain Fox* (1975); after *The Heart's Townland* (1947), McFadden did not publish a full-length volume until *The Garryowen* (1971); John Gallen was killed in a climbing accident in 1947. Barring John Hewitt, little happened in Ulster poetry after 1948 until the appearance of John Montague, who was in no simple sense an Ulster poet. It was really with Hobsbaum's Belfast Group that Ulster poetry reawakened.

28. See Hobsbaum's articles, 'The Present State of British Poetry', *Lines Review*, No. 45 (June 1973) and 'The Growth of English Modernism', *Wisconsin Studies in Contemporary Literature* VI (1965).

29. From 'The Sea in Winter' in *Poems 1962–1978* (Oxford: OUP 1979). Like Larkin, Mahon peppers his verse with vulgarisms: in both cases they are there less to shock than to re-establish a lost connection with readers.

30. 'I Am Raftery', of course, is an updating of a Gaelic original.

31. 'The Attic' in *Poems*, p. 102.

32. *The Ironic Harvest: English Poetry in the Twentieth Century* (London: Edward Arnold 1974), pp. 142–3. Larkin has like Mahon gone beyond poetic self-irony into a more literal self-irony. If Mahon refrains from projecting in his poetry much more than a voice, certainly not a self as rounded as that in, say, Heaney, Larkin preceded him in this and may have worked his influence. In 'Absences', Larkin imagines, suddenly, attics cleared of himself. (Such self-effacement seems a twentieth-century rather than Romantic imagining. The Ulster poet Michael Longley has made his Larkinesque 'perpetual absence' from a hearsay island a form of homage: see the epigraph poem to *The Echo Gate*, 1979.) And it is Larkin who in 'The Less Deceived' imagines fulfilment as a desolate attic. The connection between Larkin's terminal image and Yeats's reference in 'Anima Hominis' to the 'hollow image of fulfilled desire' may be worth pondering. Yeats's belief, stated in the same place, that the anti-self was accessible only to those who were no longer deceived by life, and not to sentimentalists who seek momentary happiness, might illuminate Larkin's poem (indeed, his entire *oeuvre*), and suggest that Larkin had not left his Yeats phase behind as decisively as he thought.

33. The class dimensions of the Movement are too complicated to be gone into here; suffice it to say that I think the lower middle-class nature of the Movement has been somewhat exaggerated and that I would describe Larkin's background as thoroughly middle-class.

34. Morrison, p. 93.

35. Where Heaney is concerned, the angular approach may derive as much from the example of Patrick Kavanagh: see my essay 'The Poetry of Patrick Kavanagh', printed below.

36. 'New Lines in English Poetry', *Hudson Review* IX, No. 4 (Winter 1956–7), 593.

37. I have discussed the connection between Calvinist and Movement aesthetics in 'The Dissidence of Dissent,' an essay in which I suggest Donald Davie (Movement poet, ex-Baptist) as the mediating figure between Nonconformism and the Movement. Hewitt, the ex-Methodist Ulster poet, shows in his verse some Movement characteristics, but would have been too regionalist for Movement poets and critics.

38. And it *is* just a literary posture. The no-nonsense approach is not serviceable in the most serious arena of Ulster life – the struggle over the national identity of the province – for the writers are not extremists or even highly committed politically, and it is hard to maintain a tough pose in the cause of moderation.

39. James Fenton has recently satirized Alvarez's critical posture in 'Letter to John Fuller', a poem in *Children in Exile: Poems 1968–1984* (New York: Vintage 1984).

40. See Hughes's *Poetry in the Making* (London: Faber and Faber 1967), pp. 55–8.

41. See my essay 'The Poetry of Seamus Heaney', printed below.

42. To be fair to Heaney, stanza nine of *An Open Letter* suggests that it is simply the offending word *British* in the Penguin title that has caused his dismay (possibly even his sense of betrayal, if Heaney granted permission under the impression that the anthology was to be called *Opened Ground*, a phrase that is Heaney's own). Would Heaney's pamphlet not have appeared then if Motion and Morrison had taken Michael Schmidt's precaution of calling his alternative anthology *Some Contemporary Poets of Britain and Ireland* (1983)? Possibly, though the word *British* is sometimes a hard one to replace (as in *the British Isles*) and often means less than it implies. In any event, its use by Motion and Morrison is as debatable as the national identity of Northern Ireland; Longley would probably not baulk at its use in the title of the anthology; but Muldoon or even Mahon might (but then again they might not). And how many of the Ulster poets contemplated reversing their decision to appear in the anthology, before or after Heaney's verse epistle? In the light of the problematic involved, the word *British* seems less a text than a pretext for Heaney's *Open Letter*. This pamphlet, after all, fits the pattern established by the first six Field Day pamphlets, which all contain an apparently prerequisite anti-colonialist attack on Britain.

5

THE POETRY OF SEAMUS HEANEY

With three full-blown volumes and several pamphlets to his credit, Seamus Heaney has already assembled a body of work of extra-ordinary distinctiveness and distinction.[1] At the age of thirty-four he has been proclaimed an exciting talent by many and a possibly major poet by several. Single-mindedness of purpose, a fertile continuity of theme, high competence in execution, a growing unmistakability of voice: these are Heaney's strengths and they place him in seriousness and maturity beyond hailing distance of most younger British poets.

These make him sound dull, whereas Heaney writes a verse that achieves, but does not depend upon, immediate impact. The most eye-catching feature is a use of rawly physical metaphors for things in and out of the physical world: frogs are 'mud grenades, their blunt heads farting'; granary sacks are 'great blind rats'; a quiet river wears 'a transfer of gables and sky'; a pregnant cow looks as though 'she has swallowed a barrel'. Heaney's metaphors are so right, so conclusive that they generate within the poem and across the canon an axiomatic quality that is perilously close to being self-defeating; they can even in cumulation constitute their own kind of preciosity. In consequence, the poet occasionally gives the impression of a man hastening to patent a style. Craft, with which unlike most poets today Heaney is preoccupied, is not merely honest skill but also Daedalean cunning. He will seemingly not be deflected from working his enviably rich vein as he strikes deeper and deeper towards some unseen mother lode. The metaphor is apt, for Heaney's theme thus far has been 'working the earth', and his exploitation of this coincides with the 'whole earth' movement in Britain and the United States. Just as important, it coincides with the attempts of several writers in Northern Ireland to delve beneath the violent surface of life in the province into lore, history and myth, on the principle that the poisonous plant can best be understood by its roots. Heaney may have been engaged upon this before terror struck in 1969, but the 'Troubles' have surely lent his poetry urgency and authenticity.

Troubles or no, digging deep has always been a hazardous business in Ulster, for it is to resume the dark, in Heaney's phrase, and the dark is fearful. It is arguable whether or not the fear with which Heaney's poetry is soaked is justified by the trove he has brought back from the Ulster heart of darkness. The impersonal insights are undeniable and remarkable, but the poet's degree of emotional involvement is more problematic. And has the poet up to now worked deep, in conceit and extended metaphor, at the expense of modal variety? These are questions not to be answered until the tangy and peculiarly seasoned quality of Heaney's poetry has been savoured. Should he reach perfection in his present mode, he will have become a notable minor poet. Should he instead widen his themes, break into new modes, and learn to trust his feeling, Seamus Heaney might well become the best Irish poet since Yeats.

I

Early Heaney poetry startled with its physicality. What a pleasure it was to come upon for the first time imagery so bluff, masculine and dead-on:

> All year the flax-dam festered in the heart
> Of the townland; green and heavy headed
> Flax had rotted there, weighted down by huge sods.
> Daily it sweltered in the punishing sun.
> Bubbles gargled delicately, bluebottles
> Wove a strong gauze of sound around the smell.

Heaney's first volume, *Death of a Naturalist*, whose titular poem I have just quoted, is as heavily laden with assonance, alliteration, imagery of touch, taste and smell, and with synaesthesia (the buzz of bluebottles visualized as gauze) as the flax is with sods. Extensive description of a static scene can, as we shall see later, lead Heaney into confusion, despite a Ted Hughes-like vividness. Heaney is on firmer ground when recreating the *processes* of the earth and how man interacts with nature through ritual, custom and work. Not only are Heaney's poems about manual work on the farm – ploughing, planting, harvesting, horse-shoeing, etc. – but they are themselves manuals on how the work is actually done. It is amusing, for instance, to set 'Churning Day' beside E. Estyn Evans's account of churning in *Irish Heritage* (1942) and *Irish Folk Ways* (1957). Heaney in such a poem is folklorist, recalling old customs that survived into his native Londonderry of the 1940s. Of course, by dint of education, travel and rural changes, Heaney is no longer at one with his rural origins and so his rehearsal of the customs he witnessed or participated in as a child assumes the quality of incantation and commemoration. The poems, he would have us believe, are substitutes for the farmwork he was once close to. In 'Digging', the first poem of his first volume, and one that functions as a crude but effective manifesto, the poet recalls his father, like *his* father before him, expertly cutting turf on Toner's bog, and says:

> But I've no spade to follow men like them.

The ex-peasant, newly urbanized, newly middle-class poet proclaims his alternative.

> Between my finger and my thumb
> The squat pen rests.
> I'll dig with it.

In one respect, Heaney has been fairly literally true to his word. If the early poems are about the use of tools – the churn-staff, the bill-hook, the spade, the hammer – they themselves are verbal mimicries of tool-using. From his evident reading and the intimacy of his recall, one senses Heaney's preparation before each poem, like that of the thatcher (in the poem of that name) of whom the poet writes:

> It seemed he spent the morning warming up.

Heaney plainly likes to execute each poem, once preparations are complete, with 'the unfussy ease of a good tradesman' ('The Outlaw'). The poem's rhythm can imitate the rhythm of the body and lungs during the work – the curt clauses echoing the blows of a riveter's hammer in 'Docker', chopped lines and caesurae imitating turf-cutting in 'Digging', variable line length contrasting the actions of setting and lifting fishing-lines in 'A Lough Neagh Sequence'. But though craft is manual, there is scope in its circumspection for delicacy, pride and even, as 'Thatcher' demonstrates, magic:

> Couchant for days on sods above the rafters
> He shaved and flushed the butts, stitched all together

> Into a sloped honeycomb, a stubble patch,
> And left them gaping at his Midas touch.

No less than 'Digging', 'Thatcher' is a poem about writing poetry, and Heaney admires not merely the craftsman's cautious preparation and paced execution but also his sense of participating in a long tradition. Heaney's own traditions would seem loosely to be those of English (or Welsh) rural intimacy (John Clare, Thomas Hardy, R. S. Thomas), Ulster rural regionalism (John Hewitt, John Montague), and the post-Movement at its best (Larkin's expert verse-turning – learned from poets as diverse as Donne and Owen – spiced with Ted Hughes's menace).

Heaney has taken Yeats's advice to heart and striven to learn his trade. *Death of a Naturalist*, fine book though it is, is very much an apprentice's book, shot through with extravagances and infelicities. In 'Trout' we are asked in the space of a few words to envisage the fish as a 'fat gun-barrel' (a curious cartoon image) and at the same time as a tracer-bullet, a volley and a ramrod, images vivid in themselves but odd in combination. In 'Docker', something more important is being said and garbled in the saying.

> There, in the corner, staring at his drink.
> The cap juts like a gantry's crossbeam,
> Cowling plated forehead and sledgehead jaw,
> Speech is clamped in the lips' vice.

This is a startling caricature not just of any docker but of a laconic Belfast docker and therefore a Protestant, as Heaney makes clear in a second stanza that proved prophetic:

> That fist would drop a hammer on a Catholic –
> Oh yes, that kind of thing could start again;
> The only Roman collar he tolerates
> Smiles all round his sleek pint of porter.

Belfast's fundamentalism is clinched to the city's industrial lifestyle:

> Mosaic imperatives bang home like rivets;
> God is a foreman with certain definite views
> Who orders life in shifts of work and leisure.
> A factory horn will blare the Resurrection.

So far, so excellent, but then Heaney images the docker as a Celtic cross, an unwitting incongruity or misguided stroke of ethnic ecumenism. The sharp vision of the Belfast Protestant docker is further blurred with concluding lines that could be used of working-class family men other than dockers and which are therefore anti-climactic:

> Tonight the wife and children will be quiet
> At slammed door and smoker's cough in the hall.

II

It might be said that in *Death of a Naturalist*, with its prolific use of elementary poetic devices and overplus of image-making, Heaney was merely learning how to handle the turf-spade. It is likely, however, that the spade, wielded with whatever expertise, is too restricted a tool for Heaney's intellect and sensibility. At any rate, his second and third volumes evidence the pen metamorphosing from spade back again to pen.

Yet digging in one form or another remains the archetypal act in Heaney's poetry. What is found when the earth is overturned is sometimes good, such as the cream-white healthy tubers in 'At a Potato Digging', though in the same poem we are reminded that this was not always so and that 'wild higgledy skeletons/scoured the land in 'forty-five,/wolfed the blighted root and died.' Deeper down, finds are liable to be more interesting. Because of the strange power in bog water which prevents decay, much of Ireland's past has been preserved within the three million acres of bog – utensils, jewellery and most characteristically the wood from Ireland's vanished oak forests: 'A carter's trophy/split for rafters,/a cobwebbed, black,/long-seasoned rib/ /under the first thatch' ('Bog Oak'). The laid-open turf-bank is also a memory-bank, permitting us to read 'an approximate chronological sequence of landscapes and human cultures in Ireland going back several thousand years'.[2] Digging turf can often be inter-rupted – or continued – to become excavation. Since the investiga-tion of Irish bogs was conducted under Danish leadership,[3] it is fitting that Heaney's imagination should be fired by P. V. Glob's illustrated account in *The Bog People* (1969) of the preserved bodies of Iron Age men found in Danish and European fens. The first documented bog body came, with reciprocal appropriateness, from the North of Ireland in the eighteenth century, but no body yet found compares in state of preservation with the man from the Tollund fen in Denmark, now on exhibition, and about whom Heaney has pledged:

Some day I will go to Aarhus
To see his peat-brown head,
The mild pods of his eye-lids,
His pointed skin cap.

It is a rhetorical vow fulfilled in its making. There is no reason for Heaney to leave Ireland. As he has concluded in 'Bogland', which begins by noting that Ireland has 'no prairies/To slice a big sun at evening',

Our pioneers keep striking
Inwards and downwards.

These two lines look like a recipe for provincialism, but the objective correlatives for striking downwards are manifold in Heaney's poetry – digging, ploughing, drawing well-water, taking soundings, fishing, divining. Analogies too are fertile. If 'going down' is in one sense going, pioneer-fashion, into the unknown, it is also 'going home', an equation punningly contained in the word 'gravitate' indirectly exploited in 'Gravities' from Heaney's first volume and 'The Salmon Fisher to the Salmon' from his second. In Heaney's poetry things tend to revert, to resume by descent their dark primal condition.

Death of a Naturalist was Heaney's preliminary and noisy spade-work, the clearing of brush and scrub. Gradually there is a movement towards the spare and vertical shapes of *Wintering Out*, serious attempts to sink shafts narrowly and deep. Between the surface clatter of *Death of a Naturalist* and the striking downwards in *Wintering Out* comes the intermediate task in *Door into the Dark* of striking inwards, recognizing the inner fears to be overcome before the real digging is begun. To go home and to go down are both finally to confront the dark. Darkness resides in the crevices and recesses around the farm, in stable, forge and barn. It was childhood fear of this dark, as much as subsequent education and urbanization, that contributed to the poet's 'death' not only as a 'naturalist' but also as the unthinking accomplice of the earth that we regard the peasant farmer as being. Less literally, the dark conceals the subterranean violence of Irish life which through history has erupted into warfare ('Requiem for the Croppies'). And it is close to the centre of religious faith – the darkness of confessional and monastery, both projections in space of the dark recesses of the soul. When he steps into the early Christian stone oratory of Gallarus on the Dingle peninsula, Heaney is possessed by compulsions to descend and return:

You can still feel the community pack
This place: it's like going into a turfstack,
A core of old dark walled up with stone
A yard thick. When you're in it alone
You might have dropped, a reduced creature
To the heart of the globe. No worshipper
Would leap up to his God off this floor.

Excessive respect for the dark is shared not only by children and religious adults, but by primitives. The dark blurs the distinction between pagan and Christian. Raised a Catholic, an upbringing that has shaped 'In Gallarus Oratory', Heaney has nonetheless kept intimate traffic with the elder faiths of the Irish countryside which lie, bog-like, beneath the visible Roman Catholicism that has often co-opted them. Such traffic arises from the poet's actual experience in youth: 'Personal Helicon' recounts the same fascination with wells that presumably lay at the heart of ancient Irish well-worship.[4] Then there were the hearth stories about the supernatural, celebrated in 'Fireside'. And also, one suspects, wide reading in the literature. 'The Blinker' is a so far uncollected poem admonishing us to take traditional steps to ward off malign people or spirits who could '"blink" a cow so that its milk would yield no butter' (Evans) or who can, as Heaney has it, 'steer venom from his rimmed eye/ /Until the milk is bile and gall'.[5] Heaney's precautions are identical to Evans's: the use of a holed flint, smearing a ball of butter on the wall once the butter breaks, driving a coffin nail into the churn, twisting a rowan twig around the churn.[6] Heaney appropriates Evans's material and shapes it into the likeness of fear, not merely of bog-sprites and evil people but also – through the reader's ability to make the imaginative leap – of the evil that stalks Northern Ireland today, usually under cover of darkness as befits dastardliness.

Door into the Dark is not a sustained assault upon the dark but a series of forays. Poetry as sortie (and therefore usually short) is suggested in Heaney's remark that poetry is a kind of raid into dark corners, a remark Benedict Kiely used as the title of his spirited essay on Heaney's first two volumes.[7] 'All I know is a door into the dark,' proclaims Heaney in 'The Forge', but at sonnet's end he has yet to open that door, and stands transfixed upon the threshold, dumbly witnessing the blacksmith go back into his grotto-like forge. Likewise he recalls watching Kelly's unlicensed bull in 'The Outlaw', who, after the businesslike conception, 'resumed the dark, the straw'. No one would expect the child to brave the dark, but few of the poems in *Door into the Dark* are childhood recollections and yet the dark remains unchallenged by the end of the book. Heaney has a marked reluctance to strike inwards, to cross the threshold, to explore the emotional and psychological sources of his fear; and fear therefore outweighs understanding in his work, as darkness out-weighs illumination. We might choose to see his Roman Catholic upbringing coming into play here. Heaney's feeling in Gallarus oratory is indistinguishable from the penitent's desire to confess inside the dark confessional or pray inside the monastic sanctum. (The suggestion of defiance in 'No worshipper/Would leap up to his God off this floor' surely stems from Heaney's being native to a fundamentalist corner of Ireland whose majority abhors kneeling and the monastic tradition.) But Heaney is no readier to confess his personal feelings to his readers than the penitent is to discuss his confession with anyone other than his priest. The privacy of religious belief becomes the privacy of poetic feeling. Furthermore, the rites of confession and absolution, like the need for orders and retreats, assume man's severely limited direct access to his God. Much must be taken on trust. By an unavoidable analogy, Heaney's description of the oratory as 'a core of old dark walled up with stone/A yard thick' is an apt image for the tabernacular resistance Heaney's poetic mystery puts up in the face of comprehension and analysis, both his and the reader's.

In the meantime, the poet remains masterly at composing the signals and symptoms of fear into verse as compactly layered as good turf. At the poetic centre of *Door into the Dark* is a fine group of poems called 'A Lough Neagh Sequence'. Accounts of how the lough fishermen catch eels, interwoven with accounts of the life-cycle of the fish, are brilliant public metaphors for that psychic disturbance in Heaney's poetry whose precise meaning remains as intractable as bog oak. The sequence also interweaves the key Heaney motifs of descent, homing and darkness in the fashion of a metaphysical conceit. The eels travelling overland at night form a 'horrid cable' that encircles the poet's world of experience, threatening it with mysterious and malign power yet defining its shape and continuity. The completed circle of eels is also an 'orbit' of fears, and this implies a gravitational tendency to descend as well as to circumscribe.

The conceit lies at the heart of *Door into the Dark*. The volume is a marked improvement over *Death of a Naturalist* in terms of surer control and more effective conservation of energy. But the tautness of the conceit and the dramatic distancing it involves can obscure psychic and emotional issues as readily as immature and uncontrolled fertility. Moreover, the particular conceit of Heaney's choice – that of the circle or orbit – threatens to make his poetic philosophy a closed system, a state of affairs which is not helped by what I earlier called the axiomatic rightness of his images.

III

Thus far, Heaney has sought not to understand but to propitiate the fearful dark. Commemoration of the experiences of a rural childhood is also an attempt to exorcize. In *Death of a Naturalist*, fear was generated and exorcized inexpensively. The trouble began with the first couplet of the first poem:

> Between my finger and my thumb
> The squat pen rests; snug as a gun.

Since the poem is about digging, the image of the gun introduces a piece of gratuitous menace. Often with equal gratuity, images of ballistics and detonation pepper the volume. Frogs are 'mud grenades' in the titular poem; crocks are 'pottery bombs' in 'Churning Day'; 'Dawn Shoot' is about shotgunning foxes; when the poet slaps the animal in 'Cow in Calf' the blows 'plump like a depth-charge'; the fish in 'Trout' is a gun-barrel and a bullet; sea explodes, wind strafes, and space is a salvo in 'Storm on the Island'; the spectrum of colour on the canvas bursts, 'a bright grenade', when the painter 'unlocks the safety catch/On morning dew' in 'In Small Townlands'. The menace of the book, however vindicated in the gun-law of Ulster society since, is unearned. So too are the exorcisms. The poet is a trifle arrogant and facile in 'Follower'. 'An Advancement of Learning', about the poet's face-off with an embankment rat, is a piece of Wild Westernese. In 'The Early Purges' the poet remembers as a six-year-old seeing kittens drowned in a bucket, but has since, despite the nostalgic irony, overcome the trauma:

> living displaces false sentiments
> And now, when shrill pups are prodded to drown,
> I just shrug, 'Bloody pups.'

Why? – 'on well-run farms pests have to be kept down'. The child's feelings were impractical, yes, but surely not false either in the sense of being counterfeited or of being superficial. Throughout Heaney's poetry one senses beneath the hard-boiled exterior a certain shyness or shame about deep feelings which are dramatized away from the poet when not disavowed altogether.

The reader might reasonably expect at least to find the poet humanly vulnerable and open-hearted in matters of love. Until *Wintering Out* – and there only fleetingly – he would be disappointed. The love poems in *Death of a Naturalist* are placed coyly at the end of the book and they are, moreover, removed in a metaphysical style from immediacy of feeling. 'Valediction', 'Scaffolding', 'Poem for Marie' and 'Honeymoon Flight' are all conceits and, while clever and even beautiful (for example, 'Scaffolding'), keep the reader outside the taut, stave-like lines of their stanzaic compounds. There are no first-person love poems in *Door into the Dark* (sex in this volume is associated with the seasons and with rural rites) but Part Two of *Wintering Out* contains several marital love poems in which for the first time Heaney seems emotionally unsure of himself and therefore capable of poetic *moods*. The beautiful but brittle assurance of 'Scaffolding' is now, in 'Summer Home', an entire curve of emotion from premonition through revulsion, placation, passion and recrimination to the final chastened assertion:

> Yesterday rocks sang when we tapped
> Stalactites in the cave's old, dripping dark –
> Our love calls tiny as a tuning fork.

This poem may be the signpost to Heaney's future poetry, but for most of *Wintering Out* he is still content to impersonalize his feelings. If, for instance, natural and preternatural fears are more honestly evoked and allayed than in either of the two previous books, it is by dint not of greater emotional investment but of sounder analogies. Glob concludes that the bog people were participants in fertility rites and then sacrificed to a fertility goddess, and Heaney seizes on this. The encouragement of fertility through violent death is an ancient irony and one senses in 'The Tollund Man' its appropriateness for contemporary Ulster. Heaney's fear of the dark becomes in *Wintering Out* a fear of the violence in what Evans calls 'the immemorial peasant tradition which dominates the heart of Ireland' and of the way this violent and sacrificial past fingers out through analogy and recurrence to the present. Other poems in *Wintering Out* are concerned not with depth-readings of the Irish earth but with topography. The signatures of the past are inscribed for us to see above as well as below the ground. In these 'topographical poems' which are also 'language poems', parts of speech and parts of landscape are identified as a Catholic Ulsterman looks and listens around and considers what he has gained and lost by living in the planted North. It is a kind of respite on the sidelines of conflict; it is interesting to note that Heaney has given up his post at Queen's University, Belfast and become a full-time writer in the South of Ireland, far from the war zone. But as the title phrase from 'Servant Boy' implies, there is also in the book a notion of endurance, for everyone from Northern Ireland is at the moment 'wintering out/the back-end of a bad year'.

Poems such as 'Fodder' and 'Oracle' furnish locality and custom with the tongues and ears of dialect. The 'soft blastings' (ex-plosives, we might say) of the words *Toome, Toome* summon up for the poet 'a hundred centuries'/ /loam, flints, musket-balls,/fragmented ware,/ torcs and fish-bones'. Things are equally interesting above the ground. 'Anahorish' posits a phonological as well as physical topography:

> *Anahorish*, soft gradient
> of consonant, vowel-meadow.

'Gifts of Rain' likens the modulation of the rich vowels in *Moyola* to the Derry river itself. Heaney's use of a slow-moving river to image the Anglo-Irish dialect is endorsed when we read elsewhere that 'for both plosives and fricatives [in Anglo-Irish dialect] affricate consonants with slow separation of the organs of speech, are often heard'.[8] The river in flood threatens livelihoods but it has for the poet female allure as it breathes its mists, like an old chanter, 'through vowels and history'. 'Broagh' is another small hymn to a Londonderry placename which also rehearses in sound the landscape it labels. Rain in the poem ends suddenly

> like that last
> *gh* the strangers found
> difficult to manage.

Strangers are those outside Ireland who have trouble, unlike the Irish (Protestant *and* Catholic), with the guttural spirant.[9] Irish names and pronunciations are survivals, for since Spenser's day the native Irish have had to come to terms with the Anglo-Saxon culture. Heaney is realist enough to know that to talk of the Irish language as a living thing is to take 'the backward look'. The poem of that name images the failure of the Irish language as the staggering flight of the snipe. The snipe's trajectory is simulated in the poem's slender, irregular form, from the bird's startling explosion when flushed through its feinting flight until it disappears into available cover some distance away. The snipe flees 'its nesting ground' as the Irish language and culture fled from their sure origins 'into dialect,/into variants'. The linguist in the 'nature reserves' of controlled field-work who transliterates Irish and English (such as the variant Irish names for the snipe, '*little goat of the air,/of the evening,/ /little goat of the frost*') is re-enacting the actual, unconscious and continuing linguistic process among the people. The snipe drums an elegy for the Irish language and culture as it slipstreams behind the vanished bittern and wild goose.[10] At poem's end, the snipe disappears among 'gleanings and leavings/in the combs/of a fieldworker's archive'.

Heaney's feelings about all this are typically enigmatic. 'Traditions' begins with a flat assertion:

> Our guttural muse
> was bulled long ago
> by the alliterative tradition,
> her uvula grows
>
> vestigial.

For Heaney then the Irish language and culture are, after Joyce, not merely a river but female – vowel-vaginal, we might say, unlike the Anglo-Saxon tradition, which is male, terrestrial, phallic-consonantal. The imputation of rape is reinforced by the suggestion of coercion in the first line of the second part of the poem:

> We are to be proud
> of our Elizabethan English:
> 'varsity', for example,
> is grass-roots stuff with us.

Is the poet resentful? Is he bridling at the pride of Ulster Protestants in the Elizabethan cast of Ulster dialect? Seemingly, and yet feeling in the poem fizzles out. In the third part of the poem Heaney will have no truck with the passion-rousing problem of identity. The 'whingeing' Macmorris in *Henry the Fifth,* identified by Thomas Flanagan (to whom 'Traditions' is dedicated) as the first stage-Irishman,[11] who asks 'What ish my nation?' is answered, 'sensibly', according to Heaney, by Leopold Bloom who said, 'Ireland, I was born in Ireland.' Neither in emotion nor logic are we prepared by the first two premiss-parts of the poem for this flat conclusion. 'Traditions' is a broken-backed syllogism and poem.

Heaney's conceit (landscape = body = sex = language) and the way it sabotages emotion leads him into such difficulties throughout these language-poems. In 'A New Song' the poet meets a girl from Derry-garve, which placename recalls for him the Moyola's 'long swerve . . . And stepping stones like black molars/Sunk in the ford'. At first the girl is merely a 'chance vestal daughter' evoking a 'vanished music' and pouring 'a smooth libation of the past'. This realistic acceptance of irrecoverable history is where 'Traditions' and 'The Backward Look' conclude. 'But now', claims the poet,

> our river tongues must rise
> From licking deep in native haunts
> To flood, with vowelling embrace,
> Demesnes staked out in consonants.

Does 'must' mean 'shall inexorably' or 'ought to'? Is the stanza blue-print or prophecy? Instead of acceptance there is the promise of resurgence, and the military metaphors of the last stanza are ominous:

> And Castledawson we'll enlist
> And Upperlands, each planted bawn –
> Like bleaching-greens resumed by grass –
> A vocable, as rath and bullaun.

This is a difficult stanza to paraphrase, elliptical to the point of being cryptic. It seems to say this: Castledawson, Upperlands and other bawns (or fortifications) established by the seventeenth-century Scots planters will be enlisted in the cause of resurgence. The planted bawns, whose names were originally foreign and 'furled' consonants in the Irish 'language-scape', have been rendered obsolete (like bleaching-greens – used by the planters in their linen trade – resumed by grass), for the planters have in the course of time become Irishmen. The 'furled consonants of the lowlanders' have become merely Irish sounds (vocables) similar to 'rath' and 'bullaun', equally obsolete native Irish objects (rath a fortification, bullaun a ritual basin-stone). For Heaney, obsolescence can be a primal state and, insofar as the obsolete is preserved in custom, speech or bog, can exert an influence on the present. It is this obsolescence-primality-nativeness of the Irish that will resurge.

When we have figured this out, we have yet to decide if Heaney is referring to a linguistic or cultural resurgence (or both) and what form it is to take. Is the poem a veiled reference to the possibility of Protestant and Catholic Ulstermen solving their political problems on the heels of the possibly departing English (whose 'demesnes' are to be flooded)? It is impossible to tell. Unfortunately these resourceful poems are so cerebral that when they fail as arguments (not necessarily by being false but by being unclear), they fail ultimately as poems.

VI

The ambiguity of the language-poems does, however, reflect Heaney's dilemma as a poet, suspended between the English and (Anglo-) Irish traditions and cultures. Correlatives of ambivalence proliferate in his verse: the archetypal sound in his work (and to be savoured in the reading) is the guttural spirant, half-consonant, half-vowel; the archetypal locale is the bog, half-water, half-land; the archetypal animal is the eel, which can fancifully be regarded (in its overland forays) as half-mammal, half-fish.

There is good reason for Heaney to be Janus-faced. He was reared in the countryside of Northern Ireland and was steeped in its lore, yet he served his poetic apprenticeship in a Belfast chapter of the Group, a subsidiary of that most English of holding companies, the Movement. Philip Hobsbaum, unofficial head of the chapter, has since tried to appropriate Heaney's work in the name of an essentially English tradition. In a recent article,[12] Hobsbaum claims the wedding sequence from *Wintering Out* as the best of Heaney so far, and places it firmly within that mainstream of contemporary English verse that he describes elsewhere as relating back to Owen, master of the half-rhyme, and through him back to the Keats of 'The Fall of Hyperion' and back to Shakespeare. Another line through the same tradition could, he says, be traced 'through Redgrove and Hughes through [Edward] Thomas and Rosenberg to the blank verse fictions of the Romantics, Shakespeare and even back to the medieval poets. Either way, it's the central line of English poetry.'[13] I have no quarrel here with Hobsbaum's concept of the English mainstream but rather with the way he seems in his general criticism to permit considerations of membership to this historic club to stifle the individuality and in some cases un-Englishness of contemporary British poets who write, after

all, at least equally in response to their personal and social circumstances as in response to their conceptions of English poetic tradition.
Particularly, one would imagine, an Irish poet. If metre and rhyme
are not our sole considerations – and even indeed if they are – we
need to discuss Heaney against the backgrounds of poetry and life in
Ulster and the rest of Ireland. (And where, incidentally, fits Yeats into
Hobsbaum's scheme?)

Philip Hobsbaum is rightly credited with having single-handedly
galvanized Ulster poetry into its present vibrant state. The province's
cultural debt to him is immense. Yet I wonder if the fact that so many
of Heaney's poems are tight as clenched fists, coiled springs without
emotional release, is not due in large part to the influence of the
Group. It is an influence that has encouraged formal excellence (an
essay could be written on Heaney's rhyme alone), but has had the
side-effect of encouraging Heaney's Irish, perhaps Catholic Irish,
impulse to keep self-revelation and emotional openness for situations
other than poetic; perhaps too it has encouraged Heaney to be the
'big-eyed Narcissus' he repudiated back in 'Personal Helicon', staring
into the recesses of the Irish landscape and past, cleverly rhyming
simply to see himself, 'to set the darkness echoing'. If Heaney becomes
the best Irish poet of his generation, it will be because he has
remained true to as great an Irishness in diction, setting and theme as
he has already achieved, while taking the emotional risks of his great
antecedent Yeats and his contemporary Thomas Kinsella. His sure
sense of miniaturist form, learned from the English poets of the 'fifties
and 'sixties, is a solid foundation from which he needs to launch into
a variety of modes. Time, shall we say, to lay aside the spade and
bring out the heavy machinery. In the meantime, there is little
contemporary poetry that has bettered the quality and fruitfulness of
Heaney's solitary digging; few poets have enlivened their work with
a more remarkable gift for seeing afresh the physical world around us
and beneath us.

[1974]

NOTES

1. The volumes are: *Death of a Naturalist* (1966, 1969), *Door into the Dark* (1969,
   1972) and *Wintering Out* (1972, 1973), all published in London by Faber and
   Faber; the second date is in each case that of the second or reprinted edition I
   have used.

2. Evans, *Irish Folk Ways* (London: Routledge & Kegan Paul 1957), p. 185. As background to 'Bog Oak', cf. Evans's further remark: 'In the past, too, considerable use was made of buried timber dug from bogs, of oak for roofing beams . . . '.

3. Evans, *Irish Heritage* (Dundalk: Dundalgan Press 1942), p. 24.

4. For an account of Irish well-worship, see W.G. Wood-Martin, *Traces of the Elder Faiths of Ireland* (London: Longman's 1902), II, Chapter III; Wood-Martin is invaluable background material for the reader of Heaney, illuminating such elements as the lough legendry in 'A Lough Neagh Sequence' and the mandrake-root in 'A Northern Hoard'. (I have discussed 'A Lough Neagh Sequence' at some length in an article published in *Eire-Ireland* XII, 2 (1977), 138–42 – JWF.)

5. 'The Blinker' appeared in *Fortnight: An Independent Review for Northern Ireland* (July 1972).

6. Evans, *Irish Folk Ways*, pp. 304–5.

7. Benedict Kiely, 'A Raid into Dark Corners: The Poems of Seamus Heaney', *The Hollins Critic* (Virginia), VII (1970), 1–12; the editor's biographical and bibliographical information in this article is unfortunately garbled.

8. G. L. Brook, *English Dialects* (London: André Deutsch 1963), p. 112.

9. Heaney implies that the velar fricative *gh* (pronounced *ch* [x]) was a native Irish rather than English sound that was adopted by the Scots planters, but in fact it was also an English sound that disappeared early in the Modern English period: J. Taniguchi, *Irish English* (Tokyo, n. Eng. d.), p. 240. According to J. Braidwood, the Scots spirant is stronger than the Irish, 'Ulster and Elizabethan English', *Ulster Dialects*, ed. G. B. Adams (Holywood, Co. Down: Ulster Folk Museum 1964), p. 75.

10. The wild goose has not, of course, disappeared from Ireland as has virtually the bittern, but this may be an allusion to the 'wild geese', Irishmen who fled the island from the Elizabethan age onwards and who formed Irish Brigades in continental armies.

11. Thomas Flanagan, *The Irish Novelists 1800–1850* (New York 1959).

12. 'The Present State of British Poetry', *Lines Review* 45 (June 1973).

13. 'The Growth of English Modernism', *Wisconsin Studies in Contemporary Literature* VI (1965), 105.

6

THE POETRY OF PATRICK KAVANAGH

It is little more than ten years since the death of Kavanagh. That his stature is uncertain is not surprising since, as we know, a poet's reputation frequently dips soon after his death. But in Kavanagh's case, circumstantial evidence for a judgment is more than usually inconclusive. A handful of memorable poems are regularly conscripted into English school and college anthologies, but none was drafted for *The Penguin Book of Contemporary Verse* (1950), edited by Kenneth Allott, or *British Poetry Since 1945* (1970), edited by Edward Lucie-Smith. In *The Oxford Book of Twentieth-Century English Verse* (1973) Larkin represents Kavanagh only by the first canto of *The Great Hunger*, but might seem to accord him greater status – the entire work being implied by the part – than those poets whose sole entry is a complete poem. Readers and teachers, if not critics, must, however, have continued to pay him attention since before his death, for his *Collected Poems*, published in 1964, has been in print on both sides of the Atlantic since 1973.[1]

'I have never been much considered by the English critics,' Kavanagh began his 'Author's Note' to the *Collected Poems*, in a tone poised, like so much of his writing, between truculence and self-pity.[2] If not, this was in part because he was a maverick – 'brother to no man' as he claimed with customary bravado in an early poem – apparently working in a siding off the main line of British poetry successively dominated in his lifetime by the Auden group, the New Apocalypse and the Movement, with all of whom he nevertheless had distant relations. Perhaps it was in part because he was Irish and English critics could not appreciate his importance in Ireland. Yet he also seemed eccentric to those readers in Ireland for whom Yeatsian concerns and the proper concerns of an Irish poet were one and the same. What reputation he enjoyed was wrested from Yeats's ghostly eminence. But Irish poets are no longer haunted by this eminence, and this is partly to Kavanagh's credit. Irish poets now under forty who made their own reputations since Kavanagh 'handed in his gun' have, in a recent and gathering revaluation of twentieth-century Irish poetry, championed the Ulster poet as a mentor and at some small expense of his far greater predecessor's reputation. This might not on the face of it prove anything more than that Kavanagh is the most credible stalking-horse of those Irish poets threatened by the achievements of the Irish Literary Revival. Yet because of the unexpectedly rich state of current Irish poetry (Heaney, Mahon and Longley who once made elbow-room for themselves alongside Kinsella and Montague now in their turn must allow Muldoon and Paulin breathing-space), it is crucial evidence in any attempt to make fast the reputation of a puzzling, exasperating and compelling figure.

Slender to the eye and rarely taxing to the mind, Kavanagh's early poems arise like prayers from the fields of his native Monaghan. That he could find 'a star-lovely art/In a dark sod', as he claimed in the first and title poem of his first volume, *Ploughman and Other Poems* (1936), was not unusual if we remember how John Clare and James Stephens – two poets early revered and referred to in his first work (but the latter afterwards and characteristically repudiated) – likewise turned the land into lyricism. It was no transmutation of poverty into poetry, however: the recurring word 'rags', like so much else in the volume, is allegorical rather than descriptive (somewhat in the manner of Frost, whom Kavanagh admired), and the landscape has a Georgian luxuriance instead of the expected Irish scant. Kavanagh often claimed to be poor, but in Dublin, not in Monaghan; and even when referring to his life in the city – or, indeed, to his poetic reputation – Kavanagh, one suspects, may have been 'pleading the poor mouth', an Irish tropism immortally satirized in *An Béal Bocht* (*The Poor Mouth*) by Flann O'Brien. What fibre the best verse in *Ploughman* possesses derives not from rural realism but from an unabashed musical paganism. He addresses the blackbird:

> O pagan poet you
> And I are one
> In this – we lose our god
> At set of sun.

The Irish countryman's adherence to the elder faiths underlies Kavanagh's Catholicism, just as Gaelic lyricism echoes behind the

acquired rural English song. In a later poem, 'Father Mat,' he eloquently remembers

> ancient Ireland sweeping
> In again with all its unbaptized beauty:
> The calm evening,
> The whitethorn blossoms,
> The smell from ditches that were not Christian.

In his autobiography, *The Green Fool* (1938), Kavanagh described
himself as 'a night-coward and full of tremulous faith in uncanny
things'.[3] This might convince us of the sincerity of the poet's
paganism in *Ploughman*, save that Kavanagh later repudiated *The Green
Fool* for its fake Irishness: did that include a fake paganism? In
addition, the autobiography is fictionalized and therefore uncertain
testimony. Either way, the sincerity of *Ploughman* seems, because so
artful, the sincerity of craft rather than of morality, and does not
resolve this issue of which Kavanagh became conscious, as the
opening couplet of a later poem, 'Auditors In', makes plain: 'The
problem that confronts me here/Is to be eloquent yet sincere'. For
there is in *Ploughman* little consistency of belief. A pagan manifesto,
'The Goat of Slieve Donard', rubs shoulders with 'I May Reap', the
piety of which is uncomfortably reminiscent of the letters the poet
was writing at the time to his sister in an English convent, letters
written in a strained and assumed voice.[4] The truth is that Kavanagh
never decisively made the choice he offered himself: '"The domestic
Virgin and Her Child/Or Venus with her ecstasy"' ('Father Mat').
And while it is to be expected that it is the Christian and not pagan
poems in *Ploughman* that suffer from a cloying devotionalism, the one
kind probably meant as much to the poet as the other, since they
achieved equally effective concealments of self. From poem to poem
in the volume, Kavanagh could be as protean as he was to prove from
decade to decade.

This is not to impugn, of course, the lyrical integrity of any single
poem, and though of the thirty-one poems in *Ploughman* I find myself
returning only to about ten of them, three or four of these, including,
naturally, 'Inniskeen Road: July Evening', are among the best poems
Kavanagh ever wrote. Yet even in an otherwise discountable poem,
small shoots of 'greenful loveliness' burst forth, tiny miracles of wings
opening out of clay and startling the poet, one feels, as much as the
reader. The poet never lost this gift, and in odd poems from start to

finish we happen upon metaphors of pure delight that remind us how true a poet was this Monaghan small farmer. From 'Shancoduff':

> My hills hoard the bright shillings of March
> While the sun searches in every pocket.

and from 'Spraying the Potatoes':

> The axle-roll of a rut-locked cart
> Broke the burnt stick of noon in two.

Perhaps the rarity of such lines (and he seems a discoverer of lines more than a fashioner of poems, far less the architect of a canon) ought not to enhance their preciousness (for Kavanagh's Midas touch failed him often), but it does, and the unpredictability of magical lines is part of Kavanagh's gauche charm, his very unevenness conveying the excitement of prospecting, as Seamus Heaney, a Kavanagh admirer, has suggested.[5]

The turning of brass into gold was Kavanagh's enduring theme and pursuit (changing his own shape was perhaps less voluntary), and he expressed it variously: 'the thrill/Of common things raised up to angelhood'; 'To smelt in passion/The commonplaces of life'; 'name for the future/The everydays of nature'. That the poet is a kind of alchemist is an old idea, likewise the notion that in being such the poet is foolishly venturesome; when in his note to his *Collected Poems* he said that 'somehow or other I have a belief in poetry as a mystical thing, and a dangerous thing', he was echoing what Dylan Thomas said in a note to his own *Collected Poems* as well as getting off a wingshot at the Movement. The outcast that Kavanagh claimed in that same note poetry made him is another, equally venerable kind of fool, and the figure that the dabbler in verse cut in Mucker, Co. Monaghan is yet a third:

The people didn't want a poet, but a fool, yes they could be doing with one of these. And as I grew up not exactly 'like another' I was installed the fool . . . At wake, fair, or dance for many years I was the fellow whom the jokers took a hand at when conversational funds fell low. I very nearly began to think myself an authentic fool. I often occupied a position like that of 'The Idiot' in Dostoevsky's novel. I do not blame the people who made me their fool; they wanted a fool and in any case they lost their stakes.

Being made a fool of is good for the soul. It produces a sensitivity of one kind or another; it makes a man into something unusual, a saint or a poet or an imbecile.[6]

Kavanagh's cunning assumption of the role of fool (be it poet-mystic, poet-outcast, poet-clown or even poet-ploughman and poet-cobbler) should not be overlooked. Very often Kavanagh connived at his own folly, calling himself a 'high dunce' in his first volume of verse. His folly in its various guises is bound up, for example, with his celebrated and thought-out distinction between parochialism and provincialism:

Parochialism and provincialism are direct opposites. A provincial is always trying to live by other people's loves, but a parochial is self-sufficient. A great deal of this parochialism with all its intended intensities and courage continued in rural Ireland up till a few years ago and possibly will continue in some form forever.[7]

Parochialism as a self-assured way of life became for the poet a conscious theory of art (the parochial writer 'is never in any doubt about the social and artistic validity of his parish'), with the danger that the theory would appear as obsolete as the way of life. Certainly it is connected in Kavanagh's verse with a certain passivity and inwardness (despite the bluster), a stubborn sedentariness and unadventurousness (despite the claim to dangerous mysticism), a shrinking from life that is like a wilful refusal to mature.

> Out of that childhood country what fools climb
> To fight with tyrants Love and Life and Time?

he asked in 'Peace', neatly returning the name of fool. Moreover, one suspects that Kavanagh secretly might not have been entirely convinced by his own distinction between parochialism and provincialism. It may have been to some extent a rationalization or compensation in the face of the nationalist success of the Revival, and when provincialism shaded into cosmopolitanism (from which he perhaps felt outcast as an ill-educated countryman) as a thing to be detested, he may have been expressing his own provincial mentality that, as he himself said, attacks what it secretly worships. For he may after all have secretly worshipped cosmopolitan reputation such as the chief Revival writers enjoyed.

Yet Kavanagh felt with some justification that to be parochial is to be most truly Irish. In 'Dark Ireland' he asserted:

> We are a dark people,
> Our eyes are ever turned
> Inward.

These lines are echoed in Seamus Heaney's 'Bogland' from *Door into the Dark* (1969): 'Our pioneers keep striking/Inwards and downwards,'[8] by a poet who has proved Kavanagh's distinction a viable one and at base a good one and who has in practice brought it closer to perfection than Kavanagh himself, who spent much more time preaching it. And on the older poet, parochialism conferred a fitful sense of freedom and authority that gave his lines a lyrical spring at once confident and giddy: 'A road, a mile of kingdom, I am king/Of banks and stones and every blooming thing' ('Inniskeen Road: July Evening'), the fool imagining, but with the poet's higher purpose of art, his parish a kingdom. The parish fool can even superstitiously imagine himself immortal, as in 'Innocence': 'I cannot die/Unless I walk outside these whitethorn hedges'. A handful of very good later poems, notably 'Intimate Parnassus', 'Epic', 'Kerr's Ass', 'On Looking into E. V. Rieu's Homer', 'Innocence' and 'On Reading a Book on Common Wild Flowers', are variations on the rich Kavanagh theme of the parish as the world and the poet-clown as king or god, the least truculent and most charming guise of Kavanagh's Messianism.

The poet, then, is not always to be confused with the fool, though I think Kavanagh was sometimes unwillingly made to look foolish. History, for example, made him her butt by having him follow the high accomplishments of Yeats and the Literary Revival. In order to make room for himself, Kavanagh had to misread the Revival writers, for to see Yeats, Synge and O'Casey as other than great writers is surely to misread them. Kavanagh found himself engaged in tactics of reaction, some wise, some perverse, all understandable. Where Yeats magnified Ireland into the world, Kavanagh shrank Ireland into Shancoduff; where Yeats saw in the fate of Ireland universal spirals and gyres, Kavanagh saw 'the habitual, the banal', lowly coltsfoot rather than right rose trees; where Yeats cultivated Lear, Kavanagh cultivated the Fool and took advantage of the Fool's immunity to peck at Yeats's reputation as the Fool taunts his distracted king. Much of this, I believe, was desperate role-playing and wastefully against the grain of Kavanagh's talent and personality, though of course he thought (or affected to think) that tragedy if allowed to ripen ripened into comedy. He found himself, in defiance of his mythopoeic impulses, pursuing the anti-heroic and anti-mythic, for had he emulated the Revival in cherishing heroism and mythology he would have been history's provincial, 'trying to live by other people's loves'. For a while he was pre-empted by the Revival wherever he turned, for example in the west, and so he professed to dislike Sligo and Connemara, wisely in this case shrinking back into and tilling the unsung fields of his unpicturesque native Monaghan. And luckily for him, Dublin was a large enough city with a venerable enough literary tradition to absorb the Irish Literary Revival and still leave room for a strayed reveller like himself.

For walk outside the whitethorn hedges Kavanagh did, moving to Dublin in 1939, three years before the publication of *The Great Hunger*. If in his own accounts of this 'hegira' in *The Green Fool, Tarry Flynn* (1948) and his letters, he appears as a kind of Irish Dick Whittington, he had a more serious precursor in William Carleton (who also had his foolish side), the nineteenth-century Ulster novelist of the peasantry whose work Kavanagh championed against the claims of the Literary Revival (somewhat pointlessly, since the tireless Yeats also championed Carleton). *The Great Hunger*, his longest and rightly famous poem, proved that Kavanagh had Carleton's courage in exposing the dark injustices of the land that bred him. It was too much, though, to expect he could sustain the authority of the simultaneously casual and oracular beginning:

> Clay is the word and clay is the flesh
> Where the potato-gatherers like mechanised scarecrows move
> Along the side-fall of the hill – Maguire and his men.
> If we watch them an hour is there anything we can prove
> Of life as it is broken-backed over the Book
> Of Death? Here crows gabble over worms and frogs
> And the gulls like old newspapers are blown clear of the hedges, luckily.
> Is there some light of imagination in these wet clods?

Little but what the poet can provide. From 'the streets of nineteen forty', Kavanagh recalled in Monaghan no Wordsworthian or Yeatsian landscape, but a place where men suffered not potato famine but sexual famine ensured by the domineering interference of aged parents and sexless priests until at last hunger became listlessness and impotence. The narrative voice is that of an insider who knows the small farmers so intimately that we suspect he is uncomfortably close to being Patrick Maguire 'whose spirit/Is a wet sack flapping about the knees of time'; the tired casualness of the tone, of which Kavanagh was justly proud (playing 'a true note on a dead slack string'), enacts the impotence of which the poem speaks and is its passive lyricism. At the same time, the speaker is an outsider eager to dissociate himself from Maguire ('Watch him, watch him, that man on a hill') with a truculent knowingness – sometimes breaking into jeering song – that holds Maguire at bay like a contagion. This is the poem's satire directed at Maguire who fails to resist his captors. Yet Kavanagh's greatest scorn is reserved for those who victimize Maguire: the speaker is an enlightened insider indignant that the futility of such a life as Maguire's should be permitted; this is the poem's covert didacticism and overt compassion: '*The Great Hunger*', said Kavanagh disapprovingly, 'is concerned with the woes of the poor.' Pity, contempt, anger and self-hatred vie like roles for supremacy:

> the peasant in his little acres is tied
> To a mother's womb by the wind-toughened navel-cord
> Like a goat tethered to the stump of a tree –
> He circles around and around wondering why it should be.
> No crash,
> No drama.
> That was how his life happened.
> No mad hooves galloping in the sky,
> But the weak, washy way of true tragedy –
> A sick horse nosing around the meadow for a clean place to die.

Kavanagh, who repudiated more of his own work than almost any other writer (perhaps out of insecurity hoping to obviate the hostile criticism of others), dismissed *The Great Hunger* for its compassion and didacticism and for its being mere tragedy. The poem is not tragedy except in the market-place sense of involving wastage, for it contains no resistance to circumstance. It is ultimately pathos, and though Yeats would have disapproved ('passive suffering is not a theme for poetry', he commented in *The Oxford Book of Modern Verse* [1936]), the pathos is stiffened into success by the outspokenness of the speaker's social indictment and the theatrical ambivalence of voice that lends the poem a deceiving simplicity. One cannot help seeing, however, in Kavanagh's repudiation a characteristic rejection of 'the Irish thing' for which he developed a nose. In the 'Author's Note' to *Collected Poems* he alleged: 'Had I stuck to the tragic thing in *The Great Hunger* I would have found many powerful friends,' an allusion to those who wished the culturally saleable tragic note of the Revival to be sustained. But I'm not sure Kavanagh's claim is justified, even if *The Great Hunger* were tragedy. *The Great Hunger* denies the view of the Irish countryside taken by many writers of the Revival and which we might call romantic primitivism. Kavanagh believed that the Revival image of the peasant was English and Protestant and imposed

THE POETRY OF PATRICK KAVANAGH

on the Catholic peasantry from without:

My misfortune as a writer was that atrocious formula which was invented by Synge and his followers to produce an Irish literature. The important thing about this idea of literature was how Irish was it. No matter what sort of trash it was, if it had the Irish quality. And that Irish quality simply consisted in giving the English a certain picture of Ireland.

[Synge's] peasants are picturesque conventions; the language he invented for them did a disservice to letters in this country by drawing our attention away from the common speech whose delightfulness comes from its very ordinariness . . . Synge provided Irish Protestants who are worried about being 'Irish' with an artificial country . . . [9]

Though unfair to Synge and undiscriminating when he listed Padraic Colum, Austin Clarke, F.R. Higgins, James Stephens and the Kavanagh of *The Green Fool* as Synge's children, Kavanagh is on target in his remarks about the nationalism and conventionalism of the Revival and about the Irish Protestants. He wouldn't, naturally enough, willingly suspend his disbelief in the Yeatsian myth of the Anglo-Irish aristocracy who with the peasantry and artists composed the fearless symmetry of a desired world. 'I came to a great house on the edge of a park,' he wrote in 'An Insult',

> Thinking on Yeats' dream Great House where all
> Nobility was protected by ritual
> Though all lay drunk on the floor and in the dark
> Tough louts and menial minds in the shrubberies lurk
> And negative eunuchs hate in an outer hall.

It was no class envy. Having already shown his qualified contempt for the Patrick Maguires of Ireland and 'the narrow primitive piety of the small huxter with a large family' that characterized the Irish mind,[10] he described the Dublin artisans as 'the most offensive class of all' ('Living in the Country: I'), thereby making it hard to accept O'Casey's ravaged but poetic Dublin slums.

Throughout his career Kavanagh burned all the bridges to group acceptance he could find, partly in delusion of his own greatness; 'only poetasters form schools' he wrote in 'The Paddiad'. By rounding not only on the Revival view of the peasantry but on the peasantry itself, he put himself in *The Great Hunger* beyond the pale not only of Anglo-Irish cultural nationalism but also of Gaelic-Catholic cultural nationalism. Kavanagh refused a consistent opinion on political issues on which all Irishmen were and are supposed to be clear – republicanism, Free Statism, the IRA, the Catholic Church, partition; rather he preferred to don whatever mask the occasion demanded (usually opposition or evasion), taking the measure of life in Ireland as Maguire takes the measure of heaven, 'angle-wise'. Maguire's life and death are full of twists: his sexual frustration is a 'twisted skein'; perhaps there is divinity in his clayey fate since the 'twisted thread' of his life is nonetheless 'stronger than the wind-swept fleece'; and the poet is determined to

> watch the tragedy to the last curtain,
> Till the last soul passively like a bag of wet clay
> Rolls down the side of the hill, diverted by the angles
> Where the plough missed or a spade stands, straitening the way.

Kavanagh's poetry up to his third volume, *A Soul for Sale* (1947), is veined with the imagery of crookedness. It is the crookedness of slanted Ulster hills on which straight furrows are difficult, but it is also the crookedness of people who have accommodated themselves to this angled landscape, captiously weaving deception, 'The half-talk code of mysteries/And the wink-and-elbow language of delight', into a compensating texture of living. Kavanagh turned such crookedness into art, for in his poetry he felt the need, as Maguire does, to 'cross-plough' difficult ground. Even his lyricism which looks merely casual actually proceeds 'skew-ways' like the mare in 'Art McCooey'. Unpossessed of Yeats's authoritative directness, Kavanagh desired instead, as he explained in 'Bluebells for Love', to look 'sideways at the bluebells in the plantation/And never frighten them with too wild an exclamation'. This strategy works time and again, not merely through theme but also through point of view: what is the answer to the question posed at the close of 'Shancoduff', for example? And also through imagery: Kavanagh was a man who used to notice such things as Yeats simply failed to see – a hare that 'sits looking down a leaf-lapped furrow', 'an old plough upside-down on a weedy ridge', the wet leaves of cocksfoot that polish a farmer's boots. To see such things, the poet had to look down and sideways, which came easy to a man who knew what it was to wrest a livelihood from the soil; perhaps, too, it came easy to a man of the peasantry whose ancestors habitually looked down in a gesture of servility.[11] In any case, Yeats's gaze was clearly directed head-high and above, and his imagery belongs to an imaginary middle distance of private and public symbolism. Crookedness also works formally in Kavanagh's verse: the way, for instance, he uses three-beat lines, with their suggestion of self-mockery and facetiousness, to undercut four-beat and five-beat lines, as in 'Kerr's Ass', in case his lyrical gift should tempt him into looking at the bluebells directly. Or the way Kavanagh achieves precarious verbal balance in 'Inniskeen Road: July Evening' to which Seamus Heaney draws attention with the expertise of a fellow craftsman.[12] Heaney, equally aware of the crookedness of his people ('O land of password, handgrip, wink and nod'),[13] has learned from Kavanagh the value of 'cross-ploughing' and of the angled approach to life's intractabilities (such as the Ulster crisis) that will not be simplified without falsification.

The poems in *A Soul for Sale* proved that *The Great Hunger* had not exorcized the crooked Ulster landscape and, as the poet confesses in 'Temptation in Harvest', that 'clay could still seduce my heart/After five years of pavements raised to art'. Despite the fact that Kavanagh predictably came to reject *A Soul for Sale*, as 'thin romantic stuff not worth a damn',[14] those poems that sing in thraldom to a Monaghan childhood, such as 'Bluebells for Love', 'Temptation in Harvest', 'A Christmas Childhood' and 'Stony Grey Soil', are among the best that Kavanagh wrote, rich in mingled tones of love, regret, despair and adulation:

> O stony grey soil of Monaghan
> The laugh from my love you thieved;
> You took the gay child of my passion
> And gave me your clod-conceived.

The sense of grievance is deep but is given lyrical tongue. There is a struggle throughout Kavanagh's work between caring (and saying so) and not caring (and singing so). 'A true poet is selfish and implacable,' he said, when turning on *The Great Hunger*. 'A poet merely states the position and does not care whether his words change anything or not.' The interest of the Irish police in those parts of the poem that hinted at Maguire's habit of masturbation the poet came to believe justified: 'For a poet in his true detachment is impervious to policemen. There is something wrong with a work of art, some kinetic vulgarity in it when it is visible to policemen' ('Author's Note', *CP*). Clearly the policemen were right in detecting a realistic and anti-'nationalistic' exposé of the peasantry, but the vulgarity was theirs and not the poem's; they could not have understood the poem's angularities of attitude. Besides, the charge of vulgarity is more applicable to Kavanagh's later essays in satire, a mode whose *raison d'être* is visibility.

Kavanagh found Dubliners, especially literary Dubliners, even crookeder than small farmers, and the increasingly combative and litigious side of his personality responded by assuming by turns the roles of helpless poet victimized by philistine officialdom and of Gaelic satirist pouring vitriol on Irish literary provincialism (e.g. 'The Defeated') from that latter-day *cúirt*, the Dublin literary pub. To call his vitriol satire is to flatter it, for it rarely rises above uncooked invective and lampoonery and is an example of a poet caring superficially and in the wrong way. The satire in *Come Dance with Kitty Stobling* (1960) fails because it springs from self-pity rather than social indignation, and I suspect that this prevented it from raising on the faces of its victims the traditional three blisters of reproach.

Whether it ought to have or not, the urge to care less, which he frequently couldn't, produced Kavanagh's truer poetry, though the ever-present danger was that uncaringness would become carelessness. What he came to admire above all was repose, uncaringness poised artfully above the kinetic vulgarity of wanting to change the world, an aesthetic ideal he shared with James Joyce, whom he revered. *The Great Hunger*, he alleged, lacked 'the nobility and repose of poetry'. He remembered his mother, on the contrary, as having been 'full of repose', and in 'Question to Life' instructed himself to 'be reposed and praise, praise praise/The way it happened and the way it is'. The poet's authority, he claimed in 'Intimate Parnassus' – as though recalling the visit of the Irish police, or thinking perhaps of the Russian 'dissident' poet Yevtushenko, whom he disliked and who was then giving readings in the West –

> Is bogus if the sonorous beat is broken
> By disturbances in human hearts – his own
> Is detached, experimental, subject matter
> For ironic analysis, even for pity
> As for some stranger's private problem.

The poet's goal is to be 'Passive, observing with a steady eye'.

Repose of a sort was for Kavanagh hard-won, which suggests that in praising it he wasn't merely re-posing. In the mid-1950s he had an operation for lung cancer and wrote afterwards that when convalescing on the banks of the Grand Canal he lost his Messianic compulsion: 'My purpose in life was to have no purpose' ('Author's Note', *CP*). Subsequent poems like 'Canal Bank Walk', 'Lines Written On a Seat On the Grand Canal' and 'The Hospital', all sonnets from

Come Dance with Kitty Stobling, are lyrically poignant yet with the muffled irony (oddly Movementish) repose makes possible ('A year ago I fell in love with the functional ward/Of a chest hospital'). Fear of impotence and failure of will, which I believe haunted Kavanagh for most of his life, are in these sonnets turned to artistic account; necessity is triumphantly turned into the virtue of fine poetry. To hear the radio recording of Kavanagh reading 'Lines Written On a Seat On the Grand Canal' is a moving experience; his voice seems to come from a long distance away (farther even than Athy and other far-flung towns), the poet, unmasked by illness and the effect of years' drinking, uncaring at last. Yet in 'The Hospital', Kavanagh in one inspired phrase described as the poet's purpose what he had in fact been attempting all along in his best poems – snatching out of time 'the passionate transitory'. It is a phrase bold enough to accommodate Kavanagh's own contradictions and perversities.

During the Movement, Kavanagh's poetry seemed as aberrant as that of George Barker and Dylan Thomas (eccentricity assumed to be a fault!), but this is no longer the case. Kavanagh's impatience in 'To Hell With Commonsense' with 'secular/Wisdom plodded together/By concerned fools' anticipated A. Alvarez's strictures on Movement poetry in the preface to his 1962 anthology, *The New Poetry*. In Ireland, Kavanagh's poetry and poetic are now being seen as of especial importance. Kavanagh's was the dissenting voice of Catholic countrymen raised, like the dissenting voice of the Catholic middle class (heard in James Joyce), against the Literary Revival. Now too we hear in Kavanagh the corrosive voice of an Ulster ignored in the Revival's Dublin orientation. His reaction against the myths of the Revival has become the more reasoned reappraisal by poet-critics like Seamus Deane and Seamus Heaney, who also happen to be Catholics from Ulster.[15] In practice, Kavanagh's use of rural colloquialisms and his implied notion of a regional word-hoard bound up with manual work on the land have been extended by Heaney, whose previously unsung Broagh, Anahorish and Derrygarve lie north-west of Kavanagh's previously unsung Mullahinsha, Drummeril and Black Shanco. His parochial image in 'Kerr's Ass' of 'the God of imagination waking/In a Mucker fog' and his self-reminder, when he fears provincialism, that Homer made the *Iliad* from such local rows as Kavanagh records in 'Epic' –

who owned
That half a rood of rock, a no-man's land
Surrounded by our pitchfork-armed claims.

– appeal greatly to younger Irish poets. Heaney's title 'Personal Helicon', for instance, echoes Kavanagh's 'Intimate Parnassus'. To open 'The Ministry of Fear', dedicated to Seamus Deane and published in *North*, Heaney cites the first lines of 'Epic': 'Well, as Kavanagh said, we have lived/In important places.' Both poems have an ironic sense of the remote Ulster parish as actually *un*important. In Kavanagh the irony is unintended and renders the parochial claim slightly brittle. In Heaney, however, the irony is superficial, beginning with the jaunty citation that seems (but only seems) to scoff at Kavanagh. But underneath, Heaney is thoroughly convinced that where he grew up *was* important: the way Kavanagh's 'I' becomes 'we' signals the conviction. What makes where he grew up important is the present violence in Ulster which he now sees was latent in the 'forties and 'fifties ('all around us, though/We hadn't named it, the ministry of fear').[16] Kavanagh's conferral of importance on his native parish is also retrospective, but in his case the scuffles of the parish are *contrasted* with another, larger scuffle, 'the Munich bother'. Heaney's conviction, then, stems in part from what Kavanagh forswore: world attention; for Heaney's North is important these days without the poetry. But Kavanagh himself would have found it difficult not to confront – as Heaney confronts in Part II of *North* – the moral dilemmas of Ulster life, beyond the parochialism, had the Ulster of his time suffered the ravages of today, even if he could have resisted exploring the mythic parallels and historic origins that attract Heaney. In any case, Kavanagh's parochialism has no doubt contributed as much as the Ulster crisis to Heaney's confident belief in the social and artistic validity of his parish. *Death of a Naturalist*, published before the present Troubles began, is proof of this.

There is, nevertheless, a good deal to John Montague's celebrated remark that Kavanagh liberated Montague's generation, but into ignorance. Certainly Kavanagh was vulgarly disrespectful towards greater artists; in a 1963 radio discussion, Yeats is pronounced 'all right', Synge a phoney and O'Casey 'overrated'. Certainly a sense of history is conspicuously absent from Kavanagh's poetry, something that would have enriched *The Great Hunger* as it enriched Montague's more ambitious long poem of the rural Catholic Irishry, *The Rough*

Field (1972), though Montague has generously called Kavanagh's one of the four best long Irish poems since the eighteenth century. And certainly Kavanagh was foolhardy in ignoring a Gaelic heritage that belonged more rightfully to him than to Yeats, who inherited only his own fanciful version of that heritage. Devoid of history and cultural mythology, Kavanagh's parish (the lean parish of his art, to adapt Montague) could not provide him with sufficient fodder and we often have to settle in his poetry for mere gestures towards universality, repetitive discussions of possible topics, endless warming-up with very little energy left for the competitive leap. It got worse towards the end, as 'the wish without will' caused him to flail around for subjects and to confess sadly in the last poem in the *Collected Poems*:

> I am here all morning with the familiar
> Blank page in front of me, I have perused
> An American anthology for stimulation . . .
> But I have no message and the sins
> Of no red idea can make me pregnant.

But in earlier years, when the leap was made, it was done so with an illusion of effortlessness, as though he were some country champion who had never heard of training, with a lightness that the heavy responsibility of an historical awareness might indeed have prevented.

It is hard not to see Kavanagh as a somewhat comic scapegoat, bearing in his figure that vulgarity, ignorance, sense of inferiority, disrespectfulness and country cuteness that had to be purged before the culturally dispossessed Catholic rural writer could come into his own. This was Kavanagh's liberating legacy to the generation of Heaney and Deane. Kavanagh was conscious of his role of scapegoat, of 'the undone/God-gifted man', as he described himself in 'Love in a Meadow', but not of its poetic implications. A stable identity and consistent voice, lyrically expressed, might seem to have been Kavanagh's supreme and tragically wasteful sacrifice, yet it ironically enabled him to become a pivotal figure in twentieth-century Irish poetry, as significant for his influence as for the score of lovely and entangled lyrics and *The Great Hunger* that were his more immediate achievement. But perhaps Kavanagh should have been even more faithful than he was to his thwarted dramatic and mythopoeic drives, thwarted because he believed himself at bottom a lyricist. The impulse was there. Critics such as Warner and Deane who see Kavanagh as always himself, 'a bare-faced poet' who has 'no masks', would do

better to see him as never himself. For which is the truest poetry –
the allegorical filigree, the lyrical remembrance, the social indictment, the scathing doggerel, the alleged repose? Kavanagh knew
himself cannily, but the self he knew was always his previous role into
which he believed himself seduced, and never the current role from
the point of view of which the previous role was repudiated. It is
fitting that in one of his finest poems, the sonnet 'Come Dance with
Kitty Stobling', he should recall a previous self as a circus performer,
plying his art loftily above the clod-conceived:

> Once upon a time
> I had a myth that was a lie but it served:
> Trees walking across the crests of hills and my rhyme
> Cavorting on mile-high stilts and the unnerved
> Crowds looking up with terror in their rational faces.

and characteristic that he should qualify, in a last, dramatically
hedging word, repossession of the inspiration that led him aloft:

> I had a very pleasant journey, thank you sincerely
> For giving me my madness back, or nearly.

[1979]

NOTES

1. *Collected Poems* (New York: Norton 1973). All quotations from Kavanagh's
   poetry are from this edition.
2. Ironically, an English critic began around the same time a study of Kavanagh's
   work, only to incur the poet's displeasure. *Clay is the Word* (Dublin: Dolmen
   Press 1973) by Alan Warner is a useful book that lacks, perhaps understandably,
   enthusiasm. Another short and useful study, Darcy O'Brien's *Patrick Kavanagh*
   (Lewisburg: Bucknell UP 1975), appears in Bucknell's Irish Writers Series.
3. *The Green Fool* (London: Martin Brian & O'Keeffe 1971).
4. *Lapped Furrows: Correspondence 1933–1967 between Patrick and Peter Kavanagh*
   (New York: Peter Kavanagh 1969).
5. 'The Poetry of Patrick Kavanagh: From Monaghan to the Grand Canal' in *Two
   Decades of Irish Writing*, ed. Douglas Dunn (Cheadle: Carcanet Press 1975).
6. *The Green Fool*, p. 11.
7. *November Haggard, Uncollected Prose and Verse of Patrick Kavanagh* (New York:
   Peter Kavanagh 1971), p. 69. For an extended discussion of Kavanagh and
   provincialism, see Michael Allen's contribution to Douglas Dunn's symposium.
8. (London), pp. 55–6.
9. These two paragraphs, respectively from a note supplied to the *Poetry Book
   Society Bulletin* in June 1960 and *Kavanagh's Weekly*, no. 9, are quoted by Warner
   on pp. 28 and 81.

10. *Lapped Furrows*, p. 58.
11. 'Down-looking', incidentally, is an Ulster description of someone whose gesture of servility, now that there is no social need for the gesture, must be crookedness, or perversity, in disguise.
12. In Dunn, pp. 106–7.
13. 'Whatever You Say, Say Nothing', *North* (London: Faber 1975), p. 59.
14. *Lapped Furrows*, p. 197.
15. See, for example, 'The Literary Myths of the Revival: A Case for Their Abandonment' by Seamus Deane, in *Myth and Reality in Irish Literature*, ed. Joseph Ronsley (Waterloo, Ontario: Wilfrid Laurier UP 1977).
16. *North*, p. 65.

7

'THE DISSIDENCE OF DISSENT': JOHN HEWITT AND W.R. RODGERS

Although he was interested in poetry during his student years at Queen's University and Presbyterian College, W.R. Rodgers did not write his first poem until the age of twenty-eight. A mere four years later, in 1941, his first volume was published to acclaim, to be followed after eleven years by his second and last. Since it appears that he wrote but a handful of poems between 1952 and his death at sixty in 1969, Rodgers's sustained verse-writing occupied only fifteen years, his poetic maturity something less than that brief span. Yet it was enough time for Rodgers to attract a significant British and American following. 'Everyone should read him', Stephen Spender wrote, 'because he is a poetic phenomenon.'[1] In the 1940s and 1950s Rodgers worked in the heady atmosphere of the BBC in London and was friend to MacNeice and also to Dylan Thomas, whose poetry Rodgers's occasionally resembles. But Rodgers has suffered a decline in reputation almost as steep as his rise to prominence, and, sadly, probably no one protested against his omission from *The Oxford Book of Twentieth-Century English Verse* (1973), edited by Philip Larkin.[2]

In sharp contrast has been the career of John Hewitt. Born in 1907, two years before Rodgers, Hewitt's latest volume of verse appeared in 1983. Since he reached back as early as 1932 for his *Collected Poems* (1968), Hewitt's poetic career has been better than a half-century long. There has been a slow but steady incline in reputation, and if he was denied representation in the mid-century collections that sported Rodgers,[3] he was rewarded with an entry in Larkin's Oxford anthology. In the wake of his recently bestowed honorary doctorates and Freedom of Belfast, Hewitt could if he chose recall with personal satisfaction what he once remarked (perhaps with mild rebuke for his own times) of nineteenth-century Ulster: 'in the earlier years of the last century the poet had some claim to prestige and status in his community'.[4]

More substantial differences between Rodgers and Hewitt will occupy me in this essay, but it will be worthwhile registering them only if we first note the resemblances. The two poets were almost exact contemporaries, a convenient fact if we wish to contrast them without confusing the chalk and cheese of different historical periods. They were both Ulster-born, and born Protestants, descendants of planters from Scotland and England. The Protestantism of the Irish writer, we tend to assume, is a nominal, at most an anomalous affair. After all, for anyone from Ulster of dissenter stock, as both Hewitt and Rodgers are, to *be* a writer, he must deny or ignore the religion he grew up with. The father of this assumption was Matthew Arnold, for whom dissent and genuine culture were mutually contradictory.[5] Donald Davie has admitted the justification of Arnold's strictures on nonconformism *for Arnold's own day*, while convincingly showing that the history of dissent has not at all been, nor need it be, a chapter in the history of philistinism.[6] And perhaps even Davie's cultural defence of dissent, revealing as it is of Davie the poet and critic as well as of Davie the English Baptist (a point I will return to), is too limited.

We tend to assume, too, that whereas the Catholic Irish writer weathers an artistically fruitful crisis of faith before apostasy, his Protestant counterpart simply walks away from his religion and finds other matters of literary concern. Yet even without a crisis of faith – and Rodgers, who left the Presbyterian ministry to become a professional writer, must have had a profound one – no one completely escapes a religious upbringing, especially an Ulster nonconformist rearing. Perhaps the poetry of Hewitt (the lapsed Methodist) and of Rodgers (the lapsed Presbyterian) bears Arnold out *too* apparently, for if we look closely, we find the poetry demonstrates that nonconformism, even when disavowed or ignored as a religion, can be a powerfully cultural, even aesthetic, and therefore pervasive affair that has its roots in the doctrines ignored or disavowed. Even in reaction, or especially in reaction perhaps, strong sectarian traces, hampering as well as beneficial, stylistic as well as thematic, remain in the verse of Hewitt and Rodgers. These help to define the verse in each case, and to explain the differences as well as the resemblances between the two poets. It is not just that Protestantism in Ulster is bound up with politics and culture, but that a religious upbringing establishes habits of mind which clothe the secular and, openly or secretively, the creative life.

It is against this rudimentary similarity between the poetry of Hewitt and the poetry of Rodgers that I want to set down the real differences, which are the more instructive because each poet to my mind represents, in the refracted ways of literature, one of two traditions of Ulster nonconformist experience. Joined at the loom, each tradition is a braiding of identities and attitudes we normally consider apart but which I would like to consider together in the discussion that follows.

I

John Hewitt has always been acutely aware of his planter heritage. Under shelter of talking about the Roman colonization of Britain, he speculates in 'The Colony' on the development and effects of the Ulster Plantation, writing from the point of view of a colonizer who stayed. Although at moments in the poem Hewitt satirizes the planter attitude towards the natives, because he is the descended equivalent of his Roman, however enlightened both might be, the satire is on a nervous rein. Hewitt's Roman is Ulster's Protestant – arrogant, patronizing and fearful; he finds the Catholic Irish in need of redemption, yet is perversely sure that he too is Irish: 'for we have rights drawn from the soil and sky'. The insistent last lines of 'The Colony' perfectly capture the planter's brittle certainty with its soft centre of despair:

> we would be strangers in the Capitol;
> this is our country also, no-where else;
> and we shall not be outcast on the world.[7]

The brittleness and despair originate in the recurring, often violent reminders of incomplete plantation. 'The Colony' was written in 1950; in 1971 the renewal of sectarian hostilities spurred Hewitt to write 'The Roman Fort' (collected in *Out of My Time*) in which he likens Ulster to a Roman colony beleaguered by 'stubborn barbarians', a phrase as brittle in its irony as loyalist response to this fresh threat to their dominance. It all adds up to a kind of 'non-conformist conscience' on Hewitt's part about the possible wrongs committed by those who carved modern Ulster out of Ireland, and to a puritan belief that warfare is wicked and distasteful but sometimes unavoidable. The conscience is acute enough for him to have suspected his own motives for fraternizing with native Irish culture. He has written:

> Maybe, at some dark level, grown aware
> of our old load of guilt, I shrink afraid,
> and seek the false truce of a renegade.[8]

Like his Roman, then, Hewitt is conscious of having an alien heritage in his own country, and is yet determined to have it recognized that it *is* his own country. The strain and confusion in this are evident. On the one hand, birth, residence and buried ancestors in Ulster define nativeness for Hewitt as surely as racial descent. He admits in 'Conacre', though, that country and nation are not synonymous, that his nativeness is incomplete: 'This is my home and country. Later on/perhaps I'll find this nation is my own.'[9] For that to happen, the power of the Roman Catholic Church would have to be curtailed. He admits in 'The Glens' that (as a nonconformist, it is implied) he finds repugnant the authoritarianism and spectacle of the native creed:

> Not these my people, of a vainer faith
> and a more violent lineage . . .
> I fear their creed as we have always feared
> the lifted hand between the mind and truth.

On the other hand, Hewitt seems to sense that birth and residence are *not* sufficient and, unable to fall back on race or religion, turns to landscape (as J.C. Beckett and Seamus Heaney were to do long after him) in order to join native and settler (see 'The Frontier'). Yet the 'sectarian landscape' remains and is a prominent feature of Hewitt's world. His poetic locales look largely Protestant – the fertile parts of the Antrim glens and the fertile corridor of the Lagan valley – but provide opportunities for the planter poet to ascend into the older native culture. Only there, as his Roman reminds us,

> among the hills with hare and kestrel,
> will you observe what once this land was like
> before we made it fat for human use . . .

And it is there that resides the dark permanence of ancient forms (to borrow from John Montague) that constitute true Irishness, and that can only be perceived (in Montague as well as in Hewitt) by the pagan, not Christian, faithful; these forms pre-date Catholicism and are therefore accessible in theory to Protestants. But although he claims in 'May Altar', from *The Day of the Corncrake*, that his heart 'hankers for the pagan thorn', Hewitt is rather self-consciously the pagan (requiring as he does to reverse his ancestral puritanism), and brings to the Irish countryside something of a folklorist's attitude, recording rural customs when they strike his urban eye as different. Such an attitude is at work in 'The Swathe Uncut', a fine, much-anthologized poem that expresses the depths and limits of Hewitt's paganism and therefore of his sense of his Irishness. The folk custom recorded in this poem is the mower's leaving uncut a last angular swathe of grain. Into this swathe the frightened hare retreats, 'crouched back, the last at bay'. The belief behind the custom is that the corn-spirit resides in the last swathe and must be killed and her husk scattered to ensure fertility the following year. In his last ringing stanza Hewitt assigns the uncut swathe a national symbolism:

> So I have figured in my crazy wit
> is this flat island sundered to the west
> the last swathe left uncut, the blessed wheat
> wherein still free the gentle creatures go
> instinctively erratic, rash or slow,
> unregimented, never yet possessed.

The west of Ireland, it seems, rather than Ireland as a whole (though there is an ambiguity), is the last swathe, an uncultivated refuge for the free and fugitive. Yet Hewitt's is Montague's rough field only in its desirable aspects; 'The Swathe Uncut' is Scots-Irish pastoral, cele-brating what is ideally unharvested and unkempt. One cannot imagine Hewitt inhabiting the rough field as one can imagine Montague, for Montague's field is rough with native grievance and the shards of Gaelic culture with which Hewitt never grew up. Hewitt's rough field is situated at the back-end of the field and the island, with psychic acreage of planted soil between himself and the uncut swathe. It is a legitimate part of his patrimony, but only in the guise of a mystery his folkloristic empathy can never quite penetrate. For this poet whose trust is in empiricism ('Press on the thought till every word is proved/by evidence of sense')[10] what he takes to be essential Irishness has been roped off and made out of bounds.

But it is precisely *because* his Irishness is problematical that Hewitt's worrying of the matter for decades has enabled him to forge the conscience of the Scots-Irish in Ireland, and this may be his chief significance.

Hewitt has told us that the ceremonial cutting of the last standing sheaf of grain is frequently celebrated in the nineteenth-century country verse of Antrim and Down.[11] The rural bards were poets strongly attached to their locality and in this Hewitt is their descendant. They were journeymen or craftsmen, and thought of their verse too as a species of craft or work. Hewitt has likened his own verse to carpentry:

> I wrought
> along the grain as with a steady tool,
> its clean edge tempered and allowed to cool;
> no surface scored by any wristy trick,
> I have, obedient to my sober thought,
> disdained the riper curves of rhetoric.

The poem in which these lines occur, 'Ars Poetica', could as easily be entitled, as he entitled a poem from the same volume (*The Rain Dance*), 'The Poet's Trade'.

Many of the rural Ulster bards were, in fact, weavers, and not only did they weave livelihood, verse and locality together, but the community of which they wrote Hewitt compares to fabric: 'It would seem that it is no threadbare metaphor to talk of the warp and weft of that closely wrought society. But, with the years, the fabric disintegrated.'[12] Weaving may be the central metaphor of Hewitt's entire endeavour as a man and a poet; he has tried to 'weave' his poetry and to interlace the parts of his life out of which the poetry comes. He has also tried to knit together (in the end unsuccessfully, alas) the rebellious fabric of Ulster society; when in 1974 he defined his famous hierarchy of identities, he was engaging in a bit of weaving too fine perhaps for the wear and tear of life in Northern Ireland.[13]

Hewitt's admired 'rhyming weavers' were of Scots descent and frequently democratic, displaying what E.P. Thompson has noted in their English counterparts, 'a deep social egalitarianism'.[14] They were also of dissenter stock and tended to be, in Hewitt's reading, independent men, like the country joiner Hewitt in 'Ars Poetica' takes as his model, a man who is dependable, circumspect, and 'no man's pensioner', a man exhibiting the archetypal qualities of the nonconformist.[15]

The rhyming weavers Hewitt dubs 'Vernacular' poets, because they were lowly born and wrote in Scots or Ulster-Scots dialect and often in Scots versification. (Hewitt himself has been Vernacular in spirit, even though he uses dialect words sparingly.) He distinguishes them from the 'Colonial' and 'Provincial' poets of Ulster who wrote in standard poetic English. Among these poets are those who, beginning with Samuel Thomson in 'Lyle-Hill' (1799), worked in the topographical tradition that had its heyday in England in the eighteenth century. Part-Provincial, part-Colonial, Hewitt in many respects is heir to the topographical poets, and elsewhere I make the claim more fully.[16] The genre is neoclassical and Hewitt is at home with it. The genre is also, in its taxonomic and generic perspectives, scientific; despite his alleged freedom from science (his escape from vaccination as a child he takes as symbolic), Hewitt is comfortable with the genre's rationalism. Like topographical poetry, his own verse is ameliorist and basically conservative, in style and attitude. What he claims as his radicalism strikes me as a venerable and gracious democracy of spirit, at best a radicalism stiffened by tradition and nostalgia into conservatism. He names as custodians of his tradition Keir Hardie, Jim Larkin, Karl Marx, 'John Ball, the Diggers, the Levellers, the Chartists, Paine, Cobbett, Morris',[17] but of this vigorous (and predominantly English) company Hewitt is a mild and mannerly member, at least if we take his verse as an exclusive source of evidence. His 'thirties socialism (the Labour Party and Left Book Club) rings truer since it is ratified outside the verse in activities on behalf of social justice.[18] But beneath the nonconformist independence, conscientious vigilance and egalitarianism, one senses – though this need not be an ideological contradiction – a Protestant belief in reason and steady progress.

The Augustan cultivation of Hewitt's poetry has its analogue in the planted landscape of Protestant Ulster. The Augustanism of his verse also accords with Hewitt's methodical and emotionally subdued personality. He admits in 'Clogh-Oir: September 1971' to seldom naming the stirrings of love and in 'On the Canal' (from the same volume, *Out of My Time*) claims he is 'equipped/for report, comment, comparison'. It is personality as well as philosophy that underwrites his moderation in face of extremes – terrain (dull planter prosperity, broken native hills), emotion (anger, passion), and politics (Ulster loyalism, Irish nationalism). The moderation and the flirtation with extremity are more telling than we might think. Hewitt is the townsman drawn to a countryside that remains, I imagine, uncongenial, and the planter drawn to a native culture that is at root equally uncongenial. He is the craftsman who believes himself a Romantic, a democrat who believes himself a radical, a rationalist who believes himself anti-scientific, a traditionalist who believes himself a maverick. There is some harmless self-delusion here, but even were there not, the profile is still of a nonconformist of vintage stripe. It is true that he is a lapsed Methodist, but for someone who believes himself an infidel (of which he takes his escape from christening as symbolic evidence), he demonstrates a great many nonconformist traits. And if it is true that he sees himself as a solitary (the last poem in *Kites in Spring* is entitled 'I Lie Alone'), this paradoxically confirms his identity, since as early as 'Once Alien Here' (1942) he referred to the 'stubborn wisdom individual' of the dissenters who planted Ulster.

To the puritan traits I have already mentioned, we may add a congenital tidiness, a desire for 'redding up' we find not only in his title *Loose Ends* but also in that rehearsal of endings, including funeral orations, he owns up to in a poem he titles, oddly, 'The Romantic':

> since I am for completeness,
> never having learned to live at ease
> with incompleteness.[19]

He refers in 'Sonnets for Roberta', from *The Rain Dance*, to 'the sober fabric of my life', and from the son of a lifelong, unswearing abstainer we can take this literally. Regularity, tidiness, sobriety: the list of puritan virtues lengthens to include frugality, industriousness, humility (even self-criticism), integrity and honesty. Personality and philosophy lie behind Hewitt's aesthetic, which it would hardly be going too far to describe as Calvinist, displaying as it does simplicity, sobriety and measure, 'the qualities that Calvinist aesthetics', as Davie tells us, 'demand of the art-object'.[20] Davie goes on – and we can bear in mind Hewitt's Augustanism – 'just as there is a necessary and compelling and often noted connection between Methodistical evangelicalism and Romanticism, so between Calvinism and "classicism" there is a connection no less binding'.[21] Although he was brought up a Methodist (but in a congregation impervious to the eloquent importunities of hellfire preachers, as the sonnet 'Evangelist' from *Kites in Spring* tells us), Hewitt seems more in tune with pre-Wesleyan Old Dissent. Indeed, he has expressly rejected Wesley, and if he has also expressly rejected Calvin, it is in favour of the Quaker George Fox (and, more oddly, Blake).[22]

There is little that is Blakean about Hewitt's style; indeed, his verse employs 'the art of sinking', a phrase Davie borrows from Pope to describe and commend the way Isaac Watts deliberately pitched his 'composures' (a telling pun if we apply it to Hewitt's poems) above flatness and below boldness to reach an entire congregation. It is an ethical as well as aesthetic pitch, retrieving modesty and moderation from the circumspect contemplation of sensuousness and licence. Even if the old man who in 'Frost', an early poem, prefers winter to summer (because 'a tree is truer for its being bare') is not quite the man Hewitt has become, we know that he will have no truck with obscurity or sleight-of-hand: 'Give me instead', he says in 'On Reading Wallace Stevens' *Collected Poems*', from *The Rain Dance*,

> the crisp, neat-witted fellows,
> sharp and laconic, making one word do,
> the clipped couplet, the pointing syllables,
> the clean-beaked sentence, the exact look.

If this poetic ideal has always been Hewitt's, it most assuredly was never W.R. Rodgers's.

III

In 'Ars Poetica', Hewitt compares 'the thresh and welter' of his words to 'spring's gale of singing birds', but the description and the comparison evoke far better the verse of W.R. Rodgers. *Awake! and Other Poems*, his first volume, appeared to enthusiastic acclaim from those who responded to the spendthrift use of language that is the arresting quality of his poetry.

> Always the arriving winds of words
> Pour like Atlantic gales over these ears,

begins the second poem in the collection.[23] This new poet believed that for the poet words lead to ideas (whereas for the prose writer the process was reversed), a belief he later ascribed to Yeats, whose early line 'Words alone are certain good' might be the motto of Rodgers's entire output. 'I write for my own kind,' said Hewitt, 'I do not pitch my voice/that every phrase be heard/by those who have no choice.'[24] Not so Rodgers. 'I feel strongly that poetry should be read aloud,' he said. 'So often nowadays words are treated like children that should be seen and not heard. But I think poetry should be heard. As Yeats once said to a friend, he said, "If you are writing poetry, write it as if you're shouting to a man on the other side of the street and he has to hear you.""[25]

If Hewitt occasionally resembles a patriarch, there is something in Rodgers of the prodigal son. Hewitt captures this quality of Rodgers in his fine memorial sonnet (in *Out of My Time*) where, taking his cue from Rodgers's own poem 'Beagles', he also sees his friend as the hare hunted down after years of eloquent flight.[26] Rodgers, we might say, embodies the corn spirit of the rough field, wild, instinctive, unpredictable, unappropriable, finally exotic – and, if we connect the memorial sonnet back to 'The Swathe Uncut', Celtic. The author of *Awake! and Other Poems* was not backward in making a similar claim himself, and in one of his best-loved poems, 'Ireland', he identifies himself and his poetry with his country more brashly than Hewitt has ever done:

> O these lakes and all gills that live in them,
> These acres and all legs that walk on them,
> These tall winds and all wings that cling to them,
> Are part and parcel of me, bit and bundle,
> Thumb and thimble.

Rodgers was a blithe spirit in claiming without reservation his Irishness and it is in sober contrast that we read Hewitt's careful exploration of his cultural traditions, his self-questioning and the slow march of doubts; it is a contrast between Rodgers's cavalier assurance and Hewitt's roundhead conscience.

The poems in *Awake! and Other Poems* are self-consciously Irish in spirit and technique. 'The faculty of standing words or ideas on their heads – by means of pun, epigram, bull, or what-have-you – is', he later claimed, 'a singularly Irish one . . . To the English ear, which likes understatement, it is all rather excessive and therefore not quite in good taste. But to the Irish mind which likes gesture, bravado, gallivanting, and rhetoric, it is an acceptable tradition.'[27] (It was indeed lapses in taste for which the English poet Stephen Spender took Rodgers to task, and rightly, amid his general praise.) To say that Rodgers is 'Irish' or 'Celtic' where Hewitt is 'English' may be to say, however, that he is Romantic, where Hewitt is Augustan or neoclassical.[28] Linguistic verve and dash, for example (a verbal play in contrast to Hewitt's workmanship), Rodgers shares with his contemporaries George Barker and Dylan Thomas, and this suggests that these qualities are not 'singularly Irish'.[29] Moreover, Rodgers is a 'thirties Romantic with the apocalyptic vision of some of his contemporaries. More specifically, the poems in *Awake! and Other Poems* register a response to the opening salvoes of World War II (the volume's American title in 1942 was *Awake! and Other Wartime Poems*), which from Loughgall, Co. Armagh, where Rodgers was Presbyterian minister from 1935 to 1946, could almost sound inviting. Many of the pieces are explicitly war poems, written by a noncombatant innocent of bloodshed, whose knowledge is filtered through newspapers and newsreels. The war is an unavoidable, if distant, fact that can spoil an otherwise ebullient day ('Stormy Day'), but, as 'Escape' suggests, 'You will be more free/At the thoughtless centre of slaughter than you would be/Standing chained to the telephone-end while the world cracks.' It can also attract the poet who feels isolated in a rural pocket of existence and dreams of the 'calamitous terminus' he flirts with in the opening poem of the collection.

The title poem of Rodgers's first volume begins with a highly emotional appeal to the wind of apocalypse to destroy a wretched world, leaving man 'like Noah afloat in his ark/On a single sea, looking for landmark'. According to the poet, however, no lenient God will spare man when Doomsday occurs, for man has hastened its advent by ensuring that the world moves . . .

> not with meant and maintained pace
> Toward some hill-horizon or held mood,
> But in great jags and jerks, probed and prodded
> From point to point of anger, exploded
> By each new and opposed touch.

We will have to save ourselves from the inevitable holocaust, and those who do so will be those who awake before it is too late and stand calmly to windward in the shelter of their foresight.

This is heady millenarian stuff, and it repeats itself in Rodgers's poetry; behind it one senses the pressures not only of World War II and 'forties neo-Romanticism but also of the Protestant evangelical tradition. As a strain of that tradition, millenarianism has typically looked for 'sudden divine intervention to destroy the existing order' and as a corollary desired radical and instantaneous social change to ensure the survival of the worthy.[30] It is a venerable strain 'stretching back', in the words of J.F.C. Harrison, 'to the sectaries of the seventeenth century, and embodying (via popular mystics, antinomians, prophets and prophetesses) an alternative to the dominant rational assumptions and teachings of the Enlightenment'.[31] It has had a poetic dimension, which Blake exhibits in his prophetic verse. There is something of the prophet in Rodgers, though his effusiveness shows a millenarian abandonment, even desperation, without the underlying discipline of a Blakean symbolic system.

There is, perhaps, some irony in the fact that Rodgers the Presbyterian minister displays some of the features of that enthusiasm we associate with Wesleyan Methodism and splinter or independent millenarian sects, while Hewitt, Methodist-born, appears more Calvinistic and representative of Old Dissent. Nevertheless, the millenarian features are there in Rodgers: a view of history not as continuity but as a series of ruptures: the prophecies and revelations; the inclination to catastrophes, but also to redemptions and resurrections; the partiality to myths and dreams. The spirit of God that inspires millenarian prophets (and presumably inspired the young Rodgers contemplating orders) is, as it were, replaced in Rodgers's verse by the muse, and while it confers freedom from constraint it can also warm an 'overweening brain', that Locke said caused enthusiasm.[32] After he resigned his ministry in 1946, breaking not only with the Church and with Loughgall and with Ireland, but also with his wife, Rodgers lived a semi-bohemian life in London, a life dedicated to writing, as a metropolitan literary figure to Hewitt's local bard. The poetry continued as exuberantly as ever, and one might trace in it (as in the life) an antinomianism in which poetic grace takes the place of Christian grace, and in which a vague pantheism fuels the exuberance.

IV

The apocalyptic voice in *Awake! and Other Poems* assumes various tones – rebuking, admonitory, euphoric, evangelical. The sense of an ending seems an attempt on Rodgers's part to resolve the growing oppositions in his life. The resolution is in many poems premature and shows little of Hewitt's efforts to hammer out a unity. Rodgers in fact cherished the oppositions and 'through-otherness' of Irish life, even though he believed he could fashion oneness merely out of his love for Ireland and in the finitude of his poems. Life is, or ought to be, a kind of perpetual trinity in which 'The idiosyncratic I' constantly confronts the dishevelment of the world, their union producing the son, Christ, love, truth, poetry, a union that heals 'The split that was in man since time began'.[33]

Rodgers was born into an awareness of duality, for life in Ulster has always been at one crucial level twofold, Protestant and Catholic. The Protestant is even divided against himself. 'Gay goes up and grim comes down,' he wrote. 'The Puritan pepper and salt, if it looked like granite tasted like drama. It had two sides to it. Everything in Belfast had two sides.'[34] Later he ascribed this duality to the entire island, and he considered that all the subjects of his celebrated radio profiles displayed a 'bi-partisan Irish background'.[35] Moreover, the contributors to the profiles proved to him, as they busily contradicted each other out of earshot, that life could be a matter of opposing truths. But he had known this: 'As a Presbyterian clergyman, I had learned to listen to a husband's and a wife's talk, each contradictory in every respect, yet each compulsively true and equally convincing.'[36] The troubling duality of marriage is successfully captured in 'Paired Lives', a brief and almost metaphysical poem in which, like swing doors, husband and wife present 'one smooth front/Of summed resistance' to outsiders, while each door in reality

> Is hung on its own hinge
> Of fear and hope, and in
> Its own reticence rests.

And since Rodgers so closely identified Ireland and poetry, it is not surprising that he considered poetry itself to originate in a violent duality: 'I think that all poetry is written out of conflict, out of a clash between two opposites, that that is where articulation comes from.' That he has a somewhat crude version of Yeats's antinomies in mind is made clear when he adds, 'As Yeats said, "Out of the quarrel with ourselves we make poetry."'[37] Duality pervades all aspects of Rodgers's poetry, from unhappy portmanteau coinages (grotesticled, eider-downtrodden, tip-toadying) through tandem phrasing (thumb and thimble, turn and trundle) to theme itself, and even sensibility (tastelessness vying with sound judgment).

Not merely duality but more specifically paradox is central to Rodgers's vision, and he pays only lip-service to the ultimate order and orderly progression in which Hewitt believes. It is not without interest that Davie has noted the same centrality of paradox in Charles

Wesley and the frequency in his poetry of its rhetorical figure, the oxymoron.[38] The essentially paradoxical nature of Christianity is something that exercises both Wesley and Rodgers. Nor did Rodgers lose sight of it when he ceased being a minister and concentrated on being a poet; indeed, as a poet he was freer to express publicly, to the point of heterodoxy, the provocative contradictions in the Christian story. 'Lent', for example, from Rodgers's second volume, *Europa and the Bull and Other Poems* (1952), is a powerful poem in which Mary Magdalene, 'that easy woman', goes back to her old ways after two days of Lenten self-denial and in doing so makes possible the rebirth of the dead Christ, who has been planted in her womb. Reborn, He returns to her the raiment and scents of her true and sensual self. Other poems, too, reinterpret New Testament episodes, often translating them into the incongruous currencies of the everyday.[39]

Altogether, *Europa and the Bull* is a more ambitious if less brash performance than the first volume. There is a wealth of sensuality in the verse, and on occasion a worldly and confident treatment of sexuality. 'The Net', for example, is cleverly poised in the manner of the Caroline poets between metaphysical conceit and innocent relish. Hewitt's utilitarianism of the heart ('stranger to passion, never strongly moved/by those emotions use has not approved')[40] bears little resemblance to Rodgers's verbal courtship displays. An unabashed paganism pervades the ambitious narrative poems 'Europa and the Bull' and 'Pan and Syrinx', as well as 'Apollo and Daphne'. All three poems celebrate lives paired in sexual pursuit, the provocative clash of desiring opposites, revelation through violent intercourse. Each is a *tour de force* partly because Rodgers's language was peculiarly suited to what in 'Pan and Syrinx' is called 'the subterfuge of flesh'. But they are weaker in insight than in celebration. Rodgers, in the words of Kathleen Raine, 'is never dull, never flat – except when he has something to say of a philosophic nature, when he drops into bathos – but this seldom happens'.[41] For Rodgers, words are the beloved daughters of earth *and* heaven, thoughts the sons cast out from his universe.

Rodgers's liberties, abandonments and superfluous energies might be laid at the door of a transposed evangelical fervour. If so, one of his last poems – one written early enough in Ulster's current Troubles to qualify as prophecy – is ironic in its eloquence. 'Home Thoughts from Abroad' is a backhanded greeting from California to the Reverend Ian Paisley, the Free Presbyterian minister and political firebrand who was, when the poem was written, achieving his notoriety. 'I think of that brave man Paisley', Rodgers writes, using a two-edged Ulster adjective,

> eyeless
> In Gaza, with a daisy-chain of millstones
> Round his neck . . .
> . . . I like his people and I like his guts
> But I dislike his gods who always end
> In gun-play.

For Rodgers, Paisley is the last of the Irish giants who, after their passing, live in shrunken form in the memories of the people. A pity this diminution, but necessary, especially nowadays, and in the light, or darkness, of Paisley's 'borborygmic roars/Of rhetoric'. The poem is a eulogy that would prefer to be an obituary. For Rodgers as poet and sometime minister must have nursed a secret envy of Paisley's rhetorical powers. Rodgers repeatedly professes in his poetry a hatred of humbug and hubbub, and in 'Words' (the second of his two poems of that title) he speaks of 'the empty shop-fronts of abstraction', 'the vendors of puffs', and 'the tricks and tags of every demagogue'. A measure of irony has to be registered here. At his worst, Rodgers has personified abstractions stalk through his pages, and when he berates Paisley for 'the blatter of his hand-me-down talk', we have to overlook Rodgers's own numerous borrowings. Rodgers's loud insistence on the orality of words, his repeated anticipation of doom, and his rhetorical use of language all have their preacherly and demagogic aspect. Did he not claim he was 'born to the purple passage,/Was heir to all that Adamnation/And hand-me-down of doom'?[42] We might contrast his style with Hewitt's, seeing echoed in that contrast two styles of preaching by dissenters, the nineteenth-century evangelical 'pattern of red-hot exhortation and dramatic religious demagogy' (Rodgers) into which the seventeenth-century 'pattern of patient and formal exposition' (Hewitt) evolved (or, as Davie would have it, degenerated).[43]

Perhaps, too, Rodgers's liberties and unmoorings could be interpreted as his reaction against a Calvinist rearing, the cocking of snooks at Ulster puritanism; his courtship displays may have been in reality distraction displays. He was, after all, born into an Ulster Presbyterian family and had the upbringing then widespread in the North of Ireland. His parents were, as the Ulster phrase has it, 'good living', and they barred Shakespeare, full-length mirrors and alcohol from their home. 'Sunday dinner was cooked on Saturday,' he recalled, 'and the Sunday boots were polished the night before, and profane books and music were put away till Monday, and nothing, absolutely nothing, was allowed to disturb "the Day of Dreadful Rest", as we restless children called it.'[44] The repression resulting from such a rearing extended itself into Rodgers's maturity, and when the reaction came it was in direct proportion to its belatedness and the longevity of the repression. A law of the excluded middle seemed to operate in the life and, to its immediate advantage but ultimate detriment, in the poetry. The puritan boasted of his freedom and in his boast denied it; and it was too easy maybe to interpret his exuberance as an Irish cultural tradition instead of his own unease. Ironically, tradition was there, but it was not the tradition he fully acknowledged; had it been (and I refer to Ulster evangelicalism), he would surely have questioned its relationship to the Celticism he unreservedly embraced, and its relationship also to his neo-Romanticism. But this is speculation. The rich disclosures and concealments of Ulster Protestant traditions, in Hewitt as well as Rodgers, are enough to be going on with, and help to explain the different and differently vigorous compass of their verse.

[1985]

NOTES

1. Quoted in *Twentieth Century Authors: A Biographical Dictionary of Modern Literature, First Supplement*; ed. Stanley J. Kunitz (New York: H.W. Wilson 1955), p. 836.

2. Although at the height of his fame Rodgers had been disfavoured by certain schools of poetic thought, the reversal in his reputation really began with the attacks on him by Donald Davie and Kingsley Amis in 1953. Davie and Amis were, of course, two of the Movement poets who reacted against the neo-Romanticism of the 'forties. Larkin, too, was a Movement poet whose literary tastes dictated the inclusions and omissions in his Oxford anthology.

3. For example, Rodgers appeared in *The New British Poets* (1949), edited by Kenneth Rexroth, and in *Poetry Now* (1956), edited by G.S. Fraser; Hewitt does not appear in either book. Rodgers also appears in the influential *Penguin Book of Contemporary Verse*, edited by Kenneth Allott in 1950, and survived into Allott's 1962 revision of his anthology. Given Allott's anti-neo-Romanticism, Rodgers's inclusion is a measure of his popularity; by the same token, it is perhaps a surprise that Hewitt turns up in neither version of the anthology. However, Hewitt does appear in *Poetry of the Present* (1949), an anthology edited by Geoffrey Grigson, with whom Allott had been associated in the late 1930s. Grigson, whose anti-neo-Romanticism was well known, gives Hewitt two poems to Rodgers's one. Generally speaking, Hewitt turns up in collections that wanted regional repre-

sentation, such as *Poetry Scotland*, No. 1 (1944) or *A New Romantic Anthology* (1949), edited by Stefan Schimanski and Henry Treece, two writers connected with the new Apocalyptic and Personalist movements who might otherwise have been supposed indifferent to Hewitt's work (Hewitt's poem was in fact grouped with other Irish poems, all chosen for the volume by Patrick MacDonogh).

4. *Rhyming Weavers and Other Country Poets of Antrim and Down* (Belfast: Blackstaff Press 1974), p. 10.

5 . I am thinking of the relevant portions of *Culture and Anarchy* (1869). The motto of the *Nonconformist*, borrowed by Arnold in his book, gives my essay its title. The phrase was originally Burke's, however, and can be found in his speech, 'On Conciliation with the Colonies'.

6. *A Gathered Church: The Literature of the English Dissenting Interest, 1700–1930* (London: Routledge & Kegan Paul 1978).

7. 'The Colony' appears in Hewitt's *Collected Poems 1932–1967* (London: MacGibbon & Kee 1968). Quoted poems by Hewitt appear in the *Collected Poems* unless, as indicated in my text, they appear in one of the following volumes published after the *Collected Poems* : *The Day of the Corncrake: Poems of the Nine Glens* (Belfast: The Glens of Antrim Historical Society 1969); *Out of My Time: Poems 1967–1974* (Belfast: Blackstaff Press 1974); *The Rain Dance: Poems New and Revised* (Belfast: Blackstaff Press 1978); *Kites in Spring: A Belfast Boyhood* (Belfast: Blackstaff Press 1980); *Loose Ends* (Belfast: Blackstaff Press 1983).

8. In 'Sunset Over Glenaan' from *The Day of the Corncrake*. Compare these lines from 'The Colony': 'Among us, some, beguiled by their sad music,/make common cause with the natives, in their heart/hoping to win a truce when the natives assert/their ancient right and take what once was theirs.'

9. In 1971 the poet decided he *had* found his nation, though in 'The Scar' (from *Out of My Time*) the word might be used for its half-rhyme with 'vision' more than for its precise difference from 'country'. The poet claims that when his great-grandmother caught famine fever from a beggar (presumably a wandering 'native' or 'Catholic'), her death 'conscribed me of the Irishry forever/ . . . in that woman's death I found my nation'. I'm not sure nationality is infectious, however fine Hewitt's sentiment.

10. In 'Ars Poetica' from *The Rain Dance*.

11. *Rhyming Weavers*, p. 37. The custom was called 'the Churn', and Hewitt furnishes extracts from a poem of that name by Henry McD. Flecher, one of the better country poets. Among the other interesting country poets Hewitt anthologizes are Francis Boyle, Robert Huddleston, Samuel Thomson and James Orr.

12. *Rhyming Weavers*, p. 27.

13. 'I'm an Ulsterman, of planter stock. I was born in the island of Ireland, so secondarily I'm an Irishman. I was born in the British archipelago and English is my native tongue, so I am British. The British archipelago consists of offshore islands to the continent of Europe, so I'm European.' Hewitt wrote this for a symposium in *The Irish Times* (July 1974); it is reprinted in *The Selected John Hewitt*, ed. Alan Warner (Belfast: Blackstaff Press 1981), p. 6.

14. *The Making of the English Working Class* (London: Gollancz 1963), p. 295.

15. Hewitt also described himself as 'no man's pensioner' in 'Conacre'. Joyce parodies the type in *Ulysses* in the Protestant Mr Deasy who always pays his way.

16. In 'The Landscape of Planter and Gael in the Poetry of John Hewitt and John Montague', *Canadian Journal of Irish Studies* I, No. 2 (1975), 17–33. Among the best of the Colonial and Provincial poets (I don't distinguish them here) were William Hamilton Drummond, William Drennan, James Stuart and William Carr.

17. *The Selected John Hewitt*, p. 4.

18. See *The Selected John Hewitt*, pp. 4–5. The moves to have Hewitt made a Freeman of Belfast were instigated by Paddy Devlin, a socialist (and Catholic) politician of long standing.

19. From *The Rain Dance*. A recent *Belfast Telegraph* profile of Hewitt tells us that every poem Hewitt has ever written 'has been transcribed neatly into note-books which he keeps in a metal strongbox in his study. There are 33 of them now, all dated and with an index at the back giving the number of lines written per month.'

20. Davie, *A Gathered Church*, p. 25. Davie is borrowing from Henry R. Van Til's *The Calvinistic Concept of Culture* (1959). Calvinist aesthetics happen to resemble the virtues of Movement poetry that Davie wrote and commended in the 1950s. (John Holloway once described the Movement writers as nonconformist in background during a review of Davie, Larkin and Conquest in the *Hudson Review*.) Hewitt displays some of the characteristics of Movement poetry (moderation, empiricism, traditional metres, craftsmanship, limitation, ratio-nalism, Augustanism) without having been associated with the Movement.

21. Davie, p. 26. Davie's preference for Old Dissent (the Baptists into which he was born are descendants of Old Dissent) limits his defence of dissent. That prefer-ence parallels his preference for Augustan poetry which limits his tolerance for Romanticism, especially when it coincides with evangelical enthusiasm.

22. *The Selected John Hewitt*, p. 3.

23. The lines quoted are from 'Words'. All poems by Rodgers that I quote are from his *Collected Poems* (London: Oxford University Press 1971) which brings together the poems from *Awake! and Other Poems*, the poems from *Europa and the Bull and Other Poems*, and some otherwise uncollected poems.

24. 'I Write For – ' in *Scissors for a One-Armed Tailor: Marginal Verses 1929–1954* (Belfast: privately printed 1974). The title of this slim collection suggests that Hewitt has collected verses written as early as 1929.

25. Quoted in *The Poet Speaks: Interviews with Contemporary Poets*, ed. Peter Orr (London: Routledge & Kegan Paul 1966), p. 209.

26. Clearly the personalities of the two poets were very different, and Hewitt, one feels, has greater fellow-feeling for the 'slow private man' he celebrates in 'William J. McClughin (1900–1971)', also in *Out of My Time*.

27. *Irish Literary Portraits* (London: BBC 1972), pp. 132, 176.

28. However, in a brace of first-rate early sonnets, 'Two Irish Saints', Hewitt proved he could at times write lines energized by the devices Rodgers loved, alliter-ation, assonance and the rest, 'Yet loud with Leary, dominant with druids,/ passing with stags tall-antlered down the valley,/was happy only when his text-vexed eyes/saw the flat Lough from Slemish as before,' and could marry a Romantic sonority to the Romanesque Celticness of an Austin Clarke.

29. Despite Kenneth Rexroth in *The New British Poets* (Verona: New Directions 1949), p. xxi.

30. J.F.C. Harrison, *The Second Coming: Popular Millenarianism 1780–1850* (London:

Routledge & Kegan Paul 1979), p. 7.

31. Harrison, p. 84.
32. Harrison, p. 16. Terence Brown makes an adjacent point when he notes Rodgers's 'association of poetic inspiration, romantically conceived, and a Calvinist's notion of divine election', *Northern Voices: Poets from Ulster* (Dublin: Gill and Macmillan 1975), p. 119.
33. 'Resurrection: An Easter Sequence' in *Europa and the Bull*.
34. Quoted in Darcy O'Brien, *W.R. Rodgers* (Lewisburg: Bucknell UP 1970), p. 22.
35. *Irish Literary Portraits*, p. 138.
36. *Irish Literary Portraits*, pp. xii–xiii.
37. *The Poet Speaks*, p. 210.
38. Davie, p. 51.
39. 'The Journey of the Magi' is more verbose and less successful than Eliot's poem of the same title (unless, unwisely, he intends parody), from which Rodgers shamelessly borrows in his beginning. 'Resurrection: An Easter Sequence' is an unedited version, as it were, of Christ's death, and again the reporter's angle serves to highlight a contradiction in tone of events, if not in doctrine, between the sacred and the profane. Auden, as well as Eliot, is the creditor in this sequence, and one poem lifts freely from 'Musée des Beaux Arts'. (See, too, in this matter of borrowing, 'A Last Word' that surely takes from Hardy. Perhaps by his second volume Rodgers's inspiration was badly flagging.)
40. 'Retreaded Rhymes' from *Loose Ends*.
41. Quoted in *Twentieth Century Authors*, p. 836.
42. In 'Epilogue' (while at the same time and in the same poem claiming that he was heir to a taciturn people, the Ulster Protestants, who distrusted Southern Irish volubility).
43. Davie, p. 60, is actually quoting from Erik Routley's *English Religious Dissent* (1960).
44. Quoted in Darcy O'Brien, pp. 19–20.

8

YEATS AND THE EASTER RISING

The seizure of principal buildings in Dublin by Sinn Féin on Easter Monday, 1916, took by surprise the Executive authority and the city's inhabitants, many of whom were making holiday. Yeats was staying with Sir William Rothenstein in Gloucestershire when the outbreak occurred. Not only was he, too, taken aback, but he smarted that he had not been consulted by the rebel leaders.[1] The reason the poet fretted is disclosed in a letter of 23 May to John Quinn: he assumed some responsibility for the Rising. This was an idea he never forsook and its most famous, and characteristically scrupled, expression was in 'The Man and the Echo' (written in 1938):

> I lie awake night after night
> And never get the answers right.
> Did that play of mine send out
> Certain men the English shot?

While no one can doubt that Yeats was genuinely shocked by occurrences in Dublin ('I had no idea that any public event could so deeply move me,' he wrote to Lady Gregory on 11 May),[2] it is equally difficult to doubt that 'Easter 1916', the poem on which he was working when he wrote to Lady Gregory and John Quinn, is in one sense a formidable attempt at appropriation. The poem registers the annoyed surprise and somewhat contrived responsibility Yeats felt as a private individual and public figure, before offering a canonical image of the Rising that establishes the importance as much of Yeats to the Rising as of the Rising to Yeats.

Indeed, the importance of the Rising to Yeats the poet is an aspect of the strategy by which Yeats tries implicitly to prove his importance to the Rising, its symbolism, impact and aftermath. In 'Easter 1916', the public demand that the executed architects of the Rising be paid homage is qualified by a personal demand for a more urgently felt response. The personal response is voiced not only by the poet as Irish citizen and literary man harbouring doubts about a headstrong display of physical force, but also by the poet as composer of an intricate canon challenged (or granted the opportunity) by a violent public event to absorb it and still retain coherence. The Yeatsian aesthetic, in 'Easter 1916' and other Yeats poems inspired by the Rising, is the bridge between the personal and the poetic (the conventionally poetic, that is), between reaction and rhetoric, and the tensions in that bridge that the troubled gap between opposing shores creates are both revealing and rewarding to contemplate.

I

'Easter 1916' shares with most other contemporary poems about the Rising an acknowledgment of the rebels' self-sacrifice. Yeats seems to have felt more eloquently, if not more deeply, the guilt many mockers began to feel as the executions followed their horrifying course. Like others, Yeats seems to have initially thought the rebellion premature and divisive, and a national setback: 'I am very despondent about the future,' he wrote to Lady Gregory. 'At the moment I feel that all the work of years has been overturned, all the bringing together of classes, all the freeing of Irish literature and criticism from politics.'³ He refers in his letter to the probable efficacy of the insurrectionists' 'sacrifice', but he is paraphrasing Maud Gonne, who had written to him before 11 May and who shared none of his early bewilderment. (According to Joseph Hone, she found 'Easter 1916', read to her in August on the seashore in Normandy, 'wholly inadequate to the occasion'.)⁴ The notion of sacrifice does in fact pervade the finished poem, but this is perhaps because the guilt engendered by the executions that dragged on and made seeming mockery of premature anti-rebel sentiment sought exorcism in praise of what the leaders had surrendered.

In any case, the initial personal doubts remain in the poem and both vie with, and translate into, the Yeatsian and the conventional. In 'Easter 1916' we are given both the admission of guilt and the transforming sacrifice (transforming both the dead rebels and – it would appear – the poet himself), but it is through the very utterness and unexpectedness of the change that Yeats allows himself a roomy middle ground in which to question the *wisdom* of the sacrifice, both personal

> Too long a sacrifice
> Can make a stone of the heart.
> O when may it suffice?

and political

> For England may keep faith
> For all that is done and said

while leaving untouched the *fact* of the sacrifice and its sudden awakening of guilt in the minds and hearts of bystanders. That fact, after all, is like a stone beneath mere speculation, as the Rising will henceforth lie like a stone in the midst of Irish history. The brute, ineluctable fact of the rebel leaders' swift disappearance from the face of the earth did not nullify but instead seemed to validate, in some elemental, inarguable way, their venture. But while registering willingly that self-evident truth, the poet confesses himself in the grip of more human considerations.

The perplexities Yeats is wrestling with mount and multiply. The fanatical and idealistic hearts of the rebels may have turned to stone (*may* have: 'Hearts with one purpose alone/ . . . *seem*/Enchanted to a stone': 'Too long a sacrifice/*Can* make a stone of the heart' – my italics), and this surely was an unwise thing to have let happen. A human heart turned to stone, deaf to human petition, is a very different matter from the stonelike effect of an historical occurrence and denies (by wrong example?) the very world it seeks in its impassibility to improve and make more human. (Later, in *Autobiographies*, Yeats in a hostile mood compared nationalist opinion to 'a part of the mind turned to stone'.) Yet the nature of sacrifice is such that what is most prized is surrendered that it might be ultimately secured and guaranteed for others; what is held to be good has its value magnified by being squandered. If the rebels' hearts have been enchanted into stones, presumably this occurred before the Rising that the enchantment in fact made possible (even though transformation into stone also suggests the rigor mortis into which the executed rebels stiffened). The stonelike hearts of the rebels may even belong to our world after all, for they 'trouble the living stream,' not merely by causing anxiety in us but also by disturbing us into living movement. Living or dead, it is the changed hearts of the rebels that in turn, by ushering in a new order, change *us*. (One recalls those in Shakespeare's sonnet 94 'Who, moving others, are themselves as stone,/ Unmoved, cold, and to temptation slow.') And if the cold passion of the rebels has put them insensitively beyond nature, it is Yeats himself who completes that process by his concluding epitaph that chisels their names on the national gravestone. Indeed, we know that elsewhere Yeats himself desired flight from nature, most famously in 'Sailing to Byzantium' (1926), and even considered the stone in 'The Fisherman' (a poem written before 'Easter 1916', in 1914) 'dark under froth', the foundation of a substantial and passionate life.

In a similarly ambidextrous way, Yeats permits us to associate the executions of the rebels with the crucifixion of Christ (by relinquishing judgment of each sacrifice to 'Heaven') – an association early established by other poets such as Seumas O'Sullivan, AE and Eva Gore-Booth[5] – while leaving it unclear if the sacrifices would be ultimately benign or malignant (the beauty born of the crushed insurrection is, after all, 'terrible'), an ambivalence possibly towards Christ that we later find in 'The Second Coming' (1919). As always in his 'annunciation' poems, Yeats is unsure of the future ('Easter 1916' like 'The Second Coming' poses questions to enormous rhetorical effect) while being certain that rupture is inevitable and frightening, whatever order it ushers in. The ambidexterity, troubling to Yeats and the reader alike, finds perfection of expression in the poem's key phrase, 'terrible beauty', to which I will return.

II

Yeats's problem was to contrive and occupy a no-man's-land between personal involvement and doubt, on the one hand, and public admiration, on the other, while seeming not to do so. The process by which the solution is achieved *is* 'Easter 1916'. Because Dublin was a small and intimate city, the rebel leaders were familiar to Dubliners and were acquainted with Yeats and other poets. In his poem 'Dublin (1916)', Seumas O'Sullivan laments 'the absent faces/ In the crowds that pass me by', and mentions MacBride, MacDonagh and Pearse.[6] For his part, Yeats in 'Easter 1916' affects to see an unsentimental poignancy, even cold marvel, in the manner in which mere acquaintances suddenly assumed a new status, a martyrdom and imperishability, though it is Yeats who is in part directing the assumption. Whereas the names of Connolly and Pearse are given to complete a rhyme and grace a monument, the sea-change they have undergone by execution is unexplored because Yeats knew better other rebel leaders. In the poem's second part Yeats devotes no lines to Connolly, two impersonal lines to Pearse, five to MacDonagh, seven to Constance Markievicz and nine to John MacBride, reversing the relative historical importance of the participants while roughly reflecting Yeats's degree of involvement with each. Personal acquaintance creates guilt whereas the impersonal roll-call that concludes the poem defers to the public and unevadable fact of execution. How Yeats bridges this gap is the genius of the poem. He begins with the anonymity of faces and disguising costume ('motley'), moves through the recollection of imprisoned or executed acquaintances who are unnamed, merely 'numbered', yet readily identifiable by the reader, and reaches the appropriate and identifying finality of rhythmic last names. The unique, essential and superbly strategic Yeats, I suggest, is to be found in the middle of the poem, moving in that somewhat enigmatic territory between the named and the anonymous, broadcasting his part-condescending, part-mythicizing demonstrative pronouns – 'That woman's days', 'This man had kept a school', 'This other man I had dreamed/A drunken, vainglorious lout.' By choosing to allude rather than refer to the rebels he had met, and by pitching his allusions between the daily and the legendary, the familiar and the reverent, Yeats leaves room to insert himself into the event. In the middle of the poem it is Yeats not history who chooses magisterially which of his acquaintances will be numbered in the song. The final outright naming of MacDonagh and MacBride and Connolly and Pearse is the reluctant but obligatory conventionalism the poem shares with other poems about the Rising. 'England had bullets and burning lime,' Seumas O'Kelly wrote in 'The Seanachie Tells Another Story', 'And Ireland has names that march with time.'[7] 'Easter 1916' ends by dutifully honouring that platitude.

The speed with which the names of the executed were canonized and, in Donagh MacDonagh's phrase, 'petrified in history',[8] was due to the fact that an enlargeable and hospitable pantheon awaited them. M. J. MacManus, like others, called the rebellion 'a Fenian rising, an insurrection in the direct tradition of '48 and '67'.[9] On 11 May, even before Connolly and Mac Diarmada were executed, Yeats wrote to Lady Gregory from Gloucestershire: 'I am trying to write a poem on the men executed – "terrible beauty has been born again".'[10] The day before that, George Bernard Shaw wrote in the *Daily News*: 'The shot Irishmen will now take their places beside Emmet and the Manchester martyrs in Ireland . . . and nothing in heaven or earth can prevent it.'[11] 'An Irishman knows well how those who met their deaths will be regarded,' wrote Padraic Colum in 1916, '"They shall be remembered for ever; they shall be speaking for ever; the people shall hear them for ever."'[12] Colum of course is quoting Yeats's own Cathleen Ni Houlihan; through that character Yeats had bolstered the notion that Irish posterity would unquestionably honour patriot martyrs; at the close of 'Easter 1916' Yeats could express that sentiment almost by reflex.

Indeed, in a more complicated and allusive fashion than did his poetic contemporaries, Yeats seems to have taken some of his cues in 'Easter 1916' from Pearse's life and writings. It was the poetry and philosophy of Pearse that indicated, before the fact, the prescribed response to the Rising. Joan Towey Mitchell has caught echoes of Pearse in Yeats's writing, a reminder that the popularity of 'Easter 1916' may well be due in part to the sop it offers to conventional Irish feeling.[13]

The motley and 'casual comedy' of pre-Rising Dublin, as Yeats saw it, was changed utterly, but it is unclear if it became in his eyes tragedy ('casual' in that case being a redundancy) or, instead, comedy to be reckoned with ('casual' in that case meaning without serious intent). Probably both: certainly there is the suggestion of folly and redundant gesture in the poem's last part ('Was it needless death after all?') and of 'all that delirium of the brave' Yeats missed in 'September 1913' ('What if excess of love/Bewildered them till they died?'). In a letter to Lady Gregory on 8 May, Yeats wrote of the 'heroic, tragic lunacy of Sinn Féin'.[14] Pearse gladly accepted the name of fool and thought that the patriot and hero had to be reckless and spendthrift.[15] In his poem 'The Fool', Pearse wanted his countrymen to be as foolish as he, and predicted (over-optimistically, as it turned out) that they would be, and that they would call for a miracle, a prediction Yeats seems to validate when he offers the executions of the rebels as utter and radical transformations, sudden intersections of the natural order by the supernatural, one guise of which is that legendry into which Pearse and the executed have been assumed.

'Prudence is the only vice,' Mary Colum remembered Pearse saying, and she remembered too her friends in New York excoriating the insurgents for their folly and recklessness.[16] Pearse thought it the recklessness of wayward children who held the secret of innocence and purity and godliness and freedom. Yeats's comparing in 'Easter 1916' the poet's naming of the dead rebels to a mother's naming of her tired child has always seemed odd to me, but it is perhaps borrowed from Pearse's exaltation of mother and child in general and from his eve-of-insurrection poem 'The Mother' specifically, in which Pearse's mother gaily sends out her two sons 'in bloody protest for a glorious thing':

> But I will speak their names to my own heart
> In the long nights;
> The little names that were familiar once
> Round my dead hearth.

In turn, other lines in 'The Mother' echo Yeats's Cathleen:

> They shall be spoken of among their people,
> The generations shall remember them,
> And call them blessed.

Yeats in 'Easter 1916' repeats Pearse's mother's prediction and bids fair to fulfill it. Yeats's telling of the names of the dead is the bard's obligation but it is also, we might say, something of an Easter duty and is echoed by the speaker of Lady Gregory's poem 'The Old Woman Remembers', familiarly personified ancient Ireland, who begins her remembrance of the rebel dead of seven centuries, including those who fell in Easter Week, by saying, 'a rosary of praise': 'Now on the beads I'll tell out names,/And light a candle for the dead.'[17]

There are other echoes of Pearse in 'Easter 1916'. 'We know their dream; enough/To know they dreamed and are dead': that is precisely how Pearse perceived the quixotic pursuit of Irish independence from Britain, and in 'The Fool' he rejected the politic words he thought were withering his Rose Tree: 'O wise man, riddle me this,' he taunted, 'what if the dream come true?' And what if excess of love bewildered the rebels till they died? Pearse had anticipated the last, unanswered question of Yeats's poem when he adopted as one of his mottoes the famous words of St Columcille: 'If

I die, it should be from the excess of love I bear the Gael.' In the light of this, Yeats's question seems redundant and even half-hearted, which Yeats may have sensed and so left it to move swiftly to the poem's epitaph. In that epitaph he repeats the poem's famous phrase – 'a terrible beauty'. It has been assumed that this is an oxymoron, but this is not necessarily the case since it is arguable that beauty can be terrifying. Perhaps Yeats means by it that the beauty of attempted independence was achieved at a terrible cost in human lives. This was hardly an original idea, nor was the idea that might furnish a second interpretation: that a terrible failure was because of its nobleness transformed into victory. 'O'Connell Street', a poem by Francis Ledwidge (killed in France a year after the poem was written), includes the lines

> And, more than Beauty understands
> Has made her lovelier here, it seems

in which 'here' refers to the still-smoking ruins of Dublin's main thoroughfare. Still, when we set Yeats's phrase beside others he offers us elsewhere – 'excited reverie', 'murderous innocence' – we appear indeed to have a deliberate oxymoron and as such the most compact verbal vesture of Yeats's philosophy and fertile duplicity, embodying as it does in two words thesis and antithesis. Yet Mitchell traces it to a phrase in Pearse's play *The King*: 'the terrible, beautiful voice that comes out of the heart of battles',[18] Fr Francis Shaw finds an even more chilling and reminiscent statement in Pearse, from *The Story of a Success*: 'It is murder and death that make possible the terrible beautiful thing we call physical life.'[19] This seems clinching, though (for the record) G. F. Dalton has directed us to Sheridan Le Fanu who uses the exact phrase but in unrelated fashion:

> Fionula the Cruel, the brightest, the worst,
> With a terrible beauty the vision accurst,
> Gold-filleted, sandalled, of times dead and gone . . . [20]

III

'Easter 1916', then, is an astonishing weave of the Yeatsian and the borrowed, much of it from Pearse. Elsewhere in Yeats we find Pearse apparently endorsed or echoed, in 'The Rose Tree' (1917) and 'Three Songs to the One Burden' (published 1939), with their seeming celebration of blood sacrifice, and in 'Under Ben Bulben' (1938), with lines that might have had the Easter rebels in mind:

Even the wisest man grows tense
With some sort of violence
Before he can accomplish fate . . .

But it is of course the Yeatsian hesitations, evasions, ambiguities, the querying qualifying the declamatory, that set 'Easter 1916' off from its contemporaries among poems about the Rising. Moreover, the poem is as concerned with modifying and advancing a canon as with celebrating an event, and assumes the insurgents into the Yeatsian scheme of things in a vivid, complicated and arresting way.

'Easter 1916' has been accurately called a palinode to 'September 1913', a retraction of that poem's lament, 'Romantic Ireland's dead and gone,/It's with O'Leary in the grave.'[21] Equally could the poem be called a palinode to other poems of Yeats's forties, 'To a Wealthy Man', 'To a Shade', and 'At Galway Races' in which Yeats pines for that heroic time

Before the merchant and the clerk
Breathed on the world with timid breath.

In 'Easter 1916' it is precisely the merchant and clerk who usher in a new dispensation, having maintained behind 'counter or desk among grey/Eighteenth-century houses' their 'vivid faces' which on Yeats's hindsight and to his surprise were evidence not of fatuous but of justified self-importance. Perhaps he ought to have been neither surprised nor annoyed by the Rising, if the poems of his forties had been meant to goad middle-class Ireland and to provoke or invite acts of denial that Romantic Ireland *was* dead and gone. Yet the poem's indirection and less than wholehearted response to the rebellion may have had their start in some class disappointment (he was later to seize on The O'Rahilly as an aristocratic and swashbuckling participant in the Rising) or in some Revival disappointment that the insurrection originated in the city and not the country (as if in consolation, the poem's central imagery is in a reversionary way rural).

The nature and extent of the change, the poet's change of heart and Irish history's change of direction, are, however, more difficult to gauge than the word 'palinode' suggests. It is not clear, for example, if Yeats commits himself in 'Easter 1916' to the view held by many of his contemporaries that an old heroism has been revitalized at the GPO, Jacob's biscuit factory and elsewhere in the city. 'Easter 1916' speaks of birth, not rebirth ('A terrible beauty is born'), though in his 11 May letter to Lady Gregory terrible beauty has been born 'again'. Romantic Ireland succeeded to what in 'All Things Can Tempt Me'

(1908) the poet called a 'fool-driven land' and from which the poet tried to stay aloof. Has Romantic Ireland returned, or has a third and unknown thing been born? Has the tragedy of Parnell that gave way to mere comedy been restored? (The terror of the beauty born may be one of Aristotle's two tragic emotions – in which case beauty is equivalent to Aristotle's pity – for in his letter to Lady Gregory Yeats quotes Maud Gonne in a letter to him: 'tragic dignity has returned to Ireland', a sentiment that may have influenced or inspired the phrase 'terrible beauty'.) Or has something new, neither tragedy nor comedy but a disconcerting mixture, been created? Has the reality of Parnellite Ireland that was followed by the mere play-acting of his successors (that Joyce mocks in 'Ivy Day in the Committee Room' and Yeats recalls at the beginning of 'Easter 1916') been reinstated by the Rising, or has a new, strange and troubling play the prologued? (When MacBride resigns his part in the casual comedy, does he leave the theatre for real life or accept a different role?) In short, is the Easter Rising violent antithesis (more accurately, the antithesis of an antithesis, a reversion) or is it violent synthesis, a monstrous combination of two orders (one remembers the sphinx in 'The Second Coming') whose appropriate trope is the oxymoron?

We can think of these difficult questions devolving upon another famous phrase in the poem, 'All changed, changed utterly'. By 'all', does Yeats mean 'all of the present' or 'all of the present *and* the past' (including the Ireland that preceded the deaths of O'Leary and Parnell)? Strictly speaking, 'all' refers only to the rebels themselves, and they inhabited, until their deaths, the present. They have been changed 'Now and in time to be', which suggests that they have reached an ultimate, unchangeable condition; this condition, new and final to them, may, however, be a periodic transformation recognizable throughout Irish history. The order such men inevitably usher in may, unlike them, be destined itself to change, even, indeed, if it is unprecedented; even should the content of Irish history have been newly minted by the Rising, its form – its heroisms, defeats and apotheoses – may well have been reconfirmed. Certainly it is difficult not to read 'Easter 1916' alongside 'The Phases of the Moon' (1918), especially remembering Yeats's reference to the 'heroic, tragic lunacy of Sinn Féin'. It is as if Pearse and the others had been summoned to adventure by the first crescent of the moon, become heroes by the twelfth phase, and then on the eve of the Rising become 'creatures of the full [moon]', with

body and soul
Estranged amid the strangeness of themselves,
Caught up in contemplation, the mind's eye
Fixed upon images that once were thought . . .

Echoing 'Easter 1916', Robartes says 'all is changed' when the moon begins to wane, with the soul that had sought 'itself' before the full moon now seeking 'the world', as thoughts in Ireland must turn after the executions from the rebels to Ireland.[22]

As Robartes sings for Aherne 'the changes of the moon once more', the poet is in his remote tower finding mere images, like Yeats in Gloucestershire at Easter 1916 grappling with the first images of his poem. But in time Yeats discovered that the first image that came to him – 'terrible beauty has been born again' – was the image that could best convey the fresh instance of changelessness that the rupture of the Easter Rising represented. And he discovered this, I suspect, by repeating it to himself, as he repeated it in his finished poem as refrain, until it became an incantation, an enchanted phrase in the midst of all other phrases and images that thronged in his mind about the insurrection. Sound, imagery and meaning became one, became symbol, when he wedded the historical (and historic) event to his extant poetic, when he transformed his initial phrase by repetition into opaqueness (that the phrase was an oxymoron helped) and thence to its revisualization as an image of stone. We witness this transformation by proxy when in the architecture of his poem Yeats has the dissimilar third part lie like a keystone in the midst of the surrounding arch of similar parts.

When he speaks of the stone that can induce changes in the substances around it, Yeats the student of alchemy may have in mind the philosopher's stone. Less debatably, Yeats in 'Easter 1916' was surely remembering, or rediscovering, what he wrote in 1910 in 'The Symbolism of Poetry': 'We should come to understand that the beryl stone was enchanted by our fathers that it might unfold the pictures in its heart, and not to mirror our own excited faces, or the boughs waving outside the window. With this change of substance, this return to imagination . . . would come a change of style . . . '.[23] 'Our own excited faces': we might think of the 'vivid faces' of the Easter conspirators, forever altered now beyond excitement; and 'the boughs waving outside the window' is an image comparable to that in 'Easter 1916' of 'the birds that range/From cloud to tumbling cloud', changing minute to minute, the world the conspirators inhabited, which we know really to be fixed and changeless were we to have the key image. And Yeats does: that of the stone lying on a stream-bed, a Heraclitean image we can regard as conjured out of the poet's fused ambivalence to the rebellion or lying on the bed of the poet's memory, awaiting a new, disturbing flux of events.[24]

Were we to 'stand' upon this stone we would, like the fisherman, know wisdom, calmness, a childlike simplicity. Yeats wanted to write for his dreamed fisherman a poem worthy of the fisherman's contemplative and coldly passionate pursuit, as he wishes to write a poem worthy of Pearse and MacDonagh and their calm, unswerving dedication to an imagined insurrection. To do so, the poet had to trace a similar, though non-violent, path as the conspirators (and the fisherman). 'Easter 1916' concerns as much the direction of Yeats's poetry as it does a political cataclysm. Like the rebels Yeats believes he must direct his attention away from subjective expression ('our own excited faces') and objective observation of the natural world ('the boughs waving outside the window') to essential images. But the poet does not have the rebels' singlemindedness, and were he to, it would only be through their example; hence the tone in 'Easter 1916' of reluctant admiration of, and gratitude for, qualities the poet feels he lacks, perhaps fortunately. My guess is that Yeats found it exceedingly difficult, indeed impossible, to write the desired poem, and that he was as finally unsatisfied with the result as was Maud Gonne. For Easter Week was *not* a dream, despite its dreamlike, or nightmarish aspects, and the possibilities of political folly ('Was it needless death after all?') and human misguidedness ('what if excess of love/Bewildered them till they died?') kept muddling the issue some way into the poem and forced the poet to desist prematurely from contemplating these possibilities and to re-pretend at the poem's conclusion that he *had* dreamed it. But then, we could argue that his lifelong, evolving and eloquently failing search for essential images *was* the poetry of W. B. Yeats.

However ancient or new, then, seemed the Easter Rising to Yeats, it was swiftly but painfully absorbed into a philosophy, a symbolism, an aesthetic. Antithesis or synthesis, objective or subjective, the Rising became one of those permanent images Yeats, looking back on his career, refers to in 'The Municipal Gallery Revisited' (1937) and as such took its place in an unfolding process of development.

IV

In 'Ego Dominus Tuus', written in 1915, Yeats had opposed the world of undeceiving action to the deceiving world of rhetoric and sentimentality. The Easter rebels, we might say, seemed to be rhetoricians and sentimentalists but proved to be actors. 'Actors' is the operative word. It appears from 'Easter 1916' that Yeats thought of the rebels with whom he was acquainted not just as men of action but as players who exchanged one role before the Rising for a completely different one during the Rising. (Common currency, oddly enough, shares this duplicity, since we talk of 'staging' a rebellion.) Like Ille in 'Ego Dominus Tuus', MacDonagh and MacBride and Connolly and Pearse called to their opposites in the GPO and Jacob's factory, fashioned from their opposites an image of an heroic Ireland to which they were ready to sacrifice immediate reality. There is, as it happens, some biographical justification for Yeats's extension of his already formulated theory of the mask and antiself to events during Easter Week. Fr Shaw calls Pearse a revolutionary *malgré lui* who was by temperament a conservative and traditionalist. To Colum, MacDonagh was 'the thoughtful man become revolutionist' who courted in opposition to his own first nature 'the fierce conflict and the catastrophe'.[25] And we know how Connolly relinquished his socialist grasp of historical change for Pearse's mystical concepts of gesture and sacrifice.

Yeats's idea that the rebels were actors in a play was made clearer in the lines he devoted to Easter 1916 after his first great utterance. The Pearse and Connolly who agree in 'The Rose Tree' on the necessity of blood sacrifice are engaging in a stage dialogue – like Robartes and Aherne in 'The Phases of the Moon' – whose artificiality gives a greater chill to their words, the unreality of the exchange accentuating the reality of what happened. In a late poem, 'Three Songs to the One Burden', Yeats makes no bones about calling the rebels 'players' who fought in a 'painted scene', thereby claiming them as characters in the Yeatsian drama. All of these poems, together with 'Sixteen Dead Men' (written in 1916 or 1917) – with its sprightly opening, 'O but we talked at large before/The sixteen men were shot' – have about them something of a jesting desperation. This effect is heightened in 'The O'Rahilly' (1937) and 'Three Songs to the One Burden' by the oddly irrelevant refrains ('*How goes the weather?*', '*From mountain to mountain ride the fierce horsemen*'),[26] a device Yeats enjoyed, especially in his later poems, perhaps because it helped to create a careless and theatrical tangency to logic and story. The somewhat unhinged effect is there in all of Yeats's verse references to the Easter Rising, pitting as they do 'MacDonagh's bony thumb' (the alogical fact of sacrificial death) and 'all that delirium of the brave' against reason and politic words.

It could be that in these poems Yeats was trying to suggest an impersonal music of tradition, to capture that mysterious quality that in folktales Colum called 'reverie'.[27] The chilling effect in 'The Rose Tree' is enhanced by the fact that Pearse and Connolly speak in a jaunty ballad metre. It is as if they were ghosts speaking with a simplicity conferred by the grave. ('Easter 1916' likewise summons ghosts from the immediate past, especially in its opening lines.) The ballad form is suggested too in 'The O'Rahilly', a poem bidding us in traditional style to commemorate a man who died the death of a ballad hero.

Yeats had always been interested in folk forms, and had hoped to have some of his work become popular and folk currency. Easter 1916 offered him the opportunity to pursue this interest and to promote his insertion into tradition. He must have been aware of his competition. The Rising spawned many ballads and songs, though none to compare, as far as I know, with Ingram's 'Who Fears to Speak of Ninety-Eight', which was imitated after 1916 ('Who Fears to Speak of Easter Week?'). Georges-Denis Zimmermann writes: 'In 1916, the song tradition maintaining the cult of the dead patriots probably swelled the popular reactions to the sequel of the rising. Though the ballads were of a lesser quality than some poems on the same subject, they were soon copied by hand or typewritten and handed around.'[28] When Yeats was not absorbing the events of Easter Week into a philosophy that was constantly widening in a gyre its applicability, he was gesturing in his own peculiar way towards the collective and obligatory simplicity of song. Although the poems written after 'Easter 1916' are more evident essays in a kind of balladry, we can see the pull of legend and song in 'Easter 1916', especially in its concluding, memorable six lines which Yeats offers to us as a detachable sestet that invites itself to be chanted or sung. The lines have the authority of a poet laureate as well as of popular sentiment enshrined by tradition. They appear to resolve the doubts entertained in the preceding parts of the poem ('enough/To know they dreamed and are dead'), but it is debatable if when we set down the poem they resound more powerfully than the questions which seem in their urgency merely to postpone their own answers.

[1985]

NOTES

1. According to Rothenstein, quoted by Joseph Hone in *W. B. Yeats 1865–1939* (London: Macmillan 1965), p. 300.
2. Quoted in A. Norman Jeffares, *A Commentary on the Collected Poems of W. B. Yeats* (London: Macmillan 1968), pp. 225–6.
3. Quoted in Jeffares, p. 226.
4. Hone, p. 304.
5. See 'The Leaders' and 'Dublin Castle 1913' by Seumas O'Sullivan, 'Heroic Death, 1916' by Eva Gore-Booth and 'Sackville Street, 1917' by AE.
6. O'Sullivan's poems can be found in his *Collected Poems* (Dublin: The Orwell Press 1940).
7. O'Kelly's poem appeared in a slim anthology of poems about the Rising published in 1917 as *Aftermath of Easter Week* and edited by Father Paddy Browne.
8. The phrase occurs in 'The Veterans', a poem included in Roger McHugh's miscellany, *Dublin 1916* (London: Arlington Books 1966), p. 394. The phrase suggests yet another meaning for Yeats's stonelike hearts.
9. *Adventures of an Irish Bookman* (Dublin: Talbot Press 1952), p. 159.
10. Quoted by Jeffares, p. 225.
11. Quoted by Desmond Ryan in *The Rising: The Complete Story of Easter Week* (Dublin: Golden Eagle Books 1957), p. 263.
12. Introduction to *Poems of the Irish Revolutionary Brotherhood*, eds Padraic Colum and Edward J. O'Brien (Boston: Small, Maynard 1916), p. xxxv.
13. Readers should consult Joan Towey Mitchell's illuminating article, 'Yeats, Pearse, and Cuchulain', *Eire-Ireland* XI, No. 4 (1976), 51–65.
14. Quoted by Hone, p. 299.
15. Mitchell in her otherwise well-documented discussion of Pearse's concept of folly might have quoted the following lines from Pearse's play, *The Singer* (1915):

> *Diarmid*: We thought it a foolish thing for fourscore to go into battle against four thousand, or maybe forty thousand.
> *MacDara*: And so it is a foolish thing. Do you want us to be wise?

16. Mary Colum, *Life and the Dream* (Dublin: Dolmen 1966), p. 206. However, Yeats valued folly as early as *The Celtic Twilight* (1893) for in 'The Queen and the Fool' he wrote: 'fools may get . . . glimpses of much that sanctity finds at the end of its painful journey'.
17. Reprinted in McHugh, pp. 387–9.
18. Mitchell, pp. 61–2.
19. Francis Shaw SJ, 'The Canon of Irish History – A Challenge,' *Studies* LXI (Summer 1972), 137.
20. The phrase occurs in *The Legend of the Glaive*, quoted by G. F. Dalton, 'The Tradition of Blood Sacrifice to the Goddess Éire,' *Studies* LXIII (Winter 1974), 350. In 'The Municipal Gallery Revisited', Yeats uses a variant phrase when he describes the Ireland represented in the portraits as 'terrible and gay'.
21. By V. K. Menon, cited by Jeffares, p. 225.
22. Yeats was fond of the phrase 'all is changed' and its variants. In cumulation, they invest its occurrence in 'Easter 1916' from outside with negative import at odds

with the poem's declared sentiment. 'All's changed' in *On Baile's Strand* (1904) refers to the loss of heroism and sanctifying folly; in 'The Wild Swans at Coole' (1916), 'all's changed' refers to the poet's loss of heart; Robartes's 'all is changed' in 'The Phases of the Moon' refers to the coarseness the soul puts on after the full moon (though this is a cyclical state of affairs); while in 'Coole Park and Ballylee, 1931', 'all is changed' returns us to a loss of aristocratic heroism. (For the dating of these works I have consulted Jeffares's *Commentary* and *The Variorum Edition of the Poems of W. B. Yeats*, eds Peter Allt and Russell K. Alspach [New York: Macmillan 1957].)

23.   *Essays and Introductions* (New York: Collier 1977), p. 163. O'Casey may have had 'Easter 1916' in mind when in *Juno and the Paycock* he used the key phrase 'Hearts o' stone.'

24.   Cf. Plato in *Cratylus*: 'Heraclitus somewhere says that all things flow and nothing remains still, and comparing existing things to the flowing of a river, he says that you would not step twice into the same stream.'

25.   Introduction to *Poems of the Irish Revolutionary Brotherhood*, p. xxxi.

26.   According to Jeffares, the original refrain to 'The O'Rahilly' was not '*How goes the weather?*' but the more understandable '*Praise the proud*', Jeffares, p. 471.

27.   Padraic Colum, *Story Telling New and Old* (New York: Macmillan 1968), pp. 14–15.

28.   Georges-Denis Zimmermann, *Songs of Irish Rebellion: Political Street Ballads and Rebel Songs 1780–1900* (Hatsboro, Pa.: Folklore Associates 1967), p. 72. Zimmermann cites examples of songs about the Rising from *Songs and Poems of the Rebels Who Fought and Died for Ireland in Easter Week*, a volume that appeared in 1925. Elsewhere I have come across 'Easter Week (The Song of 1916)', 'Easter Monday', 'The Flag on the GPO' and 'The Heroes of Easter Week'.

9

THE LANDSCAPE OF THREE IRELANDS:
HEWITT, MURPHY AND MONTAGUE

'No man shall be without a patrimony'
John O'Dubhagain, fourteenth century

'if way to the Better there be, it exacts
a full look/at the Worst'
Thomas Hardy, 'In Tenebris'

Baffled, like all of us, by the divisiveness of Irish life, Seamus Heaney
has recently seized in desperate hope upon a remark by the Irish
historian J.C. Beckett: 'We have in Ireland an element of stability –
the land, and an element of instability – the people. It is to the stable
element that we must look for continuity.'[1] I am afraid, however, that
in literature – and I suspect in history (that is, in the re-telling of
events) – landscape is a cultural code that perpetuates instead of belying
the instabilities and ruptures Beckett the Protestant chronicler and
Heaney the Catholic writer would prefer to escape. This can be
demonstrated with reference to the work of three contemporary Irish
poets, John Montague, John Hewitt and Richard Murphy, all three
conscious of their representative status as, respectively, native, planter
and Anglo-Irishman. Some years ago, Hewitt and Montague jointly
gave in various parts of Northern Ireland a poetry reading entitled
'The Planter and the Gael'. In their poems the land is a sustained
metaphor for the cloven Ulster psyche. Naturally we would expect to
find different landscapes in Hewitt and Montague by mere virtue of
the fact that they hail from different Northern terrains. And there is to
be expected the appropriation by two (three, if we add Murphy)
unique and poetic sensibilities of landscapes that are, literally, public
domain. Yet what is most significant is the cultural shaping of these
poets' perception of the land by their sectarian membership and
experience. Out of the social geography of Ireland – the broad

historical tendency of Protestant and Catholic to inhabit different terrains and sites – has developed what we might call a sectarian landscape which these three poets have inherited and which is duly painted in their verse. Even their decision to explore uninherited landscape is, when it happens, telling. There is, it should be said, something which blurs as well as sharpening the dividing contours of this sectarian landscape, and that is the influence of those traditions of landscape poetry to which the three poets belong. If the reader is insufficiently relieved to hear this (and I do not have space here to discuss those traditions),[2] I may add that without exploring as honestly and sympathetically as possible the cultural differences between Protestant and Catholic, I believe we may never forge a genuine cultural synthesis in Ireland.

I

In 1972 many of John Montague's poems reappeared in *The Rough Field*, a long poem in ten sections and an epilogue and subtitled 'Ulster 1961–1971'.[3] It is Montague's most pondered poetic statement to date, a way of returning in poetic spirit to his native land at the hour of its agony. *The Rough Field* in fact appeared the year Montague returned from Paris to live again in Ireland; and the poem's slight narrative pretext is the poet's earlier return visit in 1961 to the townland where he was reared, the poem's first section being appropriately entitled 'Home Again'. Here, then, is the journey back from exile to the native fields, a journey rehearsed time and again in the Irish myths. More than this, it is a journey *west*, from Belfast through Lisburn, Lurgan and Portadown. These are 'solid British towns' that cause the poet to feel he is journeying through an alien latter-day Pale, beyond which lies safe native terrain. And of course Tyrone, the poet's destination, was beyond the Pale during the stormy career of Hugh O'Neill who is mourned in 'A Severed Head', the fourth section of *The Rough Field*. The journey through 'the Pale', therefore, is also a journey back in time, variously to the Flight of the Earls, the Ulster Plantation, the Siege of Derry, the Famine, the Home Rule Crisis and the Irish Civil War, parallels to all of which Montague seeks in contemporary Ulster on the justification that his return is 'To what seems still, though changing'.

Fittingly, the poet reaches home in darkness, for throughout *The Rough Field* Montague sees his mid-Tyrone landscape as either dark or pale.[4] It is a sombre and sepulchral landscape, incapable of stirring up Romantic recollections of childhood fellowship and delight:

> No Wordsworthian dream enchants me here
> With glint of glacial corrie, totemic mountain,
> But merging low hills and gravel streams,
> Oozy blackness of bog-banks, pale upland grass.

This upland landscape, compelling the returning poet to ascend, is not merely dark but rough, with its 'bleak moors of dream', bogland and 'small, whin-tough hills'. 'The Rough Field' is itself, as Montague tells us in a headnote, the English translation of the Gaelic name of his native townland: Garvaghey, *Garbh achaidh*. The Garvaghey terrain is seen as uncultivated, an image enacted, as it were, by the physical impression of Montague's entire poem, its own rough field of varying line-lengths, breakage into sections and insertions of historical documentation. *Garbh* also means 'turbulent' and therefore in the light of Tyrone's bloody history that Montague exploits seems doubly appropriate. Montague makes the landscape of Garvaghey embody as well as produce the turbulent Irish spirit (of 1969 as well as 1594) of which the poem as a whole is in sombre celebration. Yet *The Rough Field* is also an elegy, a recognition of how often the wild Irish spirit has been temporarily broken. The journey home is a reminder of that: the rough field is an insurrectionists' graveyard, vault as well as cradle of tribulation. Hence one of Montague's epigraphs, lines from the Afghan that provide yet another meaning for the rough field:

> I had never known sorrow,
> Now it is a field I have inherited, and I till it.

The Rough Field is not only a rightful claim of inheritance on the ancestral fields by a returning native son, but in addition an almost wilful tillage of an exhausted soil that has already yielded to Irish poets without respite the sorrows of the past. When as epigraph to 'The Bread God', Montague calls this Tyrone landscape 'the lean parish of my art', it is as if he acknowledges how hard the contemporary Irish poet must labour to husband the soil of grievance and past oppression: on occasions *The Rough Field* betrays, with its documentary aids to a flagging imagination, this sense of desperation and strain.

Readers who have read other Catholic writers from Ulster will not be surprised that Montague's Garvaghey is a landscape in decay. Decay originates in defeat of the Irish nationalist spirit at each of the climactic historical moments of Montague's journey back in time. Behind therefore the poet's description of the impoverished landscape he encounters in the 1960s lies the notion that he returns at a time when the nationalist spirit is again under siege. Montague's Tyrone landscape is a cacography of loss, its untidy topography – and typography – spelling out the remnants of a mislaid, and an overlaid, culture. Most conspicuous by their absence are the people themselves:

> Like shards
> Of a lost culture, the slopes
> Are strewn with cabins, deserted
> In my lifetime.

And the lost language: in 'A Severed Head', the poet recalls that his grandfather had as a child the English tongue forcibly grafted on to his native Irish, with the result that his grandson's speech 'stumbles over lost/syllables of an old order'. He also recalls poignantly the last Gaelic speaker in the parish pathetically deluding himself that school Irish would keep the language alive. It is not, then, that the landscape alone has changed by having its nativeness overgrown, but that the Irish people, for whom the landscape has become only partially legible, have themselves changed:

> The whole landscape a manuscript
> We had lost the skill to read,
> A part of our past disinherited;
> But fumbled, like a blind man,
> Along the fingertips of instinct.

And along with the lost language and lost population, the lost leadership forever symbolized in the fate of the O'Neills – the severed head of Irish kingship and sovereignty (tongue and all) separated from the peasant body that was reduced to that impotent lament imaged in 'Patriotic Suite' as 'A weaving/melancholy, like a bird crossing/ moorland . . . lost cry/of the yellow bittern!' *The Rough Field* is on one level that hopeless cry of the peasantry once more.[5] In one moment of bitter defeat, Montague endorses his father's exile: 'you were right to choose a Brooklyn slum/rather than a half-life in this/by-passed and dying place'.

Montague's landscape of loss and decay has a certain factual justification. Garvaghey is inconveniently uphill from the fertile Clogher valley which in turn is even called by one geographer 'one of the many Irish backwaters, entirely agricultural and not unprosperous but off all the main routes'.[6] But equally factual is the evidence in Montague's townland of what some would call progress; when the poet ascends the mountain through ancestral fields he observes of one farmhouse:

> Our farmhands
> Lived there, wife and children
> In twin white-washed cells,
> An iron roof burning in summer.
> Now there is a kitchen extension
> With radio aerial, rough outhouses
> For coal and tractor.

Are not things then getting better? Does the poet not also come upon an unfinished dancehall, latest manifestation of the burgeoning Irish entertainment industry that supports (as the poet tells us in a documentary headnote) a hundred thousand people? But no, the poet will have no truck with an industry that is, as he sees it, 'built/on loneliness'. But if not that industry, what of others? As though in answer, Montague in 'Hymn to the New Omagh Road' launches a bitter satiric attack on a new motorway running through his townland. The poet believes I misread here, that I fail to see the humour of this section (and it *is* grimly humorous, I admit) or its suggestion of what he describes to me as 'an elegiac cheer'. Still, it is difficult not to detect in *The Rough Field* a Catholic cultural dilemma in Ulster. The Ulster Catholic writer has lived for so long with the imagery of land-decay and land-loss that he has become addicted to it; and so when he encounters evidence of that reversal of decay which his verse has implicitly called for, he baulks at it. There are other reasons for his baulking. What he wants often seems not to be progress, a forward-looking reversal of decay through agricultural improvement, but rather a return, the recovery of a politico-spiritual impossibility – a mythic landscape of beauty and plenitude that is pre-Partition, pre-Civil War, pre-Famine, pre-Plantation and pre-Tudor. Such a landscape is cherished the more because it is impossible of realization. How could any improvement by mere agriculture hope to fulfill such an expectation? Hence the stylistic importance of bathos and the emotional importance of disillusionment in *The Rough Field*. Moreover, one suspects that Montague finds agricultural and industrial progress alien and unwelcome in part because it is Protestant-inspired. But if this is the case, might not a resolution of his dilemma be to turn to the South of Ireland for evidence of national fulfilment without submission to the planter mentality and with the dream of pure nationalism still realizable? True, Montague in 'Patriotic Suite' notes tartly from the evidence at a Fleadh Ceoil in Mullingar that

> Puritan Ireland's dead and gone,
> A myth of O'Connor and O'Faolain

which suggests a degree of emancipation. But he also notes in Southern schoolrooms 'the gloomy images of a provincial catholicism' and, on a train-ride from Belfast to Dublin, 'row after row of council cottages' with 'the wild flap/Of laundry in a thousand backyards'. Clearly the revolutionary ideal has he believes shrunk into a grocer's republic with censorship and other symptoms of inwardness. Montague observes that the visitor to Coole Park – symbol of a high order presumably betrayed like its predecessors – will find a lake 'bereft of swans' and 'high wire/to protect the famous beech-tree/ from raw initials'. The 'Pale' can at this point in the poem be seen as a psychic habitat occupied just as firmly by Southern politicians and industrialists as by planters and Tudor colonialists. Like the snow in James Joyce's 'The Dead', reasons for disillusionment are general all over Ireland.

In 'Driving South: An Epilogue', Montague does belatedly allow, contrasting contemporary rural progress with past rural poverty, that

> Only a sentimentalist would wish
> to see such degradation again

but, yet, he insists, 'something mourns'. It is

> a world where action had been wrung
> through painstaking years to ritual.

Here is something visible and real, genuinely endangered by progress, and which is deserving of Montague's powers of bitter lament. It is now the poet too fleetingly but movingly transcends his sectarian landscape by mourning a ritual that was not only Catholic ('when the priest blessed/the green tipped corn') but Protestant ('or Protestant/ lugged pale turnip, swollen marrow/to robe the kirk for Thanksgiving'). Montague invokes at the end of *The Rough Field* Goldsmith's Auburn in lamenting

                    Our finally lost dream of man at home
                    in a rural setting!

(Goldsmith: 'Even now, methinks, as pondering here I stand,/I see the rural virtues leave the land.') The dream's loss is the more deeply felt, perhaps, by the returning native son. The exile's longing for home and his inability truly to come home is an old Irish theme, and we find it in as early a work as the seventh-century *Voyage of Bran*. It reappears both in *The Deserted Village* ('I still had hopes, my long vexations past,/Here to return – and die at home at last.') and in *The Rough Field* ('with all my circling a failure to return'). Like *The Deserted Village*, *The Rough Field* depicts a fallen rural paradise victimized by commerce and wealth and decayed into overgrowth and useless fertility. But the difference is that the ritual, folk belief and sense of community Montague mourns seem ironically dependent upon, even indistinguishable from, the darkness, decay and roughness of the landscape that he wants at the same time to use in indicting those who wish to alter the landscape in the name of progress. For if on the one hand Montague sees the rough field as the result of his ancestors' oppression and victimization (the roughness of bad land and poverty-enforced neglect), on the other hand he sees it as the repository of ritual and community (the roughness of indigenous folk-spirit) that are being destroyed by latter-day oppression – industry and improvement. While this may look like the poet's having it both ways, the rough field is a symbol sufficiently rich to absorb ambiguity and contradiction. And so at the same time as he laments the decline in folkways, Montague expresses fear of the folk-spirit, witness his excellent 'Like Dolmens round my Childhood, the Old People', and seems relieved when dark childhood dreams dissipate in manhood, which is also the metamorphosis of dream into myth ('the dark permanence of ancient forms'). Thus *The Rough Field* demystifies as well as mythicizes: a figure who might have stepped out of 'Like Dolmens', the *Cailleach* who terrified the poet when he was young, is seen at the close of *The Rough Field*, when the poet visits her years later at her decayed cottage, as pathetically reduced to 'a human being/merely, hurt by event'. The choice it seems is between dark dreams, impersonal mythology and shrunken reality.

In 'A New Siege' Montague's central site and symbol is expanded into near-mythic proportion as the poet senses 'the rough field/of the universe/growing, changing/a net of energies/crossing patterns/

weaving towards/a new order/a new anarchy/always different/ always the same'. But in *The Rough Field* it is violence, defeat, darkness and grievance that are emphasized. I confess to finding the landscape of the poem too exclusively brooding and insufficiently celebrated, and the poem's message concerning the state of the land today needlessly pessimistic. Be that as it may, *The Rough Field* is undoubtedly a powerful and tenebrous work, and in it an entire and venerable poetic tradition – one typified by its version of the sectarian landscape – is brought close to fulfilment. That the poem can be comfortably made to stand in such a representative and model role is a measure of its achievement.

II

John Hewitt's poetic locales lie east of Montague's hilly and Catholic Tyrone, in the green Glens of Antrim and the fertile corridor of the Lagan valley. They are largely Protestant locales, lying on a clear day in view of the mainland that peopled them, though providing, in the Antrim moors and glens, opportunities for the planter poet to ascend into the older native culture. Unlike Montague, Hewitt is a city man (from Belfast); the countryside, however, is a mere stroll away for him, and each stroll is a small trip back in time. There is no dramatic use of the journey in his work; the equivalent in Hewitt of Montague's urgent and nervous journey *through* the planter Pale is the brief and scrupulously observed country walk, the carefully planned expedition *from* the planter Pale. Hence there is in Hewitt's poetry no pungent or dramatic sense of exile (even though he lived out of Ireland for a longer uninterrupted period than Montague), but rather a sense of continuous emotional traffic with his native island. Hence too there is no great sense of personal nostalgia deepened by time, none of Montague's preoccupation for example with childhood. In 'Conacre' Hewitt tries to discover

> why a man,
> townbred and timid, should attain to peace
> with outworn themes and rustic images,[7]

ignoring the progressive clamour of his native Belfast, with its chimneys, ships, trains and resounding flagged streets. Though the real answer is obscure, he knows the answers that are false:

> It is not that like Goldsmith I recall
> some shabby Auburn with a crumbling wall
> seen through the sparkling lens of exile grief
> that gilds the lily of a child's belief.

That Montague should associate himself with, and Hewitt dissociate himself from, Goldsmith is ironic since in technique and world-view Hewitt is closer to Goldsmith than he is to Montague. Unlike Goldsmith, Hewitt in 'Conacre' may have no illusions about country people ('I know my farmer and my farmer's wife,/the squalid focus of their huxter life'), but he does have an eighteenth-century belief in the rural improvement to which Montague in *The Rough Field* pays mere lip-service.[8] He celebrates a farmer who 'turns no back on progress' and whose rural collectivist philosophy (to which Hewitt himself undogmatically subscribes) yet reminds one of those dreams of rural improvement in English landscape poetry of the eighteenth century:

> dreaming still
> of the broad tractors sweeping up the hill,
> and the great binder worked by equal men
> lifting its swathes of fat collective grain.

Hewitt's avowed and somewhat unfashionable 'thirties socialism seems less important to me than his identity as a planter and city-dweller. Hewitt writes as a planter for whom progress is bite and sup, and as a city-dweller whose timeless vision of the countryside (not located like Montague's before some mythicized historical trauma), whatever happens on the land, cannot be fundamentally altered.

This is not to say that Hewitt's landscape is unrealistic, that it is cold pastoral. If it is rich, various and chromatic, this is in part because of the greater actual fertility and variety of the Antrim glens and Lagan valley over Montague's Tyrone. But it is also in part a matter of poetic vision shaped by cultural experience. Montague's dark and pale landscape is like a negative, undeveloped because the aggrieved poet feels incapable of merely celebrating the beauty of the land but must always freight it with melancholy cultural meanings. In compensation, Montague's presentation of the land is more tactile and visceral than Hewitt's, as though mere visual and aesthetic appreciation were a denial of past oppressions, were somehow *of the Pale*. Hewitt's poetry for its part has at its best a painterly quality which does suggest a certain privileged detachment and a leisurely capacity for withdrawing from history in order to contemplate the land's beauty. We find this quality particularly in *The Day of the Corncrake* (1969), poems that celebrate the Glens of Antrim. There, as in the Lagan valley, is a leaved and berried landscape which really exists and is no picturesque fantasy. Yet even in the glen poems, fertility never runs riot but has been harnessed by generations of planters. The valleys and slopes of the glens are, Hewitt tells us in 'Sunset Over Glenaan',

> a rich country mastered long ago
> by stubborn farmers from across the sea,
> whose minds and hands were rich in husbandry.

But the planters have sacrificed spiritual intimacy with the land, set as they are in drilling

> the very soil
> into a dulled prosperity that year
> by reckoned year continues so.

The tamed landscape of Hewitt's planter localities, so different from Montague's rough field, is paralleled by the self-imposed restraints on Hewitt's own subject-matter and style. Visually his lines are tidy furrows across neat fields of poems; aurally his iambic metres have the regularity of expert but easy ploughing and his rhymes the limiting effect of paling. Stylistically he never and thematically he rarely strikes out into rough terrain and this leads ironically to a certain dulled prosperity of verse. On the other hand, it also promotes careful craftsmanship and lack of arrogance: Hewitt like a good husbandman is always conscious of 'the utmost limits of [his] chosen ground', which in 'Sunset Over Glenaan' happen appropriately to be an array of dark and native peaks.

Hewitt is aware of his alien and planter heritage, yet equally aware that since birthplace and habitation define allegiance as much as dubious ancestry, he is at the same time Irish. Hewitt's Irishness, therefore, is problematical. But then, less obviously, so is Montague's: he was born in Brooklyn; the poet is no longer a practising Catholic, crossing himself 'from rusty habit' when sensing in Paris the death of his grandmother in Tyrone; there have been the years of exile; his name, *Montague*, is for the Ulster Protestant the very synonym of Catholic, yet is I believe the anglicization of an anglicization, MacTeige (Gaelic, *Mac Taidhg*). The difference is that Hewitt as a planter cannot fall back on race or his religion in the cradle to define his Irishness and so (like Beckett and Heaney) turns to the landscape that seems on occasions to join the sects. In 'The Frontier' the speaker and his friends pass from one jurisdiction to another, 'expect new postage stamps, new prices, manifestoes,/and brace ourselves for the change. But the landscape does not alter;/we had already entered these mountains an hour ago.' Yet, of course, the sectarian landscape remains and though it is part of the fund of folk-mythology upon which Ulster poets and novelists draw, it has some basis in fact.[9] In Hewitt's Antrim glens, the fertile land tilled by Catholics is a 'rim of arable' topographically hemmed around by hill and sea. But the hills and sea are not alien to the Catholics; rather they represent a spiritual hinterland of ancient memories of freedom and passion. Paradoxically it is the planter, to whom the hills *are* alien, who is marooned in his more extensive sea of fertility: the colonizer is trapped within his own psychic stockade.

To his credit, Hewitt has ventured out of the stockade into unsurveyed territory where planter writ does not run, even though he fears the vainer native creed and the violence of native lineage. Hewitt's poems are full of small expeditions of ascent to the hill-farms of Antrim Catholics whose culture is not lost for him, at least in the 1940s, but rather living, mysterious and fascinating. 'The Hill-Farm' records how the poet found himself one night outside a Catholic cottage, overheard the family at their rosary, and felt excluded, not only from Irish Catholicism but from Irishness itself. Sixteen years later Seamus Heaney wrote the same poem from the point of view of one of the Catholic children at prayer and published it as 'The Other Side' in *Wintering Out*.[10]

III

Only sparingly does John Montague recognize his Plantation patrimony of which John Hewitt and his planted landscape are inextricably a part. He agrees this is so, but directs me to 'The Errigal Road' in *A Slow Dance* (1975), a fine but lonely poem. Hewitt for his part has tried to penetrate the mystery of his own Irishness but in a way that constitutes a Protestant formula and motif. While no other Irish poets have fashioned the intervening terrain so comprehensively or so readably, it will be left to other poets to render imaginable the insights that lie the far side of the sectarian landscape. An obvious candidate for contemplation is Richard Murphy, who is known – a hopeful sign – as 'a poet of two traditions'.[11]

Murphy's first tradition is that of the Anglo-Irish. We find in his poetry the topography of Big House, demesne and, beyond (vaulting the intervening reality of native Ireland), of empire. This Ascendancy setting is a social recoil from the rough field ('Quiet music and claret cups,/Forty acres of green crops')[12] or else a military sortie into it for the purposes of bringing the mere Irish to heel. Circumscribed in space, it proved also to be so in time. Unlike Yeats, Murphy was born too late (1927) to give us anything but glimpses of the floruit of the gentry. By the time of his christening, the 'garrison world' has bred eccentricity and a symbolic deafness and, in 'The Woman of the House', senility and madness. The gardens have become overgrown, a Protestant motif in Murphy and other Irish writers suggesting reversion, disorder and fertile decay.[13]

Murphy participates in the psychic and racial decline of the Anglo-Irish (swifter once under way than the chronic diaspora of the native Irish that appals Montague); he is like aftergrass to the Ascendancy's spent harvest. Murphy shares with Montague, then, a patrimony of scatter and decay at the hands of modernization (vividly imaged in the chainsaws that level the trees in Murphy's demesnes) and of historical reversal that Hewitt's settlers – perhaps because they planted and did not merely reap – have not suffered. In 'Auction' and other poems, the world of the Ascendancy is finally disassembled and offered for sale. But the poet needs no money to buy the gazebos, the yew-hedges, the sacked gardeners. It is Murphy who is in possession of his people's past, not the people themselves. He would without doubt subscribe to Montague's claim that it is the people 'who are being taken away from what they had, and it is I who am the possessor, and with the older people, the guardian, of what had been there'.[14] At the close of *The Rough Field*, Montague carries with him into renewed exile as cargo and for safekeeping (an exile in time as much as of place) the past, not in its original historical order but in the order (at once found, remembered, even misunderstood, and artistically shaped) that is the poem itself. Murphy like Montague is committing in his poetry an act of salvage even when, indeed because, the past is perceived as irreversibly fragmented and irretrievably submerged.

Yet more obviously for Murphy than for Montague, the inherited past, in Murphy's case Anglo-Irishry, is insufficient personally and poetically: little wonder, since it was insufficient even for Yeats who dreamed its Georgian bloom. Like his great predecessor but with a rather stronger racial claim,[15] Murphy has availed himself of another tradition, crisply versing the disparity between the two in 'The Woman of the House', a poem in memory of his grandmother who inhabited a Big House in the west of Ireland:

> The bards in their beds once beat out ballads
> Under leaky thatch listening to sea-birds,
> But she in the long ascendancy of rain
> Served biscuits on a tray with ginger wine.

That disparity is offered the metaphor of landscape in Murphy's long poem *The Battle of Aughrim* (1968), in which two armies, two cultures confront one another:

> Deep red bog divided
> Aughrim, the horse's ridge
> Of garland hedgerows and the summer dance,
> Ireland's defence
> From the colonist's advance:
> Twenty thousand soldiers on each side,
> Between them a morass
> Of godly bigotry and pride of race,
> With a causeway two abreast could cross.

It was the Battle of Aughrim in 1691 that signalled the defeat of one of two cultures contending for primacy and the virtual end of the Gaelic order. Since then, the Gaelic order has been betrayed, it would seem, by its own posterity which decreed that a Celtic cross on the battlefield commemorate 'no battle/But someone killed in a car, Minister of Agriculture'. Insult, as it were, added to injury. But Murphy seems less disapproving of modernization than Montague, possibly because of his residual Protestantism. In both poets, in any case, betrayal is countered by history's custom of repetition. 'The past is happening today,' writes Murphy in 1968 at the end of the first section of *The Battle of Aughrim*; writing in 1970 during the early days of the present Ulster Troubles, Montague laments towards the close of *The Rough Field*: 'Once again, it happens.'[16]

As a venue of defeat, the historic landscape of *The Battle of Aughrim* is not unlike Montague's rough field; each is a battlefield of cultures. But Murphy has also gone west (farther afield than Montague and even beyond mainland Galway where in fact Murphy was born) to find the geographic and psychic origins and vestiges of his adopted tradition. Confronted by the decay of two lordly cultures, the Gaelic and the Anglo-Irish, Murphy has sought the primitive fountainhead of one while being content to elegize the other. Like Synge and other Protestant Revivalists, he has pursued a consolation of western islands: Omey, Inishbofin, Clare, High. Out west is the far edge of the rough field and when he stands on it, Murphy faces a task no different from that which faced St Fechin on Omey Island when he built his church: in the words of Murphy's poem, 'Walking on Sunday' (from *High Island*, 1974), how to tune cacophony 'to make/Harmony in this choir'. Murphy is a man who apparently feels Catholic and Protestant, Irish and Anglo-Irish (his very name a racial descant), but because the strands of his patrimony are separable, his job, wherever he is in Ireland, is 'to make it integral'. *The Battle of Aughrim*, with its mixed choir of voices, is Murphy's most successful attempt at harmony as far as a sustained yet artistically contained effort is concerned. The poet had forebears on both sides at Aughrim, and so that decisive fork in Irish history that was the Williamite campaign was also a decisive fork in Murphy's ancestry and was the origin of the Southern Irish equivalent of the dissociation of sensibility, the Northern Irish equivalent of which we have already met in Hewitt and Montague. Yet one feels that this long poem, though it asks to be compared with *The Rough Field* (even if it cannot quite bear the comparison) is insufficient for Murphy in itself since it seeks to reharmonize his historic and not his everyday existence. He has sought the prehistoric site of his psychic harmony in the west and there decided 'to make it integral'. The phrase ends 'Little Hunger' from *High Island*, a poem that tells of his plans to build a granite house in the west, using pink stone from native cabins 'Hollowed with exility', employing the methods of one culture on the materials of another to create an inhabitable space and shelter.

Aughrim is the rough field in time, in the past. In the far west is the rough field in space, now. Murphy's journey there, psychic as well as physical, is best commemorated in 'Sailing to an Island' (in the volume of the same title, 1963) and is a more startling version of Hewitt's upland walks. It is the conscious Protestant reversion to an honorary native Irishness and it is appropriately hazardous, there being no convenient causeway between these two cultures. His journey is 'Across the shelved Atlantic groundswell', past 'crags purpled by legend', an acropolis of cormorants. Murphy has a Syngean fascination with drowning, and its symbolic significance seems clear: in reversion is the threat of self-oblivion; his object is to make contact with 'the other side', sea-changed and newly selved, yet recognizable, harboured. 'The other side' is the distant safe shore but also, in Heaney's (that is to say, the Ulster) phrase, members of the other tradition, in this case a reception committee of courteous fishermen. 'Here is a bed,' the tired and grateful pilgrim ends 'Sailing to an Island', thinking as well perhaps of the poetic seed-bed the west might become, and has indeed become for Murphy. The boat, then, is Murphy's symbol of two-way passage between one tradition and another, of the precarious safety which one can at best ensure during such passage, of continuity and at the same time threshold.

'Through our inheritance all things have come,' we are told in 'The Woman of the House', but inheritance is a personal and active as well as passive and genealogical transaction. The poet must buy in some sense the auctioned remnants of Ascendancy culture. Likewise, if he would claim the other tradition – a tradition equally in a state of disintegrity – he must move with even greater effort into possession of it, to be able to answer the question 'Who owns the land?' (a question that opens *The Battle of Aughrim*) with an unequivocal 'I do.' (He will not admit the possibility that joining the two traditions in this way is either a new psychic colonialism or a form of psychic treason. Yet the traitor looms so large in *The Battle of Aughrim* that one senses an over-compensation. One recalls, too, Hewitt's worry that his non-sectarianism is not what it appears to be: 'Maybe, at some dark level, grown aware/Of our old load of guilt, I shrink afraid, /And seek the false truce of a renegade.' There seems to be no Catholic equivalent of this Protestant anxiety, no doubt because Catholics cannot 'revert', and only a scant few ever 'turn', i.e. convert to Protestantism or adopt the planter mentality.) Whereas Hewitt shies away from claiming imaginative possession of the rough field, and whereas Montague's repossession of it is entirely imaginative, enjoyed in exile, Murphy claims possession of the west partly by living and building there. The Galway fishing-boat he bought is his chief symbol of selfless appropriation and the harmonizing of two traditions. In 'The Last Galway Hooker' (from *Sailing to an Island*), we are given this boat's biography – its chequered ownership by fisherman, priest and lobsterman; when he bought it, the poet 'chose to renew her, to rebuild, to prolong/For a while the spliced yards of yesterday'. The Protestant poet has taken the opportunity of the disrepair of the native tradition, as it were, to insinuate himself by contribution into the tradition (as Yeats sought to do before him), altering to some degree that tradition, be it of boatmanship, house-building or poetry.

By trying to refit the native tradition, Murphy has striven to produce a new and third integrity.

Murphy is aware of the difficulties, of the perils of extremes, domination or surrender. His background bespeaks order, for the Anglo-Irish were dominant only as long as their organization was superior to that of the Irish. Faced with the wild or primitive, his instinct is to tame or educate, and he has devoted several poems to the danger in this. The young feral goat taken by the poet from her treeless hills above Glencolumbkille in 'Care' dies when her atrophied instinct allows her to eat poisonous foliage; she is killed by misguided charity and domestication. The young illiterate given instruction by the poet in 'The Reading Lesson' is more recalcitrant:

> A neighbour chuckles. 'You can never tame
> The wild-duck: when his wings grow, he'll fly off.

But Ludwig Wittgenstein, whose stay in Rosroe, Connemara in 1949 is fancifully recounted in 'The Philosopher and the Birds', *does* tame the wild birds in Murphy's poem. These are the wild birds of rampant metaphysics and illogic, but the wild birds too of an untamed Irish landscape. When Wittgenstein leaves, however, hordes of village cats massacre the birds the philosopher tames, a revenge against order that seems under the circumstances to be aboriginally Irish. Theodore Roethke visited Murphy on Inishbofin in 1960 and is recalled in one of Murphy's best poems, 'The Poet on the Island'. Unlike the young illiterate, the kid, and the wild birds of Rosroe, the American poet actually wants to be relaxed and tamed by the islanders: 'To be loved by the people, he, a stranger, hummed//In the herring-store on Sunday crammed with drunks/Ballads of bawdry with a speakeasy stress.' But this in an already unstable man is a kindly delusion, and his mind so to speak goes feral, disordered under the influence of this savage rock:

> He'd burst the lyric barrier: logic ended.
> Doctors were called, and he agreed to sail.

Murphy seeks in theme more than in form that precarious balance between the feral and the tame. In the short poems I have just mentioned, a balance is only briefly struck before being lost, the poems eloquently mourning the loss. Perhaps it is necessary that the poet fail in some sense and at some stage to make it integral that he might succeed as a poet. The poem may flourish in what it bemoans (and perhaps wrongly bemoans). And Roethke, after all, goes mad by following his poetic impulses to their (alas, illogical) conclusion by breaking the lyric barrier, as a pilot, though he incurs no such penalty, breaks the sound barrier. Like Roethke, and Synge before him, Murphy has found on islands the irreconcilable loneliness of existence. In 'Seals at High Island', 'Nocturne', 'Stormpetrel', 'High Island', Murphy achieves a lyricism that precedes and succeeds alphabets and order, that world 'beyond omega shade' and 'before alpha' that haunted his Wittgenstein. In flight from an exclusive Anglo-Irishness, Murphy has discovered its polar opposite, a landscape of rock, darkness, sea, burrow. Murphy, who began with a sense of his own incongruity in Ireland, has reached a profounder incongruity. Perhaps this was in the cards. Wittgenstein at Rosroe, Roethke on Inishbofin – are these not anomalous and lonely figures? Has not Murphy himself been Roethke all along, a stranger in the west humming vainly to be loved by the people?

The difficulty is epic as well as lyrical. Perhaps a sustained and worthy balance is impossible between competing cultural traditions which vigorously demand separate identities, prize contradictory aspects of life, and have very different archetypal landscapes. Hewitt's synthesis fails, in any case, I think, because it is not a true balance; it is a rather intellectual and domesticating concept of *concordia discors* that is inherited from the topographical poets ('where order in variety we see', as Sir John Denham put it in *Cooper's Hill*) and is entirely Protestant and English. If Murphy succeeds better, in *The Battle of Aughrim*, for example, this would only make him a superior poet to Hewitt and to Montague (who does not tackle head-on the problem of reconciliation) were all else equal. Besides, to be a poet of two cultural traditions may be less difficult if one of the two traditions – in this case that of the Ascendancy – is no longer viable. Memories can be juxtaposed with the present in hopes of avoiding that clash between countryman and aristocrat whom Yeats fondly believed he could unite. Indeed, the radical dissimilarity between the Anglo-Irish and native traditions makes their union more speciously attractive and febrile. Consider the more genuine and pressing difficulty of reconciling the middle classes with the 'peasantry', or dissenters with Catholics. From the Revival onwards, the decline of the Anglo-Irish has provoked among their writers a somewhat programmatic flight into violent antithesis in hopes of a union, a headlong rush into the arms of the elemental west in order to escape the ogres of history and class and the guilt they engender.

A fusion of traditions and cultures has eluded all three poets, then. It might be possible to judge this a kind of success, of course, and to recall Hugh MacDiarmid's contempt for fusion and the composite. The Scottish poet cherished what G. Gregory Smith called the 'Caledonian antisyzygy', and it would be easy to posit its Hibernian equivalent, a creative state of mind ultimately at home with contrast, contradiction and inconsistency, though as Smith reminds us, as if inverting the English Denham, 'disorderly order is order after all'.[17] But the synthesis we might choose to perceive in Irish poetry and the culture it projects, whose chief metaphor for us has been the land (and it was a 'synthesis of the potential contributions of the various elements' in a culture that MacDiarmid desired to see),[18] cannot avoid the divisiveness of Irish life, that often murderous divisiveness that drives the best minds in Ireland to despair. We will have basis for hope only when the synthesis can be seen working in individuals, as Mac-Diarmid, rightly or wrongly, saw it working in himself. In the meantime, there is rich consolation. Among other things, there is the peculiarly vivid way in which we can inhabit, in the poetry of Hewitt, Murphy and Montague, the warring topographies of the Irish imagination, that landscape in whose parts all of us in Ireland at times find ourselves strangers and afraid.

[1975/85]

NOTES

1. Quoted by Seamus Heaney in *Preoccupations* (London: Faber 1980), p. 149.

2. For Montague and Hewitt, I discuss these traditions in 'The Landscape of Planter and Gael in the Poetry of John Hewitt and John Montague', *The Canadian Journal of Irish Studies*, Vol. 1, No. 2 (November 1975), 17–33.

3. John Montague, *The Rough Field* (Dublin: Dolmen 1972). I have used the 1974 second edition. *The Rough Field* includes poems from *The Planter and the Gael*, *Poisoned Lands* (1961), *A Chosen Light* (1967), and *Tides* (1970), together with *Patriotic Suite* (1966), *Home Again* (1967), *Hymn to the New Omagh Road* (1968), *The Bread God* (1968) and *A New Siege* (1970) in their entirety.

4. The poet has countered in a letter to me (Easter Tuesday, 1976) that Hardy's adjectives would make a gloomier list than his; he reminds me I have overlooked his descriptions of flowers in 'The Source', part of 'A Good Night', the sixth section of *The Rough Field*.

5. Montague spent a year in Berkeley and there attended the first or second reading of *Howl*. *The Rough Field* we might regard, *mutatis mutandis*, as an Ulster Catholic equivalent of Ginsberg's poem. See an interview with Montague entitled 'Global Regionalism' in *The Literary Review*, Vol. XXII, No. 2 (1979), 157.

6. T.W. Freeman, *Ireland: A General and Regional Geography* (London: Methuen 1972), p. 495.

7. This poem and other Hewitt poems I quote from appear in his *Collected Poems 1932–67* (London: MacGibbon and Kee 1968). A few, however, appear only in *The Day of the Corncrake* (Belfast: Glens of Antrim Historical Society 1969).

8. I discuss Hewitt's relation to Augustan poetry in the *CJIS* article I have already cited.

9. For fact, consult Rosemary Harris, *Prejudice and Tolerance in Ulster* (Manchester: Manchester University Press 1972). For fiction, consult my own *Forces and Themes in Ulster Fiction* (Dublin: Gill and Macmillan 1974).

10. That is, sixteen years after the appearance of *The Day of the Corncrake* in which 'The Hill-Farm' was collected. *Wintering Out* was published by Faber in 1972.

11. The phrase is Maurice Harmon's in his Editor's Preface to *Richard Murphy: Poet of Two Traditions* (Portmarnock: Wolfhound Press 1978).

12. The lines are from 'The Woman of the House' in Murphy's *Selected Poems* (London: Faber 1979), p. 20. The poems I discuss and quote from appear in *Selected Poems* unless, as indicated, they appear in *Sailing to an Island* (London: Faber 1963), *The Battle of Aughrim* (*and The God Who Eats Corn*) (London: Faber 1968) or *High Island* (London: Faber 1974).

13. See my account of the motif in Ulster Protestant fiction writers in *Forces and Themes in Ulster Fiction*.

14. 'Global Regionalism' in *The Literary Review*, p. 165.

15. See Harmon's Introduction to *Richard Murphy: Poet of Two Traditions* entitled 'The Poet and his Background' and Harmon's 'Biographical Note on Richard Murphy' in the same volume.

16. From 'A New Siege', the ninth section of *The Rough Field* published two years before the assembled long poem.

17. Quoted by Hugh MacDiarmid in 'The Caledonian Antisyzygy and the Gaelic Idea' in *Selected Essays of Hugh MacDiarmid*, ed. Duncan Glen (London: Jonathan Cape 1969), p. 58. See also MacDiarmid's poem, 'The Caledonian Antisyzygy' in *Complete Poems 1920–1976* (London: Martin Brian and O'Keeffe 1978), p. 1052.

18. *Selected Essays of Hugh MacDiarmid*, p. 62.

10

HEANEY'S REDRESS

CONSTITUTING POETRY

'Seamus Heaney might well become the best Irish poet since Yeats'. A year after I wrote that, Robert Lowell decided the subjunctive could be dispensed with when,verbatim, he attributed *North* (1975) to 'the best Irish poet since W. B. Yeats'. Mention of Yeats in these circumstances unavoidably implied in Heaney a comparable gravity of *oeuvre*, since it is difficult to think of Yeats without thinking of the weight and dimensions of his body of work. It was, of course, an accumulation of arresting individual poems that won Heaney's early reputation, and they were the irrigating intervention in the British poetry scene: with *Wintering Out* (1972), Heaney released a flow of talent in others with his homely wheatstraw lapped round the frozen pumps of hinterland hippocrenes. But now it is the *tide* of his work that commands respect and influences poetry, inside and outside Britain, through elements that are broader and deeper than style. The Yeats comparison is at once more justified than in 1974, and less relevant to Heaney's increasing autonomy.

It is a small measure of the continuity of Heaney's poetry, of the tenaciousness of its preoccupations, that much of what I wrote in 'The Poetry of Seamus Heaney' throws modest light on what Heaney has published since *Wintering Out*. The tenacious and indeflectible were in evidence even then, so that by now there is a faint suggestion of inexorability or manifest destiny, in the trajectory not just of the work but also of its reception and reputation. If in 1974 my impression was of an apprentice hastening to patent a style, my impression today is of a poet who has patiently strengthened and clarified his 'technique', which in a lecture delivered in the same year he said involves 'not only a poet's way with words, his management of metre, rhythm and verbal texture', but also 'his stance towards life, a definition of his own reality'. In an essay the following year, Heaney attributed the definition to Patrick Kavanagh who, always an acknowledged inspiration and influence, has become, in Heaney's 1985 re-evaluation of him, one of ten or a dozen poets whom he holds up to us. 'A spiritual quality, a condition of mind, or an ability to invoke a particular condition of mind . . . a method of getting at life'. These are Kavanagh's words, applicable to a later poet who has been single-mindedly defining his own reality volume by volume, and while doing so, developing by dynamic repetition and advance a formidable fiction or mythography that invites us to engage with it on its own terms.

There are stances Heaney does not adopt (a radical scepticism, a basic sense of absurdity, a readiness of wit) and major forms of life he doesn't 'get at' (the modern experience of the city, for example); still, his poetic experience is an enviable globe and he employs his criticism in its making. The essays in *Preoccupations* (1980) and *The Government of the Tongue* (1988) perform less to illuminate a variety of writers, though they do this impressively, than to verify 'the reality of poetry in the world', and the writers are chosen, increasingly as the criticism proceeds, for their ability to do this. His use of the word 'poetry' is honorific to the highest degree, and the essays exist also to fortify Heaney's own claim to the name 'poet'. 'As is so often the case when a poet is diagnosing the condition of another poet', he remarks in one essay, 'Hopkins is here offering us something of a self-portrait'. The idea invites itself that the running exemplars (Kavanagh, Yeats, Wordsworth, Lowell, Mandelstam and the others) are tendered partly as inducements to join Heaney in celebrating and, if we are poets, emulating them, but partly to draw attention tactfully to the exemplary nature of Heaney's own project. In their simultaneous impressionism and close reading, the essays are collectively not only a reader's manifest but also a poet's manifesto. This is an aspect of their considerable interest, though the drawbacks are that the analyses become somewhat repetitive, occasionally self-serving, while the pronunciamentos threaten to outweigh the concurrent poetry in the scale of Heaney's enterprise.

The threat to the poetry has so far been averted by the way in which each volume of Heaney's poetry accrues added value from previous volumes by a kind of compound interest. The building of an *oeuvre*, a major body of work that has not simply parts but parts which voice kinship, is the product of technique in Heaney's sense of the word. When reviewing *Field Work* (1979), I drew attention to the plaiting into the verse of Heaney's exemplars, but also to the remarkable self-referring going on, by which, for example, the Glanmore sonnets expressly generate themselves in part out of poems in *Wintering Out*. By then, Heaney's poetry had reached the Yeatsian stage of being an ingredient in its own fodder, and though I suggested airily he keep in mind James Stephens's complaint that Yeats sometimes hung around in his own poems, clanked about in his own rhymes, the poetry now conveys an enhanced impression of self-determination, and the advantage of this will become clear in a moment. In his T.S. Eliot Memorial Lecture on Sylvia Plath in 1986, Heaney saw her 'interweaving of imaginative constants from different parts of the *oeuvre*' as a mark of high accomplishment. Heaney's weave has by now surpassed hers in intricacy, for his is consciously a priority.

'The reality of poetry' is its legitimacy, its *raison d'être*, its autonomy, but the idea has excited copious and fascinating qualification. Heaney's mission has been nothing less than to identify and inhabit poetry's authentic element. He has tried to establish, we might say, the constitutional status of poetry, to his satisfaction and ours. In casting his practice and theory of poetry in a political light, I have taken my cue from the poet himself. I could easily have chosen other generic metaphors for poetry that extend and equate themselves throughout his work: sexuality, grammar, the physical world, kinship, religion. These play their part in any discussion of Heaney's poetry (where they are ubiquitous), but the political is perhaps the most revealing metaphor, because Heaney's master theme since *North* (1975) has been the possibility of poetry's self-determination, its freedom from, first one, then two, necessary captivities. Many individuals poems are lyrical dwellings in captivity and lyrical daydreams of escape, but together they chart in verse what the essays chart in prose observations of other poets: Heaney's changing idea of what constitutes poetry, and how it can be appointed to its proper dignity and office; *how*, in other words, it can be constituted. The dynamics of the political metaphor repeat those of the other chief metaphors to reveal an interesting pattern of redress. And if on his mission Heaney retreads the major issues in literary apologetics since Aristotle, that in itself is part of the redress in which he has been engaged.

The political metaphor differs from the rest, however, because politics are not merely a useful figure for poetry; to poetry politics represent a challenge, an opposition, but also a possible constituent.

That being the case, redress takes on literal guises and disguises;
Heaney's mission to constitute poetry is finally inseparable from his
own status as an Ulsterman of native and Catholic stock who grew up
on an island where questions of constitutional status have hung for
centuries in the air.

SEXUAL POLITICS

In the first phase of Heaney's career, brought to something like a
climax by *Field Work* (1979), *Selected Poems* (1980) and *Preoccupations:
Selected Prose* (1980), poetry was largely defended in the criticism and
comported itself in practice as a passive and defaulting affair,
maintained by secrecy, chance and instinct. Certainly it was *there*,
even if its wellsprings were held to be mysterious; indeed, in
Heaney's case it was there in a rawly physical fashion; but it seemed
to refuse the civil and ethical demands of society in favour of the self-
ratifying processes of the natural, into which history, itself the
repository of spent societies, eventually flows. Grauballe man who
'seems to weep//the black river of himself' is an apt figure for the
poems in Part I of *North* and many of the poems in *Wintering Out*.
They are stanzaic steps down and back through origins, declensions to
what they grew up and out of. They give the impression (but it is
only an impression) of being self-engendering, receptive to their glut
of imagery with minimum designing interference by the poet. Their
matter is Ireland and the way in which Heaney sees her as having
yielded almost naturally (even when compelled) to a series of violations.
These violations are both historical couplings and fertile analogies for
Heaney's own poetry as well as for language and culture in Ireland,
especially in Ulster, and even for poetry, language and culture in
Britain. But the poetry resides in some archetypal way more
authentically in the reception than in the invasions and progenitures.
Poetry is aboriginally female; so too is Ireland: through persistence
and ingenuity Heaney revivified the discredited feminizing of his
island, though not without some demurral among his compatriots.
Even Antaeus, a presiding figure, although male, still suckles at
Nature's breast; like Heaney at this stage of his career Antaeus 'cannot
be weaned/Off the earth's long contour, her river-veins'. It is from
'our mother ground', the Irish earth, that Heaney sees the strength
and inspiration of his verse deriving.

The male column in Heaney's ledger is occupied variously by the English, the Vikings, Ulster Protestants, and the Anglo-Saxon language. It was the invasions and colonizations of Ireland, including the Elizabethan settlements and the Ulster Plantation (eventuating in Nothern Ireland), that opened the cleft in Irish culture, and in Heaney's work and world-view. In a different key, forces and entities that oppose poetry or seek to govern her are also male: politics, society, the times, with their vocal importunities. These request action or commitment, and when thwarted can induce in the poet conscience and even penitence which in turn can incite but also inhibit powerful verse.

Complicating the issue further is Heaney's belief that poetry can itself be sexed: in *Preoccupations*, poets such as Jonson, Hopkins and Yeats are seen as rejecting linguistic and other kinds of mothering in favour of rhetorical mastery; as writers they are imperially male. Yet such is Heaney's desire at this stage to wrest the passive out of the active that even Yeats is interpreted (unconvincingly) as having come in the end to 'a mothering kindness towards life', therefore ultimately more like Wordsworth (and Shakespeare, Keats and Kavanagh) than like Yeats, allowing in himself 'a wise passiveness, a surrender to energies that spring within the centre of the mind', disavowing 'composition as an active pursuit by the mind's circumference of something already at the centre'. Three times in *Preoccupations* we are offered Shakespeare's poet's definition of poetry as 'a gum which oozes/From whence 'tis nourished' (like a river weeping itself?), an ungoverning of the tongue, a kind of verbal undress. Heaney admits there is another kind of poetry (like fire struck from a flint), an equestrian rather than pedestrian poetry (pedestrianism being a virtue), but there is no doubt that in *Preoccupations* Heaney deems the first kind prior in origin and merit.

Kinds of poetry and poets do not exhaust the forking of Heaney's thinking on poetry in *Preoccupations*; it runs from top to toe and is the formal principle of everything he has to say on the subject. His essays are remarkable exercises in binary opposition and are vividly structuralist despite the plethora of brilliantly couched impressions and metaphors. All to do with poetry is fissionable and this lures him at times into a procrusteanism which causes him, for example, to equate the English, the Anglo-Irish and the Ulster Scots as imperialists. It also equates Romantic, Symbolist and Modernist poetry on one side of a Great Divide, and discountenances Yeats (who is on the other side of the Divide) as a Symbolist poet. And in general it tacitly requires the reader periodically and without guidance to transpose Heaney's cloven ruminations to make sense of the biformities.

The distaff side of things is the essence of the matter.[1] Poetry is primally for the ear more than for the eye; its verbal texture is privileged over design, and states of feeling over statement; its purpose is evocation before address; its appeal is to the senses more than to the mind. Heaney's early poetry rehearsed these priorities in startling viscosities that quickly became his signature.

It is true that Heaney's poetry eloquently versifies its own difficulties in reaching and inhabiting the self-trusting, distaff side. Heaney has chosen to acknowledge (and makes poetry out of the acknowledgement) that much of his inherited culture, including his literary culture, is twofold, that he lives much of the time between columns. His 'forked root' in an Anglo-Irish culture, the daily Ulster necessity of being 'fork-tongued on the border bit', not to speak of his own native caution – all have tempted him not just to hang fire and sing lyrically dumb in the matter of politics but to worry out loud about doing so. He has not willingly or candidly accepted society's government of the tongue, nor has he willingly or candidly refused it. Actually, Heaney has been sufficiently forthcoming both on the Ulster turmoil and his failure to *be* forthcoming to render his worry a little brittle, as though it were a personal trope. The two Parts of *North* represent respectively the cultural analogizing *away* from the turmoil into vatic poetry, which makes nothing happen, and the cultural address, albeit introspective, half-hearted, *of* the turmoil in civil poetry, which at least contemplates making a difference, even if it gives up on trying.

In *North*, as in subsequent volumes and in *Preoccupations*, the ambivalences I noted in my 1974 article have continued richly to proliferate. It was in *North* that Heaney famously characterized himself as 'an inner émigré', as an 'artful voyeur', as a man spancelled by his 'responsible tristia', a Hamlet, 'dithering, blathering'. He reminds himself in Part I to accept poetic revelation as a 'long foray' (a phrase that suggests the slow action of a river rather than an ambitious military excursion) and not fret over the absence of a 'cascade of light'. Still, in Part II he regrets that he cannot 'come on meteorite!' and grasp 'the diamond absolutes'. He berates himself for merely

Imagining a hero
On some muddy compound,
His gift like a slingstone
Whirled for the desperate.

He daydreams of a dangerous political poetry decisively intervening on behalf of his embattled tribe, the Ulster Catholics ('muddy compound' evokes Long Kesh internment camp), like a David challenging the Goliath of Britain and Protestant Ulster; of writing a male poetry discharging civil obligations but in order to defend the female side of the historical and bloody transaction between Britain and Ireland.

However, the role of political poet is only briefly entertained, and refused; Part II of *North* is considerably shorter than Part I and chiefly versifies the inherited trammels on action – the poet's temperament, his upbringing, and the 'tight gag of place' in which, to prevent sectarian trouble, whatever you say you say nothing. Politics are simply not his element; his element is the gradual ease by which politics – essentially conflict between invading and defending groups – become history which in turn resumes the earth as artifacts and detritus, only to be exhumed and renewed in the poet's imagination which imitates in its own workings this natural process. Heaney's poet is a kind of archaeologist (bringing cultural remnants up from below the surface) whose job it is to take the long view of civilization; but poetry is an archaeology whose end is art – with its immediate sensuous gratifications – not knowledge, much less judgement. His view is an aesthetic gaze generating pleasing images and figures, a looking on: 'I am the artful voyeur//of your brain's exposed/and darkened combs,/your muscles' webbing', he confesses to the dug-up adultress of the bog.

He feels troubled about this because his identical posture is reprehensible when taken in front of living equivalents, Catholic girls tarred and feathered by their own (in the early 1970s) for fraternizing with British soldiers, whose punishment cries out for something other than the silent and fascinated observation which is all that Heaney can offer; this might render by analogy contemplation of history's atrocities equally reprehensible. The living example makes the exhumed example more than artifact, makes it relive as a moral event, pitting in retrospect standards of civilization against apparent necessities of tribe. Ought one to relish beauty in a casualty of what was then a ritual punishment but today would be assessed as barbarity? Instead of answering 'no' Heaney implies that the assessment is reversible, with today's barbarity perceivable as ritual and as having its own terrible beauty. The adultress' state of undress and poetry's verbal undress are somehow equatable. Heaney's poetry up to *Field Work* apparently inclines to the aesthetic away from the moral. He is caught in the middle only to the extent that he uses the occasions for civil poetry in order to produce vatic poetry, a poetry of autonomous and lovely speech.

It would seem that his penitence functions chiefly to defray the living expenses of the vatic verse in the harsh economy of the 'real' world of social morality, and to prevent such verse becoming mere self-indulgence, a kept woman. A poetry of penitence, according to Heaney's own standard raised in *Preoccupations*, is a second-order poetry, as is all poetry of conscience. But it is a lesser poetry than the poetry of protest which at least turns conscience to active account, as in the outcries of Wilfred Owen. Failing to achieve decisively the male side of things, penitence though passive yet hampers a poetry of true relish, a truly wise passiveness and surrender to the poet's half-conscious energies. This on the whole Heaney's early poetry achieves, it runs like a slow tide into acquiescence, and is endorsed by Heaney's discussion in the early essays of about what constitutes the truest poetry.

Yet it would be a mistake to take this at face or Heaney's value. The melt into the natural, the aesthetic, the feminine, the vatically poetic is inseparable from Heaney's native Irishness (just as his recurrent note of penitence is inseparable from his cradle Catholicism); the swerve from politics is not a swerve from culture, the deep structure of Irish politics. The truest poetry hearkens to the depth-summons of the tribe, other poetry to the shallower summons of civility. Heaney's swerve from politics is chiefly his swerve from moral condemnation of violent elements of his own tribe, while the transgressions of his tribe's opponents are inscribed in their crude masculine enactments. In this fashion Heaney has it both ways: he can be apolitical and yet in an Irish sense profoundly political, and his ambivalence is a strength beneath its apparent irresolution.

In 'Ocean's Love to Ireland' and other poems, Heaney has raised to emblematic status the interpretation of Irish history as a procession of suffered violations and defeats. He has recourse to two conventional nationalist ideas: that Ireland is female and that Ireland has been periodically ravished by invaders, latterly England. What is remarkable is the thorough and delighted way in which Heaney in the 1970s developed and exploited these conventional representations, as though as a Northern Ireland Catholic he had been insulated from Irish nationalism and had lately discovered them. It is likely indeed that an emblematic and anthropomorphic nationalism was possible for an Ulster Catholic at a time that it wasn't for his Southern counterpart. In any case, Heaney belatedly imported north of the border these representations that were prevalent during the Irish Literary Revival, and Catholic Ulster was made an imminent Eve to Protestant Ulster's unsuspecting Adam:

> Gunfire barks its questions off Cavehill
> And the profiled basalt maintains its stare
> South: proud, protestant and northern, and male.
> Adam untouched, before the shock of gender.

It is oddly generous for a twentieth-century Catholic to forfeit maleness to the ancient enemy, especially at a time when Ulster Catholics were – to borrow Heaney's frame of reference – putting on their manhood. Still, between 1972 and 1975 it may have seemed that the procession of defeats was endless. From the sidelines of that procession, Heaney (or strictly speaking, the narrator of his poems) felt helpless, unmanned, a voyeur capably male but rendered passive, in some sense womanly. But Heaney was a poet and poetry, too, is female in her conventional embodiment. The thorough way a late-twentieth-century poet developed and exploited this convention is likewise remarkable: it is not only inspiration (the muse) that can be sexed, but poetry's numerous constituents, including its grammar. Even though poetry is international, there is in Heaney's work the conventional idea that despite her political indeed, it is implied misfortunes, Ireland still has her poetry; indeed, it is implied that poetry is her form of redress. She actually survives by dint of those misfortunes, for she has become, like her bogs, ineradicable because absorbent of aggression. The forms and even content of the various penetrations are preserved, but posthumously, on the terms of the ravished goddess. This too is a conventional trope of Irish nationalism. Donagh MacDonagh wrote about the Normans in 'A Warning to Conquerors':

> This soft land quietly
> Engulfed them like the Saxon and the Dane
> But kept the jutted jaw the slitted eye:
> Only the faces and the names remain.

Conor Cruise O'Brien rightly comments that to Ulster Protestants these lines would seem like a sequence in a horror film. Heaney's bog poems are a longer sequence in that horror film.

For Heaney, then, up until and including *North* and *Preoccupations*, poetry and Ireland share an origin and essence in secrecy, mystery, triumphant receptivity, wise passiveness, darkness, earth, primal femininity; their identity is their aboriginality, not their subsequent reformations. Poetry is like the colony of Ireland that typically (but not always) outwardly acquiesced in its colonial status, but by being abstentionist passively opposed the colonizer (society in the poetic version of the metaphor, England and Protestant Ulster in the political version) and never more than when 'going to earth', returning to origins. From the colonizer she withholds the essence of herself; she exacts the revenge of nativeness and asserts by default the 'natural rights' of her original inhabitants (or practitioners). Heaney's poet is the colonized who accepts the role superficially and refuses the role of the anti-colonialist. But in reality he is neither internee nor informer, a native – and nativist – who rehearses his freedom beneath the notice of the colonizer; like Antaeus, while he stays earthbound he can't be beaten.

It is wrong to assume, therefore, that abstention – a tactic favoured tactic by Irish nationalists and one for which Heaney as a poet has been taken to task, ironically *by* nationalists – must always be defeatist in effect; it can be a sign of patience, strength and self-confidence. In his early phase Heaney sees poetic creation 'as a feminine action, almost parthenogenetic' ('The Fire i' the Flint'). Almost parthenogenetic: despite his acknowledgment of the split culture of Ulster, Heaney is disinclined to explore the Scots-Irish, the majority population of Northern Ireland, and offers them as representations of 'the others'. His unfashionable reverence for manual work and handcraft to the contrary, Heaney has largely ignored the Protestant making of north-east Ulster into its once-distinctive industriousness. 'Docker' is an early, lonely, unflattering portrait of the Protestant workman. Heaney admires those who 'beat real iron out', but in Ireland it was most commonly the Ulster Scot who beat real iron out and who took fierce pride in workmanship. I sometimes fear that in future Heaney and Ulster will become synonymous, the way Yeats and Ireland became synonymous for American scholars who took their Irish history from the poet. In fact, large tracts of Ulster, both literal and figurative, are simply missing from the sizeable acreage of Heaney's two hundred-odd collected poems.

Similarly, marriage, for which Heaney has an unfashionable reverence, does not assume symbolic significance as a possible union between Ulster's warring communities or between Ireland and Britain; instead, these relationships are seen as rapes or, at best, weddings attended by violent ritual ('The Betrothal of Cavehill'). Native Irish culture, we are unavoidably induced to agree, is almost parthenogenetic, requiring few fertilizations from 'the others'; in Heaney we can detect a nostalgia for pre-colonial unity, a recurring strain in Ulster Catholic writing.

It is difficult to decide which femininity came first in Heaney's case. Did his exploration of poetry's femaleness encourage him to dwell on the enduring passivity of Ireland's role in history? Or did his acceptance of that role, and Ireland's femaleness, encourage him to see poetry in a caressing stare as essentially female and supine? And did the strong residue of Heaney's Irish Catholicism reinforce a deceptively passive posture of compliance, resignation and hospitality? The pagan-inspired imaginative forays of *North* could not answer this last question, but the Christian-inspired sedentariness of the next volume could.

OUR BEADSMAN IN ULSTER

'I incline as much to rosary beads//As to the jottings and analyses/Of politicians and newspapermen', Heaney confesses archly towards the end of *North*. In *Field Work* (1979), piety is expressed but is prevented from enacting itself because Heaney's Catholicism is apparently instinctive and remembered, not practised. He recalls the converging gravities of Celtic Ireland, medieval Catholic Ireland and contemporary militarized Ulster bearing down on him one day in Fermanagh: 'Everything in me/Wanted to bow down, to offer up,/To go barefoot, foetal and penitential.' (Later he would do this, in 'Station Island'.)

Yet the volume begins in two places – its opening poem and the first sonnet of the Glanmore sequence – very differently, with the determination of a fresh start. *Field Work* is the harvest of the poet's four-year domicile in County Wicklow away from the city of Belfast where pressures were heavy on him not just to witness the Troubles but to intervene as a writer. He arrived in a mild early spring after the relative emotional tundras of *Wintering Out* and *North*, and did so with his lea already 'deeply tilled' and prepared for sowing (an irony, one hopes, to prevent an immodesty). He was a poetic Antaeus, fortified at ground level, believing 'art a paradigm of earth new from the lathe/Of ploughs'. Craft, possibly technique, in place, he wished in some poetic field-work to plough his vowels (Heaney' s signature sounds which he fancifully thinks of as native Irish and female) into fresh soil, the 'other, opened ground' of Wicklow, not the raw 'opened ground' of colonized Ireland ('Act of Union'), i.e. the fresh wound of Ulster. For the conscriptions of Ulster and of poetry there, he would substitute the 'free state' of the South and achieve it for his verse. Strength and revelation perhaps lie underfoot south of the border. He wants to 'break through' what he had 'glazed over/With perfect mist' in the Derry placename poems of *Wintering Out*.

The change in point of view from compliant earth to burly ploughman suggests that Heaney's dissatisfaction with his earlier idea of poetry was rankling. Poetry as a resinous product of the organic sensibility, recollection in tranquillity, was free, but free largely in the act of self-pleasuring. That it was in retreat from society was not the problem: Heaney had not left Ulster in order to tackle the province's problems from the vantage of distance. Rather, such poetry was not in command even of itself but was in servitude to its own fertility of imagery, figuration and sound, its own pleasing patterns of shape and stanza. Now, he tells us in 'Oysters', the fine opening poem of *Field Work*, he wanted to be 'quickened' (a word he uses four times in the collection) 'into verb, pure verb'. Verb is the grammatical vehicle of action, whereas Heaney's poems have been heavily nominal, given his veneration for objects.[2] He daydreams of potentiation by eating oysters – a musal aphrodisiac, as it were – that when opened exhale, in a seductive but oddly bisexual phrase, the 'philandering sigh of ocean'. In Heaney's poetic geography, the sea is aggressively male, and it was in pursuit of a figuratively masculine, verbal, oceanic mode and key that Heaney retrospectively (but indirectly) interpreted his move from Ulster to be. He coveted the *sprezzatura* and accipitrine vision he saw in another artist ('In Memoriam Sean O'Riada'), and Robert Lowell's fearlessness ('Elegy'); he wished to come on meteorite, to make a decisive lateral move across the ledger to that male poetry (the poetry of more than merely rhetorical mastery?) that requires the writer – the whole human being in verbal expression – to take governance and captaincy of his art as a skipper would his ship across a possibly ungovernable sea.

The athlete's eve-of-competition readiness that opens *Field Work* and the Glanmore sequence within it explains in hindsight Heaney's 1974 review of Mandelstam's translated *Selected Poems*. In it he wrote: 'Mandelstam's life and work are salutary and exemplary: if a poet must turn his resistance into an offensive, he should go for a kill and be prepared, in his life and with his work, for the consequences.' Since Mandelstam actually *died* at the hands of a totalitarian regime, it seemed a bit armchairish for Heaney to call on poets (including himself) to emulate him, especially since Heaney had by then decided that political poetry was not for him. However, it was a summons to arms made unfortunate and confusing by the choice of metaphor, since the 'kill' Heaney was talking about, it comes as a jolt to realize, is not fearless baiting of a repressive government, or even political poetry at all, but the oblivious, single-minded pursuit of poetry, whether in the Soviet Union, Northern Ireland or the becalmed shires of England: art for art's sake, in fact, but in no effeminate or Ninetyish way. In other words, the pure verbal drive wished for in 'Oysters'. If Owen is the exemplary poet of conscience, Mandelstam is the exemplary poet of unimpeachable truancy.

As it turned out, there was no falconry of swoop and kill in *Field Work*. There are some short-line poems (usually trimeter) in the style of *Wintering Out* and *North*; but while the thin poems in those two volumes were almost hieroglyphic representations of penetrating phallo-cultures, they represented simultaneously the sinking of those cultures after a surface hegemony ('the soft-piled centuries') and their preservation in the defeated, undefeatable Irish earth. The thin poem has proved no reining of Heaney's remarkable and enviable vocabulary. And generally, *Field Work* permits itself a looser, longer line (often pentameter), as though the poet's tongue had indeed become 'a swung relaxing hinge' ('Triptych'). Most of the verse shoals thickly with images often rich, religious and redolent (a favoured word), despite the book's opening line, from 'Oysters' – 'Our shells clacked on the plates', a line dead right, clinched with a pure verb of the kind the poet hopes for at poem's end but that the intervening lines and the rest of the volume fail beautifully and consolingly to deliver.

There is at times in *Field Work* a too sweet and devotional fascination with ritual, a luxuriant iconography. Clearings are brief and unexpected. Stoup, scapular, shroud, statue, surplice, spire, soutane, asperged, chasuble, censed – the sibilant apparatus of Catholicism furnishes this volume in an almost *fin-de-siècle* fashion.[3] It is not the quick who dominate *Field Work* but the dead, commemorated in a 'recital of elegies', poems of distressing beauty owing some of their inspiration to 'the master elegist', Lowell. Since many of the dead are Ulster dead, Heaney is returned to that wintry 'opened ground' of the North, and his verse to the status of 'colony'.

Surely, then, the striding of ghosts into Heaney's consciousness cannot be what he means by quickening into pure verb. Rather, the uninvited revenants have distracted him from taking command. Yet some doubt remains.

> Old ploughsocks gorge the subsoil of each sense
> And I am quickened with a redolence
> Of the fundamental dark unblown rose.
> Wait then . . . Breasting the mist, in sowers' aprons,
> My ghosts come striding into their spring stations.
> The dream grain whirls like freakish Easter snows.

Are those full stops stepping-stones, and the advent of the ghosts the ritually induced apparitions in Heaney's séance? Perhaps if the poet can really be quickened with a redolence (though the Blakean, Yeatsian rose might provide a necessary mystical animation), he can imagine the coming of ghosts as an active not passive occurrence. Or are the full stops a surprised pause ('hullo!') and the ghosts' advent an imminent deflection of prepared energies? Is he once again 'pinioned by ghosts' (*North*), obliged to suspend his unspecified poetic project for the quasi-priestly offices of censing, asperging, anointing, once again a teller of images, our beadsman in Ulster?

Certainly there is in Heaney an instinct for propitiation and spiritual intercession as deep as his instinct for retreat and neutrality, a desire to turn dew into holy water, to make poetry a ceremony of assuagement. This derives from his Catholicism in which, like Joyce, he is steeped whether he believes or not; like Joyce he has retained something priestly in himself. Ministration may look like ritualized subjection, but there is strength of a particular kind in Heaney's instinct. There may be in the elegiac mode of *Field Work* a disguised penitence for the poet's reluctance to participate instead of interceding, but such poetry has its own power. At times Heaney can resemble those priests who kneel to minister to dying street casualties of terror in Northern Ireland without inquiring as to sect but with attention only to a departing humanity. They tacitly acknowledge in the rite the reality of politics but also in their disregard of the civil power divorce Church from State, spirituality from the bruised and torn flesh. (The instincts for intercession and neutrality are not, therefore, incompatible.) When the Church in question is the Roman Catholic Church, and the State Northern Ireland or the United Kingdom, the symbolic divorce of Church from state unavoidably implies in the secular circumstances disapproval of the State, itself an oblique political statement. In *Field Work*, poetry bears an analogous relationship to the State and society. There is, moreover, a notion of durance that we might suggestively equate with Catholic Ireland's self-image. Field-work: a structure of defence, a redan.

I for one am grateful for the spiritual comfort Heaney has offered us in Ulster. Only a poetry whose craft is equal to its largess of humane love can suggest an ennobling resemblance to religion. It seems churlish to remark, then, that the priest and poet can be regarded as 'auditory voyeurs', listeners-in, but I do so on cue of Heaney's own evolving, declared poetic. Heaney described Wordsworth as a listener-in and Yeats as an actor-out, at a time when his preference was for the earlier poet, who is a major presence in *Field Work*. But Heaney is listening in not to the workings of earth or to his own nature, but to the sufferings of others; his poetry in its profound respect for dead friends fails nevertheless by Heaney's own high standards (it seems a harsh judgment on extremely moving verse) to be a poetry of self-respect.[4]

The expressed fatigue with a verse of ministration shows in the occasional world-weariness of the poems, which can come off as affected. Watching young people leaving a discothèque, 'I felt', he writes, 'like some old pike all badged with sores/Wanting to swim in touch with soft-mouthed life.'[5] Heaney would have been thirty-eight or -nine when he wrote many of the poems in *Field Work* and it was when he was thirty-eight that Lowell began to 'affect a fatigued, world-weary tone of voice and . . . would usually seem older than his years'.[6] Heaney's emulation of Lowell is pervasive beyond his fine elegy for the dead American, who is addressed as though he were living, since Heaney's ghosts 'live'. In the elegy Heaney voices admiration for Lowell's masculine boldness in 'riding' the dangerous sea of his life like a sea-captain, in being a fearless fisherman capable of landing the dolphin, in 'bullying' out love sonnets to his women. The subtext of the elegy, like a photographic negative, is Heaney's self-chiding and self-rallying, a kind of concealed penitence for not so far having emulated the master. In a reversal of roles, it is Heaney who becomes implicitly the petitioner, the other the ministrant. Lowell is an exemplar of a superior kind of poetry whose pursuit Heaney has had to set aside – in the fiction of his developing *oeuvre* – in order to write a poetry that sings the sad music of what has happened in Northern Ireland. Poetry in *Field Work* is for the most part, if we accept Heaney's implied estimate, a kind of chaplaincy deflected from its truer ('peacetime') offices by the warfare outside it. Lowell's very different 'empery', which is the poetry neither of relish nor of protest (much less penitence), we can leave unspecified for the moment.

REHEARSALS OF DEBTS AND BETRAYALS

Heaney began translating *Buile Suibhne* when he went to Wicklow in 1972, so it is not surprising that Sweeney makes a fleeting appearance in 'The Strand at Lough Beg', a poem in *Field Work*. Nor is it surprising that in his Introduction to *Sweeney Astray* (1983) Heaney should see the medieval tale as suspended between several of the binary oppositions that lattice *Preoccupations* – Celtic temperament/ Christian ethos; free creative imagination/religious and political constraints; relish/penitence; Ireland/Britain; myth/history; and, of course, Irish language/English language. Sweeney himself is suspended like his story, a legendary, i.e. half-mythical, half-historical figure. Like Antaeus in defeat, he inhabits in his punishment two elements, and at his death his spirit flies to airy heaven, his body returning to Nature's earth. If *Buile Suibhne*, even in translation, is independent of the rest of Heaney's work, *Sweeney Astray* is both a verse recapitula-tion (with progressive modifications) of Heaney's preoccupations and a melodious intermezzo between original movements.

In the beginning the banished Sweeney is like a wood-kerne escaped from the battle at Moira: this must have gratified Heaney who in *North* had described himself as 'a wood-kerne//Escaped from the massacre', a description visualized by Edward McGuire's painting of the poet that closes *North*. McGuire portrays him as long-haired, thoughtful and ensconced, yet backgrounded by an encroaching Nature transformed indoors into the wood of the furniture and fenestration that the poet's clothes in turn mimic, weave imitating grain imitating vein and feather. By the time of the Glanmore sonnets in *Field Work*, Heaney had implied a similarity to Sweeney beyond a rhyme of names, by imagining a house in the boor-tree to which he resorts to ponder 'roots and graftings', the stuff of his poetry. But as far back as 'Oracle' (*Wintering Out*), Heaney had associated himself with trees, on that occasion a willow, hedge-school for the auditory imagination, its woody cleft merging with the young poet's ear and throat, registers of the soft vowels of the landscape out of which the remembering adult voices his distinctive poems, The remembered self is partly responsible to human society (his family 'cuckoo' his name, *Seam-us*, as he hides in the tree), partly a genius of the woods, a recent version of those 'geniuses who creep/"out of every corner/of the woodes and glennes"/towards watercress and carrion' in Spenser's Ireland recalled in 'Bog Oak', also from *Wintering Out*. The tree, be it oak, willow or boor-tree, is the emblem of aboriginal Ireland: the latter is called elderberry in England, that name, we are taught in a Glanmore sonnet, conjuring 'shires dreaming wine'. And as 'Bog Oak' implies, it is impoverished, dispossessed Ireland whose banished natives are made exiles in their own country, inner *émigrés*, as it were, a phrase equally applicable therefore to native Ireland and the singleton Heaney styles himself.

The tree is a female emblem (that 'woody cleft' is suggestive), and at once the inspiration, imagery and language of poetry – a vatic, vaginal poetry older than the phallic poetry of conscience, protest, social responsibility. In being banished to the branches, Sweeney has not only rescaled the male, Christian Tree of Knowledge[7] (in the end 'His soul roosts in the tree of love') but more importantly has also discovered in his punishment, in his self-division, the proper site of poetry, is given tongue, and sings accordingly. In a 1978 radio talk, 'The God in the Tree', reprinted in *Preoccupations*, Heaney discusses medieval Irish nature poetry, including *Buile Suibhne*, and locates the origin of poetry in the pagan, feminine mysteries of the grove.

Sweeney is informed, it seems, with the free, aboriginal spirit of poetry. But simultaneously he is challenged by the obligations of a religious and secular world outside poetry. We might claim, then, that Sweeney's plight is, among other things, a poet's, that he is caught (as his translator sees himself caught) between the summonses of two kinds of poetry, one of celebration (pagan nature poetry) and one of responsibility (Christian hymnody). Sweeney towards the end sees himself as 'crucified in the fork of a tree', a melodramatic figure, if we choose, for Heaney's eloquent crucifixion in the fork of a dilemma. Sweeney may have escaped from the battle but he is plagued by awareness of it. He is a melodious cataloguer of Nature's excellences and a believer in her assuaging powers, but out of guilt he is a distributor of blessings, a voicer of lamentations: an archetypal Heaney, in short. In his Introduction Heaney appears to make displacement native to the artist (of which he sees Sweeney as a medieval type), the guilty incapacity (or unwillingness) to satisfy extra-poetic demands, the challenged yearning merely to sing mother earth's exhalations. Both as a wood-sprite who listens in on Nature and as a wood-kerne escaped from the battle and eavesdropping or gazing on conflict and human affairs, Sweeney is the spirit of poetry. In his very predicament Sweeney embodies the familiar Heaney equation of colonized Ireland, Nature, femininity and poetry. But the verse remains twofold and this must have qualified for Heaney this vicarious resolution of his dilemma as he searches for a unified voice and mode in his own poetry.

Besides, it would be extravagant to liken Sweeney's penance to his translator's, or his 'wild career', exile from God and madness to Heaney's milder and poetically profitable travails as an artist.[8] 'I could risk blasphemy', Heaney claimed in 'The Tollund Man', but instead of doing so he has daydreamed of poetic *alter egos*; if Sweeney is fictional, Mandelstam, for example, was real, but an *alter ego* nevertheless.

Yet Heaney has pressed the analogy between Sweeney and himself by including as the third part of *Station Island* (1984) a sequence of original poems, 'Sweeney Redivivus'. But in any case, the king whose wanderings turn out at the end of *Buile Suibhne* to have been a pilgrimage, and whose roosts as a bird-man are 'hard stations', is re-incarnated in 'Station Island', the second part of the volume, as Heaney himself. The poet on his Lough Derg pilgrimage seeks to pour his troubles back into the forms of Dante and his own cradle Catholicism, to turn those troubles into sins, confess them, do penance for them, and be shriven, but also to hear explanations of them (from himself, of course, from the mouths of ghosts conjured up as oracles and advisers) and receive directions for escaping or transcending them. In atonement may be at-one-ment, the end of self-division and accession to a final, resolving condition.

The poetic-personal 'sins' Heaney confesses in 'Station island' are perhaps over-familiar to Heaney admirers, sins characteristically midway between commission and omission: a 'timid circumspect involvement', failed obligations, evasion miscalled artistic tact, a nature 'biddable and forthcoming', sleepwalks 'with connivance and mistrust'. Despite their dramatic quickening within the framework of a pilgrim-age, the dialogues with ghosts in 'Station Island' are essentially 'old rehearsals/of debts and betrayals' ('Sweeney Redivivus'), the failure to come on meteorite or 'seize the day' ('Shelf Life'; see also 'The Strand at Lough Beg').

There is little suggestion of a fresh start in the first two parts of *Station Island*; it is largely unfinished business; the first poem in the volume, 'The Underground', in microcosm uses (like *The Divine Comedy*) the Orphean adventure through the Underworld to find the Lost Lady. Indeed, the failure to make a fresh start is itself scrutinized in a poetry that raises penitence to the highest pitch available to what in Heaney's evaluation is a second-order creativity. If Lowell in 'Elegy' is Heaney's confessor, he is joined in 'Station Island' by other writers, principally William Carleton and James Joyce. Through these ghosts, Heaney tells himself that no penance or absolution is required. He is impatiently enjoined by 'Joyce' to shed himself of guilt and stake his claim to the troubling no-man's-land he frequently inhabits instead of trying to flee it, thereby taking possession of it as the writer's authentic element and turning the poetry of penitence into the poetry of self-command.

Heaney's celebration in his early volumes of thatchers, black-smiths, diviners and the rest was a celebration of 'lives in their element', to borrow a phrase from 'Away from it All' (*Station Island*). As a writer who grew up in their world, Heaney was a fish out of water from the start. Antaeus is taken (and overcome) 'out of his element' by the intelligence of Hercules that is like 'a blue prong graiping' the giant off the vivifying ground ('Hercules and Antaeus', *North*); he is reborn as the forked-up lobster in 'Away from it All', forked up out of his element, fortified yet a 'hampered one, out of water'. The poet can't return to his native habitat, nor can he – in the words of Czeslaw Milosz quoted in the poem – fierily 'participate/ actively in history'.

Out of his native element, Heaney early made 'exile' his writer's chosen ground, making poignant poetry out of 'a dream of loss//and origins' ('Hercules and Antaeus'), out of penitence and relish, but continued to tell a story in which he was dissatisfied with origins and loss, became hampered by them, and sought a third element clean and clear beyond. In 'Station Island' that dissatisfaction reaches a belated climax. 'Joyce' imagines the writer's true element as a sea, that poet-made, masculine environment inhabited by Heaney's Lowell and which 'Joyce' directs Heaney to fill with his unique signals, like 'elvergleams', a simile that reinvests 'A Lough Neagh Sequence' in

Door into the Dark (1969) with meaning.[9] This would require courage and independence; such a poetry of the future – for it is unachieved, of course, in 'Station Island', and meant to be unachieved – would apparently come less naturally than the poetry of relish; the poet has to create the element his poetry occupies (and perhaps his readership, as Heaney might in the future be required to do).

What might all this mean in political terms? Heaney is not thinking of political poetry in which conscience dictates protest, nor of penitence, but in Heaney's case, politics, culture and the poet's mind are not easily separable. Heaney tells 'Carleton' that he, Heaney, was raised in a biddable nationalism (of the kind represented by the Ancient Order of Hibernians) that obediently accepted Protestant ascendancy in Northern Ireland while making ritual noises of dissidence, and not the unforgiving nationalism of those Fenian inheritors, the republicans. Heaney has often berated himself for the obedience he was taught and temperamentally subscribed to, and often expresses the desire to disobey. Politically this would mean a rejection of constitutional nationalism (female) in favour of republicanism (male). In fact, the political dissatisfaction appears to have been sublimated in a change of 'party poetics', away from the neighbourhood of party politics. If poetry in one pure state is like a colonized country, in its less pure state it is a kind of constitutional nationalism in permanent opposition, or, if you will, a Free State that accepts limited home rule and the *status quo* of boundaries which it settles for endlessly negotiating. That in its turn is less satisfactory than the stealthy subterfuges of the *colonizés*.

Station Island is a busy, ambitious and multifarious work, but it is so because the familiar trammellings and hamperings are paradoxically given free rein. There are a dozen superb poems in Parts One and Three – 'Sloe Gin' and 'In the Chestnut Tree' are two of them – that will take their place in the anthologies in time to come and whose re-creative power of imagery and metaphor replenishes our deep delight. Must we know it again? By all means! But during Part Two, the title sequence, the Heaney veteran might be tempted to cry out, 'hold, enough!' There is a taxing round-up of impedimenta and enablings, for the reader an experience of *déjà lu*, before the deliberate (and welcome) culling and retrenchment in his most recent volume.

A COPERNICAN REVOLUTION

Even though it has been fitfully anticipated from the start, there has been one decisive shift in Heaney's thinking about poetry, a shift registered in his second book of criticism and to a lesser extent in his poetry from *Station Island* onwards. (The earlier discovery of Glob's book and the possibilities of bog deepened what had already been there; it did not change the direction or element of Heaney's imaginative field work.) To telegraph the shift: poetry's proper element is no longer seen as earth but as air; poetry is no longer a door into the dark but a door into the light; it must climb to its proper light, no longer descend to its proper dark.

It is possible that Heaney is responding to a new weather in Ireland created by revisionist historiography, that renders his earlier gender-based nationalist mythography suspect. Or perhaps he has grown uncomfortable with the warmly reassuring presence he now is for the Common Reader who, alienated by much modern poetry and by the ideological stridency and theoretical introversions of criticism, has, judging by the enormous sales of Heaney's books, found in him a haven, the hammered shod of a bay. In any case, when 'Sweeney' describes his previous earthbound life as his 'old clandestine/pre-Copernican night' ('Sweeney Redivivus'), it is Heaney describing his own sensuous miring in the Ulster countryside. The Hughesian raid into darkness, the troubling secrecies underfoot, rich opacities of sound, rootedness: these that brought Heaney his fame are to be subjected to a Copernican revolution, a shift from earth's centrality. If the requisitions of society have always been one potential captivity for the poet, then those of origin and background have by now become another, from which his poetry must also lift itself clear.

Still, chiefly through his adoption since *Sweeney Astray* and *Station Island* of the tree as a major site and symbol, Heaney has attempted to seam smoothly his two poetics. One gains the air only through the agency of the rooted.[10] From the tree 'Sweeney' can launch himself into the air more than a stone's throw beyond those who would have him return to their battles. Heaney in 'Sweeney Redivivus' imagines the banished king as a poet (like himself) who wrote of conflict, was taken to task for doing it in the way he did, turned his back on auxiliary art, then 'upped the ante' in the poetry stakes:

I was mired in attachment
until they began to pronounce me
a feeder off battlefields

so I mastered new rungs of the air
to survey out of reach
their bonfires on hills, their hosting

and fasting, the levies from Scotland
as always, and the people of art
diverting their rhythmical chants

to fend off the onslaught of winds
I would welcome and climb
at the top of my bent.

In this eloquent wish-fulfilment, 'The First Flight', the reference to hillside bonfires establishes an Ulster dimension of meaning.

The plant of honour in that beautifully swagging poem, 'In the Chestnut Tree', has cropped up in Heaney's work before. In his 1977 lecture at the Ulster Museum, 'The Sense of Place', reprinted in *Preoccupations*, he recalled 'the green chestnut tree that flourished at the entrance to the Gaelic Athletic Association grounds' and that 'was more abundantly green from being the eminence where the tricolour was flown illicitly at Easter or on sports days'. It was, if you like, a symbol of that constitutional nationalism (cutting a republican dash on ritual occasions) I have remarked on. In its implied femaleness it also stood over against the male totem of the Protestant red, white and blue (manmade) flagpost at Hillhead. Tree = Nature = native Ireland = femininity: the familiar equation is familiarly extended when the tree in 'In the Chestnut Tree', gorgeously female, is earthed and breathes *like poetry*. In 'The Placeless Heaven: Another Look at Kavanagh', an essay collected in *The Government of the Tongue*, Heaney writes of a family chestnut tree planted the year he was born and with which he connected his own life (and, I surmise, on hindsight his poetry). The tree was cut down and forgotten about.

Then, all of a sudden, a couple of years ago, I began to think of the space where the tree had been or would have been. In my mind's eye I saw it as a kind of luminous emptiness, a warp and waver of light, and once again, in a way that I find hard to define, I began to identify with that space . . . Except that this time it was not so much a matter of attaching oneself to a living symbol of being rooted in the native ground; it was more a matter of preparing to be unrooted, to be spirited away into some transparent, yet indigenous afterlife.

That is the occasion and most succinct explanation of Heaney's one revolution in thought, and *The Haw Lantern* (1987) is the chief result in verse to date, though it is continuous with some of the poetry in Part Three of *Station Island*. The implication is that in Heaney's future verse, Sweeney's chestnut tree is doomed in its reality and therefore in its gorgeousness: it is to be immaterialized and purified; and so must the poetry, too, be translated into a new spirituality, a different tonality, a 'neuter allegiance' to use Sweeney's words in 'The Cleric', the adjective carefully displacing the word 'neutral'.

At the heart of *The Haw Lantern* is a suite of eight sonnets in memory of the poet's mother who died in 1984. The last sonnet commemorates the felled chestnut:

> I thought of walking round and round a space
> Utterly empty, utterly a source
> Where the decked chestnut tree had lost its place
> In our front hedge above the wallflowers.

He remembered (or contemplated) doing this in response to the death of his mother recalled in sonnet 7. At her last breath

> The space we stood around had been emptied
> Into us to keep, it penetrated
> Clearances that suddenly stood open.
> High cries were felled and a pure change happened.[11]

The suite of sonnets is called 'Clearances'. The title suggests all manner of changes: endings – the cutting down of trees, emptyings, sweepings clean; and also middles – clarifications and respites. And beginnings too – necessary preparations for actions, buildings, fresh starts. It even suggests transcendence: more than unhamperings or leaps over hurdles, clearances can mean those absences caused by death but turned by love into their luminous opposite; clearances are translations, not extinctions. In sonnet 4 the poet remembers his mother as 'hampered' and out of her element in the presence of her educated son, and though this is merely on the face of it a minor fond memory, the repeated word 'hampered' echoes earlier poems and enriches the sonnet as a stage on the way to the suite's resolution of the problem faced by those in Heaney's world – including himself – who are hampered, out of their element.[12] The resolution resides in a change of element, and if that is beyond the power of his mother and, say, Antaeus and the 'unshorn and bewildered' countryman in 'Making Strange' (*Station Island*), Heaney now intends it to be within his power as a poet. The achievement of sonnet 7 is the poet's transformation of his mother's death into an alleged double liberation, of mother and poet, without with crassness or disrespect and with only the opportunism inherent in art.

The unsolicited and uncontrollable 'clearings' in *Field Work* can be on occasions in *Station Island* and *The Haw Lantern* deliberate acts of individual will, performed, for example, by the hermit in 'Sweeney Redivivus':

> As he prowled the rim of his clearing
> where the blade of choice had not spared
> one stump of affection
>
> he was like a ploughshare
> interred to sustain the whole field
> of force . . .

This is the burly poet-'ploughman' of the early Glanmore sonnets speaking. Increasingly since *Field Work*, Heaney's real fields have turned into fields of force, and in doing so have become a metaphor for the kind of poetry he has professed to admire. A poem's unsayable 'field of force' has become a favourite figure in the critical essays collected in *The Government of the Tongue*. Once cleared, the hermit's field is brutally ploughed now (no more wise passiveness! no more Mr Nice Guy!) and the deep replenishment we associate with Heaney's poetry, in subject and effect, is a reward now for power.[13] This is largely a thematic mutation as yet, though the single sustained breath of 'The Hermit', its nine lines of strenuous exhalation and its three lines of recuperative inhalation, is something of a formal enactment. Of the ploughing hermit, Heaney writes:

> the more brutal the pull
> and the drive, the deeper
> and quieter the work of refreshment.

In 'Clearances' the poet recalls his response to his mother's fear of affectation that made her exaggerate her own ignorance: 'So I governed my tongue/In front of her . . . '. This is a tact which Heaney pays its rightful due in 'An Ulster Twilight' (*Station Island*), a rewriting to some extent of 'The Other Side' (*Wintering Out*); in both cases the tact is displayed by neighbours from different sides of the sectarian divide. It receives spiritual elevation in 'Shelf Life' from *Station Island*:

> I make a morning offering again:
> *that I may escape the miasma of spilled blood,*
> *govern the tongue, fear hybris, fear the god*
> *until he speaks in my untrammelled mouth.*

Heaney is rightly admired in Ulster for his tact and courtesy as he steps through the sectarian minefield, but he is aware of their involuntary origins and their profitable aesthetic possibilities:

> Two buckets were easier carried than one.
> I grew up in between
>
> My left hand placed the standard iron weight.
> My right tilted a last grain in the balance.

In 'Terminus' Heaney's straddling of divisions is at last raised to its own myth and the condition is given its own deity, the Roman god of boundaries.

Here the middle ground is redefined as success, not failure or dereliction. Yet it has always dissatisfied Heaney even when he has dignified it, as he appears to have done recently, as 'tilting the scales of reality towards some transcendent equilibrium'.[14] He has always expressed preference for the unequivocal utterance from the 'untrammelled mouth', female at first, and recently male. In *The Government of the Tongue* he praises Mandelstam and Nero (however unlikely a coupling) over Chekhov, Sorley MacLean and Wilfred Owen for permitting the tongue, 'governed for so long in the social sphere by considerations of tact and fidelity, by nice obeisances to one's origins within the minority or the majority', to be 'suddenly ungoverned' in art's jubilation, truancy, freedom, 'which is the antithesis of every hampered and deprived condition', including the burdensome obligation to bear witness against society's crimes.

Heaney has always championed the ungoverned tongue, a 'feminine' and permeable resistance to the 'masculine' demands of society. In *Preoccupations* the ungoverned or unhampered tongue is the Wordsworthian organ of origins, roots, background speaking the authority of primal conditions. Recently, however, Heaney has sought to describe and educe a more confident form of ungoverning for poetry. Now it *is* a problem should poetry evade challenges to it;

such ungoverning, it seems, is an oblique acceptance of the paramountcy of society. Heaney seeks self-government for poetry, self-government in the sense of sovereignty, not self-constraint, and in which the 'masculine' traits of government are appropriated by a verse that nevertheless retains or creates as a result the field of the original Worsworthian force and without being – as far as I can make out – the 'mere' rhetorical mastery of Jonson, Hopkins or Yeats. He seeks a third poetry that is not, however, the poetry of conscience and responsibility, even if the latter can achieves equilibrium between poetry and society, art and life.

The Government of the Tongue is dominated like its predecessor by the 'double nature' of poetry, and many of the previous polarities are rehearsed – art/life; song/suffering; poetry/politics; rhetoric/reality; beauty/truth; relish/penitence; artistic self-respect/submission to the times.[15] But on the artistic side of the equation, the *up*rooted is now privileged; so too are absence, placelessness, the unsaid, impersonality, weightlessness, vision, even dream – all most un-Heaney-like. Kavanagh is re-evaluated and found to have moved from a substantial, local and self-expressive poetry to a weightless, placeless self-mastery. This is not a reading that convinces me, but it aligns with Heaney's current 'stance towards life'. Indicting his earlier reading of the verse Kavanagh wrote after 'Epic', he writes: 'To go back to our original parable [of the chestnut tree], I still assumed Kavanagh to be writing about the tree which was actually in the ground when he had in fact passed on to write about the tree which he held in mind'. Kavanagh 'had cleared a space' to be filled from an inner source that could irrigate the world beyond the self.

The world beyond the self, which Sylvia Plath is judged not quite to have reached, is most authentically imagined in terms of air and light, of the vacancy left by events passed, objects removed, people departed. What I previously called the enviable globe of Heaney's experience, meaning its palpable comprehensiveness, is hollow in 'Alphabets', the opening poem of *The Haw Lantern*: a lucent and pure vowel, a sign of Heaney's times. The close of Heaney's memorial sonnet on Robert Fitzgerald the translator, despite the difference of its archer's infallible aim, might make us think of the ending of Philip Larkin's 'The Whitsun Weddings'. (The 'bright nowhere' of sonnet 8 in 'Clearances' is also Larkinesque.) Indeed, the poet who wrote 'Church Going', 'The Importance of Elsewhere', 'Poetry of Departures', 'Going', 'At Grass' and 'Next, Please' is a laureate of absence. But it is a glowing absence: the author of 'High Windows' is equally a laureate of light (an early typescript collection was entitled 'In the Grip of Light'), and the title of Heaney's essay on Larkin in *The Government of the Tongue* is a suitable borrowing from Shakespeare: 'The Main of Light'. Heaney's remarks on Larkin in *Preoccupations* are respectful but restrained, directed upon a poet 'of composed and tempered English nationalism'; in 'The Main of Light' he is reread in a critical redress (this one convincing) as a poet of visionary moments, of bright still centres with a nostalgia for a crystalline reality.

Solidities of natural object, rural implement and folk artefact, once the texts of Heaney's poems, are now asserted to be pretexts for their insubstantial consequences. One poem, 'Hailstones', writes of itself: 'I make this now/out of the melt of the real thing/smarting into its absence.' Heaney professes now to value glimmerings, traces, spoors, sensing : the after-lives rather than the lives of things.[16] He had already implied this in an earlier poem, 'The Harvest Bow', in *Field Work*, a pivotal (and well-nigh perfect) poem in the *oeuvre*. The phrase, 'The end of art is peace', borrowed from Patmore courtesy of Yeats, could be changed without loss to 'The end of art is love', for Heaney has implicitly adopted in this poem (as he has done explicitly in *The Government of the Tongue* and *Station Island*) Hopkins' claim that love is the power and spring of verse. The corn spirit, departed, has warmed and burnished the harvest bow as peace and love warm and burnish the poem, a device happily less frail than the bow, though still a memorial to fugitive virtue. The poem at its end gently vibrates with a kind of homesickness, a warm remnant of itself, and this re-enacts the poet's fingering the bow like braille and, in a crucial and memorable phrase, 'Gleaning the unsaid off the palpable'. Heaney has lately worked not just to transubstantiate the matter of his verse but *in*substantiate it, while leaving intact the palpable that enables its own weightless aftermath.[17]

Since nouns bear the brunt of ideas and determine the density of a poem's imagery, we can say that the verse in *The Haw Lantern*, with its more rarefied vocabulary of light and vacancy, lacks the consistency of earlier verse. Lines like the following, from 'Wolfe Tone', are spring-heeled and lack the solidarity (to borrow the poet's pun) that Tone wants and Heaney had.

Light as a skiff, manoeuvrable
yet outmanoeuvred,

I affected epaulettes and a cockade,
wrote a style well-bred and impervious

to the solidarity I angled for,
and played the ancient Roman with a razor.

Incidentally, the similarity between Tone and Heaney is here a kind of counterpoint: Heaney is no revolutionary and his early work was praised for its lack of affectation, its earthiness; but Heaney's speech, if not well-bred, has acquired manners like a foundling taken in by gentlefolk; and Heaney too could say with Tone, though for different reasons, 'I was . . . out of my element among small farmers'.

CHANGES OF REDRESS

Heaney's third poetry, a poetry of light, air, glimmer, manoeuvre, is still more a thematic than a formal accomplishment, partly because the palpable must be faithfully recorded in order for him to register its traces. The necessity of reification and the longing for rarefication create a fresh duality in the verse. In the parables in *The Haw Lantern*, for example, political reality is transmuted into the abstraction of its elements. However, the reality can still be made out. The sequence of moods in 'From the Canton of Expectation' – optative/conditional, and imperative – clearly grammaticizes the fortunes of Ulster Catholics before and during the Civil Rights movement: impotent desire/negotiation from weakness, and educated demands. The parable ends with an imagined Lowellian figure who stands his ground in a third, resolving mood, 'in the indicative', who affirms but does not do so supinely 'from under', but – and Heaney calls up the 'male' imagery of *North* here – actively, with uncompromising self-belief. Unlike the imagined David in a muddy compound, he is a figure ambiguously political and apolitical, 'whose boat will lift when the cloudburst happens'. (Civil war in Ulster, among other possible doomsdays in the world?) Here is a familiar ambivalence, Heaney torn between art and life, poetry and politics, but in a higher key, as it were; now the ideal alternative to danger is purity, not the messier business of a relishable antiquity. Escape from politics and life is no longer declension and absorption; the imagined boat is buoyed up and floated free by the very force that has challenged it.

The ideal – which is poetry *per se* but also a *kind* of poetry among lesser poetries – is, however, airy and masterful by turns. Here is a short poem from Part One of *Station Island*:

Widgeon

It had been badly shot.
While he was plucking it
he found, he says, the voice box –

like a flute stop
in the broken windpipe –

and blew upon it
unexpectedly
his own small widgeon cries.

The shock of identity that closes the poem tends to *en*close it and make the haiku-like resolution intransitive: the poem is its own small self, though we could murmur 'life out of death' or 'suffering's after-life'. However, the poem opens up when we nest it within the poet's ruminations in *The Government of the Tongue* on the origin of poetic composition. In his lecture on Plath, Heaney quotes from *The Prelude* ('There was a Boy . . .') to illustrate the original act of making – the young Wordsworth blowing 'mimic hootings to the silent owls,/ That they might answer him' – which has its equivalent in a primary poetry of innocent self-regard, of relish. When the owls respond, awakening the owl-life in Wordsworth, we have, according to Heaney, the origin of the second stage of poetic composition in which correspondences are provoked between poet and universe. (This would initiate, I assume, a poetry responsive on occasions to the needs and obligations of society, a poetry of conscience.) 'Widgeon' commemorates the second stage of poetic creation: owl-life has been altered to duck-life, and duck-life awakened by an accidental shamanic impersonation.

In the third and highest kind of poetry, the poet inhales in a commanding act the powers of the outer world. It is in turn a kind of knowing. In his first Oxford lecture (1989), Heaney approves of Auden's trinity of poetic faculties, making, judging and knowing, which strongly resembles Heaney's new tripartite understanding of poetry. In a recent uncollected poem, 'Quoting', he writes about the best poetry and the inadequacy *of* merely writing about it:

Talking about it isn't good enough
But quoting from it at least demonstrates
The virtue of an art that knows its mind.

If he is here imitating such poetry, then it can assume, it seems, a deceptive ease by which making is hidden by the appearance of unpremeditation (a relaxed yet firm Lowellian line) but which in reality is a poem's (and poet's) self-possession confidently born of experience and wisdom. But this poem seems like a blueprint when we recall Heaney's formulation in his Oxford lecture: 'the best poetry will not only register the assault of the actual and the brunt of necessity; it will also embody the spirit's protest against all that'. It cannot, then, be truancy or mere jubilation, despite Heaney's resort to those words; but it remains unclear if the best poetry engages politics and society on their own terms, even tactically or provisionally; it is unclear how far the imagined boat-builder whose craft (vessel and art) lifts clear has actually met the challenge of the storm.[18] In 'From the Frontier of Writing' (*The Haw Lantern*), freedom for poetry requires 'clearance' (i.e. permission to proceed) from some part of the poet's psyche corresponding to, and imaginable as, society in its starkest form, a soldier at a checkpoint of the kind with which inhabitants of Ulster are familiar with. Since the psychic checkpoint may be necessary (it is unclear), then society' s baffles in front of the artist and its permissions to proceed (clearance: official acknowledgment of guiltlessness) may too be necessary, or at least convertible to artistic profit. The three psycho-social stages way-marked in the poem can be interpreted as alluding not only to com-position but also to the three *kinds* of poetry – of subjugation (and endurance), of conscience (protest or penitence), and of freedom – discussed in this essay. Freedom, however, seems to be passively won in this poem on the psychic and social levels. In any event, here and elsewhere poetry is *figured as politics*. From early in his career, Heaney chose as his political allegory the troubled history of Ireland and, in greater detail, the history of Northern Ireland since his boyhood. He has employed this allegory even though poetry in its highest form is judged to have 'cleared' or surmounted politics. Before that, though, poetry is literally *challenged by politics*, whose challenge the highest poetry in some unspecified way meets but without self-compromise. But even if politics are in the best poetry sublimated (hence the imagery of light, air, flight?), Heaney has always intended his poetry to be, and indeed it is, a political poetry of considerable if oblique power.

Despite the passivity of the writer in 'From the Frontier of Writing', Heaney nowadays discusses the best poetry in terms of 'command', 'mastery', 'authority'. His literary history is sparsely populated by 'exemplars' whose better poems create 'fields of force' and whose best poems are 'epoch-making'. The metaphors of democracy have given way to those of autocracy. Power in poems now 'spills over', the verse exerts itself in 'mighty heaves'. The metaphors of femininity have yielded pride of place to those of masculinity. It is as if Heaney in his imagination has raided the male side of the ledger and returned with useful vials of hormone; his re-evaluations of Kavanagh, Lowell, Mandelstam and the others are critical Steinach operations on those writers. Poetry is to be virilified and set free. Sympathy has gravitated from the possessed (and passively possessing) female, and from the thwarted self-possession of the conscientious male, towards a male whose self-possession (though exclusively poetic) is only imaginable in terms of masculine empery, and which in the context of Heaney's *oeuvre* must be a kind of *re*-possession of the female by her rightful mate and not the rhetorical colonialism of a Jonson, Hopkins or Yeats.

Clearly a kind of sexual redress has been under way in Heaney's enterprise from the beginning. Veneration of the female and the repeated return to the mother, accompanied by an underestimation (or repressed overestimation?) of the male gives way, not so far to an active search for the father (Heaney's father is the subject of 'Digging' and 'The Harvest Bow' but few other poems) but to a less personal search for poetic maleness that will not offend the female deities of his poetry (Ireland, the muse, the goddess of the fen). It could be, however, that certain poets, notably Lowell, fill the role of 'father' and exhibit paternal power. The impersonality of the search leads to some confusion as to which set of imagery is primary: air, vacancy, trace (nominal images of a neuter state beyond gender but in the beginning more female than male); or lift, heave, spill (verbal images of masculine exertion). But certainly the poems in *The Haw Lantern* redress the balance (and not always with poetic profit) between features that Heaney sexed in *Preoccupations*: design is now as important as verbal texture, statement as feeling, address as evocation, appeal to the mind as appeal to the senses. (But the mighty heave, one feels, has yet to come.)

Heaney's own painstaking and ingenious equations and correspondences make it impossible for us to separate clearly sexual from political redress. The search for a justifying (and justified) masculinity is the search for power which, in political form, Irish Catholics were deprived of for centuries, and Ulster Catholics for fifty recent years. In the beginning (to all intents) was the colonization of Ireland, the turning of the island into a possessed (and passively possessing) woman; the native desire for 'male' self-possession was the desire for self-government, kept from total success, however, by the biddable nature of constitutional nationalism or the reasonable demands for mere civil rights inside the United Kingdom. Is the ideal re-possessing male not, then, the demanding republican who entertains, beyond redress, imperial designs of his own on his former oppressors? Might we even translate Heaney's stages of redress into all-Ireland terms and see a figurative passage from colony through Free State to the desired Republic? The personal nature of the search for redress – personal because it is autobiographical in origin and part and and parcel of Heaney's mission as a poet – gives a political dimension to the confusion between imageries. The nationalist chestnut tree that is later savoured in its absence is translated into a world above and beyond politics, Heaney's nostagia for pre-colonial unity and his acceptance of 'constitutional nationalism' succeed, it seems, to a desired transcendence of the constitutional issue, though perhaps in a way that accommodates, by absorbing, the colonizing or would-be colonizing forces. However, the imagery of male dominion unavoidably, in the light of Heaney's earlier verse, amounts to a potent revendication. The wish remains for a self-determination that seeks reparation for the past. Heaney has recently seemed to want to surmount his origins and tribal membership, and evade any possible imputations of regionalism or even nationalism. In one sense he has been both justified and successful in doing so, but in another he is hampered by the very excellence under his belt. Whatever purity and aloofness his poetry achieves in future, it cannot but be seen as a kind of sovereignty wrested out of subjection or home rule, thereby implicating Irish politics and the empowering, the growing confidence, of Irish nationalist culture (in the largest sense of the phrase) in its relationship with Britain and Protestant Ulster.

Nor has the broadening internationality of Heaney's poetry and criticism yet lessened his stature as the most considerable representative of contemporary Irish culture, for that internationality has been, and will be at least for a time, an aspect of the literary redress under way in his *oeuvre*. The early equation through gender of Ireland with poetry tacitly withheld from his island's English and Scots colonizers deepest intimacy with the muse, while the three exemplars of male poetry, of rhetorical ascendancy, Jonson, Hopkins and Yeats, were respectively an Englishman, an Englishman in Ireland, and an Anglo-Irishman. The American Lowell, on the other hand, inhabits that republic of poetry independent both of the kingdom of English verse and of the political state. Late Lowell represents for Heaney government *of* poetry, *by* poetry, *for* poetry, but it is hard to overlook culture and politics as both metaphor for and constituents of this independence. Meanwhile Heaney's interest in eastern European poets, founded on an implied similarity between their plight and his own, has likewise enabled Heaney to cross the boundary of the English tradition into a European community of poets. The similarity is an effective but problematical one, resting; on Heaney's debatable status as a dissident poet (or one close to danger yet capable of truant jubilation) and on Catholic Ulster's debatable status, since Direct Rule in 1972, as a victim culture.

Whereas we are familiar with a variety of Irelands in literature and in reality, we have tended to think of England as indivisible in that fashion because it was a parent and colonizing country. Therefore Heaney's 1976 lecture, 'Englands of the Mind', a novel account by an Irishman of Hughes, Hill and Larkin, was also a subtle shrinking of England to imaginative versions and mental regions of itself of the kind Irish writers have been driven in compensation and colonial division to create and inhabit.[19] As if over the heads of English writers and critics – but encouraged by them, possibly for reasons of colonial guilt among others – Heaney has taken it upon himself to 'speak for England' *en passant*, while he goes about the main business of speaking for Ireland and the world republic of Western and English-language poetry.

Establishing the constitutional status of poetry has involved Heaney in rehearsing issues debated since Classical times and which we might have thought had been settled, in any case, by Modernism. He has returned us to a state of affairs that obtained before society beckoned English poetry in the political 1930s, pseudo-vatic expression lured it in the neo-Romantic 1940s and early 1950s, and jocular scepticism threatened its self-esteem in the late 1950s and 1960s. Indeed, by confidently and repeatedly referring to Poetry in an honorific and essentialist sense, Heaney has tried to return to it the statehood which its Classical, Renaissance and Romantic apologists insisted it deserved. The tension the poet feels between the figurative state of poetry and the real state he inhabits is high in Heaney's case (though the state is Northern Ireland and Britain but not, oddly, as far as tension is concerned, the Republic of Ireland, where Heaney has primarily resided for almost twenty years and in which routine civil liberties are fewer than in Northern Ireland), but it has been equally high in many cases before his. If we wanted an almost randomly chosen resolution of the dilemma, we might recall the remark made by Chekhov, a Heaney exemplar, to the effect that artists should engage themselves in politics only enough to protect themselves from politics. This appears to be Heaney's current sentiment and it informs the political parables in *The Haw Lantern*. If we put the dilemma in terms of the temptation and reproach which action represents for the artist, then we can find it debated in 'Ego Dominus Tuus' and other works by Yeats, another Heaney exemplar. Casting it in the largest terms possible, the magnitude of art's obligation to life, to humanity, we might then think of the sentences by Keats, another exemplar, taken by C.K. Stead as an epigraph to *The New Poetic*, a book Heaney praises in both *Preoccupations* and *The Government of the Tongue*: 'I will assay to reach the highest summit in Poetry . . . All I hope is that I may not lose all interest in human affairs . . .'. The ambition and the anxiety are hardly less candid in Heaney himself. Stead's second epigraph, from Arthur Symons, restates the challenge with the greater distance of the critic: 'in this revolt against exteriority, against rhetoric, against a materialistic tradition . . . literature, bowed down by so many burdens, may at last attain liberty, and its authentic speech'. This is Heaney's hope precisely put. According to Stead, Modernist poetry synthesized and transcended two contradictory poetries: these three kinds of poetry are those which heaney, *mutatis mutandis*, Heaney has lengthily discoursed on and which he has perceived as what we might call the poetries of, respectively, undress, address and redress. And if the truest poetry discovers and possesses itself with the power that governs the world outside it, then for a striking figuration of the process we might turn to the eagle eyes of stout Cortez on his Panamanian heights, Keats's version of the imperial imagination of the artist.

To recycle these fundamental issues but in his own unique terms, as Heaney does in his criticism, is to exercise what Ellmann, drawing on law, called eminent domain. Meanwhile the growth of this poet's mind half-consciously rehearses that of the poetic mind itself. Recycling and rehearsing in ways available to the intelligent layman has generated for Heaney an authority reminiscent of that other twentieth-century, non-English culture-giver, Eliot. Like Eliot's, Heaney's vision is at base religious and this gives his 'stance towards life' an enviable firmness of footing.[20]

Religion for Heaney is no mere store of poetic metaphor, though we can readily find sources in the Bible for the various meanings of, for example, 'the government of the tongue', a metaphor that otherwise appears to be exclusively political. Zacharias' sudden onset of speech is a lyrical ungoverning: 'And his mouth was opened immediately, and his tongue was loosed, and he spake, and praised God' (Luke 1:64). The connection between vatic poetry and speech in tongues also suggests itself, but beyond prophecy and lyrical paean, the tongue, we are told, is a member whose government is necessary. Proverbs 21:23 spiritualizes, as it were, Heaney's tact: 'Whoso keepeth his mouth and his tongue keepeth his soul from trouble.' Not to govern the tongue is dangerous; James tells us: 'If any man among you seem to be religious and bridleth not his tongue, but deceiveth his heart, this man's religion is vain' (James 1:26). Of course, Heaney wants poetic government *by* the tongue in 'jubilation', a word of biblical ring.

More than metaphor for Heaney, religion is more, even, than that analogy for poetic vocation suggested in his approving use, as an epigraph to *Preoccupations*, of Yeats's claim that 'the following of art is little different from the following of religion in the intense preoccupation it demands'. No: Heaney's poetic self is by now a virtual soul, more aware of its own corruptness than of corruption in the community (Dante's City), though one is the habitat of the other. The unity Heaney seeks in poetry, and possibly (since his criticism is a creative auxiliary in a way Arnold would have approved) *through* poetry, is as convincing as Yeats's and is, odd though it sounds in the last decade of the twentieth century, the soul's unity with being. His sense of division and his quest for synthesis are Dante's rational mysticism rendered in contemporary terms: this is the spiritual narrative, the fiction, the mythography of his output to date, and it makes him a field-work against the expanding banality of our social lives.

Heaney's is a pilgrim's progress, charted in poetry that is rich donation to English letters. Even in our celebration of it, however, we ought not to overlook the extent to which it attempts to settle accounts along the way. For example, the Catholicism by which the progress is charted is a religious redress within the context of these islands where Catholicism, Ireland and minority nationalism are almost synonymous. It is, indeed, a greater righting of an imbalance than Joyce's. Joyce's work originated in Southern Ireland at a time when its inhabitants felt it to be a victim culture; Heaney's originates in Northern Ireland at a time when its Catholic inhabitants feel the same way. But if Joyce's work was slow to make impact in Britain, Heaney's has been rapid. That it is an Irishman, and an Ulsterman to boot, who is currently framing in practice and theory the constitution of mainstream poetry in these islands is a cultural redress of remarkable proportions and a testament to what Seamus Heaney has accomplished in what we hope is merely mid-career. Here is poetry – and here is poetic justice.

[1990]

NOTES

1. By sexing poetry so assiduously, Heaney leaves himself open to the charge of sexism. Sex, of course, is largely a metaphor for him, justified chiefly because of the elemental and pervasive nature of sexuality in human life; also, it is only one guise, among several, of Heaney's binary perception of much of that life. However, I leave open the question of whether the functions Heaney attributes to each sex reflect a stereotyping of sexual relationship that is detrimental to women in the world outside the poetry. Suffice it to say here that no detriment is inferable *within the poetry itself*. Whereas Heaney is tirelessly aware of sexual differences, he doesn't use those differences to discriminate in sentiment *against* the female sex even if he discriminates *between* the sexes.

2. Actually, I think the gerund and present participle are the archetypal, 'amphibious' parts of his speech: verbs dreaming themselves nouns. See my 1974 article for other 'amphibious' elements in Heaney's poetry.

3. In 'Station Island', Heaney permits his dead cousin, whom he elegized in 'The Strand at Lough Beg' (*Field Work*), to accuse him of having 'saccharined' his death. This is reminiscent of Yeats's permitting Michael Robartes (his own creation) in *Stories of Michael Robartes and his Friends* (1931) to object to the opulent style of the earlier 'apocalyptic stories' (1897) in which he had appeared, Heaney has reached this stage of profitable self-criticism; but that Heaney couches the self-criticism in a work of still rich verse and unabashed Catholic inspiration and structure perhaps lessens its impact. In Heaney forms and content of expression can contradict each other, mainly because there tends to be a wider variety of statement than of diction.

4. We needn't, of course, swallow whole Heaney's expressed or implicit valuations of kinds of poetry; they are part of the fiction of his enterprise and do not always 'jibe' with the experienced merit of an individual poem. But the valuations are so bound up with that enterprise that it is impossible not to follow them at a certain level of generality.

5. An instructive comparison to 'The Guttural Muse' is Derek Mahon's 'Rock Music', both poems generated by the same situation. Mahon wittily effaces himself (and the youngsters) by the undramatic irony of a silent earth's arched eyebrow. Incidentally, although in 'The Guttural Muse' Heaney riskily forces us to compare a tench with a young girl in a white dress, it is the poet, rather, who is the 'doctor fish' sending up its comforting oily bubbles to us.

6. Ian Hamilton, *Robert Lowell: A Biography* (London: Faber, 1983), p. 223.

7. Cf. 'In the Beech', a poem in the 'Sweeney Redivivus' section of *Station Island*.

8. Sweeney astray is Sweeney wandering, and also straying into error. But he is also 'astray in the head', as we used to say in Belfast – 'mental', deranged. Heaney is drawing on the conventional association of poetry with madness.

9. See my article, '"A Lough Neagh Sequence" by Seamus Heaney: Sources and Motifs', *Eire-Ireland* XII, 2 (1977), 138–42; reprinted without footnotes in *Seamus Heaney*, ed. Harold Bloom (New Haven: Chelsea House, 1986), pp. 45–9. The use of elvers confusingly implies that return to origins is possible.

10. Surprisingly, the idea is as old as 'Antaeus', a 1966 poem included in *North*, in which Hercules can earn the airy realm of fame only by engaging with the earthbound giant, but in 1966, as in 1975, when 'Hercules and Antaeus' was collected, Heaney's interest lay in Gaia's son and not in the Roman hero. (The tree as a connection between air and earth might recall Frost's birches, whose swingers are like both Antaeus the earthbound and Hercules the aspirant. Frost's early influence on Heaney, especially on his rural realism, escaped my attention in 1974.)

11. In a vision that translates medieval Christian depiction into terms of Celtic nature worship, Heaney in 'The Wishing Tree' has a vision of his mother as a tree assumed into heaven, 'an airy branch-head rising through damp cloud,/Of turned-up faces where the tree had stood'. As early as 'Belderg' in *North*, Heaney had given the tree a symbolic importance of almost mystical force, when he imagined 'A world-tree of balanced stones,/Querns piled like vertebrae . . . .'.

12. For a number of historical reasons, few in Ulster, Catholic or Protestant, who are not from the Higher strata of society, derive from what we might call a literary culture. This can provoke in the aspiring writer some discomfiture and even some sense of imposture. Carleton is the archetypal figure in this regard, but the literary symptoms are there in Brian Moore and Heaney himself; both writers, for example, apparently need to dramatize comforting exemplars. The ambiguities and ambivalences in these writers may be traceable in part to the colonial experience (which according to one Irish historian encouraged evasion and duplicity), in part to provincialism, in part (in Moore's case) to emigration to overseas cities or (in Heaney's case) to the effect of higher education on lower class rural or urban children. Heaney benefited from the 1947 (NI) Butler Education Act, which translated many children out of their family element. Heaney's work, like Moore's, can be seen on one level as an extended social and cultural redress of a highly personal kind.

13. A poem that reposes in contrast to 'The Hermit' is 'The Seed Cutters' in *North*, in which the work is performed lackadaisically and communally.

14. In his inaugural lecture as Professor of Poetry at Oxford (October 1989). An abridged version of this lecture appeared in the *Times Literary Supplement* (December 1989).

15. Dorinda Outram has identified binary opposition as a feature recurring (for a number of reasons) in Irish culture: 'Heavenly Bodies and Logical Minds', *Graph* (Spring 1988), 9–11.

16. One might think again of Frost, that specialist not only in the imagery of sensuous rural life, but also in the after-imagery (indeed, what we might call para-imagery) of that life.

17. Stone, for example, looms large in the recent poetry but weighs little. Like the tree it begins its career in Heaney's work as both poetic and palpable. Now Heaney emphasizes the impalpability to which stone permits passage; in 'The Stone Grinder' (*The Haw Lantern*), the grinder remarks of his material: 'I ordained capacities and they haruspicated' (a new inflection of the word, judging by the *OED*). Stone now conveys hermetic meaning beyond speech ('The Stone Verdict', *The Haw Lantern*) and has oracular power ('Shelf Life', *Station Island*).

18. Heaney's definition of the truest poetry bears some resemblance to my reading of Joyce's 'The Dead' in *Fictions of the Irish Literary Revival* (1987), in which Gabriel Conroy and his creator are seen as achieving vision by dint of fully acknowledging the claims of earth and mortality, of the living and the dead. They attain a world *beyond* the self only after *achieving* the self. Heaney, too, has apparently come to feel his tribal, communal identity, though richly sustaining, to be a ceiling on growth; in one sense it is real and promotes realism, but in another sense it is unreal and promotes romantic nationalism. Yet Heaney seems to feel that accession to a realistic individuality is both a desirable terminus and only a stage on the road to a self-transcending vision and experience of *real* freedom. In a letter, Heaney drew my attention to the resemblance, though he had in mind *Station Island* rather than his own criticism.

19. See my own 'The Landscape of Three Irelands' above.

20. Heaney's encounters with ghosts in 'Station Island' derive, of course, from Dante, but it is worth remembering Eliot's encounter with Yeats's ghost in 'Little Gidding' (and perhaps MacNeice's with the ghost of Grettir in 'Eclogue from Iceland', during which Grettir advises him on the course of his poetry).

11

A COMPLEX FATE:
THE IRISHNESS OF DENIS DONOGHUE

> 'I want to come upon an answer to
> this a little roundabout' – *We Irish*

The subtitle of this volume is something of a misnomer.* Of the twenty-nine pieces printed here, nineteen are book reviews, two are letters to journals (of the 'Letter from Ireland' variety) or commentaries from journals (of the *TLS* variety), one is a lecture, one a broadcast possibly. There are six essays proper.

This caution to the reader is no more than that, since by reviews and essays alike we can begin to take the measure of Ireland's best-known critic as a student of Irish literature. Donoghue is a man of international literary enthusiasms, like his compatriot Conor Cruise O'Brien, who haunts this volume in tentative apposition. But if politics are easy for O'Brien, they are difficult for Donoghue, and the word 'enthusiasms' is less appropriate in his case, for Donoghue's criticism is hardly passionate; his great intelligence is not combative or hostile, but neither is it warm or unduly helpful. The reader is invited, as it were, to follow respectfully an argument until it refrigerates into artifact, that object of contemplation we call 'the essay' (as distinct from the humbler 'article'). This is one reading, but I shall offer others.

For engagement there is. But it is largely underground and resisted – by the loyalty to Yeats, and to his teachers the New Critics, by the desire to write literature, not merely criticism, and by a half-repressed relationship to his native island from which he has been semi-exiled for many years. The last, I suspect, is the source of the deepest resistance, which he may have tried to overcome in part even in the act of assembling all of his more than topical matter on his troublesome country's writing.

* *We Irish: The Selected Essays of Denis Donoghue*, Vol. 1 (Brighton: The Harvester Press 1986).

'We Irish' is the title of the volume and of the introductory, synthesizing and presumably most recent essay. The phrase is Yeats's ('We Irish, born into that ancient sect'), inspired by Berkeley's repudiation in his journal of English abstractionism ('We Irishmen cannot attain to these truths'). It is also Donoghue's, reclaiming his own Irishness and that of his compatriots (more of this cultural nationalism anon), yet retaining some of the problematicness of both Yeats's and Berkeley's usage, preserving an ironic distance between himself and that identity O'Brien defined as 'being involved in the Irish situation and usually being mauled by it', or some such words.

Yeats, we are told, believed there was a special Irish mentality, deriving the idea in part from Berkeley, for whom 'the Irish', Donoghue concludes, meant powerless but prestigious upper-class Protestants. Donoghue calls the notion 'bizarre', and reduces it to a wish to counter English materialism and mechanistic philosophy. Yet he defends Yeats's preoccupation with a distinctive Irishness against Seamus Deane's attack in his Field Day pamphlets on the romantic mystique of nationhood, defending even the essentialism from which it issued. Indeed, Seamus Heaney, a Field Day man, is shown to have the same preoccupation as recently as *Station Island* (1984).

But in the discussion of Heaney, Yeats fades as a forerunner to be replaced by Joyce. Donoghue takes issue with Joyce's ghost (i.e. with Heaney) in *Station Island* who is apparently wrong to tell Heaney that the issue of Irishness doesn't matter, yet praises Stephen Dedalus in *A Portrait* (i.e. Joyce) for riskily attempting to escape his Irishness. Donoghue concludes that there *is* a distinctive Irish experience (is Yeats correct then?) but that it is an experience of proliferating division (is Yeats wrong then?). The most formidable poet of this division is apparently Thomas Kinsella who is nevertheless dealt with in a brief paragraph and is only summoned later in the volume in order to be curtly dismissed for writing poetry of the last atrocity.

The kernel argument of 'We Irish' I find baffling, and to make matters worse it is contained within the pretextual query as to what Berkeley meant by 'We Irishmen'. The essay ends with a reminder that Berkeley lost interest anyway in defining an Irish mentality and increasingly regarded himself as English. The whole, like Berkeley's quest for Irishness, reads like a pointless exercise. But perhaps not in subtext. Donoghue quotes Berkeley as he wonders aloud if it isn't the duty of the Irish after all to cultivate their love for England, and adds: 'The only way he had in view was that of being unfailingly biddable.' Is one meant to catch a nationalist sneer?

We all know that being Irish is 'a complex fate', to borrow the title of another piece in the book, but its articulation need not be confusing into the bargain. Donoghue on literature is enlightening, at times masterly; Donoghue on Ireland I find close to incoherent. On this subject he shares a peculiar difficulty of argument with the Field Day pamphleteers (bright men all, and more productive on Ireland than Donoghue because less inhibited on the subject). This, and the tactics of deferment Donoghue employs in 'We Irish' and elsewhere, may be the effect of having read the newer thinkers (Lacan, Derrida, Foucault) and refusing to press forward along a (male) line of discourse so as to close signification, as Jane Gallop says of Lacan. But such an effect may be coinciding in all these Irish critics with some kind of ethnic disturbance.

The locus of this disturbance (not the source but a Freudian cathexis) is the work of Yeats, modern embodiment of the primal father, a figure invested with an undesirable but irresistible authority. Beyond Yeats, 'nationalist' critics, it sometimes appears, can hardly advance, as neurotic sons remain all their lives, as Freud tells us, beneath the father's authority, unable to transfer their libido (in their case critical desire) to an outside sexual object. There are four pieces devoted to Joyce in We Irish, but three of these are reviews, and all pale in urgency beside the four extended pieces on Yeats. Like Jacob, Donoghue and the others are still grappling with the father to discover their real name (the name of their country), and have not begun (perhaps *cannot* yet begin) to engage with modern Irish literature in an unanxious way; in We Irish, all of the writers save for Yeats and Joyce are scrappily dealt with.

An attempt of course is made, and We Irish is a fascinating record of a chain of ambivalences (i.e. of desires and resistances). The ostensible first link is what Donoghue repeatedly sees as Yeats's own ambiguity. In 'Romantic Ireland' (1980), Yeats's lifelong Romanticism is set against the poet's recognition that Romantic values had failed. In 'Yeats: The Question of Symbolism' (1977), Yeats's symbolism, with its attraction to essence and vision, is countered by 'the scruple which prevented him from making his entire art with Symons and the Symbolists', that scruple arising from 'the roughage of daily experience, chance, choice, and history'. In 'On *The Winding Stair*' (1965), Yeats is seen as running his course between extremities, of which his dialogue between self and soul, and all they imply, is the case in point.

Donoghue attempts on Yeats's behalf to resolve these ambiguities. Yeats is seen as a legendizer, legend being a middle term between symbolism and history; he is seen as absorbing history into his *own* history, situating himself, again, between contraries. These are convincing if conventionally academic resolutions. Odder is Donoghue's conclusion in 'Romantic Ireland' that the idea of Romantic Ireland has been in Irish literature endlessly constructed and deconstructed (I think he merely means repudiated or satirized, judging from his brief examples, and if so he is right) but has now been 'sequestered', removed for a time from dispute against a calmer, more hospitable future. In 1980 I hope this appeared as much a cop-out as it appears today. Deane squarely faced the issue a few years later.

But it may be less cop-out than resistance. For Yeats's ambiguity is the objective correlative, as it were, to Donoghue's own ambivalence towards the poet. It is an ambivalence that seems to have been contracted from his younger compatriot critics, for it is most evident in the recent essays, 'We Irish' and 'Yeats, Ancestral Houses, and Anglo-Ireland'. He begins both essays with the most outrageous, most offensive anti-democratic, violence-mongering Yeats, as if challenging readers – but really himself – to rescue Yeats from obloquy, as rescue him we must, he being a great poet. When a critical obligation collides with a citizen's desire to accuse, this can contort the tectonic plates of feeling and thought of anyone engaged with literature. Donoghue's defence is that late Yeats was at the end of his tether and therefore exonerable. The poet's occasional hysteria is 'touching in its appalling way', a neat but too convenient paradox, surely. Another defence is that it was society's fault for provoking Yeats's violent anti-democracy.

Having loyally defended Yeats, Donoghue proceeds in 'Yeats, Ancestral Houses, and Anglo-Ireland' to undermine the poet's romantic conception of the Big House with a few well-chosen observations on the ground from Arthur Young, Carlyle, and Froude. Perhaps sensing some contradiction, Donoghue attaches a personal postscript, which brings to the surface a basic ambiguity in his own methodology. We are told that Yeats's politics and occultism caused the critic difficulty from the beginning, though he was reading the poet under the aegis of New Criticism, an American methodology that required the reader to extend latitude to the work of art as artifact. It is not clear, but it seems that young Donoghue accepted Blackmur's notion of doctrine-as-emotion. (Blackmur, Tate, Ransom,

Burke and Brooks appear nostalgically as mentors, their names almost as talismans, in *We Irish*.) Nowadays, Donoghue admits uneasily, latitude is denied by Marxist and Irish anti-colonialist critics alike. Rather than face the methodological, much less ideological, implications of this, Donoghue falls back on re-defending the figure in question, Yeats, while acknowledging that Yeats is resented in Ireland. A pause, a gap, longer and wider than the paragraph break it is, then this: 'My own stance is that of a latitudinarian, and I would hold to its concessiveness until a particularly extreme outrage makes me ashamed of it.'

Latitudinarianism joins sequestration as a neutral concept newly defensive in the presence of the younger Irish revisionists ('Catholic', 'Irish', and 'nationalist' in origin like himself) with whom he is engaged in a generational rivalry, a rather rearguard engagement from his position. His ideal reader, he tells us in his Introduction, 'moves with winning flexibility' between the categories of common reader, educated public, and professional reader, 'without committing himself to any of them'. This is quite defensible and legitimate, yet there is evidence that Donoghue feels that his reader should be more or less than this, and he himself more than a latitudinarian sequestering the knottier problems of literary ideology. The work of Williams, Jameson and Benjamin (international equivalents of local boys, Deane & co.) is not taken up but their names are dropped, stones troubling the placid stream of New Criticism.

There is no doubt that Donoghue is at his best as a mainstream critic, and 'Yeats: The Question of Symbolism', for example, is a genuine contribution to our understanding of symbolism in general and Yeats in particular, and I am grateful for it. The earlier essays are written with an eloquence uncommon today. Yet Donoghue can be seen trying to come to terms with the newer criticism when he addresses Joyce, for beside the latter's materialism is set his language that 'always seems to offer itself as a counter-truth to the truth of reality' ('The European Joyce', 1985). It transpires that Joyce's work is as ambiguous as Yeats's, *Ulysses* projecting both 'the world of conditions and the world of desire'. In Joyce's last work, Donoghue sees desire outreaching and eclipsing conditions. 'Bakhtin and *Finnegans Wake*', written especially for *We Irish*, applies the Russian critic's notions of plurality, polyphony and dialogism to the *Wake*, a work that achieves freedom before all laws.

This potentially revolutionary terminus in Donoghue's hands resembles merely an infinite latitudinarianism, a triumphant flexibility.

Nevertheless, the readerly progress from duality to plurality would seem to be there, and it would seem to complement the progress from Donoghue's 1972 acceptance of 'two traditions' in Ireland ('Another Complex Fate') to his 1986 assertion in 'We Irish' of multiple dualities (a kind of plurality). Donoghue is reluctant to get into politics or ideology, and the struggle between New Criticism and ideological criticism is increasingly causing him to 'choke', as American coaches say of athletes who tie up in the home straight. Independent and surefooted in practical criticism, Donoghue is dependent and faltering amidst contemporary theorists. Increasingly he is torn between the world of conditions (politics and ideology) and the world of desire (literature and criticism) – like the writers he has so interpreted.

Yet ideology there is in his work, or rather two ideologies jostling for power. On the one hand, he is a proto-revisionist, inclined to a pluralist notion of Irish culture (in Ireland, revisionism and pluralism are bedfellows) and sympathetic, if a touch patronizingly so, to Field Day and *Crane Bag*. On the other hand, there is his pre-revisionism that he was honest enough to re-exhibit when he printed his original review of Field Day, above his second thoughts, in Hutchinson's hardback collection of the pamphlets. For Donoghue has merely flirted with revisionism, tied as he has remained through Yeats to cultural nationalism of an Anglo-Irish kind. In 1972 he encouraged in Irish writers the long perspective, 'mythological and historical, pagan and Christian'. In 1983 ('At Swim'), he pits the obstinate facts of Irish history against the vanishing tricks of 'revisionist pedagogy', thereby apparently re-rooting himself in the world of conditions, since revisionists' attempts to dispel facts are (writ large) like Stephen Dedalus's playful, doomed attempts to deny historical facts and objective reality. However, whereas Young's perception of Irish reality served to undermine Yeats's Romanticism, Donoghue's historical materialism can only conjure into existence revisionist idealism by a false analogy. For the historians, Cullen, Vaughan and the rest, and the new econometrists, would claim that they are unearthing real (and plural), not alleged (and simple) facts.

Donoghue's facts of history are revisionist *vis-à-vis* Yeats, i.e. anti-Romantic. But he doesn't press this because Yeats is both privileged and of a different order from other Irish writers. Indeed, Donoghue defends Romantic Ireland in 'Drums under the Window' (1976) when he claims that O'Brien's attack implicitly offers us a life without passion. Donoghue puts himself in the foolish position of appearing to believe, like many Irish, that passion belongs only to political vision, not to sexual love (or, indeed, intellectual inquiry). At the same time, his facts of history are anti-revisionist *vis-à-vis* Joyce. But Joyce's early materialism, of course, belongs to the world of the revisionists. Joyce's 'this is the way Ireland is' is like the revisionists' 'this is the way Ireland was', our ideological simplicities be damned in both cases. And it is a plural world: the Joyce of *Ulysses* might be regarded as the ultimate revisionist, unless that be the author of *Finnegans Wake*.

Donoghue may think of the Field Day people as revisionists, but as I have argued elsewhere, they too are ambivalent on the matter. Like Donoghue's, their advances and reversions spin and gyre about the figure of Yeats, who resists his own demise like Christy Mahon's da, or indeed Freud's archetypal patriarch. The battle with Yeats is beginning to resemble The Everlasting Fight. He is the nationalist the Irish critics want and the higher-class Protestant they don't want. He is the Ireland they have betrayed (either by leaving or by staying and outgrowing the old simple nationalism) and yet want to propitiate; but he is also an impostor. They fear and dislike his authority yet must accept it in order to gain their freedom from it and assume their own critical maturity. All I can suggest to them is that there are three ways in which Irish critics can cope with Yeats. They can 'kill' him symbolically, after an authentic struggle, as O'Brien has done, and walk away into freedom and maturity. Or they can engage him in the deferential, essentially exegetical way North American academics engage him. Or they can go on grappling painfully and inconclusively with him, which may be brave and honest, unless it is not being admitted that it is something else entirely they are grappling with – as I feel is the case with Donoghue. 'Protestant' critics may also be exercised about Yeats, but without the suggestion of a complex, though I may be wrong.

For fathers take many forms. The most arresting in *We Irish*, aside from Yeats, are Patrick Shea and Donoghue's own father: both figure in one of the briefest reviews in the book, entitled 'Castle Catholic', yet one that speaks, or refuses to speak, volumes. Patrick Shea published his autobiography, *Voices and the Sound of Drums*, in 1981. His father grew up in Kerry, speaking Irish and English, and joined the RIC. When partition came, Shea went north to Newry and became Clerk of the Petty Sessions. His son Patrick later entered the

Northern Ireland civil service, rising eventually to become Permanent Secretary to the Public Building and Works Department, only the second Roman Catholic to achieve such high rank in the civil service.

The Sheas' story disturbs Donoghue since it resembles and then sharply diverges from Donoghue's father's career. He too was born on a Kerry farm and joined the RIC, and he too went north when partition occurred and joined the RUC as a sergeant, a rank at which he remained because, Donoghue alleges, he was a Roman Catholic. The bitterness we glimpse at the unionist regime is projected on to Patrick Shea. Donoghue wants to know how Shea got promotion, being a Catholic, and suggests it was because he was 'amenable to his seniors', a Northern Castle Catholic (unfailingly biddable like the older Berkeley?). The question Donoghue does not ask is 'why did the Gaelic-speaking Kerryman, Shea senior, go north when the island was divided, instead of remaining in the Free State?' One would not bring in biography here had not Donoghue himself deemed it admissible. So perhaps one is entitled to wonder if he refrains from asking that question because its answer would involve his own biography. Moreover, what part does Patrick Shea's upward mobility play in Donoghue's attitude? And is it silently being interpreted as success in defection or renegation? And if so, can guilt in this matter be transmitted from father to son?

Which questions prompt me to wonder in general terms whether Catholics born or brought up in Northern Ireland inherit an ambivalence towards the South, which is inverted guilt that they were not born or brought up there but were born or raised 'in defection', as it were, a guilt the more obscure for being innocently incurred. And is Yeats the nationalist Southern Irishman the depository of that ambivalence, transformed sporadically and of psychological necessity into Yeats the Protestant quasi-fascist and (for Deane) crypto-unionist (while at the same time lovingly explicated and attended to)? 'I left Northern Ireland before it became necessary for me to deal with its wretched system,' Donoghue tells us. Was this a liberation or a doubling of guilt? What is certain is that in 'Castle Catholic' Donoghue comes close to excusing anti-government violence in Northern Ireland. 'Violence is an appalling thing,' he says, but we know that he can be appalled and touched at the same time.

We Irish has a psychological subtext: a belated and faltering redress. Quite what is being redressed is never spelled out. The subtext's provenance, however, is probably autobiographical and it breaks the surface of the text at those points where politics and ideology, even the critic's own life, demand expression, a thrashing out.* Until these demands are met, I can't see Donoghue's Irish criticism being more than fitfully impressive, which would of course satisfy a less ambitious and accomplished critic.

[1988]

---

* An autobiographical volume by Donoghue, *Warrenpoint*, was published in New York in autumn 1990 and in London in spring 1991.

12

THE CRITICAL CONDITION OF ULSTER

The critical condition of Ireland at the present time seems undivorce-able from the condition of criticism in Ireland. The failure of Irish society is the failure of criticism. First of all, the failure of objectivity, of the generosity that permits objectivity, of the sympathetic faculty that impels generosity. Secondly, the failure of reflection and self-examination. Thirdly, the failure of an intelligent assertion of legiti-mate sectarian interest, heritage and identity possible only when objectivity has been striven for. It is surely telling that whereas the island has an enviable canon of literature, a critical canon would be difficult to conjure into existence.

The reasons for criticism's poor showing occur to me as they occur to you: throughout the island a powerful and ancient Church permitting, if I may borrow a phrase from Matthew Arnold, as much play of the mind as may suit its being that; in one corner of the island a Dissenting Church dangerously confusable, as Arnold claimed, with philistinism; the presence on the island of several homogeneous groups religiously and otherwise distinctive and bent on power and survival in ways that lead to petty, occasionally forceful forms of abso-lutism (and criticism cannot breathe the air of absolutism). To these we might add the unnecessarily but understandably disabling effects of class-consciousness, province-consciousness and colony-consciousness, all imposed by the association with England. I hesitate to add that quality of life Yeats attributed (or misattributed) to us when he relished the remark: 'We Irish cannot become philosophic like the English; our lives are too exciting.'

What recognizable criticism we have had in Ireland was conducted by writers for whom England and Ireland represented, discursively, a unified field; 'critical unionism', we might say. Yeats and the Irish

Revivalists attempted to disrupt that with an anti-bourgeois, nationalist universe of discourse. To this extent the Revivalists were Partisans (interested proponents of a view of Ireland as she ought to be), yet in their recoil from political factionalism, sectarianism, and practicality, in their cultural umpirage, they resembled nineteenth-century Sages, or Olympians as I would call them. (We watch Olympian and Partisan jostling for position in Yeats's 'Easter 1916', for example.)

That public sphere from which the Olympian detached himself but upon which he depended, passed with the Revival, with the Anglo-Irish, leaving a discourse vacuum. In Ireland at the present time there is no genuine critical sphere. (Outside Ireland, of course, there is, as this conference bears witness; for in a sense this conference is taking place not in Belfast but in an international academic setting. The international academic plies a valuable trade in Irish literature, but tends to take his cultural and political cues from the writers under examination.) The passing of the Anglo-Irish has at once fractionalized, simplified and deadlocked the issue by leaving the field to two antagonistic Irelands in need of education. These two Irelands, Catholic and Protestant, Southern and Northern, nationalist and unionist, have up to now supported little criticism that wasn't Partisan.

Circumstances of course have not been felicitous. The earlier Troubles were solved when the Anglo-Irish capitulated (the metamorphoses of identity by which the leaders of the Revival disguised their capitulation became the chief works of the movement). This led the majority culture to suppose that by an internal domino principle Ulster Protestantism would follow suit. Because this did not happen, because the differences in Ulster seem unbridgeable, and because Ulster defended its integrity with injustice, the critical faculty, unused in Ireland to objectivity, is baffled. Over it Ulster seems to cast a dangerous spell. I want to demonstrate this actually happening when some of the liveliest minds in Ireland today contemplate Northern Ireland, the critical condition of which occupies me here. These are the New Partisans: inheritors of a cultural identity and political stance pulling them one way, but academic practitioners of a discipline whose various imperatives and currencies pull them, by gravity of intellect, another way. Despite the confusion this creates over Ulster, a confusion of rhetorics but ultimately of politics, I take heart from the discursive plurality, seeing in it an unprecedented promise of a genuine critical sphere in which we will one day discuss Ulster without rancour, sectarianism, radical prescription, or atavism.

I have taken as my text the pamphlets put out by the Field Day Theatre Company of Derry, a most significant critical enterprise, all of whose implications even its directors may not recognize.

I

In *Heroic Styles: The Tradition of an Idea* (pamphlet No. 4), Seamus Deane claims there are two dominant ways of reading Irish literature and history: the Romantic way and the Pluralistic way. He means also that there are two modes of Irish writing, since the first is represented by Yeats and the second by Joyce. Neither is capable of addressing satisfactorily the Northern crisis in his opinion, which he sees (in deference to current critical theory) as a linguistic or stylistic crisis. Both the Romantic and the Pluralistic modes are, he argues, at base nationalistic, fuelled by the nationalist notion of restored vitality.

In the Romantic mode, 'the restoration of native energy to the English language is seen as a specifically Irish contribution to a shared heritage'. 'Cultural nationalism', writes Deane, 'is thus transformed into a species of literary unionism.' To this extent, Deane allows no difference between Yeats and Ferguson, since both beat the strategic retreat of the Ascendancy from political and cultural supremacy. Whereas Catholic Ireland could provide Yeats with a language of renovation, the art and civilization of Yeats's new Ireland came from the political connection between England and Ireland. Deane writes: 'An idea of art opposed to the idea of utility, an idea of an audience opposed to the idea of popularity, an idea of the peripheral becoming the central – in these three ideas Yeats provided Irish writing with a programme for action. But whatever its connection with Irish nationalism, it was not, finally, a programme of separation from the English tradition.' Deane then quotes from Yeats's 'A General Introduction for My Work' to exemplify what he calls 'the pathology of literary unionism'.

With some of this I am in agreement. The problems arise when Deane seeks to import his categories into Ulster where in its special air they disintegrate (and, indeed, his argument in part requires that they do). He wants to use the old categories to explain Ulster but senses that they no longer apply: a critical point in his thinking, I believe. Since we are told that 'the cultural machinery of Romantic Ireland has ... wholly taken over in the North', the equation of

Romanticism with unionism cannot hold here (unless Ulster Catholics are seen as unionists at heart), for *both* communities, it seems, cherish a Romantic millenial faith in their eventual triumph. And if the equation is just between Romanticism and Nationalism, that might work for Paisleyism but not for Official Unionism. Indeed, Deane has to cut corners to demonstrate that the Ulster Protestants resemble the Anglo-Irish (though this stage of the argument requires that Ulster Catholics do too) in seeing themselves as an élite people, even as a lost tribe. This might be true of politicized fundamentalists (and Terence Brown and Marianne Elliott – of whom more anon – confirm this), but when applied to thoroughgoing bourgeois unionists, of whom there are thousands, it is obviously nonsense. For Deane, Paisley *is* Ulster, embodying as he does 'violence, a trumpery evangelicalism, anti-popery and a craven adulation of the "British" way of life'. The recourse of Deane's argument to caricature (of Ulster Protestants, not Paisley) betrays a reluctance to admit that Protestantisms need not be identical, to admit the possibility of an authentic, appositive culture.

Joycean separatism is not an acceptable alternative, it seems, to the romantic nationalisms (or unionisms) of Ulster, because it leads to cosmopolitan pluralism, to what Deane eloquently calls 'the harmony of indifference'. Superficially attractive though this is to Deane's critical theory, it is rendered unusable by his residual cultural nationalism. This critical theory and that cultural nationalism conspire to reject in Joyce what might have been at least entertained *vis-à-vis* the North: individualism (which Deane might be confusing with cosmopolitan anonymity), realism, and a liberal humanism earthed in tolerance and compassion. Instead, Joyce is seen as having become disenchanted even with the privacy of the individual consciousness though he is yet seen as nostalgic (in some vaguely nationalistic way) for the lost vitality of community.

Meanwhile, and despite resisting the claims of realism, Deane calls for a rejection of the romantic mystique of Irishness. To accept this mystique 'is to be involved in the spiritual heroics of a Yeats or a Pearse'. Yet to reject it 'is to make a fetish of exile, alienation and dislocation in the manner of Joyce or Beckett'. But although they represent worn oppositions, there is 'little room for choice', apparently, between the hot and cold rhetorics of Yeats and Joyce. Indeed, they are 'inescapable'. Against this defeatism, it is difficult to know how to entertain Deane's request that we reread (i.e. rewrite) all our politics and literature, and that we compile 'a comprehensive anthology of what writing in this country has been for the last 300–500 years'. Such an anthology, we are told, would expose the ultimately political stereotyping of Irish national character. The request is cast in some doubt since Deane himself is not averse to stereotyping when he addresses Ulster Protestantism. Still, such an anthology is worth a try, and Field Day might consider assembling a group of potential editors under the leadership of Seamus Deane himself. I myself would be willing to participate, just as long as the all-Ireland anthology reflected the strong Scottish and English dimensions of Northern literary culture; the compilation, which might be epoch-making, must in other words have the comprehensiveness of political neutrality.*

Deane castigates Yeats's literary unionism in order, one feels, to loosen the grip on contemporary Ireland of remaining Anglo-Irish thinking, ultimately of Protestantism and England, in fact of the British presence. Yet the real significance of his argument is that his attentiveness to contemporary critical theory has involved him in an attack on *any* Irish nationalism that recalls us to a preferable past, relies on a mystique of Irishness, and defends itself on grounds of the restoration of vitalizing unity. Given Deane's background and eminence, this is monumental. Deane has broken with one of the two distinct discourses in which the republican movement speaks, according to Richard Kearney in Field Day pamphlet No. 5 (*Myth and Motherland*). The remaining discourse is 'the secular discourse of military action, political electioneering and social work', but on the subject of a united Ireland such a discourse has been so far unconvincing. Seamus Deane, this most influential of Irish critics, must now it seems abandon the nationalist position (including the realism of its secular discourse) and describe for us the alternative space to romantic nationalism and international modernism he believes his anthology would establish. Whether he does or not, *Heroic Styles: The Tradition of an Idea* joins the lonely landmarks of Irish criticism.

II

In so far as Declan Kiberd's *Anglo-Irish Attitudes* (pamphlet No. 6) offers a realist solution to the Irish problem, it is at variance with Deane's, but the Northern terminus of the argument is familiar.

* Unknown to me, Field Day were already planning such an anthology. I was asked to participate as a contributing editor by the chief editor, Seamus Deane. The three-volume anthology will appear in 1991 – JWF.

'Antithesis', in Kiberd's opinion, 'was the master-key to the entire Victorian cast of mind, causing people to make absolute divisions not just between English and Irish, but also between men and women, good and evil, and so on.' Although as far as English and Irish perceptions of each other were concerned, this was a reciprocal arrangement, it is the English perception of the Irish that exercises Kiberd because England was the colonizing power and the Irish a minority group – like women and children whom the Irish (he provocatively tells us) were occasionally held by the English to resemble.

For some of the English, the Irish represented barbarism, a stereotype examined by Seamus Deane in Field Day pamphlet No. 3, *Civilians and Barbarians*. For others Ireland represented pastoral beauty, emotional spontaneity and spiritual idealism. Yeats accepted the antithesis but reinforced the positive stereotype, though stereotype nonetheless. In the beginning of his pamphlet, Kiberd demonstrates with a supple intelligence how Irish dramatists from the late Victorian period onwards – notably Wilde, Shaw and O'Casey – turned the stereotypes on their heads in the service of a belief in an underlying human unity. Kiberd himself rejects and reverses the English stereotypes of Ireland. He agrees with Conor Cruise O'Brien that the Irish are not pugnacious but paralysed, not idealistic but pragmatic, not passionate but cunning. At the same time, nationality is itself something close to a stereotype to be jettisoned. Kiberd would seem to write approvingly: 'As an internationalist, Shaw had mocked "that hollowest of fictions", the notion of an *English* or an *Irish* man.' Kiberd's attack on antithesis and stereotype, behind which lie his feminism and socialism, would seem to incline him to a belief in essential unity underlying exploitive and divisive stereotypes.

Oddly, though, this manages to leave his nationalism and republicanism intact. Unity is all right, unionism is all wrong. His argument leads him to diminish cultural differences between England and Ireland, and also – judging by his rather unfair treatment of F. S. L. Lyons's *Culture and Anarchy – within* Ireland. Kiberd substitutes the unifying power of cash for the divisive power of culture which he sees the English as fostering.

To do so, he has to conjure out of existence Ulster Protestantism as a cultural entity. There is no Ulster culture because there is no Protestant imagination. Protestant culture is 'unionist culture'; it is in fact the Unionist Party; no, it is (leaving for Kiberd a residue of admiration for the cash-conscious hard men) the Ulster Defence

Association. How disappointing that someone so alert, so correctly alert, to the stereotyping of the Irish by the English should resort to the very mental process he deprecates in order to solve the Ulster question. The concept of androgyny, to which Kiberd seems attracted and which makes a nonsense of the binary opposition of stereotyped genders, rests on the equality and mutual respect of the constituent sexes, not on the caricaturing and absorption of one by the other. Yet this is what Kiberd's political androgyny does. One might have thought, moreover, that the political androgyny of the Ulster people, especially of the Ulster Protestants (part British, part Irish), would have aroused Kiberd's benign curiosity. Instead, his nationalist stance turns out to be the political equivalent of male chauvinism.

Kiberd ends his pamphlet by calling on English liberals to scrutinize Ulster unionism. We suspect why: he supposes that when they find out how hideous a movement it is, they will lobby for British withdrawal. But I should have thought that the call is unearned until *Kiberd* has striven to understand 'unionist culture', its history and dynamics. The antithesis in his mind between unionist and republican might saddeningly become real, but at least it would rest upon the awareness of unevadeable cultural differences.

Besides, his enviably well-argued belief in underlying unity, especially economic unity, of Britain and Ireland (that future Anglo-Irish talks might ironically uncover or cement) surely pushes him towards a federalist grasp of the British archipelago! 'Opposition brings reunion,' he approvingly quotes Giordano Bruno at the outset of his pamphlet, a quotation bearing some irony by pamphlet's end. When he laments – albeit for familiarly tactical reasons – that unionist misrule has eroded many of the best features of British democracy, that nationalist argument threatens to backfire. The deconstructionist tendency of Kiberd's always lively criticism, enabling his attacks on antithesis and stereotype, and his contemporary feminism and older socialism ought, it would seem, to conspire to threaten his republicanism and nationalism as well as permit an attack on British colonialism; they do, I think, but not yet acknowledgeably. In the meantime, we do have a provisionally healthy plurality of rhetorics at work.

III

In each of these important pamphlets, then, there is a text splendidly handled for the most part. Seamus Deane wishes to demystify Irishness, a task compelled by the Romanticism of the Revival. Declan Kiberd wishes to dissolve racist, sexual and cultural antithesis, perpetuated by the Revival, and substitute the economic facts of predicamental similarity. In pamphlet No. 1, *A New Look at the Language Question,* Tom Paulin wishes to enhance our awareness of the linguistic unity of the island. Respectively, these are attacks on literary, cultural and linguistic unionism. To them we can add pamphlet No. 2, *An Open Letter,* Seamus Heaneys rejection of literary unionism by refusing the laureateship bestowed on him by Motion and Morrison in their anthology, *Contemporary British Poetry.*

In each case there is a subtext: repudiation of the political union of Great Britain and Northern Ireland. The Anglo-Irish are slighted, likewise (in the cases of Deane and Kiberd) the Ulster Protestants (except for the hard or wild men, praised, one suspects, as potential separatists and therefore potential republicans). The pamphlets are politics by other means, and as variations on the nationalist theme are chromatic and resourceful.

But in each case the logic of the text will not support the subtext. Deane's argument points us towards anti-nationalism, Kiberd's towards an undefined British federalism. Paulin's points us towards partition or UDI as convincingly as towards Irish federalism, but my claim will have to go unsubstantiated, I'm afraid. The moment at which the subtext threatens to surface is rather like the turn in a sonnet. In each case there is a brilliant octave on English-Irish cultural relations, followed by a disappointing sestet when Ulster is contemplated. Criticism flounders when political discourse subverts the splendidly deployed critical discourse of the octave. The process is repeated in Richard Kearney's *Myth and Motherland.* There, the *logos* of rational critique is distinguished from the *mythos* of irrational mystification (Kearney's example being the pervasive Irish myth of motherland). '*Mythos*', we are told promisingly, 'can never be insulated from the ethical critique of *logos* . . . We cannot afford to dispense with the difficult task of determining when myth emancipates and when it incarcerates.' The next stage is surely Kearney's own ethical critique of the Irish myth of motherland. In the meantime, his own lapse back into *mythos* – the language of sacrificial republicanism – does not augur well; 'The poets and [H-block] prisoners', he says, 'are there to remind us that myth often harbours memories or expectations which established reason has ignored at its peril . . . if we need to demythologize, we also need to remythologize.' His pamphlet threatens to prove alas that the longest way round is indeed the shortest way home.

These provocative pamphlets have helped us reach a critical point in Irish cultural understanding. If these and other critics can honour the logic of their text, abandon subtexts, and maintain a critical discourse in wilful neglect of hereditary or acquired political discourse, we will see the emergence in Ireland of an authentic critical sphere, a critical unionism within the island, we might say. Success will require getting behind all stereotypes, not just disfavoured stereotypes, as unearned unitary thinking seduces us into doing.

'Culture, not politics' ought to be one of our slogans, 'Criticism, not politics' another, each implying the strategic pretence that these are separable activities. By politics I mean political and constitutional scenarios, prescriptions, blueprints, programmes – and an uncritical contempt for 'the other side'. We simply do not know enough at present to prescribe or forecast the political future of Ulster, certainly not an imminent united Ireland.

And so I echo Tom Paulin's regard for the dialects and languages of Ireland, but suggest we study them without yoking them to a political prescription. I echo Declan Kiberd's call for the study of unionist culture, but let its positive as well as negative guises be studied, and by *Irish*, indeed, anti-unionist, students of culture, not just English politicians. And I echo Seamus Deane's summons to dissolve the mystique of Irishness, but I challenge him to initiate this necessary task by seeking to dissolve through understanding the negative mystique of Ulster Protestantism. In Kearney's otherwise illuminating pamphlet, unionist mythology receives one sentence, and whereas nationalism is a 'tradition', unionism is a 'camp' (whose tents he no doubt wishes were folded). If my own summons seems one-sided, that is because critics of non-nationalist background have reciprocated in advance to the extent that they are sympathetic students of that Anglo-Irish literature dominated since Joyce by 'Catholic' and 'nationalist' writers.

The Free State came about only after forty years of cultural preparation. By 1920 Ireland had asserted a sufficiently different culture, according, that is, to the people who turned out to be the ones who mattered – including, let us take note, the Anglo-Irish who studied well (if not too wisely) a culture not their own. Consider the contrasting case in Ulster. There has been no cultural preparation for a united Ireland *whatsoever*. That being the case, it is an impossibility outside its military imposition. And that being the case, I beg to differ with the *New Ireland Forum Report* which considers that any kind of united Ireland is preferable to the *status quo* and that a united Ireland is an urgent requirement. If there is anything it is not, it is urgent, unless we wish to witness the spectacle of civil war. Cultural fusion by force would result in sharper cultural fission than before. Those who wish to see a united Ireland by consent should let the cultural preparation commence, but it will require the altruism of cross-sectarian studies.

What I am proposing is something different from, but not unconnected to, what I sense happening in Ulster this weather: reversion, the return to respective corners, the equivalent in the intellectual sphere of that increasing polarization we are witnessing in the political sphere. If one guise of this is the Field Day enterprise, another is the less apologetic stance by Protestant historians and critics, which we see, for example, in the *Festschrift* Edna Longley and Gerald Dawe have edited in honour of John Hewitt, *Across a Roaring Hill* (1985). Ian Adamson, who, correctly I think, accuses the Ulster intelligentsia of failing to promote a Northern identity, has taken the stance one step further, and in his book *The Identity of Ulster* tries to provide all of the Ulster people with an ancestry, a language, a culture – a mythic base for the political superstructure of a future independence.

The authentic critical space and time lie the hither side of Adamson's prematurely independent North. In the cause of understanding, we must probe (but not press) cultural differences as far as is incompatible with sectarianism or political prescription. 'The recognition of difference, especially by Irishmen themselves,' Lyons has correctly said, 'is a prerequisite for peaceful coexistence.' We might choose to interpret such work as an inducement to the change of heart Orwell found, in the work of Dickens, as revolutionary as the call for a change in society. It might even constitute the third phase of a familiar dialectic. In phase one, two groups are invidiously conscious of their differences, with one group enjoying supremacy. In phase two, there is a liberal assumption, especially by conciliatory members of the dominant group, that the two groups are equal because similar. In phase three, there is a mutual recognition, initiated by members of the oppressed group, that the two groups are equal and mutually dependent because *different*. This, I think, has been the pattern in the women's movement and, before that, in the civil rights movement in the United States; it may with luck be the pattern in Ulster.

IV

In achieving it, we might enlist, along with pooled cultural information, the kind of thinking pioneered for us by Deane and Kiberd but applied by them only to Anglo-Irish relations. In its alertness to the deployment of opposing stereotypes, we might call this thinking structuralist. Structuralism is heavily indebted to Saussure for whom in the linguistic system there are only *differences*, with meaning not immanent but functional, the result of a sign's difference from other signs. In Lévi-Strauss, as we know, the differences become binary opposition, a state to which we in Ulster are daily accustomed. At the same time, for the structuralist the units of a system have meaning only by virtue of their relations to one another. This strikes me as an interesting avenue to explore, though we are not speaking of the liberal relief at finding underlying unity. To give but one example: to what extent is an Ulster Protestant an Ulster Protestant because he is not the Ulster Catholic of whom he is nevertheless incessantly conscious? Isn't the Ulster Catholic an inescapable element of his own identity? But if so, this is only because Protestant and Catholic stand in constant opposition to one another. The psychoanalytic (not just semiotic) implications of Self and Other couched in sectarian rather than sexual terms remain as far as I know unexplored.

For Roland Barthes, signs are deployed in codes with which we are in Ulster again daily familiar, along with a rich subtextuality of Irish discourse virtually inaudible to outsiders. 'O land of password, wink and nod', writes Seamus Heaney. 'The spurious mystery in the knowing nod', writes Derek Mahon, revising it later, with semantic if not poetic gain, to 'The hidden menace in the knowing nod', for of course such mysteries are not spurious. Barthes's musings on the class vocabulary of the French Restoration could be matched by our musings on the encodification of such words and phrases as 'the North', 'the people of Northern Ireland', 'The Six Counties', 'peace and stability of Ireland', 'cherish', 'aspiration', 'staunch', 'fervent', 'intransigent'. Among recent documents, the *New Ireland Forum Report* cries loudest for decoding.

We know, too, that for Saussure rites and customs, and for Lévi-Strauss historical facts and even myths, partake of the nature of signs. Almost at random, one might consider the Irish implications of Lévi-Strauss's claim that myths are logical techniques for resolving basic antinomies in thought and social existence, and of his reflections on the analogical processes of the archaic mind (which seems to have survived into modern Ireland).

V

To their credit, Field Day have chosen to honour a sense of difference by commissioning three pamphlets on unionist culture by writers of non-nationalist background. Unfortunately, then, it is a case of Protestants on Protestants, not the cross-cultural studies I am calling for, but it is better than nothing. Indeed, I heartily recommend the pamphlets by Terence Brown and Marianne Elliott (Nos. 7 and 8 respectively) as contributions to our knowledge of Northern Irish culture and, especially, as evidence of a rich and honourable Protestant culture in the province. Moreover, in these two pamphlets, the difference is in the end denied, one arguing for the desirability, the other for the possibility, of a unified Ireland. Protestant culture, it is alleged (as though answering Kiberd by being more truly nationalist than himself), is not unionist culture. It is unjust to accuse Brown and Elliott of some wishful thinking on the matter of a united Ireland without giving them a hearing, especially since cultural ignorance we most certainly can not accuse them of, but such I fear is the case, and the pamphlets are available for your scrutiny, perhaps as material for discussion in seminar.

Given the limitation on time, I have opted to strengthen my argument (and to obviate if I can any misunderstanding of my position) by glancing at the one Field Day pamphlet that advocates continued union and partition. My argument is a simple one: inadequacy in our cultural knowledge and our criticism vitiates our thinking on Ulster, and is encouraged by political prejudgment. It is the principle neither of nationalism nor of unification that is at issue but the concreteness of the relationship between these and cultural reality.

The liberal (or Official) unionism of Robert McCartney's *Liberty and Authority in Ireland* (pamphlet No. 9) completes the trinity of Protestant viewpoints begun with Brown's Anglo-Irish perspective (cultural fusionism) and Elliott's United Irish perspective (Protestant-led republicanism). As befits the author's status as Unionist Member of the Northern Ireland Assembly and Queen's Counsellor, McCartney's pamphlet defends partition on the grounds that only membership in the United Kingdom guarantees the liberty of the individual possible in a libertarian democracy. Unification of Ireland is undesirable (and undesirable *only*) because the present Republic is a theocratic state. Where Brown sees, since 1914, a monolithic, occasionally irrational unionist North, McCartney sees a would-be pluralist state. Where Brown sees in the present Republic a state pluralistic enough to assemble the New Ireland Forum, McCartney sees a threatening and irrational monolith, a conspiracy of nationalism and Catholicism, an authoritarian homogeny (and hegemony) that violate the frontiers of private life and individual freedom.

The dilemma of liberal unionism, according to McCartney, is its support for civil and individual rights while rejecting an Irish unity which would entail the denial of those rights. Clearly, liberal Unionism is itself McCartney's resolution of the dilemma which that political position creates. For, in fact, the dilemma as he poses it creates not one but two Catch-22s.

First of all, whereas the aspiration towards a united Ireland might be granted to Northern nationalists as a civil and individual right, that aspiration, if it is pursued too actively or successfully, will be opposed and the right rescinded. In *The Way Forward*, a recent Unionist Assembly Party discussion paper (one of the authors of which is McCartney), it is proposed that 'distinctively Irish cultural activities' be fostered in a pluralist, British Ulster. But for decades, the aspiration to unity has been part of the cultural ideology of a large part of Ireland. What Catholic nationalist believes that his culture would be sincerely fostered in a state which bases its opposition to a united Ireland partly on cultural grounds? This is a problem raised by my earlier suggestion that we strategically pretend that culture and politics are separable. Where the aspiration to unity is concerned, this could be done only if the aspiration were culturally processed as precisely that – the *aspiration* to unity. But Conor Cruise O'Brien has told us that in the Republic the aspiration has in fact already been transferred from the political to the cultural realm. If so, the status of the aspiration could conceivably change in Ulster (if it hasn't already), pending cultural preparations for its retranslation from the cultural to the political realm.

I seem to be helping McCartney solve a problem he hasn't even recognized. For the difference between North and South he labours to establish must surely hold in some sense between the nationalist and unionist populations of Northern Ireland itself. Unless he regards (like Adamson) Ulster Catholic and Protestant as mutually distinct from Southerners, then the overriding of minority and individual rights that McCartney deplores in the Republic must by definition happen – though to a lesser extent – in Ulster also. McCartney would not see the ironic parallel, since he does not see events in cultural terms. For him it is a simple question of legal rights originating in the secular democracy of the United Kingdom. Not only are Catholics and Protestants alike, but everyone is like everyone else, in desiring liberty; it is just that certain populations, for example Southerners, are denied liberty by powerful institutions, for example the Catholic hierarchy and its parliamentary puppets.

It is an unwarranted cultural assumption that everyone subscribes to the bourgeois liberal humanism McCartney tries to articulate. It is not just that Northern Protestants maintain certain democratic rights at the expense of those who do not recognize the democratic majority *as a democratic majority*, but that Ulster Catholics may not even subscribe to the values of the putative majority. McCartney assumes that Southerners groan under a political structure that isn't a full secular democracy on the British model. But if they aren't so groaning, then perhaps their Northern co-religionists are groaning under a political structure that impedes full expression of a culture that does *not* produce, or want to produce, a secular democracy. We don't know enough (or rather, I as an Ulster Protestant do not know enough) about possible differences that might ironically underwrite partition but leave the problem of Northern Ireland unsolved.

The second Catch-22 is this. The inability of Northern Ireland to accommodate the active aspirations of many of its citizens is surely one cause of its conservatism. But if Ulster cannot be truly liberal because the Republic is an illiberal state, as McCartney maintains, this is an implicit acceptance of the interconnectedness of North and South. And if the rejection of unity is based solely upon objections to state restrictions on individual freedom in the Republic, Irish unity is being rejected not in theory or principle but only in practice, on grounds of present reality in the South. Of course, McCartney believes that the theocratic nationalism of the South is synonymous with that state's sovereignty and independence, making real changes impossible.

But if we grant this, and if McCartney desires a greater liberality in Ulster, would not a forceful statement of unity as a goal and a good not encourage liberalism in the Republic (a milder form of the Protestant recolonization of Ireland with which Elliott toys) since the prospect of unification would endanger the future of the Republic as a Catholic monolith? In turn, the pluralization of the South would – using McCartney's own formulation – lift the siege in Ulster, creating conditions for the greater liberalization, not just of Ulster but of all of Ireland, bringing the island into synchrony with mainland democracy. The principle of unification, and practical discussion between North and South on its eventuation, would, then, resolve the fundamental dilemma of liberal unionism. The only snag is that it is erased as a political position in the very resolution of its dilemma.

Once again, criticism and culture, reason and reality, part company. It is not just that reason is imposing itself on someone else's culture, but that it has lost touch with, shrinks from, the culture that lies behind *it*. McCartney overlooks the possibility that another reason for Ulster's conservatism might be the nature of Ulster Protestant, his own, society. Besides the little-sung virtues of this society (and we thank Brown and Elliott and the editors of the *Festschrift* for bringing them to our attention), there are the repressions and illiberalisms, even the theocratic impulses, rooted in a culture that might or might not be very different were the nationalist siege lifted. McCartney's libertarian constitutionalism seems not always relevant to the Ulster I know, even though Brown implies that if the nationalist siege were lifted (through unification), an historical freedom of belief and behaviour would return. But the relationship might be there nevertheless. It is highly likely that McCartney holds his views for cultural rather than strictly philosophical reasons, that his philosophy is a rationalization and defence, through inversion, of Ulster reality; the legalistic argument might be the best one, not necessarily the most sincere one, McCartney can muster. Certainly his appeal to the rights of the individual is important and is to be heeded, but it must be earned *through* the past and the present in the way Gabriel Conroy in Joyce's great story 'The Dead' earns his selfhood by confronting and absorbing the cultural forces that seek to impede as well as sustain him.

VI

The early Field Day pamphlets do not consider individualism as any kind of solution to the Irish problem, crushed as it is between the anti-individualism of nationalism and the anti-individualism of structuralism. Structuralism has, of course, given way outside Ireland to poststructuralism, and if poststructuralism finds the individual no more meaningful than its predecessor, at least it stresses the plurality of meaning, an emphasis that has more in common with liberal humanism than with structuralism, as Eagleton remarks, more in common with multiculturalism than with the homogeneous social state Barthes anticipated in *Writing Degree Zero*. In structuralism is the wherewithal to understand the systemic tensions of Ulster and Irish societies. But if we are dissatisfied with the composition of these societies (and who is not?), and if structuralism is too comfortably reconcilable with the ideology of the *status quo*, then we can try to reveal the inherent contradictions and assumptions in defences of that composition. Deconstruction in particular seems, at least in its intention to undermine binary oppositions, admirably suited to meet the demands upon the critic of two looming realities in Irish life: sectarianism and sexism. 'For of all the binary oppositions which poststructuralism sought to undo,' Eagleton writes, 'the hierarchical opposition between men and women was perhaps the most virulent.' In Ulster (and Ireland) they are joined by the opposition of Protestant and Catholic, as well as nationalist and unionist (and within Protestantism, of Ulster loyalist and Ulster nationalist). But all the cultural data (including the unpalatable data) must be fed into the process of decoding, else it will be an arid academic exercise. And it is surely possible without political prescription (veiled or overt). And yet it might be in the end a truly revolutionary criticism: to say 'this is the case' might be tantamount to saying 'is it right that this should *be* the case?' Revelation, we might say, *is* revolution.

Mine is, unashamedly, the old liberal humanism (Arnold's disinterestedness, even, but strategically courted) co-opting the methods of structuralism and poststructuralism, prepared to entertain, if not permit, its own supersession. A critical programme for Ireland, after all, has to accommodate fear, brutality, unhappiness and violent death. You will recall David Lodge's character, the critical theorist Morris Zapp, surviving the ordeal of being a hostage, and expressing a revisionist belief in the individual. 'I thought deconstructionists didn't believe in the individual,' he's challenged. 'They don't. But death is the one concept you can't deconstruct. Work back from there and you end up with the old idea of an autonomous self. I can die, therefore I am. I realized that when those wop radicals threatened to deconstruct *me*.'

Besides, the autonomous individual may be a bourgeois humanist fantasy, but many of us in Ireland would like to enjoy that fantasy, thank you very much. We have had the psychological feudalism, as it were, of nationalism and oppressive religion: it would be foolish for us to embrace the psychological socialism of poststructuralism before reaping the rewards of psychological *embourgeoisment*. The anti-individualism championed by the Revival lingered long enough in much of Ireland to thwart the reactionary claims of the self staked by a line of writers stretching from O'Connor and O'Faolain to Brian Moore and Bernard MacLaverty. (And to Seamus Heaney, whose poetry richly displaces its recurrent desire into totem and taboo.) The celebration of self-realization, not just cultural similitude, is what I intend by Realism, and Realism in Ireland has not yet earned its own replacement, settling as we have had to for pathological realism, a literary mode that is nourished on its own impossibility, examining among other things how personalities are warped into what it pleases us to call 'characters'. 'Self, not system' should be another of our slogans, dangerous and outmoded in America but revolutionary here. I was gladdened to hear Declan Kiberd in Tacoma, Washington, recently, in a characteristically pyrotechnical talk, defend individualism, referring to 'modern Ireland, whose writers, whose philosophers, and whose people have never had the opportunity to become themselves. And this is because, after the Easter Rebellion, they abandoned the Irish Renaissance as a search for personal freedom.' This is the line we must walk, skirting carefully cultural insult and insensitivity.

And if we bracket for the time being poststructural strictures on Realism, let us bracket likewise those on biography and auto-biography. It is a plurality of voices we precisely need in Ireland in order to interrupt the tiresome duologue of recent history. I was heartened to come across this by Lévi-Strauss:

Biographical and anecdotal history is the least explanatory; but it is the richest in point of information, for it considers individuals in their particularity and details for each of them the shades of character, the twists and turns of their motives, the phases of their deliberations.

One is tempted to exclaim: let ungovernable choirs of dissonant voices rain down on us in Ireland; let the forests be invisible for the trees! But of course the claims of sect and heritage will remain and remain legitimately, helping as they do to form this exclamatory self. To aid us in understanding *them*, let me suggest that Field Day organize a series of public seminars up and down the island devoted to examining our cultural diversity and constituent personalities, seminars popular enough in presentation to attract the intelligent unacademic, scholarly enough not to arouse the attentions of those with a political prescription in one pocket, a gun in the other.* Before us we have the example of the Revivalists of what can be accomplished along these lines. But let us not like them prejudge the outcome of our deliberations, whose final political form none of us in any case will live to see. To those of us who wish to see a unified Ireland, it is an immense but necessary forbearance for us to accept, as I believe we must, words borrowed by Arnold from another context: the existing order of things till right is ready. And right is ready when objectivity, sympathy and generosity have been expended.

* Such seminars have since taken their rise, not with Field Day but with *Fortnight*, the Belfast magazine under the editorship of Robin Wilson, and latterly with the government-sponsored Cultural Traditions Group – JWF.

[1985]

REFERENCES

Adamson, Ian, *The Identity of Ulster: The Land, the Language and the People* (Belfast: Pretani Press 1982).
Arnold, Matthew, 'Culture and its Enemies' (1867).
Arnold, Matthew, 'The Function of Criticism at the Present Time' (1864).
Barthes, Roland, *S/Z: An Essay* trans. Richard Miller (New York: Hill and Wang 1974).
Barthes, Roland, *Writing Degree Zero*, trans. Annette Lavers and Colin Smith (New York: Hill and Wang 1968).
Brown, Terence, *The Whole Protestant Community: The Making of a Historical Myth*, Field Day Pamphlet 7 (Derry: Field Day Theatre Company 1985).
Dawe, Gerald and Edna Longley, eds, *Across a Roaring Hill: The Protestant Imagination in Modern Ireland* (Belfast: Blackstaff Press 1985).
Deane, Seamus, *Civilians and Barbarians* Field Day Pamphlet 3 (Derry: Field Day Theatre Company 1983).
Deane, Seamus, *Heroic Styles: The Tradition of an Idea*, Field Day Pamphlet 4 (Derry Field Day Theatre Company 1984).
Eagleton, Terry, *Literary Theory: An Introduction* (Oxford: Blackwell 1983).
Elliott, Marianne, *Watchmen in Sion: The Protestant Idea of Liberty* Field Day Pamphlet 8 (Derry: Field Day Theatre Company 1985).

Heaney, Seamus, *An Open Letter*, Field Day Pamphlet 2 (Derry: Field Day Theatre Company 1983).

Kearney, Richard, *Myth and Motherland*, Field Day Pamphlet 5 (Derry: Field Day Theatre Company 1984).

Kiberd, Declan, *Anglo-Irish Attitudes*, Field Day Pamphlet 6 (Derry: Field Day Theatre Company 1984).

Lévi-Strauss, Claude, *The Savage Mind* (Chicago: University of Chicago Press 1966).

Lodge, David, *Small World: An Academic Romance* (Harmondsworth: Penguin Books 1985).

Lyons, F. S. L., *Culture and Anarchy in Ireland, 1890–1939* (Oxford: Oxford University Press 1979).

McCartney, R. L., *Liberty and Authority in Ireland* Field Day Pamphlet 9 (Derry: Field Day Theatre Company 1985).

Motion, Andrew and Blake Morrison, *The Penguin Book of Contemporary British Poetry* (Harmondsworth: Penguin Books 1982).

New Ireland Forum Report (Dublin: Stationery Office, n.d.).

Paulin, Tom, *A New Look at the Language Question*, Field Day Pamphlet 1 (Derry: Field Day Theatre Company 1983).

The Way Forward: Devolution and the Northern Ireland Assembly (Belfast: Ulster Unionist Assembly Party's Report Committee, n.d.).

13

NEW REALISM:
A FUTURE FOR IRISH STUDIES

I

We are all of us tediously familiar with the two opposing and simple
views of Ireland's political and cultural history, with one of which,
and only one, we are equipped when we come to consciousness on
this island. I refer of course to the doctrines of Irish nationalism and
Ulster loyalism (once part of Irish unionism). Anyone who exchanges
one view for the other, who 'turns', is generally regarded as a renegade.
These doctrines not only determine but over-determine personal
identity in Ulster, whereby you must be Irish or British *and* Catholic
or Protestant *and* nationalist or unionist. Nationalism and loyalism, to
put it another way, are not just theories or readings of Irish history,
but beliefs that double back constantly to reinforce and 'doctrinize'
the original developments of nationalism and loyalism in history. This
is what makes reinterpretation in Irish studies fraught with implication. To reinterpret by grave complication or by denial is especially
significant.

When the nationalist view of history is so reinterpreted, the result
is called revisionism, a term first used by Marxism-Leninism of
tamperings with itself. According to Roy Foster in the opening essay
for the first number of *The Irish Review*, revisionism in Irish historical
studies has been going on for twenty years, though it has accelerated
of late. Among the revisionists Foster lists Joseph Lee, Raymond
Crotty, Vincent Comerford and Paul Bew, and we can add W. E.
Vaughan, author of the influential monograph *Landlords and Tenants
in Ireland 1848–1904* (1984). It has been claimed that Vaughan has
replaced the old picture of the predatory landlord and exploited tenant
with 'a more balanced but more puzzling one'. Meanwhile, writes
Foster, the Famine and the Penal Laws have been reinterpreted with
the aid of econometrics and other methods. In a paper to a recent

social sciences seminar in Belfast, Liam Kennedy cited George O'Brien, author of a multi-volume work, 1918–21, as the chief nationalist economic historian of the independence period; his thesis was that Irish political independence would lead to economic prosperity, a thesis requiring revision, in Kennedy's view, since independence has disproved it. Kennedy also cited Frank Gallagher, author of *The Indivisible Island* (1957) as a nationalist polemicist of the post-partition period, whose thesis was that economic disability was caused by partition. Kennedy dissents from Gallagher's view and alleges partitionist tendencies in Ireland since at least the early nineteenth century.

Before O'Brien it was Arthur Griffith who was associated with economic nationalism and the phrase 'Sinn Féin', though D.P. Moran of the Irish Ireland movement also comes to mind. Peter Neary in his RTE lecture, 'The Failure of Economic Nationalism', defines economic nationalism as the failure to recognize dependence on foreign events and ideas, and he lays at its door many of the mistakes of economic policy in politically independent Ireland between the 1930s and 1960. However, after a period of success due to the reorientation of Irish policies towards international trade and investment, Neary sees a new form of economic nationalism at work in the South, 'a tendency to exaggerate our ability to control our own destiny', in particular an over-reliance on inflexible planning and on native ideas and policies.

George O'Brien, Arthur Griffith and D.P. Moran were, as it happens, active during the Irish Literary Revival, a high point in Irish cultural nationalism and the dates of which are roughly 1880 until the early 1920s or around the time the Free State came into being. The literary revival was part of a larger cultural revival, involving the resuscitation of the Gaelic language, the collection of folklore, the setting up of dairy co-operatives and other forms of economic nationalism, and the renewal of interest in Gaelic sports, pastimes and crafts. Not only the literature but other components of the Revival exhibited romantic and traditionalist tendencies.

In the past ten years, some Irish critics have questioned the ideology of the Revival and its virtual monopoly of Irish discourse, identity and outlook down to the present day. What the Famine, landlords and tenants, and the Land War are for revisionist historians, the Irish Literary Revival is for revisionist critics. But whereas revisionist historians *tend* to be Protestants questioning Catholic nationalist history, revisionist critics tend to be Catholics questioning Protestant nationalism which they see as disguised unionism. Many of these critics have written pamphlets put out by the Field Day Theatre Company of Derry. The most readable revision of the Revival's cultural nationalism by a Field Day pamphleteer is Declan Kiberd's article, 'Inventing Irelands', which appeared in the *Crane Bag* journal. In the course of his article, Kiberd attacks the Ireland which he claims the Revival invented and foisted on posterity, i.e. on us: rural, traditionalist, conservative, anti-European, provincial and anti-individualist. I have affirmed in *Fictions of the Irish Literary Revival* that there *were* writers who were portraying Ireland as she was, but writers who were not part of the Revival itself.

The basic tenet of Irish revisionism is that a singular, nationalist reading of social, political, economic and literary history – one in which (that reading projected into the future) unionists must submit to the inevitable – is no longer tenable. Anthony Gallagher reminds us that nationalism in Ireland is a fairly recent phenomenon, without a mass base for nearly a century after the 1798 rising. He also reminds us of the variegated nature of Irish nationalism, beginning as Ascendancy Protestantism, becoming agitation for Catholic Emancipation and Repeal of the Union, then agrarianism, and only with Parnell a genuinely popular nationalism (which took cultural form, on Parnell's downfall, with the Irish Revival).

Gallagher's remarks find their counterpart in Terence Brown's rejection of the idea of a whole Protestant community having always enjoyed solidarity in face of the republican threat. According to Brown the idea holds water only after the period 1886 to 1914 when the modern unionist identity was forged. In his Field Day pamphlet, Brown contemplates the history of Ulster Presbyterianism and therein finds evidence of dissidence and debate, sedition and revolutionary action, episodes of irrational evangelical outpourings, and dissent from established authority. All of these confute the notion of a monolithic Protestant culture in Ulster lying behind and underwriting authority and reaction.

Brown is a revisionist critic of Ulster Protestant nationalism, rejecting the simple view of Ireland he was handed at birth, and counterpart of those revisionists who reject the lingering relevance of what Stephen Dedalus called cynically 'the sorrowful legend of Ireland'. Brown promotes a plural image of Protestantism *then* in order to tarnish the singular image of Protestantism *now*. He hopes, fondly, I'm afraid, that Protestant awareness of their own complex past will encourage their willingness to participate in the future in a plural but nevertheless united Ireland, detached from the United Kingdom.

II

Revisionism may mark the beginnings of Irish studies proper. In any case, it is a proliferating feature of a variety of disciplines, indicating a potentially major cultural shift. David Stevens, associate secretary of the Irish Council of Churches, has written: 'There is a crisis in all our traditional ideologies – both religious and political – at the moment,' and we can extend ideology far beyond religion and politics. Revisionism is both effect and cause of this crisis, which because it *is* a crisis is disorientating and bewildering. The unitary ideologies of nationalism and post-partition unionism are apparently in collapse and we seem to be in a post-nationalist, post-unionist transition and state of uncertainty.

Yet many of the changes in Irish society detected by professional students have, or did have, a comforting ring: industrialization, secularization, urbanization, rationalization, modernization. These are solid, reassuring words, and they imply a terminus imminently to be reached, just as 'transition' entails its own destination to which it is an ante-room or linking corridor. Richard Kearney sees higher Irish culture like this: 'Thus we may say that the modernist tendency of certain Irish writers, artists and intellectuals represents a shift away from the cultural nationalism of the revival to a cultural internationalism committed to formal and critical experimentation.' The Irish Republic, we are told, optimistically, is 'an advanced secular nation-state of the European community'. Literature and art constitute a kind of EEC in cultural terms, a multinational corporation of the pen and brush.

It is, closer to home, an artistic version of that pluralism I suspect we are likely to hear less about in the days to come, which John Brady SJ regrets the Republic will not stir itself to achieve. The catch is that pluralism when promoted by nationalists (for example, John Hume and the New Ireland Forum) is seen by unionists as republican, and when promoted by unionists (for example, Robert McCartney and the unionist reply to the Forum *Report*, the pamphlet *The Way*

Forward) is seen by nationalists as anti-unification. There is Ulster pluralism and Irish pluralism, and both are mere blueprints, and highly undetailed ones.

Nor does Kearney's pluralism (or internationalism) hold up even in literary terms. Since Yeats and the Revival there have been far more Irish realists (or would-be realists) fighting for breath in a stifling society than there have been Modernists, at least from the 1930s to the 1970s, from Frank O'Connor to John McGahern.

In Kearney's thinking there is a connection between modernization and Modernism (dubious to my mind, thinking of Pound, Eliot, Lewis and late Yeats). We are told by the editors of *Ireland: A Sociological Profile*, an influential textbook, that most studies of social change in rural Ireland are informed by modernization theory. 'Modernization', John Hickey explains, 'is the process within a society which marks the transition from a traditional folk form of structure to that of the complex social organization associated with urban, industrialized societies.' One of its effects, or attendant features, Máire Nic Ghiolla Phádraig writes, is that 'a process or train of secularisation is set in motion', and secularization, Hickey further explains, implies scepticism and the questioning of received wisdom.

However, Nic Ghiolla Phádraig notes of the South:

The approach of most Irish Catholics to their religion tends to be fairly conventional, rigid and legalistic . . . the lack of a reasoned and personalised faith and ethics and the heavy reliance on authority figures like the clergy to adjudicate on moral issues, leaves them ill-equipped to face a future in which both the church and the world have changed radically. The inertia of the old patterns still obtains and hence, on the surface, the strength of the institution is very impressive.

Meanwhile, north of the border, the bad or good news from John Hickey, depending on your point of view, is that 'Religion has not gone through the process associated with secularisation . . . it is the strength of the religious survival here which has marked off this society from most of the other modernised societies in the western world.'

The literary critic Seamus Deane might be right when he claims that 'Nationalism was reduced in this country to a caricature of itself because it could not reconcile its conservative cultural vision of itself with the economic demands of modernisation' (quoted in Pine, 1985). But the sociologists contributing to *Ireland: A Sociological Profile* query the depth of Irish modernization. They also question implicitly the optimism of the revisionists with their talk of pluralism and interdependence that will inevitably succeed the bad old monisms of nationalism and unionism.

Indeed, modernization as an explanatory theory seems to be taking a knock in Irish sociology. James Wickham, for example, analysing employment in the Republic, favours the explanatory force of 'dependency theory', which emerged in the grim circumstances of Latin America, over modernization theory, which began in the happier circumstances of the United States. According to dependency theory, underdevelopment is not a stage in the development of a society towards industrialization, but a condition imposed on under-developed by developed societies. Later it was recognized that development could still occur in the underdeveloped countries, but it took the form of 'dependent industrialization'. Wickham sees the Republic as dependent from the 1920s to the 1950s, and thereafter dependently industrial. The sociologist's interpretation is in contrast to the economic historian Neary's, which identifies the villain during the same three decades as economic nationalism.

After some judicious reservation, Liam O'Dowd aligns himself with Wickham where it comes to Northern Ireland. The economy of Ulster has followed the transition described by modernization theory from industrialization to a post-industrial service economy. Not only is the vast bulk of manufacturing industry state-aided, but the service economy is 'state-dependent'. He concludes: 'While Northern Ireland is still far removed from the status of a developing Third World country, it has become an increasingly dependent, underdeveloped economy despite attempts at economic modernization.' In accor-dance with other dependent economies, 'the Northern Ireland case is a sharp reminder that power and control may often lie outside the territorial boundaries of particular states and regions'. The reminder is gloomier coming from the sociologist O'Dowd than from the economic historian Neary who recommends Ireland's interdepen-dence with other countries.

O'Dowd entitled his contribution to *Ireland: A Sociological Profile*, 'Beyond Industrial Society'. It is a title reminiscent of *Beyond Nation-alism*, a recent book by Desmond Fennell. Whereas modernization promises a bright future, dependency does not. Yet a feature of Irish studies today, and testimony to our bafflement and hope, is a belief in an imminent third phase of Irish culture. For Kearney revivalism and Modernism are being followed by post-Modernism. For Deane it is Romanticism, pluralism, then post-Modernism. For Fennell, nationalism, liberalism, then post-nationalism. Fennell calls the third phase the 'Third Revolution'. For Kearney it is that 'Fifth Province' 'where the divisions of the four political provinces might be confronted and resolved'. These ringing phrases are rather undermined, alas, by the despairing use of the prefix 'post' which is not much more than a kind of negative.

Since a synthesis is a transformational combination of thesis and antithesis, there is always the danger that it may appear by turns and to different observers as reactionary or progressive, backlash or advance. For example, Deane rejects the cultural nationalism of Yeats, but only because it is *not* nationalism in Deane's view, instead literary unionism in disguise; for Yeats, he believes, did not wish separation from the English tradition. Then there is Denis Donoghue, who flirts with pluralism but reverts at moments into a nationalist impatience with what he calls 'revisionist pedagogy'. Fennell can sound one minute like a counter-culture guru, the next like a nostalgic Catholic reactionary. On the unionist side there are the productions of the Ulster Society, including its journal *New Ulster*, the revisions of which are in the cause of revitalizing unionist culture, and look like backlash.

As for the sociologists, it is difficult to gauge how far the rejection of modernization theory betrays a crypto-Marxist tendency, opposed both to nationalism (and its goal of independence) and the liberal humanism (and interdependence) of pluralism, or instead a disguised disappointed nationalism offended by the existence of Northern Ireland and the promiscuous multinational desires of the Republic. And Roy Foster reminds us that the historians who revised the old anti-English, anti-Protestant history have been attacked or ignored by convert, expatriate or English pro-nationalists and now had their own work readjusted.

I'm not sure to what extent the instability and confusion brought about by counter-revision come with the territory of the Third Revolution. There are theories of revision to which Irish students can have recourse, drawn from the fields of communist debate, art history, psychoanalysis and literary criticism. The work of the literary theorist Harold Bloom springs to mind. It would surely be useful for us in Ireland to contemplate what is at stake when familiar readings are split, diffused, and called into question, and what the mechanisms of this process are.

III

One problem with pluralism is that though it recognizes differences, it seeks to minimize them and render them innocuous or merely useful. Something of the same impulse can announce itself in social anthropology in Ulster, which for understandable reasons has been reluctant to stress differences within communities.

In 'Collecting Ulster's Culture: Are there Really Two Traditions?', Anthony Buckley summarizes the opinion of Wallis, Bruce and Taylor that the answer to this question is 'yes'. They point to those things that divide the communities – religion, education, holidays, marriage, residence, sport, history and politics. They may therefore, conclude Wallis, Bruce and Taylor, be considered as 'ethnic groups'.

Buckley, while admitting that most people in Ulster persist in seeing themselves as falling into one of two camps, doesn't believe that these camps are 'traditions', or that it is helpful for ethnographers to regard them as such. He writes:

I want to suggest here that there do not exist, in empirical fact, two (or three) 'traditions' in modern Ulster, and that the opposite claim that there is a single Ulster or even Irish tradition is equally false. Instead, it will be argued that in Ulster and in Ireland generally there is both cultural diversity and cultural uniformity . . . In particular, the use of the term 'tradition' in expressions such as 'there exist two traditions in Ulster', is harmful to a proper understanding of what is going on in the province.

This is because 'Most of what Catholics and Protestants do is not distinctively either "Catholic" or "Protestant",' and Buckley is interested in what people do, not think. 'I wish therefore', he says, 'to repudiate the notion that there exists a body of "Irish tradition", or "Ulster tradition", or "nationalist tradition", or "unionist tradition".' Instead, Buckley offers a detailed and busy portrait of cultural fusion, interaction, multiversity, criss-crossed by regional and class allegiances. In *A Gentle People*, he claims that in one Ulster community the reality behind this portrait has succeeded an earlier reality of division and demarcation. Things have got better, in other words, with neighbourliness, individualism, non-sectarian associations and bi-sectarian activities transcending the old confrontations.

Buckley is an ethnographer of somewhat functionalist persuasion. Such concepts as balance, reciprocity, negotiation and parallelism are crucial to his interpretation of Ulster communities. Social anthropologists in Northern Ireland, as their colleagues Donnan and MacFarlane point out, tend to see their communities as integrated mechanisms, and therefore emphasize peace, similarity and consensus over violence, difference and conflict (of a centrifugal or unravelling kind).

Elliott Leyton, for example, believes you understand division in Ulster communities not by studying bigotry and intolerance but by comprehending 'a dualistic organisation of society'. Leyton's duality is very different from Buckley's homologies, but he claims that it has prevented the Northern Ireland homicide rate during the Troubles from approaching the peace-time rate of Detroit city. Leyton does not suggest that dualistic organizations are bad because they perpetuate division, if not conflict, and so one can see the possible justice in the views of those who, according to Kingsley Davis as far back as 1959, attacked functionalism for failing to handle social change, for having a vested interest in societies as going concerns, in the *status quo*, and for paying scant attention to rupture and the struggle for power. Buckley does pay attention to social change but only by contrasting the 'folk' past with the present. And he clearly prefers his 'Upper Tullagh' to Leyton's 'Aughnaboy'; yet his preference rests on his decision (and, it seems, the decision of his informants) to ignore the role and implications of constitutional politics and likewise the psychological (private, intimate) dimension of sectarianism, indeed of all his homologies. And the contrast with 'Aughnaboy' permits us to wonder how exceptional and atypical is 'Upper Tullagh' among Ulster communities.

The disparity between the conclusions of Buckley and those of O'Dowd is in part the difference between social anthropology and sociology in Ulster. The ideology of the latter seems leftist and/or vestigially nationalist, orientated towards conflict and power, metaphorically 'Catholic' to the metaphoric 'Protestantism' or 'unionism' of social anthropology. (To ignore constitutional politics in Ulster is to be *ipso facto* unionist, which is a bad thing only if it is unearned.) Yet 'Ignoring the Implications of the Communal Divide: The Implications for Social Research in Northern Ireland', by O'Dowd, is an example of what I call the New Realism in Irish studies that might possibly constitute a genuine phase of understanding after revisionism and pluralism.

O'Dowd regards 'the communal divide' as deep and ubiquitous in Ulster society, interwoven with class, occupation, locality, economics and politics. It is distortive to perceive the divide as an abnormal growth on the normal body cultural, yet social research in his opinion has tended to do so. It has done so by employing what he calls strategies of avoidance and/or compartmentalization. One strategy is to concentrate exclusively or heavily on the Troubles: it was, after all, the violence of the 1970s 'which generated the massive interest of international social science in Northern Ireland'. Later, a second strategy evolved, the complementary one of concentrating exclusively or heavily on the 'normality' of Ulster society, its socio-economic features and problems from which the communal divide had been subtracted as a factor. This was an attempt to localize the research, a result of Direct Rule, and a product of the Ulster lay strategy of avoiding the Troubles in everyday transactions (which, we recall, Buckley is concerned with).

O'Dowd scrutinizes the arguments in favour of avoidance, including the proposition that social scientists should try to help 'normalize' Ulster society by marginalizing communal division, and finds them all wanting and obstructive. 'It remains the job of the social scientist to probe precisely why consensus is so limited – why, for example, so much well intentioned and selfless effort often appears utopian and naive. To turn a blind eye to conflict and coercion is [to] ensure that the efforts to build consensus and common interest are doomed to marginality in the long run.' For O'Dowd, class, employment, politics, sect, ethnic membership, and culture form a complex from which sect and ethnic membership cannot be subtracted without falsification. (He is close to the anthropologists Donnan and MacFarlane here.) He calls for research 'at the interface of existing social science disciplines'. He denies that Ulster society is pathological, but asks us to attend to 'the durable' – and not always negative – 'ethnic sectarian divide'. He concludes: 'Superficial assumptions and claims about common interests are counter-productive. Common interests there are but these can only be fully recognised when the obstacles to realising, expressing and working towards them are fully researched.' O'Dowd uses the word 'realistic' twice as he approaches that conclusion.

So the idea of two traditions has been reinstated, but as part of a fabric of which they are the dominant colour and weave. Many of us are aware of the growing polarization in Ulster, as larger and more sharply defined areas – geographic but also psychic – become off-limits to each of us, which must inevitably over time grow exotic.

F.W. Boal has recently studied the demography of this polarization in Belfast. Many of us may even be in some psychological or cultural way returning to our corners. Realists would recognize this and offer only the prospect of their studying our deep and widening differences, simultaneously monitoring the process, holding the line against it, participating in it, understanding it. In stressing difference, we must risk sounding superficially like the discredited voices of old, looking as if we had come full circle.

Difference has been studied in a variety of international fields – psychoanalysis, anthropology, sociology, feminism, philosophy, film theory – especially in the last two decades with the rise of structuralism, and of feminism in which differences between men and women have been foregrounded. The dualization explored by the anthropologist Hertz in 1909 and since by functionalists and others, should be supplemented by the polarity in Greek thinking recently investigated by Lloyd and, of course, by the binary opposition prominent in the work of Lévi-Strauss. For Lévi-Strauss the units of a system have meaning only by virtue of their relations to one another. What he says of societies Freud had already said of the individual, whose self is created in the recognition of difference. Freud deals in what he regarded as universals whereas we in Ulster deal with localities – *unless* the differences we are born into and with in Ulster perform a universal function. 'Anatomy is destiny,' said Freud, meaning we are born male or female and all else follows. This has been disputed by feminists; still, it sometimes seems that in Ulster sect is destiny: we are born Catholic or Protestant and all else follows. That destiny, as Irish feminists are finding out, is apparently stronger than the anatomical one, at least in the context of Ulster.

What we urgently need is a psychology of sectarianism. Without a raising of consciousness comparable to the consciousness shift brought about in America and Europe by feminism, all political prescriptions will fail because imposed from without. We could do worse than begin with Simone de Beauvoir's analysis in *The Second Sex* of 'the Other' as which woman functions for man. The man, she says, 'attains himself only through the reality which he is not, which is something other than himself', in other words woman. Although man dominates woman by withholding identity from her, she incarnates the lack in himself, and 'it is in seeking to be made whole through her that man hopes to attain self-realization'. Imagine if you will such insights generated by sectarianism. Really, and shamefully, we have not begun to understand the primary fact of our existence in Ulster.

While recognizing the complexity of the psychic relation between men and women, de Beauvoir seeks to undermine the concept of the Other, since it prevents self-realization, reciprocity and mutual dignity. Indeed, feminists have recently sought to escape the oppressive network of hierarchical binary opposition. 'This problem of dealing with difference without constituting an opposition may just be what feminism is all about (might even be what psychoanalysis is all about),' writes Jane Gallop. Having recognized and understood fully the potency of binary opposition – as we have yet to do in Ulster – the feminists have joined forces uneasily with post-structuralists to destroy binary schemes of thought. Feminists hope to substitute multiple, heterogeneous difference, 'anarchic fragmentation', as the Ulster feminist Eileen Evason calls it (quoted by Ward). This is not the facile pluralism of Ulster and Irish liberal nationalists and unionists. For the French thinker Derrida, meaning is neither instantaneous nor based on simply difference (as it is for us in Ulster) but deferred and open-ended – what he calls *différence*.

We had better pause at the deconstructionist enterprise that dominates advanced feminist and poststructuralist thought abroad. It sounds Utopian or silly in the context of sectarian meaning and identity. We can, however, promote several projects. One, the complication by students and writers, with maximum publicity, of the dualistic Ulster world-view. Two, the acknowledgment of the strength and depth of that world-view, at the psychological level, by what the Ulster feminist Inez McCormack calls 'that difficult dangerous honesty' (quoted by Ward). Revisionism and pluralism, yes, but also the realistic analysis of binary opposition.

This side of deconstruction, we might have to settle for a chorus of individual voices in Ireland to interrupt the tiresome duologue of Ulster history. (Hence the importance of autobiography and of local or micro-history.) We might have to settle for the goal of self-realization which is regarded as a liberal-humanist fantasy only by those who have already achieved it, but George Moore said that the tragedy of Ireland is that people live and die without realizing the qualities they are born with.

Women in Ireland will achieve self-realization only if they transcend sectarianism and the so-called national question. Betty Friedan in *The Feminine Mystique* encouraged women to seek self-realization, and of course she is now seen as a bourgeois feminist. Still, women in Ireland cannot be expected to jump from the experience of sexism to the successful subversion of difference without claiming and accomplishing equality *in* difference. Equality and self-realization are still the goals of Irish feminism, and women's studies ought to be a component of any Irish Studies syllabus.

Feminism exists on its own terms. But it is also a fruitful source of analogy. Read feminism and you learn willy-nilly about sectarianism – about difference, opposition, dominance and oppression, the language of difference. These two aspects of feminism could combine in Ireland if gender became a third force, a third Irish identity. Alas, twenty-five years after Friedan it looks increasingly unlikely, and it seems that as Protestants and Catholics, nationalists and unionists, British and Irish, we are still thrown back on our own slender resources.

[1988]

REFERENCES

Boal, F.W., 'Ethnic Residential Segregation, Ethnic Mixing and Resource Conflict: A Study in Belfast, Northern Ireland', *Ethnic Segregation in Cities*, eds C. Peach, V. Robinson and S. Smith (London: Croom Helm 1981).

Boal, F.W., 'Two Nations in Ireland', *Antipode* 12:1 (1980), 38–44.

Boal, F.W. and David Livingstone, 'Protestants in Belfast: A View from the Inside', *Contemporary Review* 248: 1443 (1986), 169–75.

Brady, John, 'Reflections of a Disappointed Pluralist', *Studies* 75:300 (1986), 464–7.

Brown, Terence, *The Whole Protestant Community: The Making of a Historical Myth* (Derry: Field Day Theatre Company 1985).

Buckley, Anthony, 'Collecting Ulster's Culture: Are there Really Two Traditions?' Paper delivered to the annual meeting of the British Association for the Advancement of Science (September 1986).

Buckley, Anthony, *A Gentle People: A Study of a Peaceful Community in Ulster* (Holywood: Ulster Folk and Transport Museum 1982).

Buckley, Anthony, '"You only *live* in your body": Peace, Exchange and the Siege Mentality in Ulster'. Unpublished MS.

Davis, Kingsley, 'The Myth of Functional Analysis as a Special Method in Sociology and Anthropology', *American Sociological Review* 24:6 (1959), 757–72.

de Beauvoir, Simone, *The Second Sex* (1949), trans. and ed. H.M. Parshley (Harmondsworth: Penguin Books 1972).

Donnan, Hastings and Graham McFarlane, 'Social Life in Rural Northern Ireland', *Studies* 74:295 (1985), 281–98.

Donnan, Hastings and Graham McFarlane, '"You get on better with your own": Social Continuity and Change in Rural Northern Ireland', *Ireland: A Sociological Profile*, eds Patrick Clancy, Sheelagh Drudy, Kathleen Lynch and Liam O'Dowd (Dublin: Institute of Public Administration 1986).

Donoghue, Denis, *We Irish: The Selected Essays of Denis Donoghue*, Vol. 1 (Brighton: Harvester Press 1986).

Fennell, Desmond, *Beyond Nationalism: The Struggle against Provinciality in the Modern World* (Swords, Co. Dublin: Ward River Press 1985).

Foster, John Wilson, *Fictions of the Irish Literary Revival: A Changeling Art* (Syracuse: Syracuse University Press; Dublin: Gill and Macmillan, 1987).

Foster, Roy, '"We Are All Revisionists Now"', *The Irish Review* 1 (1986), 1–5.

Friedan, Betty, *The Feminine Mystique* (Harmondsworth: Penguin Books 1982).

Gallagher, A.M., 'Identity and Ideology in Social Conflict: The Case of Northern Ireland'. Ph.D. diss., Queen's University, Belfast, 1987.

Gallop, Jane, *Feminism and Psychoanalysis: The Daughter's Seduction* (London: Macmillan 1982).

Hertz, Robert, 'The Pre-eminence of the Right Hand: A Study in Religious Polarity', *Right and Left: Essays in Dual Symbolic Classification*, ed. Rodney Needham (Chicago and London: University of Chicago Press 1973).

Hickey, John, 'Religion in the Divided Society', *Ireland: A Sociological Profile*, eds Clancy et al.

Kearney, Richard, 'The Transitional Crisis in Irish Culture', *The Honest Ulsterman* 82 (1986), 30–42.

Kennedy, Liam, 'Irish Historiography and the Ulster Question'. Unpublished MS.

Kennedy, Liam, *Two Ulsters: A Case for Repartition* (Belfast: College Park Publications 1986).

Kiberd, Declan, 'Inventing Irelands', *The Crane Bag* 8: 1 (1984), 11–23.

Leyton, Elliott, 'Opposition and Integration in Ulster', *Man*, New Series 9 (1974), 185–98.

Lloyd, G.E.R., *Polarity and Analogy: Two Types of Argumentation in Early Greek Thought* (Cambridge: University Press 1966).

Malcolm, Elizabeth, 'Irish Mental Hospitals in the 19th Century'. Unpublished MS.

Neary, Peter, 'The Failure of Economic Nationalism', *The Crane Bag* 8:1 (1984), 68–77.

Nic Ghiolla Phádraig, Máire, 'Religious Practice and Secularisation', *Ireland: A Sociological Profile*, eds Clancy et al.

O'Dowd, Liam, 'Beyond Industrial Society', *Ireland: A Sociological Profile*, eds Clancy et al.

O'Dowd, Liam, 'Ignoring the Implications of the Communal Divide: The Implications for Social Research in Northern Ireland'. Unpublished MS.

Pine, Richard, 'Reflections on Dependence and Independence', *The Crane Bag* 9:1 (1985), 96–102.

Stevens, David, 'Pluralism: A Northern Reaction', *Studies* 75: 300 (1986), 471–4.

Ward, Margaret, 'Feminism in the North of Ireland', *The Honest Ulsterman* 83 (1987), 59–70.

Wickham, James, 'Industrialisation, Work and Unemployment', *Ireland: A Sociological Profile*, eds Clancy et al.

14

WHO ARE THE IRISH?

The question 'Who are the Irish?' is not an innocuous one like 'Who are the Welsh?' or 'Who are the Finns?' asked by school teachers of pupils, who are meant to reply, 'People who live in Wales, miss' or 'People who live in Finland, sir.' Rather, it invokes the debate long in process over the respective merits of candidates for the appellation. Irishness in certain contexts is an honorific title, and as such open for claim, for bestowal (and rejection), and possibly for negotiation.

But if Irishness is a ribbon of merit, there are those who are handicapped, possibly even disqualified, if they attempt to claim it, and yet who are assailed if they do not. It is the Ulster Protestant who is perceived by members of the majority culture on this island as having the weakest case for claiming Irishness. (I don't know how they regard the embrogued boat people of the South or the Ulster-accented Chinese of the North). It is obvious that I have been asked today to speak as an Ulster Protestant, or, as Professor Lucy put it, with a characteristically eloquent turn of phrase, as 'someone outside the romantic nationalist tradition'. I have no hesitation in speaking as an Ulster Protestant, and suffer no sense of shame or even reluctance in stating dispassionately what I presumably am – a descendant of those who planted Ulster in the name of King James I all those centuries ago.

I am not proud of all that Ulster Protestants have done, or even of all that they are (they seem a rather dull group to me on the whole): all races and populations have their vices as well as their virtues, their shameful episodes as well as their finer hours. But although my sense of being an individual outweighs my sense of ethnic identity, I am proud enough of being Northern Irish, and of being Protestant – not in the churchgoing or even strict theological sense, but in the now secular, once theological sense of deriving from dissidents and nonconformists.

The weakness of the Ulster Protestant's case is due in part to the fact that whereas in some situations he accepts or claims Irishness, in vital political situations he doesn't wish to stake the claim in the first place. But it is also due in part to the racialist withholding of Irishness *from* him by the majority culture.

Certainly 'Who are the Irish?' is not a question Ulster Protestants would ask. And they do not ask it because they recognize it as a question asked by those secure in the sense of their own Irishness. The question might really be, 'Who in our midst might not be truly Irish?' and therefore have ominous overtones that the Ulster Protestant's radar picks up right away. Perhaps I am too cynical and the question is meant to encourage for the best of motives a broader definition of Irishness than at present obtains in the orthodox and majority view. Though even then the Ulster Protestant is wary in case that hoped-for broader definition is kin to the view of Irishness set down in the *New Ireland Forum Report*: secular pluralism on the outside, old-style Catholic republicanism on the inside, old wine in new attractive bottles. In short, the Ulster Protestant finds the question uncomfortable, and his answer will reflect that discomfiture. But it is surely an opportunity as well, and it is in that spirit that I will tackle it.

THREE HISTORICAL CONCEPTS OF IRISHNESS

The only two sizeable groups on the island thinking of whom it makes sense to ask this question, 'Who are the Irish?', are the Southern Protestants and the Northern Protestants. Ironically, it was the former, we are told, who forged the idea of the Irish nation, in the eighteenth century. Yeats was fond of the fashion in which George Berkeley in his journal repudiated English philosophical abstractionism, subscribing each argument with the formula, 'We Irishmen cannot attain to these truths,' a formula Yeats echoed in his line, 'We Irish, born into that ancient sect'. Denis Donoghue has devoted some difficult pages to Berkeley's formula, and has concluded:

To Berkeley, 'We Irish' meant, I think, those men, upper-class Protestants, who had no power and only whatever prestige accrued to them from their talents in philosophy, divinity, law, and natural science. Such men – Molyneux, Archbishop King, Swift, and Berkeley himself – were often provoked into sentiments that could be mistaken for those of modern nationalism.

Here, then, is one long-discredited answer to the question 'Who are the Irish?' The Irish, mark I. There were, of course, the 'mere' or pure Irish, but they were of no political consequence until much later, a reminder that the question 'Who are the Irish?' is inseparable from the question of power.

An attempt to seize power from the Anglo-Irish on behalf of the mere Irish in league with Northern Dissenters – both groups noisily disaffected – culminated in the failed rising of 1798. This revolution is commemorated today chiefly because it is thought to have been executed in the spirit of Wolfe Tone's belief in 'the Common Name of Irishman'. Catholic and Dissenter were identified in their mutual and indissoluble Irishness (the Irish mark II), and nostalgia for this identification has increased in latter years with the Troubles in Northern Ireland. According to some historians, partition and civic strife could have been averted had the golden opportunity of 1798 come to fruition.

The United Irishmen definition of Irishness was, sadly, divisive in fact if not in fiction, and there was an air of unreality about it. One sympathetic historian has it that Protestant contempt for Catholic intellect made co-operation impossible. Another has it that Catholics and Dissenters were farther apart in the run-up to '98 than nostalgic nationalists believe. The definition of Irishness at the time was one of revolutionary idealism rather than reality, and therefore its apparent inclusiveness is an illusion. The Ulster Protestants today are the philosophical product of the years between 1886 and 1914 when the modern unionist identity was forged. Paisleyism is in fact a vestige of the United Irishmen ideal, its all-Ireland republicanism evaporated, leaving only as a deposit the flirtatious Ulster (anti-Catholic, anti-Irish) republicanism of UDI – loyalism inverted and made purely nominal.

However tenable these two definitions of Irishness were before the nineteenth century, they could not survive the advent of Daniel O'Connell. From O'Connell derives our modern day-to-day image of the Irish, the majority on the island, as Catholic, English-speaking, democratic, and *petit-bourgeois* – the only Ireland Sean O'Faolain came to see as real. Incidentally, it appears O'Connell visited Ulster just once in his life. When he went to Belfast to address a Repeal Association meeting in 1841, he used an alias and travelled two days early and by minor roads. O'Connell, like most nationalists after him, knew little of the Protestant North and cared less. Clare O'Halloran has referred recently to the 'sectarian basis and southern origins of constitutional nationalism'.

Almost as much can be said of the Home Rule movement of the 1880s, which culminated in independence, i.e. partition, in 1921. The Irish Literary Revival might appear to have been the cultural arm of the Home Rule movement, but in fact it was, at least on the surface, a heady expression of an élitist cultural republicanism. W.B. Yeats had no truck with the sprawling and inconvenient reality of O'Connellite Ireland (the Irish, mark III) which he saw as a wave of his 'filthy modern tide'. When he quoted approvingly an unnamed fellow Irish poet – 'We Irish cannot become philosophical like the English, our lives are too exciting' – I believe he was quoting himself and had Berkeley's Irish in mind. For Yeats saw no excitement in O'Connellite Ireland. It was Joyce who was its chief laureate. We see it vividly in his middle-class Dublin versions (and in O'Casey's working-class, or non-working-class, Dublin versions) as a 'through-other' affair, its literature and music and received wisdom scrappy, half-English, half-Irish, handed down from above and beyond. A world without cultural, moral or spiritual integrity, whose centre is its reflex Catholicism or perhaps merely its volubility, its entertaining, consoling, hollow eloquence, all else precarious and piecemeal. Yet it is authentic and in Joyce and O'Casey oddly engaging if incorrigible, or because incorrigible. It has changed since Joyce and O'Casey, of course, but it is still recognizable: indeed, while a dominant middle class is in process of formation, O'Connellite Ireland and its Ulster Protestant counterpart are the only two Irelands that matter today, and their horns are locked.

IRISHNESS AND THE REVIVAL

Yet it is not really O'Connellite Ireland that threatens and excludes the Ulster Protestants. Exclusive Ireland is an official (indeed, constitutional) and orthodox Ireland that derives from two traditions of thinking for which we can let two men, Yeats and Daniel Corkery, conveniently, if somewhat unfairly, stand.

The two implicit criteria of Berkeley's concept of Irishness – Protestantism and high birth – would *seem* to have been abandoned by Yeats and the Anglo-Irish Revival. In the Revival we have the ennoblement of the Irish peasant, who was in practice Catholic (and who ought to be, if he was not, Gaelic-speaking).

Certainly the Revival was nominally an anti-Protestant movement. The Protestant was too readily identifiable with the distrusted merchant, scientist, industrialist, rationalist, democrat and individualist. But it is arguable that the pervasive interest during the Revival in the occult, theosophy, secret societies, ritual, was a displaced freemasonry or sublimated evangelicalism. Besides, the Anglo-Irish leaders of the Revival when they extolled the peasant discounted the lowly, workaday Catholicism of the peasant, preferring to see below this a pagan spirituality. They also tended to avoid open confrontation with the Catholic Church, chief institution of the Ireland they wished out of countenance. By this means, the Revivalists could mine under the one great stumbling-block to their own sense of Irishness – Catholicism. To this extent, the Revivalists, apparent renegades against their heritage, could be viewed as covert spokesmen for Southern Protestants trying to establish a role and identity in the dangerously changing Ireland of the 1880s onwards. In any event, there was certainly great falsification in the image of the mystical, contented, rooted peasant, which Patrick Kavanagh ruthlessly exposed later.

Also, although the Protestant Revivalists loved the peasant, they did so in part because he was seen as an aristocrat in disguise or in some way equivalent to an aristocrat. The affinity between gentry and peasantry rested on a half-historical, half-legendary conviction that the latter, or at least the seers and storytellers among them, held in protective custody the music and art of the native aristocracy dispersed with the overthrow of the Gaelic order in the seventeenth century, an idea given most vivid expression in Corkery's book, *The Hidden Ireland* (1924), but prefigured in Yeats's equation of peasant, artist, and aristocrat. All three, said Yeats, create beautiful things, enjoy long tradition, possess a special kind of knowledge or wisdom, and are above (in the case of the aristocrat), beneath (in the case of the peasant) or beyond (in the case of the artist) merely materialist concerns.

So Protestantism and high birth, nominally dropped as criteria for Irishness, were smuggled back into the Revival concept. As for the Gaelic language, the Gaelic League ensured that some genuine revival took place, but this meant introducing a qualification for Irishness that most of the Revivalists themselves, including Yeats, AE, Standish James O'Grady, and James Stephens, could not, or would not, meet, and so the qualification had to wait for proper elevation until after the Revival.

Because of these feedbacks and stratagems, it has been claimed recently by younger Catholic critics that the apparent nationalism of the Revival, long accepted by English and American academics, who take their Irish history and cultural orthodoxy from Yeats, was in fact disguised unionism. This view derives from Daniel Corkery, and, later, from Kavanagh.

But before I glance at the revision of the Revival view of Irishness carried out by Corkery, we can remind ourselves what parts of the Irish, mark IV, survived the Revival, i.e. into the Irish Free State and beyond. One, love of the land and the special status of the peasant (later farmer); two, residual respect for the aristocrat, who in the nature of things was a surviving member of the Ascendancy, titled remnant of a glory, however once-hated; three, the special status of the artist, especially the writer as lyrical idler ('words alone are certain good'!) – room, that is, for early Yeats, Alice Milligan, Colum and so on, but not for our own lapsed, ungrateful and dangerous sort: Joyce and Clarke, for example; and four, disdain for Ulster of the kind Yeats exhibited, with its nasty undisguised urbanism of Belfast, its filthy industrialism, its contemptible Protestant low-church non-conformism.

I will pause at the latter. A successful Revival required the conscious de-anglicizing of Ireland that Douglas Hyde called for in 1892. Such cultural engineering could be justified only on the ground that it would effect a return to an essential, natural and historically continuous Irishness. If the Protestant north-east were an obstacle, then partition it off in one's mind. In any case, the Ulster planters of the seventeenth century had differed disobligingly from all other invaders in refusing to be absorbed. They had damaged 'the continuity of the Irishism of Ireland . . . in the north-east of Ulster, where the Gaelic race was expelled and the land planted with aliens [*sic*], whom our dear mother Erin, assimilative as she is, has hitherto found it difficult to absorb . . .'. Whereas unassimilated Gaelicism was a virtue, unassimilated Scots-Irishness was a vice. Further comment is unnecessary, beyond reminding readers that Hyde became the first President of the Irish Republic, official embodiment of the highest ideals of the state.

Superficially, then, the Protestant leaders of the Revival were rebelling against their racial, class and religious heritage. At first, Catholic writers and intellectuals were suspicious of the renegades, viewing them as fifth columnists or playboys, but many, including Griffith and Pearse, came to accept their usefulness to the cause of an independent Ireland in providing a cultural basis for separatism. The emerging coalition developed a synthetic and triumphantly eloquent cultural nationalism; it formulated a definition not only of Irish literature but of Irish culture and Irish nationality. Certain traditions, literatures, regional identities, and subcultures were championed and others disqualified. A faction of the Anglo-Irish made common cause with a faction of the Irish, and in the process certain unwelcome and inconvenient Irelands were ignored or misinterpreted: *petit-bourgeois* and small-farmer Catholic Ireland that dominated the island in terms of population (and still does), that Ireland known intimately to James Joyce, Brinsley MacNamara, D. P. Moran, and later Flann O'Brien and Patrick Kavanagh; the genuine Gaelic culture that had once flourished and had now a precarious grip on life in the west of Ireland; orthodox Anglo-Ireland, aristocratic, mercantile and clerical remnant of the Protestant Ascendancy; and Protestant Ulster, the Scots-Irish north-east of the island.

Corkery in *Synge and Anglo-Irish Literature* (1931) dissolved this partnership unilaterally from the Catholic side. He was at one with the Revivalists in accepting love of the land and a nationalist philosophy as two qualifications of Irishness. But his third qualified the other two and in so doing distinguished his sense of Irishness qualitatively from theirs. That third qualification was Catholicism. Corkery if he deepened the concept of Irishness also narrowed it: his definition of the authentic Irish, the Irish, mark V, disqualified most of the Northern Irish as well as the Anglo-Irish. And it proved to be the winning definition.

IRISHNESS SINCE 1920

Elements of definitions one, three, four and five went to make up the definition of Irishness that has prevailed in the South of Ireland since the founding of the Free State and afterwards in Eamon de Valera's Republic. It has to be said that the definitions were formulated largely out of sound and sight of Northern Protestants, who were not responsible, in their philosophy or even in their existence, for the formulations, which would have happened without them. All four definitions exclude them. So if they do not feel truly Irish, is it any wonder, whether or not they wish to feel truly Irish? Leopold Bloom's reply to the Citizen in the Cyclops episode of *Ulysses*, that Ireland is his nation because he lives there, is clearly not a passing answer to the question if we have the Ulster Protestants instead of a lone Dublin Jew in mind. Residence is evidently not enough, even residence since Jacobean times.

When the Free State came into being, and despite the relative pluralism of the 1922 Constitution, Catholicism, the Irish language, and nationalism became essential qualifications of Irishness. Northern Protestants, as Clare O'Halloran has recently convincingly shown, were seen as fundamentally and traditionally other and alien, and long before the Government of Ireland Act, 1920. Officially, this was the case only half the time. O'Halloran says: 'unionists were to be considered Irish for the purposes of the claim for national unity comprising the whole island as the national territory, and yet foreign when their views or actions were seen as contrary to Irish nationalist ideology and stated expectations'.

As nationalist ideology developed from the early nineteenth century, there was an answering self-exclusion by Northern Protestants from nationalist Irishness, a self-exclusion that was nevertheless largely irrelevant to that ideological development, as I have suggested. Partition in 1921 was not some devilish sundering of the island imposed from without, but an almost natural consequence (however regrettable or unacceptable to some) of the culmination on the nationalist side of events long-preparing. This is why Clare O'Halloran found no evidence of the major trauma on the popular imagination or political consciousness she expected to find in the South when she began to explore the impact of partition on Southern politics. Instead she found a pragmatic Southern partitionism behind the rhetorical pretence of unambiguous irredentism (Eiredentism, I am tempted to pun). The trauma was apparently suffered only by Northern nationalists, who could find even themselves, after 1921, regarded by Southern politicians as irksome, even somewhat alien, threats to nationalist ideology.

Northern unionists were most definitely alien. It is orthodoxy now for many that there are two traditions in Ulster; there is even an organization of that name, the Two Traditions Group, dedicated to reconciliation, proclaiming the existence in Northern Ireland of the Ulster-British and the Ulster-Irish. These are categories that Desmond Fennell, the Southern writer, has used, asserting that the Ulster Protestants constitute a population separate enough that the attempt to annex them is a species of imperialism. If a label must be accepted, then I suppose 'Ulster-British' is the least inaccurate I can think of, though it is clumsy and unattractive. However, for the historical reasons I have merely sketched, the word 'Irish' has been appropriated by those who see it as synonymous with the Gaelic language (even if forgotten), aboriginal ethnicity, and the Roman Catholic religion.

OBSTACLES TO AN INCLUSIVE IRISHNESS

Clearly there is no immediate way around the distinction between planter and Gael, settler and native. It is of course on occasions absurd. Is a relative of mine, product of a Catholic father and Protestant mother, planter or Gael? To talk of mixed marriages is one thing, but mixed progeny quite another, and surely ridiculous. Still, the distinction is maintained, to the extent that I believe (or am duped into believing) that an Irish-American, born and bred in, say, Boston, bearing an Irish name and perhaps complexion, is more Irish, in some vital way, than I. Sometimes I cheerfully comply with this fiction. But fictions can have force. The distinction had to be underlined, for example, to give emotional strength to the independence movement in the South. Yet the distinction is always invidious, since nativeness implies primacy and priority. Since no one wants to claim second-class identity, Ulster Protestants, instead of claiming Irishness, prefer to let Pearse, Corkery and their nationalist successors have and hold their definition of Irishness while they claim what is first-class and incontrovertible identity: Ulsterness within or without a constitutional Britishness, though always within an ethnic Britishness (since we cannot falsify our origins).

If there is no obvious way, at present, around nativeness, equally there seems no imminent way around Catholicism, which, for historical reasons, sometimes poignant historical reasons, was identified by some with Irishness, an identification that became copper-fastened through legislation after 1921, again in 1937, and in 1983 and 1986. Even a lapsed Catholic like James Joyce, sounding like his own Citizen, told James Stephens (how much in jest?) that he (Stephens) could not understand the Irish since he wasn't Catholic. Patrick Kavanagh accused Irish Protestants of trying to 'by-pass Rome on the way to the heart of Ireland'; for him, one could not be Irish and not a Catholic. This is clearly a situation that could conceivably change when the majority of non-Protestants lapse from their faith, though even then the cultural and psychological effects of centuries of Catholicism would have to fade before Irishness and Catholicism were separated. The theological and secular reservations Protestants and free thinkers entertain towards Catholicism are actually irrelevant now to the majority's equation of their nationality and ethnicity with their cradle religion.

The Irish language is equally a stumbling-block to an island-wide Irishness, especially since the language is associated with a western rurality and the ethnic well-spring of the peasant, including his music – all impossibly remote to urban Ulster Protestants, however good-willed they are and game to fake their responses, as many self-deceivingly do. The Gaelic language and Irish music, cut the cake as you will, are simply not their heritage, and if they are essential to Irishness, then Irishness is not their heritage either. Even if I were to learn Gaelic, I would be an even greater anomaly than I already am – an Ulster Protestant who had learned Gaelic. Already I have qualms about claiming to be in Irish Studies or to study Anglo-Irish literature, when I can find myself in the position of reviewing someone whose name I can't even pronounce. Time and again at arty or academic social gatherings in the evenings, the drink flowing, the concentric circles of Irishness narrow and shrink, the *real* Irish receding, as it were, into a dark centre, starting up with the ballads of the sorrowful legend of Ireland, as Stephen Dedalus called it, breaking into the Gaelic, claiming their heritage, the more consciously if there are foreigners present, the Prods and English meanwhile affecting sheepish grins and bottomless ethnic empathy, faking away like mad! At times like that I almost feel as if your Sammy Wilson or your Ian Paisley is more honest than your polite bystanders, pluralists to a man.

But cannot one claim Irishness simply by proclaiming oneself a nationalist? William Magennis, who formed the Clann Eireann party in the 1910s, wrote: 'Anyone, I do not care what his racial origin or religion, so long as he becomes an adopted Irishman or is an Irishman by conviction, taking a national view of things, is, to me as good as anyone of an unbroken Gaelic descent.' I do not believe Magennis, since the formulation of his assertion is its own denial. Besides, 'taking a national view of things' is precisely the rub. One can be an Irish nationalist, it seems, only by accepting that Irishness resides in some commingling of nativeness, Catholicism, love of the land, and the Irish language, and that the nationalist view of Irish history is the true one. Proclaiming nationalism is not an easy *alternative* to racial origin and religion, but the paradoxical self-cancellation of one's candidature for Irishness!

THE POLARIZATION OF NORTHERN IRELAND

There is at present in Ulster a reassertion of cultural nationalism. In several Catholic areas, street names have been put up in Gaelic; there is an upsurge of interest in Irish language classes and schools; and there is a revival of enthusiasm for traditional music, this time with a decided ideological edge unlike the folksy, counter-cultural togetherness of the 1960s revival. All of these are accompanying the reassertion of political nationalism (between Limavady and Belfast the other day I counted three bright new tricolours flying from brazen vantage-points) and the translation of the South's irredentism from rhetoric into, at long last, action, with the Anglo-Irish Agreement.

This is provoking (though perhaps little provocation is needed) a cultural as well as political backlash among unionists, and there is emerging for the first time a unionist cultural spokesgroup. Its political intellectual is Robert McCartney Its mythologist is Ian Adamson. Its cultural watchman is Peter Brooke. Its journal is *New Ulster*, the journal of the Ulster Society. Its cultural backup is the rise of the various Ulster Heritage groups. A Protestant Ulsterness is now being asserted in place of Britishness, but only the sanguine can imagine that this is a halfway house to an assertion of Irishness.

Because it is a backlash, it can appear rather hysterical and right-wing, as right-wing as its republican counterpart. But there is in it, as in its counterpart, a core of populist sentiment. When partition occurred and the North and South of Ireland were locked into their respective mind-sets, Ulster did not need thinkers or apologists; it was on automatic pilot, fixed by grey and visionless men. Unionism as an intellectually or culturally defensible belief withered away. Coincident with the new Troubles of the 1970s, a rebirth of Ulster literature took place, induced first by the poets, latterly by the playwrights. But the best writers have been strictly non-ideological or apparently so. As the political and constitutional crisis worsens, this may change. I do know that a wind of change is blowing in the academy. Recently, in response to the Anglo-Irish Agreement, some eminent Protestant intellectuals have withdrawn from all-Ireland academic bodies previously seen as politically innocent or neutral. The polarization of Northern Irish society now extends ominously upwards from the back streets to the university.

Pre-emptive talk of pluralism, of cherishable traditions or varieties of Irishness is not, I am afraid, the answer, but a form of self-deception. Nationalism and unionism are not just traditions, they are *causes* and are mutually exclusive *in their present and historical form*. When I wrote elsewhere of the menacing subtexts of the *New Ireland Forum Report*, of the old idea of Irishness, thinly disguised, which it contained, I may have appeared paranoid. But now Clare O'Halloran has come to the very same conclusion in the epilogue to her recent book *Partition and the Limits of Irish Nationalism*. We are all aware in Ulster of the growing polarization in the society, as larger and more sharply defined areas – geographic but also psychic – become off-limits to each of us, which must inevitably in time grow exotic. Many of us may even be in some psychological or cultural way returning to our corners. Realists would recognize this and offer only the prospect of their studying our deep and widening differences, simultaneously monitoring the process, holding the line against it, participating in it, understanding it.

One realist has decided that the differences even now warrant their radical constitutional recognition, that the ethnic nettle should be grasped, the Gordian knot cut. In *Two Ulsters*, Liam Kennedy, a Tipperary economic historian working out of Belfast, makes the case for repartition, with a smaller Northern Ireland fully integrated into the United Kingdom, and the remainder ceded to the Republic. He does so after examining all alternative constitutional proposals and rejecting them as unworkable, not just now but for the foreseeable future.

DIFFERENCE

Although recent work by F. W. Boal supports Kennedy's evidence of demographic polarization, we apparently are not at the repartitionist stage in our thinking, which is why Kennedy's book has had a muted reception. Nevertheless, it seems clear to me that Irish studies, especially Ulster studies, must devote themselves to the examination of the difference that both divides and binds the dual communities of Ulster and divides Ulster from, and binds it to, the outside world. In stressing difference, we must risk sounding superficially like the discredited voices of old, looking as if we had come full circle. What we urgently need, for example, is a psychology of sectarianism, not a behaviourist psychology but a social-identity psychology infused with psychoanalysis and existentialism. We have to know what being Protestant or Catholic does to us and for us, and how far it produces identity and meaning into our lives. Whence cometh our fear and loathing of each other, even when they are repressed or sublimated into decency and silence?

The differences between Protestant and Catholic, unionist and nationalist in Ulster may be no shallower than those between North and South on the island. Irrespective of perception, there are objective cultural differences between North and South. These North-South differences too need airing and exploration; and they are in part differences in ideas of Irishness. But in the acknowledgment of difference may be the beginning of reconciliation. Unionists are largely ignorant of Irish history, and of the varieties of Irish nationalism. Their ignorance nourishes their paranoia. But as the graffito has it, even paranoiacs have enemies, and nationalism, however you look at it, is opposed to unionism and Protestant self-determination. And I believe that Protestants seek self-determination, wanting union with Britain (which is primarily separation from the South, in actuality) because the alternative has been defined in a way that excludes them yet desires them, and therefore threatens them.

THE NECESSARY REDEFINITION OF IRISHNESS

It is clear to me that if there is to be peace on this island, one prerequisite is the redefinition of Irishness. The onus lies on those who cherish the concept. The Republic must detheocratize itself, separate Church and State, not only in letter but in spirit, and by so doing demonstrate that a genuinely pluralist Ireland, within whatever constitutional framework, is a possibility. If you equate Irishness with Catholicism, a unified Ireland is a dangerous figment. We remember what Yeats told the Senate prophetically in 1925 when it was ratifying the outlawing of divorce: if you pass Catholic laws you will never get the North. (Yeats's phrase 'get the North' is both telling and objectionable.)

The Republic must surrender the fiction of a Gaelic-speaking nation, even the fiction of a nation all of whose citizens acknowledge it as their mother tongue, whether they are fluent in it or not. Hyde's de-anglicization failed even in the homogeneous South; it is time now for the 'de-Hydration' of Ireland. And the historians of the South must continue to revise the history of Ireland, and demystify that history, in ways that Fr Francis Shaw, Conor Cruise O'Brien, and latterly John A. Murphy, W. E. Vaughan and others, have pioneered. It would require the immense sacrifice of admitting, for example, that despite his courage and his great impact on Irish events, Pearse was in error, both in Catholicizing the struggle for independence (a struggle which many Ulster Protestants I believe would be in sympathy with) and in failing to confront the massive obstacle of Northern Protestantism. Pearse was, as we know, half-English. If anyone believes that Pearse was still more Irish than I am, then that person will never induce me to claim my Irishness.

This is much to ask of a populace largely happy in its hard-won homogeneity. It is also much to ask of a people who fought long and honourably to free themselves of English domination. But the alternative is to continue dreaming of unification, dreams that intersect fatally with reality. And I believe such a revised self-estimate could be matched by an increasingly island-centred self-definition of Ulster Protestantism, less unionist and British, more 'nationalist' if you like. After all, self-loyalty has always been the core of Ulster loyalism; eventually loyalists will have to admit the contractual, convenient, conditional nature of their fealty to the Crown.

When the reduced definition of Ulsterness crosses the expanded definition of Irishness, there may be created hopeful eddies. In the meantime we have the Anglo-Irish Agreement, which is an imposition and ought to go. But if it does not, it may prove a two-edged sword, driving a wedge between Britain and Ulster, to be sure, but eventually involving Britain in the affairs of the South as well as the Republic in the affairs of the North. If so, this will simply be a tacit recognition of the unity, on certain levels, of the British archipelago. In Saskatoon recently, at the Canadian Association for Irish Studies annual conference, there occurred what for me was a significant event. Paul Durcan, the Dublin poet who, unlike most Irish poets, inhabits the real world of Slane rock concerts and religious hype, denied the cultural partition of Ireland by decrying the categories of 'Northern poet' and 'Southern poet'. *But* he also claimed – the first time I have heard a Catholic or Southern writer do so in public – that he is British. I also recall his memorable formulation: 'Maggie Thatcher will not stand between me and John Dryden.' He had expanded the definition of Irishness, not in an act of renegation, but in an act of enlargement and freedom. And at that moment he became for me a fellow Irishman.

[1988]

REFERENCES

Boal, F. W., 'Ethnic Residential Segregation, Ethnic Mixing and Resource Conflict: A Study in Belfast, Northern Ireland', *Ethnic Segregation in Cities*, eds C. Peach, V. Robinson and S. Smith (London: Croom Helm 1981).

Brown, Terence, 'After the Revival: The Problem of Adequacy and Genre', *Genre* XII, 4 (1979), 565–89.

Corkery, Daniel, *The Hidden Ireland: A Study of Gaelic Munster in the Eighteenth Century* (Dublin: Gill and Macmillan 1977).

Corkery, Daniel, *Synge and Anglo-Irish Literature* (New York: Russell 1965).

Donoghue, Denis, *We Irish: The Selected Essays of Denis Donoghue,* Vol. 1 (Brighton: Harvester Press 1986).

Kennedy, Liam, *Two Ulsters: A Case for Repartition* (Belfast: College Park Publications 1986).

New Ireland Forum Report (Dublin: Stationery Office, n.d.).

O'Halloran, Clare, *Partition and the Limits of Irish Nationalism* (Dublin: Gill and Macmillan 1987).

15

CULTURE AND COLONIZATION:
VIEW FROM THE NORTH

I

The politics of colonization are less complicated than its cultural expressions and the psychology of those involved. The latter persist after the political apparatus of colonization has been dismantled. The prerequisite of ethnic usurpation, the motive of economic profit, the requirement of social privilege, and the necessity of political control: these do not exhaust their own subtle forms nor the post-colonial guises they can assume. And the South of Ireland, in its Ascendancy, United Kingdom, Free State and Republican forms, is less complicated to explain in terms of colonization than the North, before and after it became Northern Ireland.

Northern Ireland was the outcome in 1921 of a complex train of events, which it is easy to distort by roughcast or misnomer. Early-seventeenth-century colonizers came from Britain, the mother country: coloniarchs like the Chichesters, Hamiltons, and Montgomerys, and those who became what we might call colonialists, or what by analogy to other places we might call colons: colonial planters or farmers. Britain remained a mother country, and if we insist on profit as an essential part of the colonial process we would think chiefly of the industrialization of Ulster. There was profit for Britain in the developing Northern working class and in the factories and shipyards of the Lagan valley, a profit which has only recently drained away.

In their analysis of Northern Ireland, with the solution to the Northern Ireland problem it implies (eventual withdrawal by Britain and reunification of the island), this is where Britain (unofficially) stops, as Hugh Roberts tells us, and where Irish republicans stop, as Tom Nairn tells us. In fact, however, the Protestant community was reinforced by those who had never been part of the Plantation, who had established themselves unaided. The settlers, Roberts reminds us, 'were independent, voluntary migrants from the Scottish Low-lands . . . quite unlike the transported settlers in Australia and Algeria, and very like the first English settlers in America'.

He says this to demolish the analogy (with the solution to Northern Ireland *it* implies) some people have formed between Algeria and Ulster. The Protestant community became 'a self-conscious, advanced "frontier" society', in Nairn's terms, which he likens to the old German settlements in Central and Eastern Europe. As Nairn sees it, growing *away* from Britain in its own advance, this community *chose* the British connection when faced with the rise of peasant nation-alism in nineteenth-century Ireland. The working class that developed was closer to that of Clydeside than of Dublin and, in Peter Gibbon's words (quoted by Nairn), 'formed part of the great industrial triangle of the valleys of the Mersey, the Clyde and the Lagan'. It was British and yet not British, a small-scale, fairly cohesive bourgeois society.

These profound complications registered and the simple anti-colonialist and anti-imperialist analysis of Sinn Féin correctly confuted, we are left nevertheless with the colonial strand in Ulster's history, and with the position of the Northern Catholics in this small-scale bourgeois society and the role as natives they performed for the Protestant majority. In his wish to further the cause of Ulster Protestant nationalism (as one of the minority nationalisms he encourages in the UK that a new British socialism may emerge), Nairn rather ignores these residues. Ulster Protestants, however, cannot afford to conceal the features of the society in which they were reared that derive from a partly-colonizing past. Their acknowledgment is one of several necessary to our development as individuals. What is at stake is per-sonal, not merely cultural, self-respect and self-realization. It is also one of several acknowledgments necessary to the development of the very sense of nationality Nairn as an outsider promotes. Indeed, in Ulster, as in pre-independent Ireland (and I'm afraid, as in independent Ireland), personal and cultural incompleteness are often inseparable.

In 1921 Protestant Ulster as Northern Ireland confirmed its fairly autonomous, un-British nature. But it also confirmed its nature as a frontier of Britain, ultimately controlled by Britain (as later events made manifest) and of industrial and strategic benefit to Britain. We Northern Protestants recall the mediocrity that prevailed because the best went across the water as though back to the mother country. They left behind, to use the words of Albert Memmi, the Tunisian writer contemplating North Africa in his book *The Colonizer and the*

Colonized, 'only men of small stature beyond the pomp or simple pride of the petty colonizer'. Among the writers, for example, who left before or after 1921 and never came back, one thinks of C.S. Lewis, Robert Lynd, Helen Waddell, Joyce Cary and Louis Mac-Neice. We grew up in Lilliput, but we were aware from the start of the country of the giant Gulliver, as the Lilliputians were not.

We wished to profit from the choice our forebears made in throwing their lot in with Britain (and, in doing so, recolonized ourselves to some extent). We presented ourselves as grateful and faithful Britons, purer in fervour, truer in patriotism, more perceptive about the condition and destiny of the mother country (what Memmi calls 'the national community') than our fellow Britons on the mainland. Yet more arrogantly, we were custodians of the imagery and memory of the mother country's greatness, certainly its Protestant conscience; we were watchmen in Sion. We loved, like Memmi's North African colonialists, the most striking demonstrations of the power of the mother country, and admired its army. We basked in England's imperial glory that we presumed ours.

But we were British in a special sense. (I never heard the word mainland used of Britain when I was growing up, by the way: I think it became common usage with English commentators on the current Troubles. 'Across the water', our phrase, signified at once a lesser sense of dependence on, and a greater psychic distance from, Britain.) Because of this, we could not accommodate or accompany changes in the Britain to which we had secured our identity. It was necessary that we in Ulster freeze ourselves in time. We required of Britain, like Memmi's colonialists of France, that she constitute a different, 'never intimately known ideal, but also an ideal immutable and sheltered from time'. The colonialist, says Memmi, 'requires his homeland to be conservative'. 'Each colonialist', he adds, 'is naturally further to the right than his counterpart in the homeland.'

This of course is because of the presence of natives in whose midst he lives. His conservatism derives from the colonial situation and he is what he is in part despite himself. The continued integrity of the society requires its calcification, and the integrity of Ulster has up to now entailed Protestant dominance. Any change in that integrity would threaten that dominance, therefore we have favoured the least progressive features. Even when, like Memmi's colonialists, we have been warm friends and affectionate fathers who could have been democrats, or radicals (in our case, in Britain), we have been turned into conservatives by the perceived need to protect our identity, even existence. We approved discrimination and the codification of injustice; we have even contemplated atrocity.

I believe many Protestants resent this perversion of normal political desire, sensing perhaps the personal loss it issues in, the lack of wholeness. At the same time, they feel the political situation necessitates it. But they are caricatured by that situation; they live on the boundary of self-acceptability, which is a terrible strain.

Because of the necessity of stasis, our British nationalism is of a special nature. Our loyalty is qualified. The colonialist, says Memmi,

is seized with worry and panic each time there is talk of changing the political status. It is only then that the purity of his patriotism is muddled, his indefectible attachment to his motherland shaken. He may go as far as to threaten – Can such things be! – Secession! Which seems contradictory, in conflict with his so well-advertised and, in a certain sense, real patriotism.

This is rooted, of course, in our ambiguous nationality.

Our relations with Catholics are less complicated on the political level than with Britain, but no less complicated on a deeper level. On some shelf of our psyche sits uneasily our acceptance of our usurpation, which we justify in terms of our own merits and the demerits of the usurped. But such justification (which was translated into political and legal terms in Northern Ireland) confirmed our repressed guilt and condemned us while preserving us. We wished, like Memmi's colonialists, the disappearance of the usurped. Indeed, we attempted politically to erase them, imagining, then acting out, a Northern Ireland free from the dormant, sporadically stirring threat of sedition (hardly treason, since despite what we said, we did not really desire the loyalty of Catholics). Socially we erased them too, in a manner Memmi would understand.

The mythical portrait of the colonized [remarks Memmi] includes an unbelievable laziness, and that of the colonizer, a virtuous taste for action. At the same time the colonizer suggests that employing the colonized is not very profitable, thereby authorizing his unreasonable wages.

This is a portrait, varnished by Lord Brookeborough, of the Catholic, North and South, vestigially alive today.

Such stereotyping required that we singularize the natives, depersonalize them, to justify the social inequities we maintained. We italicized the differences between their culture and ours. These differences we removed from time and therefore possible evolution. The Catholic was essentialized, made inescapably Other.

What is actually a sociological point [claims Memmi] becomes labelled as being biological or, preferably, metaphysical. It is attached to the colonized's basic nature . . . the colonial relationship between colonized and colonizer, founded on the essential outlook of the two protagonists, becomes a definitive category. It is what it is because they are what they are, and neither one nor the other will ever change.

Yet on a deeper shelf of the psyche squatted the realization that without the Catholics we could not be what we were. We defined ourselves over against them which meant that we were in part defined *by* them. 'The colonialist's existence', says Memmi, 'is so closely aligned with that of the colonized that he will never be able to overcome the argument which states that misfortune is good for something.'

Very little of what I have said can be explained away by social class. The integrity of Protestant Ulster has transcended class to the despair of those socialists who have not acknowledged, as Nairn has, the repressed or frustrated nationalism of that community. In a remarkable insight, Nairn claims that it is as aberrant substitutes for nationalism that the two idea-systems to which the Ulster Protestant has in the past given himself, militant Protestantism and imperialism, have to be understood. And while provincialism represents a better explanation of Ulster Protestants than class, it will not suffice. Certainly Belfast is a provincial city wearing the mask of a capital, as James Joyce in 1904 said Dublin did. Yet London if truth be told is not for Ulster Protestants their capital, as it wasn't for Joyce's Dubliners. The Ulster Protestant truly accepts London as his capital only through a process of assimilation to the British 'mainland', and this requires a psychic separation from Ulster. (And a change of accent, offensive to compatriots back home: an anglicizing of our distinctive vowels, for example.) Without this process, his going to the capital to confirm his Britishness, to find the central locus of his values, solves nothing, proving that his problem is not chiefly one of provincialism, but must be one rooted in some species of colonialism or postcolonialism.

II

Yet the deviations from the colonial norm in Northern Ireland are obvious. Those in the 'colony' are not economically better off than those at 'home'. Britain the mother country is not a far country but one visible on clear days to the naked eye. The Ulster Protestant, unlike the colonialist, typically plans his future in Ulster, not in the mother country.

Indeed, any profile of colonial society matches more truly Anglo-Ireland until 1922. In the history of Anglo-Ireland we find embedded Memmi's portrait of the colonizer, despite some significant differences. With the Anglo-Irish, as Hugh Roberts reminds us, we are dealing with a social class that functioned as a ruling caste, quite distinct in this and other ways (including the distribution of religious denomination and of social class itself) from the Ulster Protestant community that was committed less to England than to itself.

One view of the Irish Revival is that it was a movement spearheaded by people, many of whom belonged to the ruling caste, the Anglo-Irish, but also belonged to Memmi's category of 'The colonizer who refuses' his role as colonialist, who knocked at the door of the colonized and found it opened in gratitude, after some initial bolting of the door by Catholic nationalists, such as Pearse. But it is clear that the Revival continued, in even more eloquent fashion than before, to 'essentialize' the native Irish; the mystique of Irishness was indeed exalted by the transcendentalism of the movement, while it was to aery thinness beat, expanded to include the troubled soul of the Southern Protestant. And whereas the stereotype was meant to convey virtue, to be racial but not racialist, there have been, and are, Catholic writers and intellectuals, from Daniel Corkery through Patrick Kavanagh to Seamus Deane, who simply could not accept it.

Moreover, the Southern Protestant in the fullness of time discovered, like Memmi's colonizer who refuses, that the colonized necessarily adopted 'a national and ethnic form of liberation from which [the colonialist] cannot but be excluded'. The *de facto* exclusion of the Protestants was inevitable since the achievement of Irish independence required the vigorous promotion of differences between the colonized and the colonizers, who were not only the English but also the Anglo-Irish. There was after 1922, but especially around and after 1937, an overt, indeed constitutional, return to religion, to Catholicism, and *de jure* exclusion of the Protestant. But Catholicism had never been away.

Formalism [says Memmi] of which religious formality is only one aspect, is the cyst into which colonial society shuts itself and hardens, degrading its own life in order to save it. It is a spontaneous action of self-defence, a means of safeguarding the collective consciousness without which a people quickly cease to exist.

Even before 1922 the original language more obviously than religion was meant to express the decolonized, making of the Gaelic Revival a different creature from the Anglo-Irish Literary Revival and a movement which tended to exclude Protestants. The Gaelic language and the Catholic religion were only two of the elements of Irish society after independence that made life difficult in Ireland for Protestants. The earlier flight from Ireland of Wilde, Shaw and Moore (an honorary Protestant), who fled the provinces to the metropolis, was succeeded by the flight to England of Moore (again) in 1911, John Eglinton (1922), James Stephens (1925), Sean O'Casey (1926) and AE (1933): a principled exodus (this time from one country to another) rarely remarked upon, even by Catholic literary historians, presumably because it throws some doubt on the indigenity of the Literary Revival.

If Pearse and others angrily rejected some elements of the English stereotype of the Irish National Character, while aggressively accepting other elements (in order to exploit the potential of difference), and if the reaction was itself conditioned by colonialism, there were other native Irish whose colonized condition was more abjectly demonstrated. These are among Joyce's subjects in *Dubliners*. As far as I know, that volume of stories has never been fully discussed for the classic profile of the culture and psychology of the colonized, of the pathology of colonialism, it actually is. Two kinds of colonialism dictate the stories – Roman and British, and every story is a study in dominance and servility, or in the latter but implicating the former. Some characters accept, by acting out, the English stereotyping of Irishness; some use the colonizers as models (what in Ireland was called shoneenism); all have their individuality limited, defined, crushed. They are even the gratefully oppressed. One or two, such as Molly Ivors, are *un*gratefully oppressed, yet do not engage our full sympathy.

And this suggests the problem Joyce's portrait of the colonized represents. Whereas his Dubliners seem incorrigible, irredeemably sunk in servility, it is difficult to demonstrate Joyce's preference for contemporary nationalism. How far he tries to liberate his countrymen from servility, and how far he reinforces the imagery and thereby the reality of Irish servility, is difficult to decide. Certainly he claimed that *Dubliners* was his own first step towards the spiritual emancipation of his country, but the value of that is hard to establish.

Perhaps this is a measure of the complexity of the colonial situation. Joyce's Dublin exhibits the paralysis, the encystment, Memmi has explained comes with the territory of the colony, a paralysis belied by the empty circularities and the meaningless commotion that overlie it. Like *Juno and the Paycock*, *Dubliners* mercilessly portrays a society without cultural (and therefore moral) integrity, and in which one talks, sings, and tells, even lives, someone else's stories and does so, moreover, in someone else's language or dialect. Joxer Daly, that human magpie, is the most striking embodiment of a culture's disintegrity; his entire humanity, it seems, subsists in the secondhand: tags, aphorisms, scraps of poems, snatches of songs. Even the pieces are in pieces; when called upon to sing a song, he can't complete it.

Joyce turned this cultural misfortune into artistic triumph by immersing himself in the condition, which *we* call the victory of stylistic multiplicity, his welter of voices. Perhaps the absence of a normative consciousness in his fiction (his language typically approximating the language of his diverse characters or of another writer or style) has this cultural explanation.

Yet despite the 'sabbath of misrule' (Joyce) and 'chassis' (O'Casey, of course) that are the reality of this colonized society, there is order of a kind. There is a spun web of native counterparts of the relationship between colonial master and servant, endlessly replicating dependence and oppression. *Dubliners* is a study in that imprisoning network. Farrington in 'Counterparts', for example, bullies his son because he himself is bullied, is a link in a chain of dominance stretching from the child to Westminster and Rome. He bullies the child because he wants to punish himself out of self-contempt, for not being his own master or even his own man. The son pathetically uses the language of one subordination ('I'll say a Hail Mary for you, pa') to escape the blows administered by proxy, by the father, to enforce the other.

III

Many Catholic Irish accepted the role of the colonized in Anglo-Ireland. But of course there were always those who refused the role, proudly conscious of the former attainments of Irish civilization and aware too of the alternative link with Rome. It was because of the

success of the ungratefully oppressed in the South that the acceptance by Catholics of a subordinate position in Northern Ireland was
unreliable. While Northern Ireland between the 1920s and the late
1960s was largely quiescent, even paralysed, there was indication in
sporadic republican eruptions that the paralysis was neither terminal
nor complete.

Indeed its precariousness was guaranteed by the fact that the
Northern majority felt itself in that condition in which the colonized
turn the tables: the condition of siege. The Ulster Protestant, unlike
Memmi's colonizer, never regarded the natives, the Catholic Irish, as
weaklings requiring protection. If Northern Ireland was a protec-
torate, it was the Ulster Protestant who felt in need of protection by
the RUC, by the Special Constabulary, by the British army:
protection from the fifth column within and their masters without.

He was in part justified. Irredentism was a constitutional fact and
often more than that. The Ulster Protestant, feeling the perpetual
threat of being taken over, already experiences in some sense, and
exhibits the symptoms of, *the condition of being colonized*. His legendary
intransigence is the anticipation of a calamity. It is true that this colonization is a mere project called reunification of the motherland, and
that the Ulster Protestants have been called Irish by the projectors.
Outside this context they are regarded as interlopers, alien, the spawn
of colonizers. They too have been stereotyped and essentialized,
invested with the aura of a negative mystique. As such, they are meet
subjects for colonization or annexation.

Because it has assumed social and cultural forms in the North, the
threat to Ulster Protestants today is at once more diffuse and more
real. Simultaneously, the relationship of colonizer and colonized that
was deeply, almost invisibly embedded in the relationship of Britain
and Protestant Ulster (by paradoxical virtue of the latter's very independence of development and spirit) has been brought to the surface
and given overt political form. Britain always had ultimate control
over Northern Ireland; but Direct Rule and, lately, the Anglo-Irish
Agreement have fully acknowledged the fact. The latter has reminded
Northerners that they are excluded from the effective governance of
the kingdom of which they are a part. They are debarred from voting
for a party with any realistic chance of forming a government. This
was always the case, but before Direct Rule Stormont was a sufficient
compensation. Now abroad in the province there is a feeling of
impotence and disenfranchisement. There is evidence that young

educated Protestants now typically plan their future on 'the mainland', as though to flee to the mother country and away from the troubled colony.

The Anglo-Irish *rapprochement* has dangerously conjoined in the consciousness of the Ulster majority the fear of Irish irredentism and the resentment towards England they always felt in their hearts as members of a truculent frontier society. By an irony of history, the experience of being infantilized, suffered by James Joyce's Irish, has been visited upon the Ulster Protestants. The fate of the infantilized is to be ignored or condescended to, at best contemptuously regarded. But the Ulster Protestant has for some time lived with a sense of his own unattractiveness in the eyes of the world (in contrast to the desirable mystique attached to the 'real' Irish), a fate that has already enveloped the white South Africans and might shortly envelop the Israelis. It can happen that the individual finds himself representative of a community, and a community that plays a role in someone else's moral drama. The role is assigned and one must play it irrespective of how far it suits; one may be in part, perhaps largely, miscast, but to protest is paradoxically to confirm one's villainy; it is self-justification, but justification of the erroneous self.

The Southern Irish themselves, of course, have been hostile, as I have said. Yeats had no time for Ulster Protestants, finding them so disagreeable that he hoped unification would never come about. (They did not in any case fit his programme for the ideal society.) And if Joyce thought that James Stephens was not truly Irish because he wasn't Catholic, how much more alien was the Northern Protestant. In 'Counterparts' it is a Northerner who oppresses Farrington as the story opens, and an Ulster student whose accent and mind so offend Stephen Dedalus in science class.

But it is the relationship with Britain (principally England) that has for obscure reasons damaged the Ulster Protestant as well as aided him. This is not the place to confess in detail to the injurious feeling of inferiority beside England with which this Ulster Protestant grew up, a feeling I believe widespread but masked by patriotism, and one not explained by mere provincial pique. Ignoring the clear historical differences, what Daniel Corkery said of the effects of an Irish education earlier this century I will let stand for an Ulster Protestant upbringing thirty or forty years later:

No sooner does [the Irish child] begin to use his intellect than what he learns begins to undermine, to weaken, and to harass his emotional nature. For practically all that he reads is English – what he reads in Irish is not yet worth taking account of. It does not therefore focus the mind of his own people, teaching him the better to look about him, to understand both himself and his surroundings. It focuses instead the life of another people. Instead of sharpening his gaze upon his own neighbourhood, his reading distracts it, for he cannot find in these surroundings what his reading has taught him is the matter worth coming upon. His surroundings begin to seem unvital. His education, instead of buttressing and refining his emotional nature, teaches him the rather to despise it, inasmuch as it teaches him not to see the surroundings out of which he is sprung, as they are in themselves, but as compared with alien surroundings; his education provides him with an alien medium through which he is henceforth to look at his native land! At the least his education sets up a dispute between his intellect and his emotions. Nothing happens in the neighbourhood of an English boy's home that he will not sooner or later find happening, transfigured, in literature. What happens in the neighbourhood of an Irish boy's home – the fair, the hurling match, the land grabbing, the *priesting*, the mission, the Mass – he never comes on in literature, that is, in such literature as he is told to respect and learn . . . In his riper years he may come to see the crassness of his own upbringing, but of course the damage is done: his mind is cast in an unnatural because unnative mould.

The only history of my own community I learned at school was the successful penetration of north Ireland by British commercial interests and settlers known as the Ulster Plantation, which was taught as belonging exclusively to the history of the English state and its expansion, eventually, into the British Empire. Did the syllabus, I now wonder, come from Westminster, or from Stormont, aping Westminster down to the choice of set texts and topics? All I know is that I was in my twenties before I read a serious work by an Ulster writer or set in Ulster. It happened to be Brian Moore's *The Lonely Passion of Miss Judith Hearne* (the English title), which will remain special for that reason. It was slowly I untaught myself that contempt for the imagination of one's own community which is a form of self-contempt.

IV

Our debt in Northern Ireland to the writers of the past twenty years is immense. They have enhanced our self-regard, if only because we can congratulate ourselves that we have produced such writers. Yet Protestant readers will look mostly in vain if they seek in the literature some reassurance that their community has any dignity of imagination.

Protestant writers of high calibre have rarely explored without inhibition the community that bred them.

Why is it that Northerners, and Protestant Northerners in particular, have blushed to assert their imaginative potential? Why has there been no intellectual class in Ulster since the nineteenth century? The answer is not to be found chiefly in the history and make-up of Protestantism, even low-church Protestantism. It lies closer to home.

When the Ulster writer this century went south, in body or in spirit, he was often taking delivery of a myth of Irishness that bloomed during the Irish Revival. Tom Nairn quotes a reviewer of Robert Kee's *The Green Flag*, who refers to

the superior attraction for the cultivated mind of the winding caravan of Irish nationalism with its poets, assassins, scholars, crackpots, parlour revolutionaries, windbags, mythopoeic essayists, traitors, orators from the scaffold, men of action emerging from so long and so great suffering of the people to impart an almost mystic quality to their often futile and often brutal deeds – the superior attraction of that to the hard, assertive, obsessive, successful self-reliance of the Ulster Protestant which has about it as much poetical imagination as is contained in a bowler hat.

The Irish reality is in one case rendered into seductive legend, in the other rendered into unprepossessing caricature. As long ago as 1913 Tom Kettle tried to puncture the myths of the Northerner with a genius for business and the dreamy ineffectual Southerner, by tracing the success of the Northern businessman to economic protectionism. But it was fruitless. The myth (the caricature of an underlying truth) remained; and whereas Kettle believed he was attacking in order to appropriate a positive fiction of the Northerner, that fiction in art and culture has been negative, signalling absence. If in the past fifteen years a counter-myth of Northern creativity has grown up, that has not prevented the Protestant writer from accepting the essential hostility of Ulster Protestantism, unlike Irish Catholicism, to art and creativity. He has fled himself, in fear of his own philistinism.

There has been, too, a connected reluctance to write about the middle class (even if the writer has come from that class) in favour of the working class. The working class, I suspect, is the artistic descendant of the peasantry of the Irish Revival. Recent drama from and about Ulster, except for that of Robin Glendinning, confirms this bias.

The aversion to the middle class (like the attraction to nationalism) has been the critics', when it has not been the writers'. How else can one explain (unless through intellectual misogyny) the neglect of a first-rate writer like Kate O'Brien, whose novels are ignored in favour of the *failed* novels of Frank O'Connor and Sean O'Faolain? Or the complete obscurity of Kathleen Coyle, the relative neglect of Mary Lavin, writers who along with Molly Keane (M.J. Farrell) are being rediscovered, but because they are women, not because they cut across and disrupt the winding caravan of Irish nationalist culture.

It is not only English script-writers and playwrights, then, who have commodified the city of Belfast, indeed all of Northern Ireland, by reducing it to one relentless image: that of a Catholic, occasionally Protestant, unemployed working class eternally turbulent and besieged. As a result, many in Ulster are estranged from their own image; they have no mirror in which to see themselves. Is this not a condition of the colonized?

Simultaneously they are erased for outsiders and the changeling cries hopelessness in tones of unreason. I wondered when I saw the film of *Judith Hearne* if the change of setting to Dublin from Belfast had not been justified, explicitly or no, on the commercial-artistic principle that Belfast could not be the setting for a Catholic middle-class crisis of faith *with no discernible connection with the Troubles*. In any case, a grave injustice was done to the city and, I believe, to the novel. Picture the outcry if *The Dead* had been transplanted to Belfast.

I will merely mention the attraction which in a vague, sentimental form Irish republicanism has for the Protestant intellectual, the unexamined assumption that whereas republicanism is intellectually respectable and artistically fruitful, unionism is intellectually barren and artistically stultifying. The shabbiness of the Unionist party is confused with the respectable philosophy of unionism, whether it take the form of devolution, power-sharing or integration. And the philosophy of unionism has itself been permitted to indict or invalidate an entire culture and heritage. The Protestant intellectual seems to flee himself, in fear of his own bigotry.

He is embarrassed, of course, by the mistreatment of the Irish by the English, and of the Catholics by himself. That embarrassment, signalling guilt, can cause inhibition and self-repression. Besides, he is separated both from Catholics and from those Protestants who entertain less conscious guilt. This can induce a kind of paralysis. Sartre, telling us that Memmi, as a Paris-educated Tunisian, was in a similarly contradictory position, reminds us that 'such rendings of the spirit, plainly introjections of social conflicts, do not dispose the individual to action'.

The embarrassed intellect of Protestant Ulster can certainly encourage an eloquent and healthy scepticism – we see it at its best in Louis MacNeice and Derek Mahon – but the danger for lesser talents can be at first ennui, and then a falling back on the diminishing resources of the self rather than of the culture. Embarrassment can also disguise itself as disclamation. The contrast with, say, Patrick Kavanagh and Seamus Heaney is instructive. In 'Courtyards in Delft', for example, Mahon finds the puritan philistinism of his lower middle-class Protestant Ulster anticipated in the seventeenth-century painting of Pieter de Hooch. Yet although the poet admits that the world in the painting and in Ulster 'is life too', this poem ends by celebrating (a trifle smugly one might think) his estrangement from that world from the beginning. His boyhood companions are simplified into killers of black Africans and Catholic Irish – good imperialists, loyalists and Fenian-bashers. By contrast, Heaney's difference from *his* tribal culture springs *from* that culture (Heaney as poet as wood-kerne) and ceaselessly laments itself.

> I grew out of all this
> like a weeping willow
> inclined to
> the appetites of gravity.

Although he might at times have been more judgmental, to the profit of his verse, never does Heaney simplify, much less caricature Catholic Ulster, and rightly so.

The gestures in Northern Ireland today towards cultural and political nationalism are animated by rejection of the Anglo-Irish Agreement, but also, I believe, by frustration at the voicelessness of Ulster unionist culture. In any case, they are perhaps less worrying when put into the context of my remarks. They don't signal a resurgence of the old discredited unionism. And they are not necessarily of the right, as some have taken alarm in thinking. They are gestures of a community reawakening after a long hibernation, after permitting itself to be colonized one way or another. Hugh Roberts, writing from the left, believes Ulster's nationality is historically rooted. Tom Nairn, also writing from the left, believes it is politically necessary, if the Northern Ireland problem is ever to be solved, for that nationality to be expressed.

Certainly the old Britishness is mortally wounded, but the new Britishness may eventually incorporate in some fashion the entire archipelago. No minority nationalism can escape the social and economic subsidences and realignments happening in these islands. Nor can it escape the accelerating process of Americanization that only a periodic visitor from North America can accurately gauge. Nairn is right, though I prefer to think in terms of cultural and psychological rather than political necessity. Only in pride can we Ulster Protestants be strong enough to conquer the anxiety that legitimate concern, about the Republic, about Catholicism, about the IRA, turns into. We are coming from behind, and have to attain ourselves before we have the confidence to extend generosity, to leave the refuge and prison that sectarianism is.

And only then will we be whole. The Ulster Protestant is asserting his differences, since those differences (to adapt Memmi) are within him and correctly constitute his true self. There would be no liberation in refusing the category of 'the Other' for oneself – in denying caricatures of oneself by demonstrating complexity – while continuing to attach it to fellow citizens. We would have assumed the posture of colonizers again. We desire wholeness without mystique. The Other, as Simone de Beauvoir said of woman as she functions for men, incarnates the lack in oneself, and it is in seeking to be made whole *through* the Other that we hope to attain self-realization. I am oddly confident that we in Ulster will succeed.

[1988]

REFERENCES

Corkery, Daniel, *Synge and Anglo-Irish Literature* (1931) (New York: Russell and Russell 1965).

Memmi, Albert, *The Colonizer and the Colonized*, trans. Howard Greenfield, Introduction by Jean-Paul Sartre (1957) (New York: The Orion Press 1965).

Nairn, Tom, *The Break-Up of Britain: Crisis and Neo-Nationalism* (1977) (London: Verso 1981).

O'Halloran, Clare, *Partition and the Limits of Irish Nationalism* (Dublin: Gill and Macmillan 1987).

Roberts, Hugh, *Northern Ireland and the Algerian Analogy: A Suitable Case for Gaullism?* (Belfast: Athol Books 1986).

16

RADICAL REGIONALISM

I

In the 1940s, regionalism was very much in the air that British writers were breathing, and was a near-synonym for the Celticism (Welsh, Scottish, Irish) that was a geographic strain of the dominant Romanticism of the period. The journal *Poetry Scotland*, for example, in which the Ulster poet John Hewitt's poems appeared, was seen as a regional counter-force to *Poetry London*. But if he inherited the idea of the region, Hewitt accorded it more urgent significance than did his fellow regionalists in Britain. This was because of the very mootness of his own native region which, in turn, he thought a communal perception of Ulster *as a region* would bring to an end. 'Ulster,' he wrote in 1947, 'considered as a region and not as the symbol of any particular creed, can, I believe, command the loyalty of every one of its inhabitants.' A sense of the region could function as an underpass between religious and political divisions and subvert their effects. That sense would be cultural in the first instance; partly recommending, partly predicting, Hewitt was of the opinion that 'there should emerge [in Ulster] a culture and an attitude individual and distinctive, a fine contribution to the European inheritance and no mere echo of the thought and imagination of another people or another land'. He wished to inhabit an Ulster to which all its people could give emotional and cultural and then, perhaps, political allegiance.

Some precision in the definition of region was required, therefore, and so Hewitt defined region for us in the pages of *Northman:* 'an area which possesses geographical and economic coherence, which has had some sort of traditional and historical identity and which still, in some measure, demonstrates cultural and linguistic individuality'. Precise, but not too precise, and not politically precise at all in the Irish north's case: indeed, if Northern Ireland or 'Ulster' (six counties) or Ulster proper (nine counties) were a region, it could not therefore be a nation but must be part of, a region of, a larger whole, as yet (in 1947, and in 1987 when Hewitt died) unachieved. That whole he would have liked to be a federated British Isles (incorporating all of Ireland – presumably the touchy adjective 'British' was negotiable), but he would have settled happily for a federal Ireland politically distinct from Britain. This put the 'constitutional question' (Protestant version) or 'national question' (Catholic version) on the back burner – wisely in my opinion – pending a peacefully but vigorously arrived at consensus as to the preferred whole.

First the regional identity itself must be won. As though to encourage us, some of it is a given. 'The grouping of counties and provinces', says T. W. Freeman, the geographer, 'implies a broad recognition of fundamental regional differences in the country as a whole.' Ulster is what Freeman calls 'a natural region', 'essentially the four river basins of the Foyle, Bann, Erne and Lagan, together with the Tirconnail country in Donegal'. According to Mary Cawley, another physical feature has given the region a kind of boundary:

The drumlin belt with its intervening marshes posed an effective barrier to movement until woodland clearance took place in the early seventeenth century. Even today, the drumlin country of Counties Cavan, Monaghan and south Armagh functions mainly as a frontier zone, with a mixed population of Catholics and Protestants, Nationalists and Unionists.

The natural regional framework of the island has to some extent supported the combination of counties and dioceses into, respectively, civil and archiepiscopal provinces.

Ulster, however, is not just a region of Ireland but a special region. 'Man's impact on the landscape,' Cawley writes, 'within the constraints imposed by the physical environment, has served to produce a series of marked regional contrasts within the island. Most notable are a broad east-west divide and the special identity of north-east Ulster which is the product of a series of exceptional cultural, economic, and political circumstances.' She continues:

The Ulster Plantation and the cultural diversification which it established more strongly than previous colonisation efforts elsewhere in the island, is undoubtedly of major importance in explaining the distinctive cultural and political character of the Northern Ireland state today,

but adds that some commentators argue 'that the distinctiveness of Ulster is of a much more ancient origin'. To the cultural and political distinctiveness we can add the economic. 'By 1850', says Thomas Bartlett, 'Ulster, or at least the north-eastern region, with its factories, mills and urban development, was more akin to Clydeside in Scotland than to the rest of Ireland. It is tempting to conclude that the roots of "Ulster's" separateness are to be found in its divergent economic development from the rest of Ireland.' The speciality of Ulster has been recognized by inhabitants of the rest of Ireland partly by their withholding of full-status Irishness from those of settler stock in the north-east. After partition this century, the two constitutional units of Ireland developed separately, in ways that O'Halloran and Kennedy have recently traced.

Northern Ireland is more debatable as a region than Ulster, in geographers' terms. If natural regions are, as Freeman tells us, 'clearly marked entities, each possessing distinctive quantities that mark them off from their neighbours', and if 'these qualities are derived from the morphology, climate, past and present space relations, natural vegetation, land use, industry and population distribution', then Northern Ireland is not a natural region. However, because Freeman is a human as well as physical geographer, he concedes: 'While the Border is in no sense a morphological divide over most of its course, the regional geographer cannot neglect this separation within Ireland as he makes his division of the country into a number of units.' What has happened is that 'a series of county boundaries have been elevated to frontier status'. The border, marching along old dividing-lines, 'has itself acquired sufficient importance in the life of the region to be, in human terms, a major geographical and economic divide, which one is obliged to accept as a limit of some human significance'.

Hewitt was similarly both circumspect and realistic. In 1947 he acknowledged, indeed seemed to approve of, the 25-year-old political semi-autonomy in Northern Ireland (he liked autonomy wherever it could be managed), and the economic accomplishments of the region. But these had been achieved before cultural integrity and emotional consensus and therefore Lewis Mumford's chronology of regional vitality had been disrupted: 'the process', Mumford had written, begins 'with a dynamic emotional urge, springing out of a sense of frustration on one hand and a renewed vision of life on the other'. Hewitt, who quoted these words, believed that art and high culture could consciously supply the emotional legitimacy of a region, but only if a popular consciousness were awakened along the way. To enable this, art and high culture were to grow from rootedness, out of traditional identity. Alert to the difficulties, Hewitt did not prescribe the precise extent of the region in question, nor the political form its expression would take. He was content to aspire and to wait. He knew too that if we had the historic nine-county Ulster in mind, current Protestant withholding of allegiance to that entity matched current Catholic withholding of allegiance to the entity of Northern Ireland. The problem was not to be solved by immediately adding back three counties to Northern Ireland.

Yet in 1947 Hewitt was hopeful about the creation of cultural regional legitimacy, and not only in Northern Ireland. In 1989 it's with a curious sense of *déjà vu* that we read his optimism over the then recent Scottish National Assembly and over the activities of Northern Irish writers and artists. Hewitt lived long enough to see his hopes dashed (not only in Northern Ireland but in the UK, where neo-romantic regionalism gave way to the witty and Little England stringencies of Larkin, Amis and the Movement), but he also lived long enough to see the hour of his outmoded ideas come around at last. I'm thinking especially of the ideas contained in his essay 'No Rootless Colonist', published in *Aquarius* in 1972 and reprinted by Tom Clyde in *Ancestral Voices*. Today, in the wake of the Anglo-Irish Agreement, it may be that the sense of frustration that Mumford mentioned (particularly the frustration of the majority in Northern Ireland) will yet force into being a renewed and wholesome vision of life in this corner of the world.

Outside Ulster, too, time might be ripening. For Hewitt, in 1947, the nation had become too complicated and estranging a mechanism; it was the region that could conceivably command a preferable and – since he was writing only two years after the war – infinitely less threatening loyalty. Neal Ascherson recently suggested that the sovereign nation is too *small* and that smaller nations realize the importance of belonging to some larger organization – but with a considerable measure of autonomy. Ascherson's small nations sound very much like Hewitt's regions, and like Hewitt, he uses Scotland as an example of the kind of entity he means. Both have in mind what Benedict Anderson – cited by Ascherson – called 'imagined communities'. Hewitt would have approved of this phrase. Ulster (Protestant and Catholic Ulster) was a community *in fact* but it remained, and remains, to be imagined by the majority of its inhabitants. Hewitt imagined it, and this made him something of a pioneer.

But there are enormous baffles to *our* imagination, I'm afraid.

Hewitt believed in 1947 that over-centralization in government, increasing standardization in commodities, and proliferating propaganda (political, commercial, ideological) were causing, in reaction, the resuscitation of regional identity and allegiance. But clearly these also oppose such resuscitation when it stirs and they have strengthened since 1947. I would like now to glance at them, to try to show just what regional culture is up against, before I attempt to rekindle Hewitt's hopes for the cultural, and in the end administrative, possibilities of regionalism in north-east Ireland. I'm assuming in what I have to say that politics and culture cannot be autonomous features of society, and that by culture we mean not only novels and poetry and paintings and works for chamber orchestras, but also the food we eat and where we eat it, the clothes we wear, the places we spend our leisure time, the popular art with which we are surrounded, the buildings we inhabit and frequent, and so on; increasingly, the distinction between mass and élite culture is blurring.

II

If Ulster is a special region of Ireland, since 1921 that part of it called Northern Ireland has been a special region of the United Kingdom. One distinctive feature has been its mode of governance, another is the fact that it commands less than full consent of its citizenry. Until the imposition of Direct Rule in 1972, this region enjoyed (or abused, some would say) considerable autonomy, after which Northern Ireland became a special region of the UK by enjoying *less* autonomy than other regions of the kingdom. Its regional identity is not, in this context, positive but negative. Power has been largely reclaimed by Westminster, by the centre, making Northern Ireland a greater victim (or beneficiary, some might say) of centralization than was the case in 1947. Increasingly, the people of Northern Ireland are the creatures of central bureaucracy; their parliamentary representation is fairly impotent and irrelevant, and they are governed in what one is sorely tempted to call a neo-colonial manner. (I'm not suggesting, of course, that this bed in which they lie is not of their own making, but the fact remains.) The bind in which the majority finds itself is that were it to object too strenuously, it would risk expulsion from the kingdom that foots its bills but does not particularly want it; loyalists are rather in the precarious position of a dissatisfied house guest. The minority, too, is in a bind, since the current price for the Irish dimension of its political life is rule by officialdom and the absence of autonomy.

The Northern Irish, then, suffer a kind of unclassified status; they are special category citizens, one notch above British Overseas Citizens. I'm led to understand, for example, that neither Northern Ireland residents nor mainlanders can collect state benefits in the others' region; paper currency issued in Northern Ireland can't be cashed in Britain. Such small indignities mount up. I am reminded of my special Britishness each time I go through Gate 49 at Heathrow *en route* to Belfast, which seems to me a threshold of that otherness (not just of security intensification) we associate with the ghettoized or colonized. That I enjoy full citizenship of Canada does not lessen the indignity, since I am still a British subject.

In 1985 regional autonomy was further depleted by the Anglo-Irish Agreement. To Ulster as an administrative region of the UK was added Ulster as a quasi-administrative region of the Republic of Ireland. Nevertheless, the current bottom line, because of the abstention of the majority and the external bureaucracy the Agreement brought in its train, seems to be one of deficit in terms of regional wholeness and political self-expression. I say 'bottom' line, because the Agreement may well have lengthened the credits column of the minority's political representation, though not in the normal parliamentary fashion.

It would be perverse to regret the aeration of the unionist crypt that Direct Rule and the Anglo-Irish Agreement represented. But one should perhaps distinguish them from the special fumes of bureaucracy that were then pumped in to replace the stale air released. The historical imperatives of a region's culture need not always be obeyed, especially when they manifestly perpetuate injustice or cruelty, but one worries legitimately about wholesale restructuring from the remote centre, particularly in the absence of full democratic representation, about the mentality behind imposed sectarian quotas, about social engineering, about rule by officials, social theorists, commissions, experts, about bureaucratic answers to cultural questions. The position is worsened when Ulster people, feeling themselves *not* to be English, nevertheless have – in the absence of regional autonomy – implemented in their community standards, policies, values (in education, say, or public morality) developed by the central administrators with entirely different communities in mind. Britishness, thus imposed, becomes an ironic backfire among loyalists, at which we can all manage a thin smile.

There have been noised abroad – and in one case tried, unsuccessfully, in 1974 – practical solutions to the problem of Northern Ireland's lack of regional political expression. The two solutions that are no longer noised abroad are Stormont as it was between 1921 and 1972, and an independent Northern Ireland (despite pockets of support for this idea). Let me list the chief contenders. One: electoral and party political integration into the UK, favoured by the Campaign for Equal Citizenship and designed to make Northern Ireland an equal region of the kingdom. Two: a power-sharing devolved administration (semi-autonomous within the UK), either with some Irish dimension (e.g. a Council of Ireland) or without an Irish dimension. Three: a regional parliament for Northern Ireland within a federal Ireland (Hewitt's second choice, though he may have had nine-county Ulster in mind, a solution even less likely since it is, or was, favoured by Sinn Féin). Four: a federal kingdom of England, Scotland, Wales and Northern Ireland. This is no longer as far-fetched as it once seemed, as the recent Channel 4 series 'Divided Kingdom' revealed. It appears, on that and other evidence, that the alienation from central government, and the wealth and power of the favoured and competitive, felt by many in Ulster, is felt by certain and diverse groups in the UK generally – blacks, the unemployed, Northerners, Scots – who are entering reservations about allegiance to England's Britain.

Ulster is decreasingly freakish and alone in its representational plight. (Current motions in the political culture of Scotland are of particular moment to Ulster people, because of the proximity of the two regions and their historical connections. Scottish autonomy appeals in Ulster to both nationalists and loyalists, and Scottish culture to both Gaelic-speakers and English-speakers of settler ancestry. The Scottish connection is part of the cultural distinctiveness of Ulster: 'contacts between the north-east of the province and south-west Scotland', Cawley writes, 'have always been strong, stronger indeed than contacts with other parts of Ireland'.) The possible break-up of Britain, to borrow the title of Tom Nairn's influential book, has been blamed on Prime Minister Thatcher's philosophy of untrammelled market forces which punishes the actual and figurative regions of the kingdom. If such a solution – a federal kingdom – came to pass the circumstances necessitating it might cause the Republic of Ireland to be involved, especially if the Anglo-Irish Agreement were to be made fully reciprocal in the meantime. So we might contemplate solution number five, Hewitt's first choice in 1947, a federation of the entire archipelago. But even a nominal monarchy would pose a problem.

Only time will tell which, if any, of these solutions will be adopted, and time will tell only when culture forces it to. Hewitt quoted W. B. Stanford: 'in Ireland a political creed needs cultural and historical roots if it is to win and hold the imagination of the people'. The historical roots of Ulster identity exist but need to be fully traced and fertilized. And if politics and culture interpenetrate, politics need not mean unthinking use of stale rhetoric, outworn slogans, sectarian catchphrases. It need not even mean simple constitutional recipes or non-negotiable demands. Politics in Northern Ireland have yet to become a culture rather than a cockfight, and so I have counselled elsewhere: culture now, politics later, meaning by politics the constitutional first principles beyond which people in Ulster cannot seem to advance.

In the meantime another regional identity for Northern Ireland, besides a British and Irish one, is in process of formation; for some time, Northern Ireland has been a region of the European Community. (A federated archipelago of the future would constitute in itself a semi-autonomous region of the EC.) Regionalism, in the sense of EC regional policy, is the principle of free market forces in reverse, and though it is intended to strengthen the overall economic power of the Community *vis-à-vis* the world market and therefore is in the ultimate interest of competitive economics, its beneficence is unarguable. Of the £300 million directed at the problems of Belfast between 1981 and 1986, the EC contributed 20 per cent or £60 million. (Let us not forget the generosity of British taxpayers who contributed the bulk of the remainder.) And it is heartening at first glance to read about the report published in 1986, 'An Economic Strategy for County Tyrone to 2001', commissioned by, among other bodies, the European Commission.* It recommended in detail an integrated plan of economic recovery for Tyrone that emphasized local initiative, maximizing 'opportunities indigenous to the area', and renewal from within; a plan that attempted to reflect 'the personality of Tyrone'.

* The Report is discussed by two of its authors, Michael Murray and Mark Hart, in 'Integrated Rural Development in Northern Ireland: A Case Study of Local Initiative within County Tyrone', a contribution to the symposium just published by the Regional Studies Association, *Regional Policy at the Crossroads: European Perspectives.*

It appears, however, that the response of central government agencies has been disappointing, leading to the authors' claim that 'within County Tyrone at present the ability of the indigenous population to involve itself in the economic regeneration of the County is weakened by centralisation of decision-making in critical areas within central government organisations and departments . . . and by the existence of four local authorities with a paucity of functions'. The claim could presumably be repeated with greater or lesser accuracy for the other five counties of Northern Ireland. (Local authorities in Northern Ireland have lesser powers than their mainland counterparts, and whereas the latter may apply for EC regional funding through Westminster, Northern Irish local authorities must apply through the EC division of the Department of Commerce.) The EC can't be held responsible for British government or local sectarian strife; and when an economy transits from a manufacturing dominance to a service dominance, as Northern Ireland's is doing, one expects a substantiation of bureaucracy, not just an increase. But it remains to be seen whether regions in the EC sense (disadvantaged areas of the Community) can be helped to regenerate themselves, rather than merely and ultimately being restructured socio-economically to contribute to an evolving EC master plan. Meanwhile, does current regional development in Northern Ireland reflect the personality of the region?

III

In 1992 Western Europe will become economically more integrated, and while we can be sure that economic patterns will be affected, it remains to be seen what impact there will be on the social and artistic culture of its regions. (How we live influences what we express and how we express it, after all.) As for Ireland, it is possible that the economic downgrading of the border in 1992 will increase the importance of regional identity rather than promote the unity of Ireland. (This might be one example of a Europe-wide reaction to economic denationalization.)* In the meantime, one is entitled to wonder if current centralized government, especially through funds and subsidies, is merely aiding the initiatives of local artists and art groups or if it is also in some way purchasing art and culture accept-

---

* The loosening of the communist bloc with the answering reorientation of the EC countries might cause the same reaction – JWF.

able to it. In Canada, the government quite clearly has set out over the past score of years to subsidize a Canadian high culture into existence, via the Canada Council, and has been far more successful than anyone in these islands realizes, simply because Canadian matters are not reported over here, while American matters are, endlessly. (Toronto and Montreal as centres of high culture outstrip all British cities save London.) Canadian culture can draw on a rich and generous corporate sector, but business, like government, expects a return for its money and a return which is to its financial and aesthetic liking. So is there a price to pay for the subvention of culture?

In one sense it depends on the autonomy granted to agencies such as arts councils, art galleries and museums. It might be worth comparing what appears to be indigenous regional culture in Ulster with culture that has been officially sanctioned by subsidy and fellowship. (Since John Hewitt was deeply involved in art galleries, arts councils and museums, it might be interesting to explore the disparity, if any exists, between his interest in native regional culture and his association with public cultural bodies funded by central government.) But in another sense, the whole question of a region's culture being subsidized by outside agencies needs to be looked at. There are those, such as Jacques Barzun, who believe that there is too much government involvement in the arts (he quotes Degas' mischievous remark in the 1890s: 'We must *dis*courage the arts'), and that funding is often misdirected at individuals, as well as (what to Barzun is more appropriate) public art, with both kinds of art suffering as a result. Northern Ireland, of course, is so far from being New York as to make comparisons risible (there are 117,000 jobs related to art in the New York metropolitan area, yielding a total income of two billion – what we used to call over here two thousand million – dollars a year). Yet Barzun's claim, that the redirection of arts funding would help regional culture to thrive since 'its qualities would be enhanced by the contributions of the more talented . . . who now vainly try for the highest places', is nevertheless worth pondering. In Northern Ireland, are we in any danger of getting 'Direct Culture' to go along with Direct Rule?

Apparently benign interventions in the culture of Ulster and Ireland are also made by international bodies. Institutes of Irish Studies and the British Association for Irish Studies have recently sprung up or expanded. These appear merely to perform academic observer roles, but the fact that they sprouted in the wake of the

Anglo-Irish Agreement – a controversial political document – and that they have the backing of the British and Irish governments suggests that they have been encouraged not only to observe but ultimately to influence and persuade. How will they affect regional culture and what is their ideological agenda?

More international still are the International Fund of Ireland and the various Ireland Funds – of America, of Australia, of France, of Great Britain, of Canada – that operate under one umbrella. The founder of the American Ireland Fund was Tony O'Reilly of H. J. Heinz. The *Ireland Fund of Canada Journal* is a lavish affair with advertisements and endorsements from leading Canadian businesses and from the Prime Minister of Canada, the Taoiseach of Ireland, the Secretary of State for Northern Ireland and the Lord Mayor of Dublin (but not of Belfast). In order to get serious money, the Fund organizers have gone top-market. Several million dollars have been distributed to projects and associations; the Canada fund alone gave out more than $100,000 in 1988. The causes are unimpeachable, and there are many, most of them cross-community or integrated. The slogan of the Funds is Peace, Charity – and Culture. The aim is to change Irish culture through the financial promotion of certain groups. I hope some local Michel Foucault will examine the ways in which government and corporations have an impact on our extant regional culture and discover if they do, as the Ireland Funds hope to, 'develop Ireland's unique cultural heritage', since that sounds like a redundant activity. Is the past being officialized and reinterpreted as 'heritage'? Is culture being drained of conviction and made to perform a socially ameliorative role? Will regional culture increasingly be required to satisfy international (i.e. North American) criteria of acceptability? Might there be cultural MacBride principles, for example?

Ulster, of course, is being internationalized in any case. The shuttle flights to and from Heathrow are crammed in the summer months with Ulster people taking continental holidays. Even staying at home, they can watch foreign television via satellite and listen to nationally indistinguishable pop music on proliferating FM stations. In architecture, cuisine, fashion and even books themselves, it is a post-modern age we live in (more so in North American cities than in Belfast or Dublin, of course) We are learning, in post-modern style, to accept 'all cultural manifestations, both high-style and populist', in the words of a *TLS* reviewer. The cultural pluralism is diachronic, and the reviewer claims that 'the characteristic fact of life in an age of information processing is a reworking of previous traditions'. Spatial equivalents of this recycling are easy to think of. There is, for example, something that has been called the Chop Suey Syndrome. This dish was concocted not in China but in the USA by Chinese immigrants. I wouldn't be surprised if Chop Suey were made in China now, for we could equally call this the Irish Coffee Syndrome. Irish Coffee was first concocted in O'Doul's Restaurant in San Francisco from where it spread around the world. (The Ploughman's Lunch, too, was recently invented, by London's Madison Avenue, a fact Ian McEwan gets satirical mileage from in his political film of that name.)

The ethnic, indigenous or regional, then, can be invented abroad or can be absorbed by the metropolitan culture. The proliferation of ethnic restaurants and menus in North America – with its sequence of fashionable cuisines – is beginning to be imitated in Ireland. The latest style in high fashion, according to the magazine *Chatelaine*, is 'tailored-over ethnic', a pluralist wardrobe of so-called 'exotica', made, paradoxically, internationally familiar. Low fashion shows how American this all is: the secret of America's cultural success is its selling of its own culture (which is pseudo-culture, mostly, or even anti-culture) as international, and even as local, i.e. yours. Once travelling Americans were unmistakable in their leisure-wear; now Western Europeans, Japanese and North Americans are indistinguishable below the neck in that regard. And as for low fashion, so for low cuisine, with American fast foods (along with the architecture and economics of their outlets) fast becoming international. 'Macu-Donarado's', as it is pronounced in Japan, has opened outlets in Moscow, where the Big Mac is as invariable as anywhere else.

One example of American culture that I predict will spread like wildfire in Ireland, funds permitting, is the mall or arcade. I won't recount its fascinating social history according to William Severini Kowinski, author of *The Malling of America*. Suffice it to say that Americans nowadays spend more time in the mall than anywhere else except at home, school and workplace. Malls are responsible for 50–60 per cent of the nation's retail sales; they are, says Kowinski, America's 'cathedrals of consumption'. They have triumphantly linked the idea of shopping with the idea of entertainment. The West Edmonton Mall in Canada is the world's biggest, though an even larger one is planned for Minneapolis–St Paul by the same Triple Five Corporation. In West Edmonton you will find under one roof 800 shops (including 200 women's shops), 110 eating places, 19 cinemas, 10 department stores, a submarine base with four submarines, the world's biggest water park with waves etc. – a vast pleasure dome. The environment of the mall is timeless, placeless, artificial, enclosed and controlled. The principles of what began as a scaled-down, sanitized version of Main Street, USA, including the principle of replication, are now implemented all over America, in condominium buildings, convention centres, domed stadia, airports, theme parks, high-tech campuses ('research parks'), office buildings, hotels, renovated waterfronts, 'festival marketplaces' (pseudo-traditional city markets). I mention all this because our future seems as far from regional culture as it is possible to get. America is being universalized, placelessness is being exported and will displace real places. One wonders if John Montague's notion of 'global regionalism' (region raised in art to universality) will not in fact transpire as its reverse (universality imposed on region) and prove as naïve as the Canadian Marshall McLuhan's idea of the global village, which will be an American village made global only because the world is America's backyard.

IV

In face of the forces of deregionalization, can we persist in trying to imagine Ulster? The *ideal* uses of regionality are obvious. In our political culture it would provide Catholic and Protestant Northerners with a common allegiance. It would provide Protestants with a buffer between them and the Republic while satisfying their desire for Irishness and (at least semi-) autonomy. It would locate Catholic (and indeed Protestant) loyalty centrally in Ulster, not in England; the governmental centrality of England is as great an imposition on nationalists as the centrality of the Republic would be to unionists. In our general culture it would resist successfully the unacceptable international features of society while admitting and absorbing the desirable features. Unlike, say, Patrick Kavanagh's parochialism, it would be no cloistered virtue but traffic with the wide world, for some aspects of international and American culture are, and will be, liberating for corners of the globe like this one.

But is a mutually acknowledged regional culture in Ulster possible? Two conditions are required. The first is that the Ulster identity be distinct from all other regional cultures in the world. But what might a regional culture of the future look like? How will the local express itself, if not only through inferior versions of international or American prototypes?* Whereas international culture will increasingly render Catholic and Protestant similar, it won't render them distinctive in their mutuality. I want to set these questions aside for another occasion and turn instead to the implications and difficulties of the second condition, that Catholic and Protestant feel, equally, *of* Ulster.

Despite the impact of internationalism, it is clear that some form of cultural reawakening is going on in Ulster and in other British regions. I mention only three home examples: the sudden rise in the popularity of local history, the resurgence of interest in the Irish language, and the burgeoning curiosity about wildlife and the environment generally. But although a fair measure of common Ulster identity can be demonstrated – in dialects, in the sense of humour, in personality traits, in daily lifestyles – is there real reason to believe that regional reawakening will reinforce that common identity? Is the Irish language *ipso facto* sectarian? Will local history uncover further justifications for hostility? Is concern for the environment an imitation of an international (rather, Western) phenomenon? Despite denials from some quarters, there are deep cultural divisions which should be studied fearlessly, the history and patterns of which A. T. Q. Stewart has charted for us in his 1977 book, *The Narrow Ground*. (These differences will at least have the merit of preventing the growth of a spurious myth of Ulsterness as the underpinning of a Northern nationalism seeking to make itself entirely independent of its own Irish and British components.) So if a political creed needs cultural and historical roots in order to win and hold the imagination of the people, how can such a creed emerge in Northern Ireland? (Can we expect at best only a forever vigilant sectarian sharing of power, rather than a fully democratic and ultimately unselfconscious participation in regional government, grounded in the Ulster inhabitants' sense that they are culturally one people?) The roots surely are roots of difference.

Yet Stewart wishes to complicate that simple assertion. He makes the case that there was greater interaction in the past between planters

* Since posing this question, I have discovered that some art critics and historians have adopted regionalism by which to define one guise of post-Modernism and to encourage opposition to what Paul Ricoeur called 'the phenomenon of universalization': see, for example, Kenneth Frampton, 'Towards a Critical Regionalism: Six Points for an Architecture of Resistance' in *Postmodern Culture*, ed. Hal Foster (London: Pluto Press 1985), pp. 16–30 – JWF.

and Gaels than hitherto acknowledged. He denies that the difference between planter and Gael is racial; it must, then, be cultural and theoretically dissoluble. At the beginning of historic times, he says, there was an already mixed population in Ulster, and the Gaelic O'Neills were as much foreigners as the Scots who later took their lands from them. There was an Anglo-Norman colony in the late twelfth century along the south-eastern coast of County Down; meanwhile, 'immigration from Scotland was fairly continuous for centuries before 1609, and was a fact of geography rather than a fact of history'. There was a wave of Scots, for example, in the thirteenth century when Highland Scots mercenaries came from the Western Isles, while the Scots-Ulster culture as we know it was really established by a natural influx of settlers rather than by the artificial planting earlier in the century. Of the Plantation itself, Stewart claims that the native Irish were not driven off the escheated lands wholesale: 'the great concealed factor in this whole "British" plantation is the part played by the relatively undisturbed Irish population in building the towns, fortified bawns and planter castles, and in developing the resources of forests, rivers and loughs'. He concludes: 'the Londonderry plantation was never, as it sometimes appears in Protestant mythology, a purely Protestant settlement which is slowly being overwhelmed by the Catholic population. It was more than half-Catholic from the very beginning.'

We have to keep in mind, of course, some historians' opinions that such interaction ended with 1641. Certainly we seem to have inherited an interaction between 'natives and newcomers' that in peacetime is carefully balanced, as Rosemary Harris showed in her study, *Prejudice and Tolerance in Ulster*, and in crisis, tense at best, murderous at worst. Yet this other version of negative regionalism is paradoxically evidence of Ulster's distinctiveness, to set beside more positive proof. Ulster is distinguished by its inability to decide whether it is primarily a region of Ireland or a region of Britain. It is of course both, a fact that has yet to assume unique cultural form. Stewart quotes Churchill's famous (or infamous) complaint in his book *The World Crisis*, that although the map of Europe had been redrawn during World War II, Ulster's had not: 'As the deluge subsides and the waters fall we see the dreary steeples of Fermanagh and Tyrone emerging once again. The integrity of their quarrel is one of the few institutions that have been left unaltered in the cataclysm which has swept the world.' *The Narrow Ground* is Stewart's history of that integrity, and since integrity means oneness, it is a history of the maintenance of Ulster's regional identity, one founded ironically on division. Our task is to promote positive formations out of this distinctive negativity.

In 1986 when *The Narrow Ground* was republished, Stewart believed that Ulster's paradoxical integrity – its peculiar regional identity – was impervious to propaganda and hostile criticism: 'nor will [it] be changed in essence by the economic, social and intellectual pressures of the contemporary world, as so many imagine'. It remains to be seen whether the external cultural forces I've mentioned prove as locally helpless as he thinks. They may well act as a solvent in Ulster's divided society, or as an adhesive. They may even be more salubrious than I've feared above. Yet I prefer to imagine, as Hewitt imagined, a primarily indigenous synthesis. I have been stimulated to do so by a metaphor from Canada, that vast country where I make my home, that perhaps most successful of democracies. Still, that democracy, and the federal-provincial arrangement that sustains it, does not entirely satisfy all Canadians, especially all Quebecois and all westerners, many of whom feel alienated. In 1981 George Melnyk published a book entitled *Radical Regionalism* which I read with great interest both as a Western Canadian and an Ulsterman. The book has proven in the last decade too optimistic for Canada, but it has provided me with some imaginative potential for thinking about Ulster.

Melnyk calls for a cultural revolution in the Canadian West; through it he believes a Western identity can be recovered. He is strenuously opposed to what he calls Ontario-based nationalism which, as he sees it, exists to reassure itself against Quebec. But he does not align himself with conservative anti-federalism. 'The right's naming of central Canada as the prime enemy rather than the United States', he says, 'has it making nationalism, not imperialism, the main stumbling block and this is incorrect.' Whereas he thinks Canadian nationalism *can* be supportive of regional expression (Melnyk's West would be a semi-autonomous region of a de-Americanized Canada), Americanism, which became imperialistic after World War II, cannot. 'The removal of American capitalism and influence is the way to a self-determining regional society.' The West in its present condition exhibits the mind of what Melnyk calls derisively 'the hinterland'.

Hewitt's belief that Ulster culture should be 'no mere echo of the thought and imagination of another people or another land' is echoed in Melnyk's claim that 'a whole people's consciousness of itself is repressed (therefore inauthentic) when its identity is determined elsewhere, when it comes from without rather than from within. A culture is inauthentic when it is the expression of the other, rather than the self.' Melnyk's region, like Hewitt's, must be no mere hinterland.

Melnyk sees the Canadian West as oppressed by the imperatives, the symbiotic imperatives, of the official Anglo-French Canadian cultures, themselves permeated by American culture. These surely have their analogues in the official Irish and British components of that identity spelled out for the Northern Irish, by outsiders, in the Anglo-Irish Agreement and before that in the New Ireland Forum, and they too are symbiotically linked and are being permeated by American culture. For a long time the Ulster people have suffered the twin psychological colonialisms of Irish nationalism and British nationality that have falsified their consciousness and diverted them from the true task of self-realization. Under this false consciousness they have persisted in perceiving fellow inhabitants of Ulster as 'them', as 'the others'. These two colonialisms rest on the demonstrably false propositions that Northern Ireland is as British as Finchley and that Ireland is, now or imminently, one country. No final peace can settle on Ulster until these ideas, which I believe most Ulster people *feel* to be untrue, are cast off; there is little dignity, after all, in wearing someone else's hand-me-downs. Under the influence of these ideas, Protestants have connived at turning themselves into ethnics and Catholics at turning themselves into natives.

Against the official nationalisms of Canada, Melnyk contemplates a Western synthesis of ethnic (i.e. immigrant but not English or French) and native (i.e. Indian and Inuit) cultures, which he envisages by means of what he calls 'the Métis metaphor'. Métis are the descendants of European (especially French) fur traders and Indian women, and they emerged as a distinct group around the Great Lakes from the 1690s onwards and on the Prairies in the early nineteenth century. They became a racial-political-cultural group with minority grievances and in 1885 staged a famous rebellion that was crushed. (Their being both newcomers and natives in extraction, one is tempted to see a 1798 parallel.) In this century, lands were set aside for Métis settlements and *The Canadian Encyclopedia* tells us that 'a distinct Métis culture combining Indian and Euro-Canadian values and modes of expression is practised in the Métis settlements, and there is a Métis dialect combining Cree, French and English'. The Métis will soon achieve a considerable measure of regional autonomy within Canada.

'Métis' is an old French word meaning 'mixed'. *Métissage* – or race mixture – has gone on in Ulster as long as it has in Canada, but according to Stewart, it was the Reformation that prevented assimilation of the Scots in Ireland, forcing mixed progeny to belong culturally to one side or the other. It has been suggested that mixed marriages are the answer in Northern Ireland, but of course they aren't unless they were too numerous for community processing, since the general culture (of which religion is an aspect) has proven stronger than mixed marriages. Ulster's is a cultural problem, then, not a racial one. So too, as Melnyk sees it, is the problem of the Canadian West, since the Métis simply function as a metaphor for him. He wishes to see a synthesis of ethnic and indigenous cultures that would eventually dismantle what he terms 'the politics of otherness', which of course is what is practised in Northern Ireland.

There is no comparable figure from contemporary life available to us in Ulster, though 1798 is a potent historical (and now largely unusable) one. So far, our writers have failed to offer us attractive and powerful metaphors for the positive intercourse of Northern Irish life, and the historians have been largely going it alone, demonstrating the degree of historical interaction. Contemplating the idea of Central Europe, George Konrád remarks of the kind of figures we seek: 'The advantage of such metaphors is that you cannot turn them into dry bones by mere analysis; they have some inner reserve, a life of their own.' We do not, of course, wish for a synthetic non-sectarian Ulster culture, which some agencies are busy trying to bring about. Rather, we want the natural culture of Ulster to be perceived and encouraged, after the veils of outside causes and dogma have been dropped.

[1989]

REFERENCES

Albrechts, Louis, ed. *Regional Policy at the Crossroads: European Perspectives* (London: Jessica Kingsley 1988).

Ascherson, Neal, 'The Religion of Nationalism', *Observer*, 2 Dec. 1988, 13.

Bartlett, Thomas, ' "What Ish My Nation?": Themes in Irish History', *Irish Studies: A General Introduction*, eds T. Bartlett, C. Curtin, R. O'Dwyer, G. O Tuathaigh (Dublin: Gill and Macmillan 1988).

Barzun, Jacques, 'A Surfeit of Art and why government need not encourage it', *Harper's*, July 1986, 45–9.

The Canadian Encyclopedia, second edition (Edmonton: Hurtig 1988).

Cawley, Mary, 'Ireland: Habitat, Culture and Personality', *Irish Studies: A General Introduction*.

Filler, Martin, 'Building in the Past Tense', *Times Literary Supplement*, 24–30 Mar. 1989; 295–6.

Freeman, T. W., *Ireland: A General and Regional Geography* (London: Methuen 1972).

Harris, Rosemary, *Prejudice and Tolerance in Ulster: A Study of Neighbours and 'Strangers' in a Border Community* (Manchester: University Press 1972).

Hewitt, John, *Ancestral Voices: The Selected Prose*, ed. Tom Clyde (Belfast: The Blackstaff Press 1987).

Kennedy, Dennis, *The Widening Gulf: Northern Attitudes to the Independent Irish State 1919–49* (Belfast: The Blackstaff Press 1988).

Konrád, George, 'Autonomies in Concert', *Times Literary Supplement,* 8–14 Sept. 1989, 972.

Kowinski, William Severini, 'Main Street in a spaceship: the covered mall', *Smithsonian*, 17 Sept. 1986, 35–43.

Melnyk, George, *Radical Regionalism* (Edmonton: NeWest Press 1981).

Nairn, Tom, *The Break-Up of Britain: Crisis and Neo-Nationalism* (London: Verso 1981).

O'Halloran, Clare, *Partition and the Limits of Irish Nationalism* (Dublin: Gill and Macmillan 1987).

Stewart, A. T. Q., *The Narrow Ground: Aspects of Ulster, 1609–1969* (London: Faber 1977).

ACKNOWLEDGMENTS

'The Topographical Tradition in Anglo-Irish Poetry' appeared in *Irish University Review* IV, 2 (1974), 169–87.

'The Geography of Irish Fiction' appeared in *The Irish Novel in Our Time*, eds Patrick Rafrodi and Maurice Harmon (Lille 1976), pp. 89–102.

'Irish Modernism' is the text of a talk given at an international symposium, 'Modernism and Modernity', sponsored by the Fine Arts Department of the University of British Columbia, Vancouver, March 1981. It appeared under a different title in *Modernism and Modernity*, eds Benjamin H. D. Buchloh, Serge Guilbaut and David Solkin (Halifax, Nova Scotia 1983), pp. 65–80.

'Post-War Ulster Poetry: The English Connection' (1985) appeared with a different subtitle in *Cultural Contexts and Literary Idioms in Contemporary Irish Literature*, ed. Michael Kennelly (Gerrards Cross, Bucks., 1988), pp. 154–71.

'The Poetry of Seamus Heaney' appeared in *Critical Quarterly* XVI, 1 (1974), 37–48.

'The Poetry of Patrick Kavanagh' appeared in *Mosaic* XII/3 (1979), 139–52.

'"The Dissidence of Dissent": John Hewitt and W. R. Rodgers' appeared in *Across a Roaring Hill: The Protestant Imagination in Modern Ireland*, eds Gerald Dawe and Edna Longley (Belfast 1985), pp. 139–60.

'Yeats and the Easter Rising' appeared in *The Canadian Journal of Irish Studies* XI, 1 (1985), 21–34.

'The Landscape of Three Irelands: Hewitt, Murphy and Montague' contains, in a different form, some of 'The Landscape of Planter and Gael in the Poetry of John Montague and John Hewitt', *The Canadian Journal of Irish Studies* I, 2 (1975), 17–33. The section on Richard Murphy was written in 1985.

'A Complex Fate: The Irishness of Denis Donoghue' appeared under a different title in *The Irish Review* 2 (1987), 107–12.

'The Critical Condition of Ulster' is the text of a talk given at the Triennial Conference of the International Association for the Study of Anglo-Irish Literature, Queen's University, Belfast, July 1985. It first appeared in *The Honest Ulsterman* 79 (1985), 38–55.

'New Realism: A Future for Irish Studies' appeared under its subtitle in *The Irish Review* 3 (1988), 75–88.

'Who Are the Irish?' is the text of a talk given at University College, Cork, July 1987. It appeared in *Studies* 308 (1988), 403–16 with a response from Alban Maginness, Chairman of the Social Democratic and Labour Party of Northern Ireland.

'Culture and Colonization: View from the North' is the text of a talk given at the annual conference of the Canadian Association for Irish Studies, Marianopolis College, Montreal, March 1988. It appeared with a different subtitle in *The Irish Times*, 29 June, 30 June, 1 July 1988.

'Radical Regionalism' is the text of a talk given at the John Hewitt International Summer School, St MacNissi's College, Co. Antrim, August 1989. It appeared in abridged form in *The Irish Review* 7 (1989), 1–15.

Initialled matter in footnotes has been added for this volume.